International Marketing Reader   1996.

This collection of articles focuses on the particular challenges and issues of international marketing. How can a company break into a new foreign market? What pricing structures should be in operation for a global product? How does one manage a multilingual advertising campaign?

The Reader combines previously published articles with new papers commissioned to update classic research in the field. With an international set of contributors and a range of international examples, the book offers a selection of critical studies that analyse each part of the marketing function. It then concludes by reflecting on the creation of the EU, of NAFTA and the unpredictable Westernization of emerging markets of Central and Eastern Europe, showing how the international marketing expert must be able to respond to the rapidly changing global environment.

Stanley J. Paliwoda is Professor of Marketing at the University of Calgary, Canada. His previous publications include *Marketing* (Prentice-Hall Canada Inc.) with Keegan, Moriarty and Duncan, *Investing in Eastern Europe* (Addison-Wesley/EIU Books), *The Essence of International Marketing* (Prentice-Hall) and *International Marketing*, 2nd edn (Butterworth Heinemann). **John K. Ryans** Jr is Professor of Marketing at Kent State University, Ohio, USA.

International Marketing Reader

Edited by Stanley J. Paliwoda and
John K. Ryans Jr

London and New York

First published 1995
by Routledge
11 New Fetter Lane, London EC4P 4EE

Simultaneously published in the USA and Canada
by Routledge
29 West 35th Street, New York, NY 10001

Typeset in Times by
Florencetype Ltd, Stoodleigh, Devon

Printed and bound in Great Britain by
T.J. Press (Padstow) Ltd, Padstow, Cornwall

British Library Cataloguing in Publication Data
A catalogue record for this book is available from the British
Library

Library of Congress Cataloguing in Publication Data
International marketing reader / [edited by] Stanley J.
Paliwoda and John K. Ryans.
    p. cm.
    Includes bibliographical references and index.
    ISBN 0–415–11400–4. — ISBN 0–415–10039–9 (pbk.)
    1. Export marketing. I. Paliwoda, Stanley J. II. Ryans, John K.
    HF1416.I634 1995
    658.8'48—dc20   94-43146
                                                     CIP

ISBN 0–415–11400–4 (hbk)
ISBN 0–415–10039–9 (pbk)

Contents

Figures

Tables

Acknowledgements

Chapter 4: 'International marketing and internationalization processes: a network approach', by Jan Johanson and Lars Gunnar-Mattsson, was first published in *Research in International Marketing*, edited by Peter W. Turnbull and Stanley J. Paliwoda, and is reproduced here with kind permission of Croom Helm Ltd.

Chapter 6: 'Multinational market portfolios in global strategy development', by Gilbert D. Harrell and Richard O. Kiefer, was first published in *Marketing Review*, 10(1): 60–72, and is reproduced here with the kind permission of MCB University Press.

Chapter 9: 'ISO 9000: the new strategic consideration', by H. Michael Hayes, is reprinted from *Business Horizons*, May–June 1994: 52–60. © Foundation for the School of Business at Indiana University. Used with permission.

Chapter 10: 'The Deming, Baldrige and European Quality Awards', by Behnam Nakhai and Jaoa S. Neves, is reprinted from *Quality Progress*, April 1994: 33–7. © American Society for Quality Control. Reprinted with permission.

Chapter 11: 'Make marketing part of the quality effort', by Joseph L. Orsini, is reprinted from *Quality Progress*, April 1994: 43–6. © American Society for Quality Control. Reprinted with permission.

Chapter 17: 'Tactical pricing', by Robert A. Garda, is reprinted from the *Journal of Business Strategy*, September–October 1991, with permission from Faulkner & Gray Inc., 11 Penn Plaza, New York, NY10001.

Chapter 18: 'Pricing for a single market', by Ralf Leszinski, is reprinted from the *McKinsey Quarterly*, no. 3 (1992): 86–94, with the kind permission of McKinsey Company, Inc.

Chapter 19: 'Developing a global pricing strategy', by Clive Sims, Adam Phillips and Trevor Richards. This paper first appeared in ESOMAR's quarterly journal *Marketing and Research Today*, 20(1), (March 1992): 3–13. Permission for reprinting this paper has been granted by the European Society for Opinion and Marketing Research (ESOMAR).

Contributors

Ulf Andersson is a doctoral student in the Department of Business Studies at Uppsala University, Sweden, where he is participating in the project on Managing International Networks headed by Professors Mats Forsgren and Jan Johanson.

Fred Burton is Senior Lecturer in International Business in the Manchester School of Management, University of Manchester Institute of Science and Technology (UMIST). He has published widely in international management and economics journals, and has acted as consultant to multinational companies and international organizations, including the United Nations Development Programme and the European Foundation of Management Development.

James Cooper is Director of the Cranfield Centre for Logistics and Transportation where he is also Exel Logistics Fellow. He is the author of several books, and many articles, two of which received 'Best Paper' awards from leading academic journals in 1991 and 1992. Professor Cooper has led major research projects for both government and industry and is currently vice-chairman of an OECD expert group on logistics and transportation.

Adam Cross graduated in 1982 with a BSc in geology and worked as an international trader for five years. In 1992 he completed an MSc in Management Science at the Manchester School of Management, UMIST, where he specialized in International Business Economics. Since then he has worked as a Research Assistant at the School and has taught on International Business courses at both undergraduate and postgraduate level. He is currently conducting an investigation, funded by the Economic and Social Research Council, into UK international franchising activity and has published a number of papers in this field.

Angie Driscoll is a PhD candidate, University of Calgary, Canada. Prior to coming to Canada in 1990, she was a Lecturer in Marketing at the

University of Otago in Dunedin, New Zealand, where she also received her MCom degree. She has worked as a marketing consultant in the public and private sectors both in New Zealand and in Canada. Clients have included the New Zealand Department of Health, Otago Area Health Board, the Dunedin City Council, Food Marketing Research Unit, Cardinal Computing, Button Up and Janis Marketing. Her current research interests include international marketing strategy, database marketing, tourism and small-business entrepreneurship.

David Elton is President of the Canada West Foundation, a position he has held since 1980. He holds a doctorate from the University of Alberta, has been a faculty member at the University of Lethbridge since 1969, and is a Professor in the Political Science Department. He has conducted research and is published in a number of areas such as resource development, transportation policy, economic development, trade, and constitutional reform. He chaired a Task Force on Canada–US trade from 1985 to 1988, and has also participated in television and radio programmes on public affairs throughout Canada.

G. Scott Erickson is Assistant Professor of Marketing at Ithaca College, Ithaca, New York. He received his PhD in Business and Economics from Lehigh University in 1993. Research interests include international retailing, the influence of the patent system on technological innovation, and the US export control system.

Mats Forsgren is Associate Professor in the Department of Business Studies, Uppsala University, Sweden. Publications include *Managing the Internationalisation Process: The Swedish Case* (Routledge) and, as co-editor, *Managing Networks in International Business* (Gordon & Breach). Together with Professor Jan Johanson, he has headed a research project on Multinationals as Interorganisational Networks (the MIN project) involving five doctoral students.

Robert A. Garda is a Director of McKinsey & Company Inc., an international management consulting firm that serves the world's largest industrial companies, service firms and healthcare organizations, as well as national governments. He has been a Director of McKinsey since 1978 and a Principal since 1972. He has a degree in electrical engineering from Duke University and an MBA from Harvard Business School.

Ursula Grüber was born in Kiel, Germany, and studied languages and economics at the universities of Heidelberg, Cambridge and the Sorbonne. A career in public relations and advertising – notably at the Ted Bates agency in Paris, where she was international co-ordinator – led her to discover a real need for a specialist service to handle foreign-language versions of advertising and promotional copy. She created a totally new concept: multilingual copy adaptation, and developed a unique approach. Today her Paris-based agency, Ursula Grüber Communication Internationale, is the world leader in the field with a network of more than 200 professional copywriters and technical consultants in 24 countries, a prestigious list of clients in consumer, business-to-business and industrial sectors, and over twenty years' experience in international communications. Ursula Grüber is a frequent speaker at international conferences and heads seminars in universities and business schools. She is co-author of the *Bilingual Dictionary of Advertising and Communication* (Dunod), and is a regular contributor to the professional and economic press.

Lars Gunnar-Mattsson is Professor of Marketing at the Stockholm School of Economics, Sweden.

Gilbert D. Harrell is Professor of Marketing, Eli Broad School of Management, Michigan State University. His international research, consulting and teaching interests focus on all aspects of strategic marketing. He has authored over fifty books and articles in areas of strategic planning, marketing and consumer behaviour. His publications have appeared in the *Journal of Marketing*, *Journal of Marketing Research*, *Journal of Consumer Research*, *Journal of Consumer Affairs*, *International Marketing Review*, and other journals. In addition, he is President of G.D. Harrell and Associates Inc., a professional consulting group specializing in systems, programmes and services for strategic marketing management, sales management and executive strategy development. The company has worked with numerous corporations in over twenty countries to create organizational change through the application of tools for effective marketing.

H. Michael Hayes is Professor of Marketing and Strategic Management at the University of Colorado at Denver, USA.

Todd Hirsch is a Research Associate at the Canada West Foundation, and has been on the staff since 1989. He received his BA in Economics from the University of Alberta, and an MA in Economics from the University of Calgary. His research and publications include topics on public deficits and debt, international trade, and the economics of constitutional reform.

Jan Johanson is Professor in International Business at Uppsala University, Sweden. His research interests are the internationalization of the firm and business networks. He is one of the co-founders of the European IMP Group. His latest publication, with Matts Forsgren, is *Managing Networks in International Business*.

Warren J. Keegan is Professor of International Business and Marketing, and Director of the Institute for Global Business Strategy at the Lubin School of Business, Pace University, New York City and Westchester. He serves as a consultant to corporations, law firms, governments and international agencies, is a frequent speaker to business audiences, and regularly appears on national and global television. He is the Prodigy-on-the-line international business bulletin board expert on international business and author of the weekly *Global Observer* commentary for *International Business*, a core feature of the Prodigy service. His previous experience includes MIT Fellow in Africa, where he served as Assistant Secretary in the Ministry of Development Planning and Secretary of the Economic Development Commission, Government of Tanzania; consultant with Boston Consulting Group and Chairman of Douglas A. Edwards, Inc., a New York corporate real estate firm. He has an MBA and doctorate from the Harvard Business School. Recent books include *Marketing sans frontiers* (with Jean-Marc De Leersnyder; InterEditions, Paris, 1994), *Marketing*, 2nd edn (Prentice-Hall, 1994). He is also the author of *Global Marketing Management*, 4th edn, *Advertising Worldwide, Judgments, Choices, and Decisions: Effective Management Through Self-Knowledge* (John Wiley) and the *Dictionary of Marketing Terms*. His newest books, *Global Marketing Management* and *Principles of Global Marketing* wil be published by Prentice-Hall in 1995.

Richard O. Kiefer graduated in 1959 from Concordia College in Ft Wayne, Indiana, with his BA, and went on to earn his MBA from Michigan State University in 1980. He has recently retired as Vice-President of Product Management at New Holland in London, England – the Fiat sector for agricultural and construction equipment. In this capacity he has had world-wide responsibility for product development. Prior to 1991, he worked with Ford Tractor in product and international marketing.

Ralf Leszinski is a partner in the Zürich office of McKinsey. He joined McKinsey in 1987 and has worked extensively with major European companies in the consumer goods and industrial sector, ranging from commodities to integrated machine systems, on issues covering strategy, operational improvements and organization. He co-leads McKinsey's worldwide pricing practice.

Therese Maskulka is Associate Dean of the College of Business and Economics at Lehigh University, Bethlehem, Pennsylvania. She received herDBA in Marketing from Kent State University in 1987. Research interests include international retailing, service quality and strategic planning.

Behnam Nakhai is an Associate Professor of Management at the

Millersville University of Pennsylvania in Millersville. He received a doctorate in management from Claremont Graduate School in California.

Jaoa S. Neves is an Associate Professor of Management at Trenton State College in New Jersey. He has a doctorate in management from the University of Pennsylvania in Philadelphia.

Joseph L. Orsini is a professor of quality management and marketing at California State University in Sacramento. He received a doctorate in management from the University of California in Los Angeles. He is a member of the American Society for Quality Control and is a certified quality engineer.

Stanley J. Paliwoda is Professor and Chair of Marketing at the University of Calgary, Alberta, Canada, and the author of several books, including *International Marketing*, 2nd edn (Butterworth-Heinemann, Oxford, 1993); *Essence of International Marketing* (Prentice-Hall, Hemel Hempstead, 1994) and *Investment Opportunities in Eastern Europe* (EIU/Addison-Wesley, London, 1994). He is also Editor of the *Journal of East–West Business* (Haworth Press Inc., New York).

Adam Phillips is Managing Director of Mass-Observation Ltd and a Director of the MRB Group. He is a member of the MRS Council, the AMSO Council and the Interviewer Quality Control Scheme Council.

Trevor Richards joined Mass-Observation in 1986 and has been particularly involved in modelling developments in pricing and new product developments. He was co-author of a 1990 Barcelona ESOMAR paper concerned with the effect of price on trial and repeat purchasing of new products.

John K. Ryans Jr is Professor of Marketing and International Business in the Graduate School of Management, Kent State University, Kent, Ohio. His particular areas of teaching and research are International Marketing and International Business. He served as the first US editor for the *International Marketing Review* and has served (or is serving) on the editorial boards of a number of academic journals, including the *Journal of International Marketing* and the *Journal of International Business Studies*. He is the co-author of *Marketing Strategies for the New Europe* (American Marketing Association, 1990); *International Business Classics* (Lexington Books, 1988); *Management of International Advertising* (Allyn & Bacon, 1984), and several other books. He has been a frequent external reviewer for recent AIB conferences, including the 1992 and 1993 annual meetings. His articles have appeared in *Journal of International Business Studies*, *Columbia Journal of World Business*, *Harvard Business Review*, *Journal* *of Marketing, Journal of Marketing Research.* He has been a Visiting Professor at Columbia University and the University of Houston, Schering-Plough Visiting Professor at Fairleigh-Dickinson, and Owens Illinois Visiting Professor at the University of Toledo.

Rajan Saxena is Thums Up Chair Professor of Marketing at the Narsee Monjee Institute of Management Studies, University of Bombay, Bombay. He has over twenty-two years of teaching, training, consultancy and research experience in the marketing area and has published fifty-five articles in leading Indian and foreign journals and a book *International Marketing: Concepts, Techniques and Cases* (Tata McGraw Hill, New Delhi). His next book, *Marketing Management: The Indian Context* is also to be published by Tata McGraw Hill. In 1990, he was awarded the Best Teacher of Management Award by the Bombay Management Association and Fellowship and the Indian Society for Training and Development. He was a Visiting Professor at the University of Calgary, Faculty of Management in 1993–4.

Jim Sherlock is Senior Lecturer in International Trade at Manchester College of Art and Technology in the UK. Following experience in UK manufacturing industry, he now specializes in export consultancy and training. He is currently Chairman of the Education Committee of the Institute of Export, and a member of the Institute Council and Executive. He has been involved in providing export training for several multinational companies, including British Steel, Unilever, Toshiba and Shell.

Clive Sims is head of Planning and Special Projects for United Distillers. He joined Cadbury's as a graduate trainee in the Market Research Department, and moved within the company to manage the Forecasting and Analysis Section. He joined BAT in 1980 as Market Information Manager, joined Johnnie Walker & Sons as Marketing Systems Manager in 1982, and was appointed Marketing Services Director in 1986.

Nükhet Vardar was born in Istanbul in 1961 and completed most of her education in Turkey. She obtained her MSc in 1985 and PhD in 1990 from the University of Manchester Institute of Science and Technology (UMIST), England, specializing in international advertising. Her work experience started on the client side at Henkel-Turyag, where she worked as a product manager 1985–7. After completing her doctorate, she moved to the agency side and worked as Research and Planning Director of Yaratim/FCB 1990–3. She is now with Young & Rubicam/Reklamevi, Istanbul, as Director, Planner. She is author of *Global Advertising: Rhyme or Reason* (PCP, London, 1992). In addition she has published more than thirty articles in Turkish and English which have appeared in scientific journals and trade magazines on international marketing, advertising and media planning. She is a member of ESOMAR and Secretary-General of the Turkish Market Researchers' Association.

Douglas West is Associate Professor of Marketing at the University of Calgary, Alberta, Canada, and was recently Visiting Professor at City University Business School, London, UK. His research and teaching interests are in the areas of advertising and marketing management. His publications have appeared in *International Journal of Advertising*, *International Journal of Advertising Research*, *Journal of Consumer Behaviour* and *Journal of Euromarketing*, among other journals.

1 Introduction

Stanley J. Paliwoda and John K. Ryans Jr

Today, international marketers are faced with a myriad of world economic changes and varying market conditions that would have seemed unthinkable as recently as the late 1980s. Not only has the European Union come into 'full bloom' and the North American Free Trade Agreement (NAFTA) got underway, but markets such as South Africa, Poland, Hungary, the Czech Republic and the People's Republic of China (PRC) have become very viable. If we couple these new market conditions with the rapid evolution of communication and computer technology, it is small wonder that marketing has become a truly 'global game', a game in which the old operational rules and principles are rapidly becoming passé.

Marketers, of course, have always had to be flexible and to be able to respond to the needs of their customers and the demands of governments, their stakeholders and even their competitors. However, today, the pace of the changing environment is simply unprecedented. In fact, many marketers have yet to comprehend the breadth and depth of these changes. To illustrate, it has long been felt that retailing was one area of marketing that tended to be essentially local or national in character; it tended to reflect cultural differences and was an unlikely candidate for 'globalization' or foreign intrusion. The sanctity of the local Harrods or Seibu (department stores), or the Tokyo toy shop or the native bazaar in Istanbul was thought to be 'safe' from the 'global' retailer. Today, even this belief has begun to be successfully challenged.

Rather than accepting this assumption regarding local retailing's omnipotence, a number of major retail organizations are now operating successfully overseas. A 1993 study by the Management Horizons Division of Price Waterhouse provided one of the first comprehensive pictures of the extent to which the 100 largest retailers had expanded beyond their national borders. This study indicated that more than one-half of the group, led by European retailers responding to the challenges of the European Union, had become international.[1] (These large European retailers were on average already operating in four countries.) Among the best examples have been Marks & Spencer, which correctly sees itself as a global department store/specialty store chain based on its Spanish,

French, US, Canadian, Japanese, etc., achievements, and Toys-'R'-Us, a US retailer which has an impressive record in Japan and Europe. These firms, as well as several other pace-setting international retailers, have shown that the competitive retail world of the mid-to-late 1990s is much different and suggest that we need to rethink many of the marketing paradigms that have stood us so well in the past.

In preparing this book, we have examined the new trends in both concept and practice that seemed to be providing future international marketing direction for consumer, business-to-business and service organizations, but we did not wish to be constrained by the traditional approaches to international marketing. Further, we did not wish to have the book limited solely to North American authors; we actively sought the views of leading academicians and practitioners from Europe and elsewhere. (This book is especially unique in that so many leaders in contemporary marketing have been willing to share their thoughts with our readers.)

In this introductory section, we will first identify and discuss several of the primary change agents that have altered the global environment of business. Then, we will note (and briefly discuss) some eight 'New Directions in International Marketing' that have resulted from this changing environment. Finally, we will 'introduce' our contributors and consider how their individual contributions offer an additional dimension and better understanding of international marketing in the latter half of the 1990s. We will then close with our challenge to international marketing to remain on the cusp of the evolving world of business in the future.

THE CHANGING GLOBAL ENVIRONMENT

Is international marketing really changing, and if so, do we see the changes as fundamental? To answer these questions, it is important to explore some of the new parameters facing international marketers and to note the reasons for the changes. In particular, we will focus on the growth of regional integration, industry concentration and technology development.

Regional integration and global organization

Since 1987, when the harmonization within the then European Economic Community began in earnest with a five-year self-imposed completion deadline (EC-92), a host of nation states have either aligned themselves with economic partners, ratified major trade treaties or simply totally altered their political structure. Historically, such massive change, such as the inception of GATT, has only occurred as a result of wars, and even then, the number of countries involved were fewer.

Not only has the EEC become the European Community and finally the European Union, but literally dozens of other countries have chosen economic partners. Canada, Mexico and the US responded to the new competition provided by the European Union by forming the North American Free Trade Association and a line of countries, which include Chile, Colombia, and so on, has quickly formed to join this regional body. Similarly, Pacific Rim countries, building to some degree on the Association of South East Asian Nations (ASEAN), began to consider ways to band together economically and the trend toward regional integration was in full swing.

At roughly the same time, the massive breakdown of the former Soviet sphere of influence took place. The USSR itself became a splintered group of republics, while other East European members of the Soviet group, including Poland, Bulgaria and Hungary, became independent as well. Then, we saw apartheid end in South Africa, and China, India and Vietnam open their doors as never before to foreign investors.

To marketers such changes have meant a great deal more than simply an increase in market opportunities. These changes have meant a reorganization of many of their overseas markets. For example, it no longer makes sense to organize market segments or sales forces or distribution patterns along national lines. In fact, many US firms have found that a sales office in Brussels or London, coupled with a warehouse/distribution facility in Antwerp or Amsterdam, may provide all the coverage needed for the European Union market. Should a production site be needed, Budapest or Glasgow might provide the best location considering the firm's need for a well-educated, but lower-cost work-force. Such firms as Ford, IBM and others have found reorganization of their European and North American operations to be vital to their future planning operations.

Industry concentration

Whether through acquisitions, joint ventures or other forms of alliances, the number of big market-share players in many of the world's leading industries has been reduced to a precious few. Whether it be gas-fired turbines (ABB, GE and Siemens) or automobile tyres (Bridgestone, Michelin and Goodyear), the degree of concentration has become startling.

An interesting case in point has been the global chocolate industry. While there still are a vast number of small, local niche firms, a few competitors, including Cadbury, Nestlé, Mars and Hershey, tend to dominate the industry. Their marketing strategy relies on global branding for several products (brands) and the maintenance of a number of locally acquired brands. The power of these major players lies in their high brand recognition, their media/agency leverage, and the economies of scale of their marketing, finance and production. In fact, many global consumer product companies, like Sara Lee, Proctor & Gamble and Grand Met, have employed an effective brand name extension approach to Europe and other markets.

All of this industry concentration has raised considerably the stakes required in order for a firm to do business overseas. It is, therefore, not surprising that marketing alliances, designed to share R&D, media and distribution costs, are on the increase.

Technology development

A third major change in the way firms do business, and particularly, conduct their marketing activities, lies in the rapid developments in communication technology. To illustrate, the fax machine has reduced the complaints of foreign sales reps that they 'lose sales due to slow responses from headquarters in the States or Canada'. Similarly, satellite television, global video-conferencing, global television networks, computer databases, E-mail, etc., have all made 'doing business today' much different.

Satellite television alone has given an enormous impetus to the use of common advertising themes in Europe, while the rapid transmission of in-house sales and customer data have altered the market research and production needs of major players and small firms alike. To illustrate the latter, Buckeye Feeds Inc. of Dalton, Ohio, sells mineral supplements used by a growing array of major racehorse breeders in the UK, continental Europe and other overseas markets. (The Queen's horses have used this supplement.) Buckeye's supplements are matched to the nutritional quality of the local grains/feeds and need to be altered regularly. The fax (and other electronic media) has permitted the firm to compete in a variety of foreign markets from its research labs in a small rural location in the States. Similarly, a Sherwin-Williams (paint), Sara Lee or other consumer products firm can monitor its global sales on a daily basis if it so desires. Life-size video-conferences between, say, a New York advertising agency and a Paris client can now be conducted from the respective cities, saving the costs of transportation and executive time. The agency can show the client a storyboard of a new commercial and obtain feedback without leaving their respective time-zones. Certainly, such immediacy has made 'time to market' (and 'time-to-marketing') much different and has, among other things, quickened the pace of competitor response.

NEW DIRECTIONS IN INTERNATIONAL MARKETING

While the aforementioned environmental changes are not comprehensive, they do provide some understanding of why it is so important today to take a close look at the new world of international marketing. To further emphasize this point, we have suggested some eight 'New Directions in International Marketing' (Table 1.1). In the main, these new directions are either self-explanatory or have been discussed earlier (or will be discussed in other areas of this book.) However, a few deserve special attention at this juncture. These include the birth of the Eurobrand and the develop-

Table 1.1 Eight new directions in international marketing

1 The full impact of the EU (and its partners), NAFTA, and economic integration in general are just beginning to be recognized by marketers. For example, Eurobrands are just beginning to gain importance.

2 The increased number of strategic alliances, especially marketing alliances, have dramatically altered new product strategy and development, especially in high technology firms.

3 More and more firms are testing the use or moving directly to standardized (or global) marketing, particularly promotion. This has increased dramatically the segmentation and pre-testing work in overseas markets.

4 Time-to-market and product differentiation (physical and psychological) are becoming even more significant in the second half of the 1990s.

5 The importance to the firm of getting immediate awareness, image and preference data from the EU, etc., has led to new types of marketing research, such as the use of omnibus tracking studies.

6 Regulation is becoming an increasingly important factor in marketing planning; the developments in GATT and the new World Trade Organization highlight this importance.

7 Greater concentration in retailing and the total channel for consumer products is underway, as is the growth of the international retailer. Business-to-business marketers are finding it increasingly difficult to identify exclusive agents and reps, as concentration is becoming stronger in most European middlemen categories.

8 Consumers in virtually all markets have shown more price sensitivity, as evidenced by the success of private brands. To date, market concentration in most industries has failed to lead to price increases.

ments relating to the standardization of marketing programmes/strategy, especially in regard to promotion.

Eurobrands

For more than a decade, the possibility of the development of branded products that would meet the *specific* needs of European consumers has been considered in public forums and company headquarters. The events surrounding EC-92, particularly the successful harmonization of so many 'sticky issues', has given a new impetus to this dialogue.

In its purest form, a Eurobrand would be a product or service developed specifically to meet the needs of the EU-wide consumer or business-to-business market. In practice, one would expect to have marketing research conducted among a EU-wide market segment to determine the unique benefits of this customer group. The whole process of product and market strategy development would proceed through the normal stages of new product introduction. What has been fairly typical in the past has been for a US, Japanese, German, etc., producer to take an existing product, i.e. one introduced in the home market, and then with little or no modification offer it to customers in the regional European market.

To the extent that European accommodation occurs, it is often in the use of European-wide media or a 'pan-European' campaign. IBM is just one of a wide number of companies that has taken a pan-European approach in order to obtain a single image in Europe.[2] (The question of product-promotion trade-offs is discussed more fully by Warren Keegan in Part III of this book.) Since Europe now provides the opportunity for significant economies of scale for a Europe-wide product, we can expect a sharp increase in the development of Eurobrands in the late 1990s. And, clearly, the availability of pan-European (and global) advertising agencies has made the promotion side particularly viable.

Centralization and standardization

For the past decade or more, there has been an on-going debate in international marketing over the question of standardized marketing (strategy and tactics). Theodore Levitt in his now classic *Harvard Business Review* article (May–June 1983) championed the standardization approach and subsequently found many corporate and academic subscribers to his 'global strategy' concepts.[3]

Recent regional economic integration in Europe, North America and, to a lesser extent, the Pacific Rim and South America, have enhanced the potential for standardized marketing efforts. Companies, such as 3M, have found the New Europe ripe for reorganizing their operations; moving away from separate national headquarters to a more centralized (Euro-manager) approach. In particular, the Single European Market has led numerous companies to rethink their distribution strategies and, for example, to initiate regional sales offices and warehouses.

Standardization efforts, of course, are typically enhanced when the multinational firm employs a more centralized organization design. Goodyear International uses a relatively global promotional campaign; an approach termed 'pattern standardization'. Initially, this major tyre producer receives inputs from its various overseas managers and tests its promotional concepts among consumers in several global markets. However, once the central promotional theme has been developed, say for its international television commercials, then its market-to-market variations are minimal. The strength of the major global advertising agencies and the advances in cross-border media have further supported standardized marketing from a centralized (headquarters) base.

As with the other new directions for international marketing, the standardized-centralized movement and the Eurobrand developments have challenged some long-held principles in the field. This is one of the reasons why a book presenting perspectives from a host of distinguished contributors provides such a unique approach to the study of international marketing. In the next section, we provide a few comments as to what the reader may expect from this book.

OUR CONTRIBUTORS FROM THE 'GLOBAL VILLAGE'

The term 'global village' was coined in 1962, before the age of electronics, by Marshall McLuhan, a Canadian who foresaw what we have today. An expert on the media, many of his statements were prophetic and so have quite justly passed into our consciousness, even if we do not remember that it was he who first came out with the words: 'The medium is the message' or Andy Warhol who first spoke of the possibility of us each being famous for fifteen minutes. We feel the 'Global Village' is an apt term to use in introducing our contributors.

As mentioned earlier, in this collection mainly of invited contributions with a few special reprints, we have sought to piece together what we consider to be a suitable reader for understanding the workings of contemporary international marketing. First, a few words about our contributors.

The world has changed and so we must reflect that change. The nation state is no longer able to command an economy on its own. At both corporate and governmental levels, strategic international alliances are both the present and the future. In this collection we begin with a chapter by Angie Driscoll on 'Foreign Market Entry Methods' which not only reviews the internationalization literature but provides a framework for strategic decision-making in this area. This is followed by Burton and Cross who focus on franchising as an entry mode.

Organizational responses to foreign market environments are crucial, and in Part II we have incorporated three chapters. First, Johanson and Mattson, who examine networks as an alternative explanation of international marketing. Next, Andersson and Forsgren discuss the use of networks as a means to determine multinational parental control of subsidiaries, and this leads us into Harrell and Kiefer who have revised and updated an article which drew a great deal of interest when first published and that deals with multinational market portfolios in global strategy development.

International product management is undoubtedly an important area of study and so to begin Part III we invited Warren Keegan to provide an update on the strategic alternatives. There will be few who have followed the international marketing literature who do not know the name of Warren Keegan or are unaware of his contribution to international product strategy. It is a delight therefore to see him here with an update on his earlier work. Similarly, we welcome the country perspectives of our contributors who add to our body of knowledge by sharing illustrations with us. We have here contributors from India, Sweden, Turkey, Britain, Canada, the USA, France and Switzerland.

Rajan Saxena, from India, examines generic product strategies for the world market. However, while this gives us a balance with Warren Keegan of a highly developed country and a developing country, any discussion of international product policy would be incomplete without reference to ISO 9000. Michael Hayes leads us through ISO 9000, indicating clearly how it has become a strategic consideration and a new requirement for doing business overseas. The two chapters which then follow focus on different but related aspects of this. Benham Nakhai and Jaoa Neves review the criteria and the measures for the US, European and Japanese quality awards while Joseph Orsini focuses on the marketing contribution to quality.

'International marketing' has developed to the point where it now has a body of knowledge and its own experienced practitioners. We are fortunate to have been able to persuade so many of them to contribute to this present endeavour. It is indeed rare to find a book such as this where the actual contributors are from different countries and not just from either Europe or North America. The expectations of readers of such books quickly evaporate, normally finding only local contributors talking of foreign markets. We have chosen to break this mould because it deserved breaking.

Take the example of international advertising. No one until now has really thought sufficiently about this topic to investigate how it may function within a Muslim country. In this volume, that has been corrected by Nükhet Vardar of Young & Rubicam, Istanbul, Turkey. Also under advertising, there are contributions on the British multinational advertising agency expansion by Douglas C. West, while Ursula Grüber, based in Paris, focuses on multilingual copy adaptation.

By now, we have already mentioned several of our contributors but we have not yet mentioned the important topic of international distribution systems. Here, we highlight the contribution of James Cooper on international logistics and mention also Therese Maskulka and G. Scott Erickson who have done a fine job for us with their piece on international retailers. It ties in well with the others just mentioned on foreign market entry and adds another level to existing knowledge of this important sector, focusing on the transferability of a competitive advantage to another country. In drawing upon the market profile of their foreign acquisitions and home market strengths, there are links also with the other contributions such as that by Ursula Grüber.

It is relevant at this stage to tell a story about the chapter submitted by Ursula Grüber. Alone of all the contributors, only Ursula Grüber picked up on the mailing address for our contributors being in Calgary, Canada and so enquired as to whether we required American or British spelling. In fact, we have allowed our contributors wide latitude here and allowed the use of whatever spelling is used in their own home country. This should also make the reader more aware of the differences that exist internationally but which do not detract in the main from basic communication but add instead a level of richness. We could have changed the spelling throughout by simply standardizing it, recommending the spelling according to a certain given dictionary, but there is another important issue that we would have simply glossed over, and that is that the meanings of words change also across countries, and that goes beyond the simple spelling. Someone from Britain may agree to 'table' a motion, meaning that he/she intends to include it on the agenda, but for an American or Canadian this would mean shelving it. As Sir Winston Churchill once pointed out, the United States and Britain are two countries divided by a common language.

When it came to the issue of pricing we selected three recent articles which had already previously been published but which we found to be of outstanding merit. The article by Sims, Phillips and Richards had already won the annual best paper prize from ESOMAR (the European Society for Opinion and Marketing Research). The other two contributions are from practitioners and it is purely coincidental that the authors concerned both appear to work for the same consultancy firm – McKinsey's – although in different countries.

The focus of too much media attention has been the degree to which the European Community has fallen short of total harmonization, envisaged in their own legislation by 1993. Instead, we should be looking at the de gree to which there is now one market rather than several, particularly since the joining of the European Union with the EFTA countries minus Switzerland and Leichtenstein formed the European Economic Area, a new enlarged free trade area greater in size than the United States of America. There are many instances now starting to emerge of the very real implications of this new market harmonization and it will have profound implications within Europe until the start of the next century, as this will affect manufacturing and so distribution policy, which in turn has to take into consideration now that there are no artificial constraints, that it is possible to manufacture in one country and sell and distribute in several without non-tariff barriers. Labelling, country of origin and even product standards have been smoothed out to an incredible degree within the last few years and the danger for North Americans is that unless similar progress is made on NAFTA, the winners of the future NAFTA will be decided upon the competitive battlefield of Europe. Witness, for example, the extent to which the German DIN standards now apply internationally. It is just not possible to sit on the sidelines and also be a leader. While the Pacific Rim grows in size and stature, the competitive response should be prepared now to form new and imaginative alliances. This opportunity will not come again. The window of opportunity exists now. As for government, the only role for government in business is to determine the level playing field for its companies. Companies trade, not nations, and in the distortion of natural competition there is a omnipresent governmental factor.

Jim Sherlock, Education Secretary of the Institute of Export, London, reviews for us the Single European Market. On NAFTA, we invited David Elton of the Canada West Foundation to write a suitable introduction. The rationale for this was to have a non-American argue the significance of this new trade agreement. Although three-quarters of Canadian foreign trade is with the United States, protectionism abounds in many forms, not only as regards cross-border traffic but within Canada itself. A bold but necessary step is what now confronts Canada faced with the challenge of NAFTA. The Mexican case is different again but would be founded more on the mainly US foreign direct investment that has taken place and again mainly in the *maquiladora*, the export trading areas. For Mexico, it undoubtedly brings investment and employment and the promise of the good life if its large population can be turned from hungry poor to affluent middle class. At the moment, Mexicans are seen by many in Canada and the US as only future threats to their own employment. The very concept of a new large market that could be larger than the new Single European Market passes most people by, as does the concept of the Single European Market itself.

The whole of Europe may be seen presently to be in a state of transition from the old to the new and uncertain world which is composed of trading blocs. On the outside looking in are four former East European countries; Poland, Hungary, the Czech Republic and Slovakia. The collapse of the former Soviet Union and therefore the empire which it controlled has had significant political and economic ramifications for the world as a whole. Tanks and missiles cannot readily be turned into ploughshares and no one would probably want them even if they could, such is the state of agriculture worldwide. However, a new trading area has been opened up to the international community as a result of these moves and new political, trade and defence alliances will ensue in their wake. Paliwoda therefore guides us through the new marketing environment as Eastern Europe moves westwards.

It is a regret that the one contribution we did not receive was that from the National Westminster Bank in London on the joint development of their expert system 'Pharos' for small and medium-sized companies seeking to enter Europe, which was developed in conjunction with Ernst & Young. This was due to the bombing of the National Westminster Tower in the City of London by the IRA, and the subsequent decanting of various banking departments across the City. Pharos is a particularly innovative development which works by asking you questions about your company in five key areas: general company profile; suppliers; internal operations; products and services; and customers. Conclusions drawn by Pharos are based on your answers to these questions. A full printed report of the analysis can be generated at the end of the consultation. Pharos presently illustrates the way in which we will be moving in future, towards ever-increasing dependence on computers for information of all kinds. What Pharos does is to assess your business at both a strategic and operational level and signal three different levels of market difficulty facing your entry to the Single European Market, from very general points to watch out for to highly specific threats such as existing or impending legislation. Pharos is designed to run on just about any type of computer and does not require the fastest or the most sophisticated to work. It is also updated twice a year and diskettes are provided to subscribers of the service as well as access to a systems helpline.

CONCLUSION

That this book was ever able to come together is due itself to the advent of modern communications. Telephone, fax, and E-mail combine to make it difficult to hide from your co-author or publisher. It has however been a very pleasant task for the pair of us, working independently, but in close agreement, to collaborate on a book such as this. We have enjoyed sharing opinions with academics and practitioners across different continents, never mind countries. We have sought to portray here a realistic representation of what constitutes the international marketing environment of today and of tomorrow. We are both open to reader suggestions for improvements in the next edition.

NOTES

1 Ira A. Kalish, Sandra J. Skrovan and Daniel J. Sweeny (1993), *Global Retailing 2000* (Columbus, Ohio: Management Horizons, Division of Price Waterhouse).
2 Diane Summers (1994), 'Forty into one does go', *Financial Times*, 26 May, p. 11.
3 Theodore Levitt (1983), 'The globalisation of markets', *Harvard Business Review*, May–June.

Part I

Foreign market entry modes

What more basic or fundamental than to begin with the decision which carries the firm overseas? Driscoll offers a literature survey of foreign market entry modes to help managers better serve customers overseas. Institutionalization of entry mode can simply perpetuate problems with a particular entry mode. Reluctance to change arises from different reasons including the inability to effect change once the wrong decision has been made. Angie Driscoll describes the different modes of entry to international markets, examines different characteristics of the various entry modes and discusses a number of situational influences and moderating variables on mode choice. Finally, a comprehensive model for understanding mode choice is presented from her own research which has several implications for managers.

F.N. Burton and A.R. Cross then take one hitherto ignored form of market entry mode – international franchising – and examine it in an international context as a form of relationship. Beyond licensing and extending beyond the domestic economy, franchising is still ill-defined. Different forms of international franchising as an entry mode are discussed as are factors which may help choice selection between these franchising modes.

Part I

Foreign market entry modes

2 Foreign market entry methods:

A mode choice framework

Angie Driscoll

INTRODUCTION

In international strategy formulation, a variety of decisions must be made. Apart from deciding on an appropriate product–market combination, an important strategic issue is the choice of an appropriate institutional arrangement, or entry mode, that makes 'possible the entry of a company's products, technology, human skills, management, or other resources into a foreign country' (Root 1987: 5).[1] That is, the firm must decide the means by which to enter international markets and to best serve their customers in these markets.

Choosing an entry mode into international markets has been identified as a critical decision facing managers (Terpstra and Sarathy 1991; Wind and Perlmutter 1977). The substantial and often lasting impact of the mode decision on the success or failure of international business operations dictates that the decision be carefully considered. Increasingly, major international companies such as Canada's Northern Telecom are making calculated decisions with respect to their international mode of entry. Yet, as other firms have discovered, an ill-judged mode selection in the initial stages of a firm's internationalization can cripple the firm's future market entry and expansion activities. Since it is not uncommon for firms to have their initial mode choice institutionalized over time as new products are sold through the same, established channels, and new markets entered using the same entry method, a problematic initial entry mode choice can be perpetuated through the institutionalization of this mode. Reluctance of firms to change entry modes once they are in place, and the difficulty involved in so doing, makes the mode of entry decision a key strategic issue for firms operating in today's rapidly internationalizing market place.

In what follows, the present paper will build an argument for the development of a comprehensive framework for understanding mode of entry choices. In separate sections the paper describes different modes of entry to international markets, examines different characteristics of the various entry modes, and discusses a number of situational influences and moderating variables on mode choice. Finally, a comprehensive model for understanding mode choice is presented along with remarks on the managerial implications of this model.

FOREIGN MARKET ENTRY METHODS

Three broad groupings emerge when one looks at the assortment of entry modes available to firms when entering international markets: export, contractual and investment modes. Any classification of entry modes is bound to be contentious because the basis for the classification determines the group to which any particular entry mode is placed, but there are some similarities among the different classifications of, for example, Anderson and Gatignon (1986), Root (1987), and Young *et al.* (1989) to support the three 'generic' groups reported here.

With export entry modes, a firm's products are manufactured in the domestic market or a third country, and then transferred either directly or indirectly to the host market. Direct exports usually involve the firm handling documentation, physical delivery, and pricing policies, for example, with the product either being sold direct to the customer or by agents, distributors, and overseas sales affiliates. Indirect export modes, by contrast, generally involve the use of intermediaries such as export houses or trading companies to perform these activities, often without the firm's involvement in the foreign sales of their products.

Contractual entry modes include a variety of arrangements such as licensing, franchising, management contracts, turnkey contracts, non-equity joint ventures, and technical know-how or co-production arrangements. Contractual arrangements generally take place when firms possessing some sort of competitive advantage are unable to exploit this advantage because of resource constraints, for instance, but are able to transfer the advantage to another party. The arrangements often entail long-term relationships between partner firms and typically are designed to transfer intermediate goods such as knowledge and/or skills between firms in different countries. Often there is limited equity investment and little direct participation by the firm in the production and marketing of the product in the international market, although, as Burton and Cross (1995) contend, this is not always the case. Franchising, they argue, can be thought of as a direct form of international involvement and one which can comprise substantial equity investments.

The final group of entry modes is investment modes. Investment entry modes typically include some form of ownership by the firm of production facilities in the host market. These facilities range in nature from assembly to manufacturing plants, and necessitate sizeable equity investments by the firm in the host market. Investments may be made through acquisitions, mergers or greenfield (start-up) investments. Acquisitions refer to the purchase of stock in an existing company in an amount sufficient to acquire control (Kogut and Singh 1988). Acquisitions allow firms to establish themselves quickly in an international market and gain access to an already developed international network. Joint ventures refer to the pooling of assets in common ownership and separate organization by two or more firms who share joint ownership and control over the use and fruits of these assets (Kogut and Singh 1988). Joint ventures thus often can be a short route to establishing a market presence. Finally, greenfield investments refer to start-up investments in new facilities. Such investments can be wholly owned or represent a joint venture between two or more parties. Start-ups can be costly and time consuming to initiate.

CHARACTERISTICS OF DIFFERENT ENTRY METHODS

Distinctions made between these types of entry modes have been manifold; several scholars have proposed that the key characteristics differentiating these mode types are the varying levels of control, dissemination risk, resource commitment, flexibility, and ownership that each entry mode possesses (Agarwal and Ramaswami 1992; Anderson and Gatignon 1986; Douglas and Craig 1989; Erramilli and Rao 1993; Hill *et al.* 1990; Root 1987).

Control

Control has played a prominent role in the mode of entry literature principally because it is seen as a means of maximizing economic efficiency and return on investment in international markets. Defined as 'authority over operational and strategic decision-making' (Hill *et al.* 1990: 118), control allows firms to safeguard supplies of essential inputs to the production process, co-ordinate activities, ensure the quality of end products, and influence the logistical and marketing activities for the product in the target market. It also enables firms to gauge more precisely the needs of the market and to design products and services in such a way as to better satisfy these needs, as well as to anticipate and respond to the moves of competitors. In effect, maintaining decision-making control allows the firm to determine its own destiny.

Dissemination risk

Dissemination risk refers to the extent to which a firm perceives that its know-how will be expropriated by a contractual partner. Since many firms' competitive advantage is grounded in their knowledge assets (whether technological or marketing related), dissemination of this know-how through expropriation by opportunistic parties can create substantial threats to the survival of a firm.[2] While dissemination risk can be combated through comprehensive contingent claims contracts, such contracts may be extremely difficult and costly to specify *ex ante*, if they can be specified at all (Williamson 1985). Protecting proprietary knowledge and speeding it to market in a stream of rapidly and continually improved products and services forms the basis of a firm's competitive advantage over other firms. Thus, preventing 'leakage' of this knowledge is a crucial element in the competitive strategy of a firm.

Resource commitment

Resource commitment refers to the financial, physical and human resources that firms commit to a host market. According to the Uppsala Internationalization Model (Johanson and Vahlne 1977; Johanson and Wiedersheim-Paul 1975), there is necessarily a commitment of resources as international business operations progress. The establishment chain of internationalization proposed by these scholars indicates that over time there is a tendency for firms to increase their resource commitment to foreign markets. This increasing commitment occurs as firms become more experienced and knowledgeable about foreign markets and thus less uncertain about committing these resources.

Committing resources to foreign markets represents a cost factor for firms. Setting up a wholly owned subsidiary, for example, requires the transfer of people and equipment, the purchase, lease or construction of offices and/or manufacturing facilities, and the development of a network of suppliers and customers. As well, there is an opportunity cost of investing resources in one country which may prevent the firm from investing resources in another country.

On top of this high capital cost comes risk. Besides the financial risk involved in committing resources, there is the ever-present threat of expropriation of resources in some countries. The recent outbreak of hostility between opposing factions in Yemen, to take one example, drove many Canadian surveying and oil and gas firms from the field. After employee evacuation, many physical assets were left idle and at the mercy of indigenous warring parties. The threat of abduction of employees also has increased the cost of committing human resources to sensitive areas of the world (e.g. Latin America, South East Asia, the Middle East and Eastern Europe).[3] With premiums for kidnap and ransom insurance running in the range of Cdn$5,000–10,000, firms are having to factor this and many other costs into their resource commitment decisions.

Flexibility

Flexibility, or the ability of a firm to change entry modes quickly and with minimal costs[4] in the face of evolving circumstances (Anderson and Gatignon 1986), is inversely related to resource commitment. Strategic inflexibility, as a result of heavy resource commitment, increases costs when exit barriers prevent firms from repositioning themselves within a market or from retrieving the value of their investments when exiting markets (Porter 1976). Being able to change entry modes quickly and efficiently can prevent firms from incurring considerable losses if the environment changes unfavourably or, conversely, may facilitate substantial gains should the environment change favourably. Since flexible organizations, with their looser organizational structures (less formalization and centralization), are better able to adapt to changing circumstances (Klein 1989), this may give a firm a 'first mover' advantage in that or other markets.

Ownership

Ownership refers to the extent of a firm's equity participation in an entry mode. Ownership of assets occurs when costs can be reduced by internalizing intermediate product markets within the firm (Buckley and Casson 1976; Rugman 1981). Full-equity ownership is optimal when the benefits of ownership (e.g. increased control) are greater than the costs incurred by shared-control equity modes (e.g. dissemination risks). In scholarly literature, ownership of an entry mode frequently is used as a proxy for the amount of control an entry mode affords an entrant (e.g. Gatignon and Anderson 1988). Therefore ownership may be important only to the extent that firms are able to control their activities. To illustrate, to many firms 49 per cent equity means no control whereas 51 per cent equity means total control. However, control may be gained through means other than equity participation. For example, McDonald's is able to have a high degree of control over its franchises without owning them. Furthermore, control of technology may be achieved without equity. What this means, then, is that while ownership has been proposed as an underlying construct influencing mode choice, the efficacy of this construct is related to the control that ownership implies. Examining the amount of control that equity participation affords an entrant may be more useful than studying ownership *per se*.

Hill *et al.* (1990) argue that these differing characteristics amongst the types of entry modes represent underlying constructs that influence mode choice. These constructs vary with the type of entry mode. Table 2.1 compares the characteristics of different entry modes across the three 'generic'

Table 2.1 Characteristics of export, contractual and investment entry modes

Entry method	Control	Dissemination risk	Resource commitment	Flexibility	Ownership
Investments	High	Low	High	Low	High
Contracts	Medium	Med–High	Med–High	Medium	Med–High
Exports	Low	Low	Low	High	Low

Table 2.2 Mean scores for characteristics of export, contractual and investment entry modes[6]

Entry method	Control	Dissemination risk	Resource commitment	Flexibility	Equity ownership(%)
Investments	22.52	14.52	20.76	11.52	95
Contracts	20.24	15.72	16.44	10.56	42
Exports	18.47	12.57	12.76	11.72	27[a]

Notes n = 117
[a] Of the 72 firms using export modes in the study, 19 report that their equity ownership in this mode is 100%.

types. Evidently, investment modes of entry are characterized by high levels of control, ownership, and resource commitment, and low levels of dissemination risk and flexibility. At the other end of the continuum of mode types, exporting arrangements are shown as having low levels of control, dissemination risk, ownership, and resource commitment, and a high degree of flexibility. Finally, sandwiched between the options of investment and exporting modes are contractual modes which are characterized by median amounts of control and flexibility, and medium to high levels of dissemination risk, resource commitment, and ownership.

In a study I recently conducted of Canadian firms active in international markets, empirical evidence supports the contention that these characteristics vary across different mode types in the manner depicted in Table 2.1. Table 2.2 reports the mean scores for the characteristics noted in Table 2.1.[5] In this table, higher mean scores represent higher levels of that characteristic for a particular entry mode.

The only difference between Tables 2.1 and 2.2 is with the flexibility construct. In the empirical study, flexibility is highest for export modes and investment modes and lowest for contractual entry arrangements. While measurement problems may account for this result, it is also conceivable that flexibility is related to the ability of the firm to unilaterally make its own change decisions without having to negotiate change with a contractual partner. Beyond this difference, there is considerable empirical support for the distinctions between the different entry mode types proposed in the academic literature.

While the characteristics recorded above do differ across entry modes, it is important from the perspective of mode choice to note that there can be differences between the *actual* level of a characteristic employed by a firm (as indicated by the entry mode used) and the *desired* level of that characteristic (Erramilli and Rao 1993; Klein 1989), and thus between desired and actual mode choice. Firms may have a desired level of control which they are unable always to attain owing to a number of intervening variables, such as government involvement or corporate policies that prevent desired levels of control being reached. In making mode choices firms need to consider what factors could affect their ability to achieve the desired level of any given characteristic.

Erramilli and Rao (1993) observe that the efficacy of entry mode choice models could be greatly improved by measuring the firm's desired level of different mode characteristics independently of the actual entry mode used by a firm.[7] Further improvements to choice models may be made by identifying and examining the impact of variables that moderate the relationship between desired and actual levels of different mode characteristics. Several of these moderating variables are considered in the next section.

FACTORS MODERATING MODE CHOICE

Some factors that can create a gap between desired and actual levels of various characteristics include government policies and regulations, size of the firm, and corporate policies. While this list of moderating variables is not exhaustive, it serves to suggest factors that can influence a firm's ability to achieve its desired level of different mode characteristics and thus its desired mode choice.

Government policies and regulations

Host government policies, which include capital controls, intellectual property laws, and monetary, transfer pricing, antitrust, labour, and trade and investment policies, may moderate the relationship between a firm's desired level of control or resource commitment, for example, and the actual level of control or resource commitment an entry mode allows a firm. Protectionist import policies in the form of tariffs, import quotas, and duties may prevent the use of export modes and favour contractual or investment entry modes. A firm wishing to use export modes because of their low resource commitment may be unable to do so because of these government policies. Similarly, when host governments prohibit 100 per cent foreign direct investment or place limits on foreign ownership so as to ensure some amount of local ownership of foreign assets or to protect strategically important industrial sectors such as telecommunications, transportation, energy or defence, export and contractual entry modes may have to be deployed instead. Again, a firm wishing to use investment modes because they allow a high degree of control may be prevented from so doing.

The now famous 'Poitiers Incident' of 1983, in which the French government deliberately routed Japanese VCRs through one poorly staffed customs office, illustrates the ability of government policies to affect a firm's desired mode of entry. Where one entry method may become unavailable as a result of government action, another entry method may be able to circumvent such intervention. With respect to the Poitiers Incident, it is interesting to note that by 1984, ten Japanese VCR plants had been announced for Europe (Hood and Truijens 1993).

Home governments also influence the relationship between entry modes desired by firms and the actual entry modes used by firms. Subsidies on outbound foreign direct investment, export controls, price controls and export subsidies all serve to increase or decrease the availability of various modes relative to each other. Many governments offer export incentives to local firms. In Kenya, export compensation of the order of 10 per cent (down from 18 per cent prior to February 1992) is available to producers of certain products (Economic Intelligence Unit 1993a). This makes exporting an attractive entry mode for many of the small Kenyan producers. While a Kenyan company may wish to enter a foreign market through some form of contractual arrangement, the incentives offered through export compensation may change the utilities of these two modes in favour of export modes.

In South Africa the government controls exports, credits and some prices, such as those on gasoline, coal, and paraffin. In 1992, the South African government also introduced new foreign exchange restrictions in an attempt to stem the tide of outbound investment from South African companies. While South African companies can invest abroad, they require the blessing of the Reserve Bank, which only grants this if the firm can show that its investment will be in the national interest through boosting exports, earning additional foreign currency, or safeguarding the source of foreign supplies. One of the biggest obstacles facing foreign investment, however, is the two-tier currency system in South Africa. Investments must be made in financial rands which trade at a substantial discount to the commercial rand (Economic Intelligence Unit 1993b). Thus, while a South African firm may wish to use investment modes of entry to foreign markets to protect its firm-specific advantages from 'leakage', the ability of the firm to use this entry mode may be compromised by the government's policy of having these investments made in the financial rand. There are many firms in other countries also in the same situation, restricted in their mode choices by home government policies.

Firm size

Size is an indicator of the firm's resource availability; increasing resource availability provides the basis for increased international involvement over time. Although small firms may desire a high level of control over international operations and wish to make heavy resource commitments to foreign markets, they are more likely to enter foreign markets using export modes because they do not have the resources necessary to achieve a high degree of control or to make these resource commitments. Export entry modes, with their lower resource commitment, may therefore be more suitable for small firms. While resource availability may limit a firm's ability to match its desired with actual levels of different mode characteristics at any given time, this constraint is not static.

Corporate policy

In some cases firms mandate the use of one entry mode over another. As noted earlier, it is not uncommon for firms to use one mode repeatedly in different entry situations, irrespective of whether this is situationally the optimal entry mode. No matter how much the entry situation influences the firm's desire or need for certain mode characteristics, historical precedent dictates the actual level achieved of that characteristic. Thus, corporate policy can have a pivotal impact on the relationship between desired and actual levels of a given characteristic and therefore mode choice.

These different moderating factors can prevent a firm from matching its desired mode choices with actual mode choices. Klein (1989) refers to this as a positive–normative gap, or the difference between what *is* (actual) and what *should be* (desired).

In addition to there being a number of variables that moderate the relationship between the desired and actual levels of different characteristics of mode choice, there are also a number of situational influences that affect a firm's desired level of a given mode characteristic – or that affect what characteristic is desired. For example, various environmental aspects, such as political and economic volatility of the foreign market, may adversely influence a firm's desire to commit resources to that market for fear that its investments will not be recovered. In the following section I will review several of these situational influences on mode choice.

SITUATIONAL INFLUENCES ON MODE CHOICE

Extant literature describes a diverse range of situational influences that could bear on a firm's desire for certain characteristics of mode choice. For expository convenience these situational influences have been categorized into two broad groupings of firm and environmental factors. Firm factors refer to any competitive advantage or skills a firm may have relative to other firms. They include any product differentiation, knowledge, or managerial experience advantages held within the firm. The strategic motivations, goals, and objectives of a firm also influence that firm's desire for different mode choice characteristics. Environmental factors include aspects such as the demand and competitive conditions in the host market, as well as political, economic, and socio-cultural characteristics of the foreign market.

Firm factors

Firm-specific advantages

Early proponents of foreign direct investment (FDI) theory (e.g. Hymer 1960; Kindleberger 1969) suggest that for foreign firms to compete with indigenous firms who possess knowledge of local customers' tastes and of the legal, business and social systems, foreign investors must detect some sort of compensatory advantage. For a firm to invest in a foreign market, these advantages must be firm-specific, must be transferable, and must outweigh the disadvantages of market and geographical distance (meaning higher transportation costs) relative to local firms. The Hymer–Kindleberger approach to FDI is one which searches for these compensatory advantages; the critical determinant of FDI, according to Caves (1971), lies in the product differentiation advantages obtained from a firm's investments in R&D.

Products distinguished by physical variations, brand name, advertising or after-sales service (e.g. warranties, repair, and replacement policies) which promote preference for one product over another (Chamberlin 1933) may allow a firm to absorb the higher costs of being a foreign firm in a foreign market. Product differentiation advantages give firms a certain amount of discretion in raising prices to exceed costs by more than normal profits. They also allow firms to limit competition through the development of entry barriers, which are fundamental elements in the competitive strategy of a firm (Porter 1980) as well to better serve customer needs and thereby strengthen the competitive posture of the firm *vis-à-vis* other firms (Levitt 1981; Porter 1980). When product differentiation advantages exist, firms seek to establish control over these advantages because they represent a 'natural monopoly' (Buckley and Casson 1979) and to protect these competitive advantages from dissemination through the use of investment modes of entry.

Unlike the oligopoly power in final goods markets suggested by Hymer and Kindleberger, Buckley and Casson's (1985) theory of the multinational enterprise (MNE) stresses the importance of firm-specific advantages in intermediate goods in explaining a firm's mode choice. In particular, an important determinant of the institutional mode of transfer is the nature of know-how. When know-how necessary to manufacture new products is *tacit* in nature – that is, when it is difficult to articulate and thus transfer – it is more likely to be transferred within the firm than in the market because firms are more efficient mechanisms for effecting the transfer of this know-how (Hill *et al.* 1990; Kim and Hwang 1992; Kogut and Zander 1993). The difficulties and costs involved in transferring tacit know-how provide incentive for firms to use investment modes of entry to foreign markets. Investment modes are better able to facilitate the intra-organizational transfer of tacit know-how by utilizing its human capital, drawing upon its organizational memory, and using existing organizational routines to structure the transfer problem (Hill *et al.* 1990: 125).

Experience

Another firm-specific factor influencing mode choice is the international experience of managers and thus of the firm (Benito and Gripsrud 1992;

Dunning 1981; Yu 1990). Experience, which refers to the extent to which a firm has been involved in operating internationally, can be gained either from operating in a particular country or in the general international environment. International experience has an important bearing on the costs and uncertainty of operating in a foreign market; Buckley and Casson (1985) hypothesize that experience reduces the cost and uncertainty of serving a market, and in turn increases the probability of firms committing resources to foreign markets.

In developing their theory of internationalization, Johanson and Vahlne (1977) assert that uncertainty in international markets is reduced through actual operations in foreign markets (experiential knowledge) rather than through the acquisition of objective knowledge. They suggest that it is direct experience with international markets that increases the likelihood of committing a large amount of resources to foreign markets.

Strategic considerations

Strategic factors also effect a firm's mode choice. Firms may enter a foreign market with a particular entry mode not because that mode is optimal for that product-market combination but because that product represents the first step toward expansion in a particular market and thus better fits the long-term or company-wide strategy of the firm. Leveraging one product against another so as to achieve overall corporate objectives (Kim and Hwang 1992) also has an impact on mode choice.

In situations where speed of entry is important, such as when firms want to retaliate against foreign competitors who have entered their domestic market or to attack competitors in a foreign market (whether or not that market is the competitor's home market), highly flexible modes such as export entry modes may be sought over other entry modes that are more time-consuming to initiate. When a firm is following a customer into a foreign market and a greater show of commitment is expected by that customer, firms may consider heavier resource commitment modes. Therefore, the strategic goals and objectives of a firm play important roles in determining what mode characteristics are desired and thus what entry mode a firm may wish to use when entering foreign markets.

Environmental factors

Demand and competitive conditions

One of the most important considerations for firms in choosing an entry method into a foreign country is whether there is a need for the firm's products and services. Moreover, is the need currently being satisfied by other firms or is it likely to be served by other firms? Demand and competitive conditions bear on the cost of serving a market. When demand is low or declining and competition intense, the cost of export or contractual modes relative to investment modes declines. Increasing competition can lead to price wars and subsequently to subnormal returns on investment. The opportunity for monopolistic pricing also may decline and thereby discourage firms from making heavy resource commitments. In a market with favourable demand conditions and few competitors, a firm is more likely to desire tighter control over their international operations. This is because tighter control gives firms more say in how to capitalize on the opportunities present in this market. Firms also have more impetus to commit resources to attractive markets. However, if strategic objectives predominate, resources may still be committed to less attractive markets (Agarwal and Ramaswami 1992).

Political and economic conditions

Unpredictability and volatility in the political and economic environment of the host market increases the perceived risk and uncertainty experienced by the firm. In turn, this disinclines firms from entering the market with entry modes requiring heavy resource commitments; flexibility is alternatively highly desired. Political and economic instability increases the risk of asset expropriation, nationalization or, worse, civil unrest leading to war. The situation in South Africa aptly demonstrates the potential effects of a volatile political and economic situation on firms' mode of entry to that country. In an environment of instability and civil discord as the country adapts to the abolition of apartheid and the transfer of power to a new multiracial government, many foreign firms are embracing a wait-and-see attitude toward investing in South Africa, preferring instead to use export or contractual modes to enter the country.

In Russia, political and economic chaos resulting from the Soviet Empire's collapse, the continuing risk of conflicts both within the Russian federation and with other former Soviet republics, and the harsh and overly bureaucratic business climate serve to discourage foreign investment at a time when investment is much needed. Although many firms such as Canadian Fracmaster Ltd have invested in Russia through joint ventures, these investments are susceptible to the vagaries of the Russian business climate. Contractual arrangements can be broken whimsically, and with no clear system through which to seek legal recourse, entering the Russian market through this type of entry arrangement can be dangerous. In this situation, low resource commitments and low risk entry modes may be preferred. Exporting is thus a primary option available here.

Socio-cultural conditions

More economic interaction, one may argue, occurs between socio-culturally similar countries than between socio-culturally dissimilar countries, at least in the firm's initial international foray (Johanson and Vahlne 1977). Socio-culturally similar countries refer to those countries that have similar business and industrial practices, a common or similar language, and comparable educational levels and cultural characteristics.[8]

Socio-cultural differences between a firm's home country and its host country can create internal uncertainty for the firm, uncertainty which influences the mode of entry desired by that firm. In particular, increasing socio-cultural distance (dissimilarity) multiplies the perceived costs of using high commitment modes as compared to lower resource commitment modes. Further, socio-cultural dissimilarity discourages investment because of the difficulties involved in transferring marketing skills, technology, and human resources to socio-culturally different markets (Davidson 1980). Being unfamiliar with dissimilar cultures creates high information acquisition costs as firms strive to acquire information needed to bridge the cultural gap between home and host country. Information acquisition costs can be lessened by sharing these costs with a contractual partner (Erramilli and Rao 1993).

Situational influences are dynamic rather than static in nature, and change with the situation presented to the firm. These situational variables affect the desire for alternative mode choice characteristics noted earlier and therefore the need for various entry modes. In the next section an attempt is made to combine the different entry modes and their characteristics, as well as the moderating and situational variables on mode choice discussed above, into a framework useful for understanding mode choice. Before presenting this framework, a brief summary of key points made in previous sections may help to recapitulate the arguments presented so far:

1 Alternative modes of entry have different characteristics.
2 These characteristics include control, dissemination risk, resource commitment, flexibility and ownership.
3 The *actual* level of each characteristic is indicated by the mode of entry used (these are summarized in Table 2.1).
4 Firms *desire* certain characteristics of an entry mode depending on the entry situation.
5 Desired and actual levels of these characteristics may differ.
6 A number of factors moderate the relationship between desired and actual levels of the different characteristics.
7 In addition to these moderating variables, various situational variables bear on a firm's *desired* level of any given characteristic.
8 Situational influences may effect different characteristics.

MODELLING MODE CHOICE

Figure 2.1 schematically summarizes the mode choice framework proposed here. It suggests that a number of situational variables affect a firm's

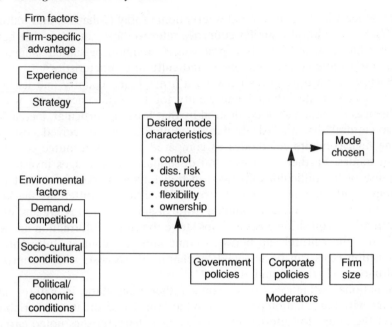

Figure 2.1 Mode choice framework

desired level of different mode choice characteristics and thus the mode desired by firms. The ability of a firm to achieve its desired mode is influenced by a number of different moderating variables. In the absence of moderating variables, a firm's desired mode is equal to its actual mode used in a given entry situation. When present, however, moderating variables can prevent the firm from using its desired mode, thus compelling the firm to select an alternative mode of entry or to reconsider entirely its entry into a particular foreign market.

To illustrate this point, it was mentioned earlier that when firms have some competitive advantage, for example in their ability to develop differentiated products, they desire a high degree of control and a low degree of dissemination risk. From Table 2.1 an investment mode might be the most appropriate mode of entry since these modes allow firms a high degree of control and low dissemination risk. However, if the host government of the country being considered for entry prohibits investment modes of entry, the firm is unable to realize its desired amount of control or dissemination risk through the use of investment modes. The firm either will enter the market using some other mode of entry that is next best in allowing them a high degree of control or low dissemination risk or opt not to enter that market. Similarly, when unfavourable demand and competitive conditions or a volatile political or economic environment in the host market decreases the firm's desire to commit resources to the foreign market but increases its need for flexibility, export entry modes may be preferred. Again, however, if host governments have strict import quotas or high tariffs and duties, or home governments have export controls, firms may not be able to employ export modes.

This model differs from previous mode choice models in several respects. First, previous conceptualizations of mode choice depict a range of situational influences directly affecting mode choice. With this type of model there is an implicit assumption that actual levels of different choice characteristics are equal to desired levels. The extent to which this assumption is valid is uncertain. It seems probable that under some conditions actual and desired levels will differ. The model developed in this paper heeds the advice of Erramilli and Rao (1993) that the efficacy of mode choice models may be improved by conceptualizing a firm's desired level of different mode characteristics independent of actual levels (i.e. actual entry mode used).

Second, this model not only considers a number of situational influences on desired mode choice characteristics, but also, because desired levels of mode characteristics are considered independent of actual modes chosen, it considers several moderating variables. These variables moderate the relationship between a firm's desired and actual levels of different mode choice characteristics.

Third, the model considers a number of alternative mode characteristics. Previous models have tended to concentrate on one characteristic, namely, control, and have assumed it to be the most important choice characteristic. While anecdotal evidence supports this focus, empirical evidence has yet to do so.

This model has several implications for managers. First, it is important that managers recognize that mode choice is a multidimensional task. Each entry mode has a number of different choice characteristics, which may be more or less important to the firm. Prioritizing the characteristics desired of an entry mode according to the firm's entry situation and understanding the compromises and tradeoffs among the various characteristics inherent in each type of entry method should be one of the initial considerations of the firm.

Second, it is important for managers to consider the impact of a number of situational influences on mode choice. These situational variables can have differential impacts on the various characteristics of entry modes. The importance of situational influences, then, is linked to the relative weight given to each of the different mode choice characteristics; the influences are more or less important depending upon the way in which they effect each mode choice characteristic and the importance of each characteristic in a firm's mode decision. For example, socio-cultural differences between a firm's home country and host country may have more of an impact on a firm's ability to retain control over its international operations than on its dissemination risk or resource commitment decisions, the latter being influenced more by a firm's level of experience. If control is the key characteristic desired by the firm, then socio-cultural conditions are the main situational variables the firm should consider. Conversely, if resource commitment is the prime consideration of the firm, the firm's experience represents the most important situational influence. Considering various mode characteristics and the way in which distinct situational influences bear on the desire for alternative characteristics may highlight the complexity of mode choice.

Third, although firms have desired characteristics and thus desired entry modes, their ability to realize these desires is influenced by numerous moderating factors. While some of these moderating factors are beyond the control of the firm, managers need to be aware of the effects of these variables on their ability to use their desired entry mode. Many international executives are acutely aware of some of these moderating variables, especially those of the role of government intervention and firm size. Less obvious, though, is the effect of corporate policy. Where corporate policy mandates the use of a standard, institutionally accepted entry mode for all entry situations, two problems can arise. First, a firm may forfeit a promising market because its institutionally accepted mode is incapable of penetrating the foreign market (Root 1987). Second, although the firm may be able to penetrate the market, its mode of entry may prevent it from fully capitalizing on market opportunities. Being aware of and avoiding the pitfalls inherent in institutionalizing entry modes may lead to more long term success in international markets.

Finally, firms need to pay closer attention to the process aspects of mode choice. Research conducted in the 1970s discovered that international market entry mode decisions are frequently based on 'judgmental reactions to a few market opportunity factors (e.g., macroeconomic and demand indicators) rather than on the use of sophisticated analytical tools' (Goodnow 1985: 17). In a more recent study of Canadian firms' entry mode decisions, Calof (1993) found that, when making a mode change decision, 33 per cent of sampled firms characterize their decision-making process as rational in nature. A further 28 per cent indicate that the decision is made on the basis of a combination of rational processes and gut feel, while the remaining 39 per cent made mode change decisions by gut feel alone.[9] Calof also found that more rationally based decision-making processes resulted in better three-year mode performance. The finding that the highest performance is achieved by firms using a combination of gut feel and rational processes rather than by firms using solely rational processes is notable; nevertheless, the difference between these two processes is not significantly different ($p<0.05$). Gut feel alone results in a significantly lower mode performance than with the other two processes. Attention, therefore, needs to be paid to more careful consideration of a number of different factors influencing mode choice. For academics, the challenge is to develop frameworks for studying mode choice and to translate these frameworks into managerially useful decision making tools. This paper goes part way toward achieving this end.

CONCLUDING REMARKS

Normatively speaking, it cannot be impressed upon firms enough the judiciousness of appraising a number of alternative entry modes when making mode of entry decisions. It is from this 'consideration set' of entry modes that the final mode selection should be made. Because there is a large number of potential entry modes to choose from and since no one mode is optimal under all conditions, firms should consider a number of entry modes rather than institutionalizing one mode of entry. When appraising different entry modes, firms need to consider the situational fit between different mode characteristics, firm and environmental factors that have an important bearing on a firm's preferred entry mode, and the variables that moderate a firm's ability to embrace its preferred mode. Prioritizing the characteristics desired of an entry mode for a given situation, and understanding the manner in which various situational and moderating influences bear on these characteristics, is crucial to selecting a situationally optimal entry mode. While some of these mode characteristics, situational and moderating influences have been considered in this chapter, there will be others not covered here that affect mode choice. These variables are dynamic in nature, changing over time and with each new entry situation. This chapter indicates a number of factors deserving of consideration when making mode choices.

Since selection of an entry mode has an important bearing on a firm's international success and can be instrumental in the future expansion activities of the firm, careful consideration must be given to this decision. The mode of entry decision, however, is not a 'once and for all' decision although an unwise choice can well make it appear so. Firms change their strategic goals and objectives, countries become more or less politically and economically volatile, and ruling governments are ousted. Separately and together these changes may motivate firms to change their mode of entry. As well, entry modes evolve. Innovation is taking place with regard to entry modes. To take one example, franchising, once the preserve of the domestic market, is now an international mode of entry. We do not yet understand what drives this innovation much less foresee the possibility of future international entry modes. It could be suggested that the international success of a firm will depend, at least partly, on the ability of that firm to use a range of entry modes to serve international markets, and to know when one mode may be more situationally appropriate than another.

NOTES

1 So as not to be misleading here, is it emphasized that international strategy formulation is not a sequential process but an iterative one.
2 It is important to note that risk may just as easily arise in developed as well as less-developed countries.

3 Kidnappings are not restricted to less-developed countries. The risk of kidnapping also is high in places such as Sicily in Italy – a developed country.
4 Costs are minimal because change is anticipated and reflected in the institutional arrangement used to enter international markets.
5 Vertical integration is not measured in this research study.
6 Control, dissemination risk, resource commitments and flexibility are multi-item scales measured by seven-point Likert scales while equity ownership is measured using an open-ended question.
7 Erramilli and Rao (1993) limit their argument to the control characteristic; however, the same argument can be extended to other mode characteristics.
8 Cultural characteristics refer to 'the sum total of knowledge, beliefs, art, morals, laws and customs, and any other capabilities and baits acquired by humans as a member of society' (Wertsch 1985: 2). Cultural characteristics of a market influence the consumption patterns of consumers – who buys what, where, when, how often, and how much. Material culture affects the level of demand for various products and services, the quality and types of products and services demanded, their functional and aesthetic features, as well as the means of production and distribution. Religion, beliefs, superstitions, social institutions etc. influence the acceptance of certain types of products and services (e.g. food, clothing, music, art) and the standards of beauty in each culture.
9 Calof (1993: 105–6) defines these three processes in the following way:

> *Rational process:* The decision to change mode and the subsequent mode choice is based on detailed analysis and discussion. The process closely approximates that suggested by classic strategy process theorists: (i) the problem is identified; (ii) on the basis of a simple and quick analysis, several options are identified; (iii) options that emerged as viable are subject to detailed study, (iv) the option whose sales potential and costs are most appropriate for the market size was submitted for approval.

> *Gut feel:* The mode decision is made at a discrete point in time without benefit of a formal study or, according to the decision-maker(s), the decision is made entirely on the basis of intuition or gut feel.

> *Combination of rational processes and gut feel:* The decision-making process contains elements of both a rational process and a gut feel process. While no formal study of mode choice is conducted and only one mode is usually considered, management does consult with outsiders and discusses options with other company personnel.

REFERENCES

Agarwal, Sanjeev and Ramaswami, Sridhar N. (1992) 'Choice of foreign market entry mode: impact of ownership, location and internalization factors', *Journal of International Business Studies*, First Quarter, 1–27.
Anderson, Erin and Gatignon, Hubert (1986) 'Modes of entry: a transaction cost analysis and propositions', *Journal of International Business Studies*, Fall, 1–26.
Benito, Gabriel R.G. and Gripsrud, Geir (1992) 'The expansion of foreign direct investments: discrete rational location choices or a cultural learning process?', *Journal of International Business Studies*, Third Quarter, 461–76.
Buckley, Peter J. and Casson, Mark C. (1985) *The Economic Theory of the Multinational Enterprise*, London: Macmillan.
Buckley, Peter J. and Casson, Mark C. (1979) 'A theory of international operations', reprinted in Peter J. Buckley and Pervez Ghauri (eds) *The Internationalization of the Firm: A Reader*, London: Academic Press, 1993, pp. 45–50.

Buckley, Peter J. and Casson, Mark C. (1976) *The Future of the Multinational Enterprise*, London: Macmillan

Burton, F. N. and Cross, A. R. (1995) 'Franchising and foreign market entry', in S. Paliwoda and J. Ryans, Jr (eds) *International Marketing Reader*, London: Routledge.

Calof, Jonathan (1993) 'The mode choice and change decision process and its impact on international performance', *International Business Review*, 2 (1): 97–120.

Caves, Richard E. (1971) 'International corporations: the industrial economics of foreign investment', *Economica*, February, 1–27.

Chamberlin, Edward H. (1933) *The Theory of Monopolistic Competition*. Cambridge, Mass.: Harvard University Press.

Davidson, William H. (1980) 'The location of foreign direct investment activity', *Journal of International Business Studies*, 11, 9–22.

Douglas, Susan P. and Craig, C. Samuel (1989) 'Evolution of global marketing strategy: scale, scope and synergy', *Columbia Journal of World Business*, Fall, 47–59.

Dunning, John H. (1981) *International Production and the Multinational Enterprise*, London: Allen & Unwin.

Economic Intelligence Unit (1993a) *Kenya*, London: Economist Publications.

Economic Intelligence Unit (1993b) *South Africa*, London: Economist Publications.

Erramilli, M. Krishna and Rao, C.P. (1993) 'Service firms' international entry mode choice: a modified transaction-cost analysis approach', *Journal of Marketing*, 57 (July): 19–38.

Gatignon, Hubert and Anderson Erin (1988) 'The multinational corporation's degree of control over foreign subsidiaries: an empirical test of a transaction cost explanation', *Journal of Law, Economics, and Organization*, 4 (2): 305–36.

Goodnow, James D. (1985) 'Developments in international mode of entry analysis', *International Marketing Review*, 2 (3): 17–30.

Hill, Charles W.L., Hwang, Peter and Kim, W. Chan (1990) 'An eclectic theory of the choice of international entry mode', *Strategic Management Journal*, 11 (2): 117–28.

Hood, Neil and Truijens, Thorsten (1993) 'European locational decisions of Japanese manufacturers: survey evidence on the case of the U.K.', *International Business Review*, 2 (1): 39–63.

Hymer, Stephen A. (1960) 'The international operations of national firms: a study of direct foreign investment', doctoral dissertation, Massachusetts Institute of Technology; reprinted Cambridge, Mass.: MIT Press 1973.

Johanson, Jan and Vahlne, J. E. (1977) 'The internationalization process of the firm: a model of knowledge development and increasing foreign market commitment', *Journal of International Business Studies*, 8(1): 23–32.

Johanson, Jan and Wiedersheim-Paul, Finn (1975) 'The internationalization of the firm – four Swedish cases', *Journal of Management Studies*, 12: 305–22.

Kim, W. Chan and Hwang, Peter (1992) 'Global strategy and multinationals' entry mode choice', *Journal of International Business Studies*, First Quarter, 29–53.

Kindleberger, C.O. (1969) *American Business Abroad: Six Lectures in Direct Investment*, New Haven, Conn.: Yale University Press.

Klein, Saul (1989) 'A transaction cost explanation of vertical control in international markets', *Journal of the Academy of Marketing Science*, 17 (3): 253–60.

Kogut, Bruce and Singh, Harbir (1988) 'The effect of national culture on the choice of entry mode', *Journal of International Business Studies*, 19, 411–32.

Kogut, Bruce and Zander, Udo (1993) 'Knowledge of the firm and the evolutionary theory of the multinational corporation', *Journal of International Business Studies*, Fall, 625–45.

Levitt, Theodore (1981) 'Marketing success through differentiation of anything', *Harvard Business Review*, January–February, 83–91.

Porter, Michael (1976) *Interbrand Choice, Strategy and Bilateral Market Power*, Cambridge, Mass.: Harvard University Press.

Porter, Michael (1980) *Competitive Strategy*, New York: Collier Macmillan.

Root, Franklin R. (1987) *Entry Strategies for International Markets*, Lexington, Mass.: D.C. Heath.

Rugman, Alan M. (1981) *Inside the Multinationals: The Economics of Internal Markets*, New York: Columbia University Press.

Terpstra, Vern and Sarathy, Ravi (1991) *International Marketing*, 5th edn, New York: Dryden Press.

Wertsch, J. (1985) *Culture, Communication, and Cognition*, New York: Cambridge University Press.

Williamson, Oliver E. (1985) *The Economic Institutions of Capitalism: Firms, Markets, Relational Contracting*, New York: The Free Press.

Wind, Yoram and Howard Perlmutter (1977) 'On the identification of frontier issues in multinational marketing', *Columbia Journal of World Business*, Winter, 131–9.

Young, S., Hamill, J. Wheeler, C. and Davies, J.R. (1989) *International Market Entry and Development: Strategies and Management*, Hemel Hempstead, Herts.: Harvester Wheatsheaf.

Yu, Chwo-Ming (1990), 'The experience effect and foreign direct investment', *Weltwirtschaftliches Archiv*, 126 (3): 561–80.

3 Franchising and foreign market entry

F. N. Burton and A. R. Cross

INTRODUCTION

One area of international marketing which has enjoyed considerable attention in recent years is the study of the various organizational structures and institutional arrangements available to firms seeking to extend their operations beyond national boundaries. There is now an appreciable body of literature (surveyed, amongst others, by Young *et al.* 1989) which describes in detail these foreign market entry modes and which attempts to analyse determinant factors behind a firm's selection of optimal mode for a given circumstance. However, within this body of literature scant attention has been paid to one particular entry method: the use of franchise contracts to establish non-domestic operations. Over the last two decades, franchising has enjoyed remarkable success as a growth strategy for domestic firms in many industrialized countries, not least in the USA, where more than one-third of all retail sales are now estimated to be sold through franchise outlets of one form or another (Bradley 1991). In a similar, though probably less dramatic fashion, franchise contracts are also being observed more frequently during the internationalization process of firms (e.g. Kaynak 1988, Falbe and Dandridge 1992). Indeed, many internationally franchising companies are today household names, and the Italian clothes retailer Benetton, the UK retailers Body Shop and Marks & Spencer, and the ubiquitous US fast-food chain McDonald's are just a few examples of many companies that have successfully expanded their operations overseas using franchising. In addition to the cursory treatment which franchising has received in the foreign market entry analysis literature, certain assumptions held of it, in particular that it involves an arm's-length transaction between independent parties equivalent to those found in international licensing agreements, have, we feel, misrepresented franchising in the limited accounts found in this literature.

In keeping with the central theme of this book, this chapter highlights the rather simplistic manner in which franchising has been treated to date in the international marketing literature and indicates how a subsequent re-evaluation may impact on our theoretical appreciation of franchising when used to enter and develop non-domestic markets. To do this, we begin by defining what we mean by international franchising and then describe how it has been traditionally regarded in the literature. Then, by outlining the variety of international franchise arrangements in use today, we show why this traditional view cannot be universally applied to the business method in practice. We conclude by discussing, in a rather conceptual manner, some of the factors which may enter into a firm's selection of appropriate international franchise arrangement for a particular situation. Hopefully, in doing so, this chapter will lay some of the groundwork that will facilitate more relevant empirical investigation. This will help to advance our academic understanding of franchising as an entry mode and enable it to be placed more accurately in the general schema of foreign market entry theory.[1]

INTERNATIONAL FRANCHISING: TOWARDS A DEFINITION

It is accepted that franchising, which literally means 'freedom from servitude', is a business concept which defies precise definition. The term has many connotations and the literature abounds with different methods of categorization, depending on, for example, what is being franchised or the nature of the relationship between the participants in the franchise contract (see, for example, Bradley 1991; Euromonitor 1987; Hoffman and Preble 1991). However, the focus of this chapter is on business format franchising (also referred to as second generation franchising) since this 'seems to be the basis of all successful [international] franchising operations during the last three decades' (Götberg 1989, confirmed by Sanghavi 1990; Welch 1989) and because market entry analysis literature almost universally concentrates on this form.[2] But before our critical evaluation of the currently held perceptions of international franchising in the foreign market entry literature can begin, an appreciation of what constitutes business format franchising (henceforth franchising) when used to cross national boundaries is required. The following description encapsulates the most important characteristics of franchising contracts when applied to international markets.[3]

International franchising is a foreign market entry mode that involves a relationship between the entrant (the franchisor) and a host country entity, in which the former transfers, under contract, a business package (or format), which it has developed and owns, to the latter. This host country entity can be either a franchisee, a subfranchisor, or it can be an entity in which the franchisor has made an equity investment.[4] The package transferred by the franchisor contains most of the elements necessary for the local entity to establish a business and run it profitably in the host country in a prescribed manner, regulated and controlled by the franchisor. Thus it can contain, *inter alia*, trade marks, trade names, copyright, designs, patents, trade secrets, business know-how and geographic exclusivity. The package may also include the right for the local entity to establish and service its own subsystem of subfranchisees within its appointed territory. In addition to this package, the franchisor also typically provides local entities with managerial assistance in setting up and running local operations. All locally owned franchisees, subfranchisees and subfranchisors can also receive subsupplies from the franchisor and benefit from centrally co-ordinated advertising. In return for this business package the franchisor receives from the franchisee or sub-franchisor an initial fee up-front and/or continuing franchise fees, based typically on a percentage of annual turnover or as a mark up on goods supplied directly by the franchisor.

THE TRADITIONAL VIEW OF INTERNATIONAL FRANCHISING

The traditional view of international franchising as a foreign market entry mode seems to be rooted in two presumptions: first, that it is basically domestic franchising which has been extended to the international environment and, second, that it should be regarded as a particular type of licence.

Managerial economists, who view franchising as being a hybrid organizational form, located somewhere between the extremes of vertical integration on the one hand and completely independent operations on the other, hold that although the parties to the franchise arrangement are independent (Adams and Mendelsohn 1986; Caves and Murphy 1976; Rubin 1978) the transactions which take place between them can be likened to those of intra-firm vertical integration (Norton 1988) because features of the contract encourage the agent (the franchisee) to act in the interests of the principal (the franchisor). These features include unilateral termination clauses in the franchise contract (Rubin 1978); the residual claimant status of the franchisee (Mathewson and Winter 1985); hostage effects and asset specificity (Williamson 1983); and reduced agency costs associated with monitoring and policing the contract (Brickley and Dark 1987).[5] It is thus argued that the franchise contract provides the franchisor with greater control than would occur in fully market located transactions whilst avoiding full integration and its associated costs. However, this perspective is derived from studies on companies that confine their franchise systems to domestic markets only. It seems fair to suggest that recent descriptions of international franchising in the foreign market entry literature merely extends, perhaps not surprisingly, this domestic experience to the international environment. As a consequence, franchised operations in host countries are generally presumed to be independent from the franchisor in respect of ownership (Götberg 1989;

Hoffman and Preble 1991; Kaynak 1988; Oman 1984, amongst others) and, inherent to this, that franchise contracts are negotiated with each franchisee on an individual basis.

Many authors working in the field of international market entry also assert that franchising should be considered as a variant of licensing. For example, Oman, in outlining a taxonomy of international market entry modes, states that 'franchising may be regarded as a particular type of licensing' (1984: 15). Similarly, Root (1987: 109) insists that 'franchising is a form of licensing in which a company (franchisor) licenses a business system as well as other property rights to an independent company or person (franchisee)'. The few foreign market entry analysts that actually specify international franchising as a discrete entry mode, such as Anderson and Gatignon (1986), Erramilli (1990) and Hill *et al.* (1990) also explicitly concur with this view. Indeed, Boddewyn *et al.* (1986: 55), in common with others, have taken this stance as far as to suggest that 'since franchising is a form of licensing, it will not be discussed as a separate type of foreign business involvement'. We feel that this kind of perspective has encouraged analysts to overlook franchising as a distinct foreign market entry mode in its own right. In so far as the term 'licensing' expresses a permission granted contractually by an entrant to a local entity for the latter to use the proprietary technology or know-how of the former, in return for financial compensation, this supposed equivalence of licensing and franchising does seem reasonable – franchising clearly involves a similar, although often more comprehensive, technology transfer from the home country entrant to the host country entity. But foreign market entry analysts consider licensing to be an arm's-length transaction that occurs in the market place between independent parties and is therefore viewed as a zero equity form of international association (Contractor 1985, 1990). When categorized as a variant of licensing, franchising is automatically but erroneously attributed with similar characteristics (Burton and Cross 1993b).[6]

It follows from both the managerial economist's domestic-only based perspective of the franchise contract and the categorization of franchising as a variant of licensing, that, when used to cross national boundaries, franchise arrangements are perceived to be purely arm's-length, contractual, non-equity, non-direct forms of international association. This is certainly how they appear to be treated in the foreign market entry analysis literature (as exemplified by Anderson and Gatignon 1986; Contractor 1990; Czinkota and Ronkainen 1988; Erramilli 1990; Root 1987; Young 1987; Young *et al.* 1989, amongst others). The descriptions in the international marketing literature of the advantages and disadvantages of using franchising to access non-domestic markets often reflects this view (see Table 3.1).

But initial observations of current international franchising activity indicates that this perspective is not entirely realistic.

Table 3.1 Advantages/disadvantages to the entrant of franchising across national boundaries described in the literature[a]

	Suggested by
Advantages	
Low risk, low cost entry mode	Brooke (1986); Götberg (1989)
Ability to develop new and distant international markets, relatively quickly and on a larger scale than otherwise possible	Götberg (1989: Bradley (1991) Root (1987; Young *et al.* (1989)
Using highly motivated business contacts with local market knowledge and experience	Root (1987); Götberg (1989); Bradley (1991)
Creating additional turnover with small investments in, for example, personnel, capital outlays, production and distribution	Götberg (1989); Bradley (1991) Young *et al.* (1989)
Precursor to future direct investment in foreign market	Root (1987); Götberg (1989); Hoffman and Preble (1991)
A standardized, worldwide company profile and brand image created generating economies of scale in marketing to international customers	Brooke (1986); Root (1987); Götberg (1989)
Disadvantages	
Lack of full control over franchisee's operations resulting in problems with co-operation, communications, quality control, etc.	Root (1987); Götberg (1989); Young *et al.* (1989)
Limitations of franchisor's profit	Root (1987); Götberg (1989)
Costs of creating and marketing a unique package of products and services recognized internationally	Götberg (1989)
Costs in protecting goodwill and brand-name	Götberg (1989)
Problems with local legislation, including transfers of money, payments of franchise fees, and government-imposed restrictions on franchise agreements	Root (1987); Götberg (1989)
Disclosing internal business secrets and knowledge may create a potential future competitor	Root (1987); Götberg (1989); Young *et al.* (1989)
Risk to the company's international profile and reputation if some franchisees underperform	Götberg (1989)

Note: This list is merely illustrative and far from exhaustive.

DIFFERENT FORMS OF INTERNATIONAL FRANCHISING AS AN ENTRY MODE[7]

We can identify two elements of the international franchise arrangement which demonstrates that this traditional view of international franchising as ubiquitously being a non-equity, non-direct form of international association is limited in scope. These are (a) the variety of mechanisms which franchising companies can use to transfer their business package to each individual host country entity; and (b) the question of ownership of the local entity to which the transfer is made. To explain, it is necessary to outline briefly, and somewhat simplistically, the five different institutional arrangements for conducting transactions available to internationalizing firms today, as described by lawyers and practitioners who have negotiated international franchise contracts (such as Abell 1990; Mendelsohn 1992).[8]

In the first of these, *direct international franchising*, the market entrant, the franchisor, does transfer the business package directly to each individual unit (i.e. the sales outlet or production facility) in the target country or territory. This can be done at arm's-length by concluding franchise contracts with independent parties (franchisees), or it can be arranged hierarchically by establishing franchisor-owned (i.e. company-owned) units. These units can be referred to as external and internal franchisees respectively. In this arrangement, all elements of service (the term 'service' here includes the provision of on-going backup and support as well as monitoring and policing activities) which these units receive is provided directly by the franchisor from the home country.

However, franchising companies also establish wholly owned branches or subsidiaries in the host country in order to service, police and monitor the internal and external units created by direct international franchise contracts. This arrangement is termed *direct international franchising with subsidiary*.

Alternatively, franchising companies also deploy 'intermediary' parties, (termed subfranchisors) in host countries and territories. These subfranchisors can be either wholly owned by the franchisor (*subsidiary international franchising*), jointly owned with a local partner (*joint-venture international franchising*) or totally independent entities (*master international franchising*). In each case the subfranchisor is granted the exclusive right, by the franchisor, to exploit the franchisor's business package within a designated territory. These subfranchisors then develop and service their own subsystem of units, which can be either owned by the subfranchisor or subfranchised to independent parties (subfranchisees).[9]

Franchising companies often deploy a mix of these arrangements in their international franchising strategy. For example, in one market the franchisor may have established a subsystem of fully company-owned (internal) units via a direct international franchise agreement, whilst at the same time developing a second market through a master international agreement (in which all units established are, by definition, external to the franchisor).

What this brief description illustrates is that franchising, when used to extend a company's activities to non-domestic markets, is a more complex phenomenon than is currently appreciated by foreign market entry analysts, and is certainly institutionally more complex than the assumption that it is merely a form of licensing presupposes (Burton and Cross 1993b). More importantly, franchisor *investment* can, and does, take place in the host country, both at the subfranchisor level (in the form of subsidiaries and joint-ventures) and at the unit level (in the form of internal units). It must therefore be unrealistic to view international franchising ubiquitously as a purely arm's length, contractual, non-equity, non-direct form of international association between entrants and host country entities.

Extending this argument further, a continuum for each foreign market penetration using franchising can be envisaged, depending on the percentage of equity that the franchisor invests at the subfranchisor level and/or the unit level. This will range from one extreme, where the percentage equity invested is zero (using master international franchising or direct international franchising with all franchisee-owned units), through to the other extreme, where all the local units and support facilities in the host market are 100 per cent owned by the franchisor (when all established units are internal to the franchisor in either direct international franchising, with or without accompanying subsidiary, or subsidiary international franchising). As the level of equity invested at both the subfranchisor level and the unit level increases along this continuum, a point must come where market penetration is effectively taking place by foreign direct investment. At this point (and possibly earlier) many of the characteristics presupposed by the traditional view of international franchising, such as it being a low-capital-outlay, low-risk and low-control market entry mode, must have their status challenged. It is this observation that undermines the traditional view of international franchising outlined above and summarized in Table 3.1.

Of course, the proportion of equity that a franchising company invests in a particular host country is not fixed, but can change through time. Direct international franchising can become subsidiary international franchising incrementally in, for example, the case of a local company-owned subsidiary that is set up first to service existing franchisees then later develops its own subfranchisees. In the same way, the proportion of internal to external franchisees or subfranchisees in each market can change. Indeed, some authors have suggested that there may well be a life cycle effect in international franchising entry strategy in this respect. For example, Hackett (1976), Young *et al.* (1989) and Welch (1989) propose that franchisors penetrate foreign markets with internal, company-owned units as a market testing strategy before 'beginning major franchising efforts'

(Hackett 1976: 71). Conversely, others concur with the domestically oriented observation of Lillis *et al.* (1976) and suggest that international franchising is an inexpensive method of testing the market potential of a country prior to making a more substantial financial commitment (Hoffman and Preble 1991; Root 1987).

It should be noted that foreign market entrance which involves a high (or total) proportion of internal to external units, or where equity is being invested in subfranchisors, should still be described as international franchising and not foreign direct investment. This is because it is merely the institutional mode of transfer of the entrant's business format that differs between hierarchical and 'arm's-length' transactions (i.e. whether the transfer takes place within the firm or in the open market). The essential characteristics of the transferred business remains the same, irrespective of the ownership status of the entity to which the transfer is made, and consumers perceive no apparent difference between franchisee-owned and franchisor-owned units in the system. Indeed, this is one of the aims of the franchisor (Sanghavi, 1990). Furthermore, the same package can be transferred to one subsystem which contains entirely internal units and subfranchisors, and to another with entirely external units, while equally, subfranchisors and individual units in one country can be transformed from being franchisor-owned to independently-owned, and vice versa, relatively easily. The term 'international franchising', we argue, embraces each of these eventualities.

POTENTIAL FACTORS INFLUENCING THE CHOICE BETWEEN THESE MODES

As already indicated, although there has been little academic effort to systematically analyse and explore motivational issues behind a franchising firm's selection of one of these various international franchise arrangements to particular situations, it would still be interesting to look briefly at each in turn and discuss their application in international markets.

Direct international franchising is conceptually the most straightforward form of international franchising. As franchising firms tend to make available to purchasers a single uniform and standardized franchise package, the franchisor will generally not modify the package nor introduce new procedures or systems for specific markets. Thus, when used as a foreign market entry strategy, direct international franchising is often merely an international extension of the franchisor's domestic franchise network (thus conforming to the traditional view of international franchising). As a consequence, direct international franchising is most often observed between firms from psychically proximate countries, such as the US and Canada, the UK and Eire, and Australia and New Zealand, where the close franchisor/franchisee relationships often fundamental to the success of this business method can be promoted (Hoffman and Preble 1991). The franchised product and/or service would probably require significant modification in order to be viable should there be significant linguistic, cultural or commercial differences between the host and home country markets, and this would be prohibitively costly to arrange contractually if a contract with each entity in the host country is entered into individually. (The burden on franchisor management, in terms of servicing units, would also increase as the number of units established directly increases.) As Abell (1990: 21) suggests, direct international franchising 'is not . . . usually suited to distant markets with a different language and business culture'.

In order to obtain closer and more effective control of franchise subsystems and their development, and to reduce servicing costs, franchising entrants can use subsidiaries in host countries. These either service existing units directly or act as a subfranchisor. These subsidiaries may also provide the franchisor with access to various forms of government grants and subsidies. However, this type of international involvement requires significant financial and managerial commitment on the part of the franchisor and a degree of commercial sophistication which many franchisors may not possess. The equity invested in the subsidiary will also increase the franchisor's exposure to political risk, which may dissuade the use of this arrangement when psychic distance is perceived as significant.

An alternative method open to franchisors to reduce their transactions costs associated with identifying suitable franchisees, negotiating with them, and servicing, policing and monitoring them, is for the franchisor to enter into a single franchise agreement with a subfranchisor in the host country. International franchise arrangements which use subfranchisors containing a proportion of host country ownership (i.e. master and joint-venture international franchising) can also use the subfranchisor's local knowledge to adapt and modify the franchisor's business package appropriately (Falbe and Dandridge 1992). This serves to minimize cultural and language problems and reduce legal barriers. However, offsetting these advantages, to an extent, are the difficulty and costs associated with selecting a suitable subfranchisor partner and what to do if this subfranchisor underperforms.

In joint-venture international franchising, the local partner's contribution to the subfranchisorship helps to reduce the investment levels associated with forming a subsidiary (so decreasing any exposure to political risk) while at the same time maintaining similar levels of hands-on control for the franchisor (Welch 1989). The franchisor may also benefit from the local party's commercial and political contacts, market knowledge, manpower and existing distribution networks (although external franchisees and subfranchisees, it could be argued, fulfil a similar role). This type of association, which can help to overcome any local prejudice on the part of government, commerce or private individuals against the franchisor, may also benefit from laws specially designed to attract joint-ventures (such as tax holidays and preferential profit repatriation regulations which might not otherwise be available to them or their subfranchisors). However, a disadvantage of joint-venture international franchising is that there may be lower returns to the franchisor since the initial and continuing franchise fees levied on individual units will now need to be divided between the franchisor and the joint-venture partner. Other disadvantages are probably those most often argued for joint ventures in general, including conflicts in business culture and management style, conflicts of interest, and high administration costs (Harrigan 1988). The operation of a number of joint ventures in an international franchise system will of course multiply such difficulties. Problems associated with terminating an unsatisfactory joint venture, and subsequent questions over the ownership of internal units that it has established, may also prove a disincentive to invest in this manner. Joint-venture international franchising would probably be employed when host country laws stipulate the presence of a local national partner, when fiscal benefits accrue, or when the local knowledge of a partner is essential to the success of the venture but when the franchisor still needs to maintain a degree of control over the franchise subsystem. In other circumstances master international franchising is likely to be preferable.

As master international franchises involve a purely arm's-length transaction with an independent entity in the host country (and as such conform closely to the traditional view of international franchising), the franchisor can establish its franchise system in foreign markets without taking on the financial and management commitment required in joint-venture or subsidiary international franchising (Hackett 1976). This minimizes the entrant's exposure to political risk and is a rapid market penetration strategy but, as with joint-venture international franchising, offsetting this is that returns are shared. Furthermore, master international franchising is very much a 'hands-off' form of international association. The franchisor relinquishes control of individual subfranchise systems to a much greater degree than with the other forms. By strictly and clearly defining the contractual duties and obligations of the subfranchisor such difficulties should be minimized, but problems can still arise. For example, exactly how and at what rate the franchise subsystem is developed is determined primarily by the financial and managerial resources of the subfranchisor and this may not tally with the wishes or requirements of the franchisor. As with joint-venture international franchising, should any disputes arise between the franchisor and the subfranchisor in this arrangement hostage effects in the parties' negotiations may develop: in many cases independent subfranchisees will have only had dealings with their local subfranchisor and may be reluctant to deal with the franchisor directly or a new subfranchisor.

CONCLUDING REMARKS

International franchising activity is often far more complex than its traditional treatment in the foreign market entry literature supposes. Firms employing franchising contracts in their internationalization process can, and frequently do, invest significant amounts of equity in host country franchise subsystems. It is this possibility that invalidates the universal applicability of many of the assumptions underpinning the traditional view of this entry mode. In each of the international franchising arrangements described above, the franchising entrant will need to structure franchise contracts tightly to reduce the risks associated with both creating a competitor (by its very nature the standardized business format package is often easily copied) and damage to the goodwill and image of the franchisor's system in both that market and (more significantly) internationally, should any entity in the franchise subsystem underperform. As these risks increase, so will the pressure on the franchising entrant to internalize overseas operations and invest equity in the host country in the form of company-owned units and subfranchisors. However, increasing internalization reduces many of the advantages previously cited for franchising, such as its low capital outlay and rapid market penetration characteristics. This is the dilemma faced by internationally franchising companies, and indeed by all internationally active companies: when to internalize overseas operations and when to conduct them at arm's length with independent parties. We have outlined only a few of the factors that may enter into a franchising firm's response to this decision and clearly there is opportunity here for detailed empirical investigation. Such investigation would, we feel, not only improve our understanding of this entry mode and help it to become clearly recognized as a specific entry mode in its own right, but could also generate fruitful avenues of research of relevance to foreign market entry theory and analysis.

NOTES

1 This chapter is a synthesis of arguments presented by the authors in three recent papers (Burton and Cross 1993a, 1993b, 1993c).
2 We note that the main characteristics of business format franchising are very similar to those of other operational forms, such as product and trade-name franchising (also called first-generation franchising), and so some of the discussion in this chapter will apply equally to all forms, particularly in respect to the different institutional arrangements of international franchising described later. But most first-generation franchises, such as those associated with car dealerships, petrol service stations and soft-drink bottlers, probably more closely resemble licensing as an entry mode than they do business format franchising and in this respect are beyond the terms of this account (see Burton and Cross 1993b).
3 We acknowledge that this description does not conflict greatly with that for domestic-only franchising, but we feel that there are significant differences between the two to warrant its inclusion here.

4 This is an important point which will be returned to later.
5 See, amongst others, Thompson and Wright 1988: ch. 4, for a comprehensive review of these principal–agent issues.
6 We do note that equity participation by licensors in licensee firms is a growing phenomenon often overlooked by foreign market entry analysts. In one international survey around one in seven licensing firms questioned indicated that they had an equity stake in the companies to which they licensed (OECD 1987).
7 Both the practice and study of franchising are impeded by the confusing terminology surrounding the subject. In order to introduce uniformity, Konigsburg (1987) presents a lexicon of recommended terminology to which this account conforms throughout.
8 This section is based on literature describing legal aspects of extending franchise systems to international markets (Abell 1990; Mendelsohn 1992) and also draws on our preliminary observations of UK-based franchisors operating overseas and non-UK based franchisors operating in the UK.
9 These various forms have received only cursory attention in the limited available literature on international franchising. For example, Welch (1989) recognizes master franchising; Hoffman and Preble (1991) subsidiary and master franchising. Hackett (1976) excludes only the subsidiary international franchising option and the possibility that the franchisor can also own subfranchisees when it has equity in the subfranchisor. However, Aydin and Kacker (1990), for example, do not recognize any of these arrangements at all, merely inferring that all activity is direct international franchising. Furthermore, there is little attempt in this literature to define the terms used, or to fully explore and systematically analyse motivations behind the deployment of these various franchise arrangements. As for franchisor ownership of units in a system, this is a well-documented phenomenon, observed in both the domestic context (e.g. Brickley and Dark 1987; Norton 1988) and internationally (e.g. Aydin and Kacker 1990; Brooke 1986). But, unlike the domestic context, again there has been little effort to explain patterns of franchisor-owned to franchised units in the international context.

REFERENCES

Abell, M. (1990) *The International Franchise Option*, London: Waterlows.
Adams, J. and Mendelsohn, M. (1986) 'Recent developments in franchising', *Journal of Business Law*, 206–19.
Anderson, E. and Gatignon, H. (1986) 'Modes of foreign entry: a transaction cost analysis and propositions', *Journal of International Business Studies*, Fall, 1–26.
Aydin, N. and Kacker, M. (1990) 'International outlook of US-based franchisors', *International Marketing Review*, 7(2): 43–53.
Boddewyn, J.J., Halbrich, M.B. and Perry, A.C. (1986) 'Service multinationals: conceptualization, measurement and theory', *Journal of International Business Studies*, Fall, 41–57.
Bradley, F. (1991) *International Marketing Strategy*, Englewood Cliffs, N.J.: Prentice-Hall.
Brickley, J.A. and Dark, F.H. (1987) 'The choice of organizational form: the case of franchising', *Journal of Financial Economics*, 18: 401–20.
Brooke, M.Z. (1986) *International Management: A Review of Strategies and Operations*, London: Hutchinson.
Burton, F.N. and Cross, A.R. (1993a) 'A reappraisal of franchising across national

boundaries in foreign market entry mode analysis', in M. Levy and D. Grewal (eds), *Developments in Marketing Science*, vol. XVI, Coral Gables, Florida: Academy of Marketing Science, pp. 638–42

Burton, F.N. and Cross, A.R. (1993b) 'A clarification of the concept of international franchising in foreign market entry mode analysis', in the Proceedings of the 20th Annual Conference of the UK Academy of International Business, Pontypridd, Wales, April, pp. 71–82.

Burton, F.N. and Cross, A.R. (1993c) 'International franchising in an East and Central European context', in *Managing East-West Business in Turbulent Times*, Conference Proceedings of the Second World Business Congress, International Management Development Association (IMDA), Turku, Finland, pp. 165–79.

Caves, R.E. and Murphy, W.F. (1976) 'Franchising: firms, markets and intangible assets', *Southern Economic Journal*, 42: 572–85.

Contractor, F.J. (1985) 'Licensing in the theory of the international firm', *Licensing in International Strategy: A Guide for Planning and Negotiations*, Westpoint, Conn.: Quorum Books.

Contractor, F.J. (1990) 'Contractual and cooperative forms of international business: towards a unified theory of modal choice', *Management International Review*, 30(1): 31–54.

Czinkota, M.R. and Ronkainen, I.A. (1988) *International Marketing*, New York: Dryden Press.

Erramilli, M.K. (1990) 'Entry mode choice in service industries", *International Marketing Review*, 7(5): 50–62.

Euromonitor (1987) *Franchising in the European Economy: Trends and Forecasts 1980–1990*, London: Euromonitor Publications.

Falbe, C.M. and Dandridge, T.C. (1992) 'Franchising as strategic partnership: issues of co-operation and conflict in a global market', *International Small Business Journal*, (10(3): 40–52.

Götberg, G. (1989) 'Franchising in international marketing', *Marketing at the Gothenburg School of Economics*, (proceedings from a symposium for Prof. Bo Wickström, BAS, University of Gothenburg, Gothenburg.

Hackett, D.W. (1976) 'The international expansion of US franchise systems: status and strategies', *Journal of International Business Studies*, 7: 65–75.

Harrigan, K. (1988) 'Joint ventures and competitive strategy', *Strategic Management Journal*, 9: 141–58.

Hill, C.W.L., Hwang, P. and Kim, W.C. (1990) 'An eclectic theory of the choice of international entry mode', *Strategic Management Journal*, 11: 117–28.

Hoffman, R.C. and Preble, J.F. (1991) 'Franchising: selecting a strategy for rapid growth', *Long Range Planning*, 24(4): 74–85.

Kaynak, E. (1988) 'Global franchising: European and North American perspectives', in E. Kaynak (ed.), *Transnational Retailing*, ch. 4, Berlin: de Gruyter.

Konigsburg, A.S. (1987) 'A compendium of franchising terms', *Journal of International Franchising and Distribution Law*, 2: 58–67.

Lillis, C.M., Narayama, C.L. and Gilman, J.L. (1976) 'Competitive advantage variation over the life-cycle of a franchise', *Journal of Marketing*, 77–80.

Mathewson, G.F. and Winter, R.A. (1985) 'The economics of franchise contracts', *Journal of Law and Economics*, 28: 503–26.

Mendelsohn, M. (1992) *Guide to Franchising*, 5th edn, Oxford: Pergamon Press.

Norton, S.W. (1988) 'An empirical look at franchising as an organisational form', *Journal of Business*, 61(2): 197–218.

Oman, C. (1984) *New Forms of International Investment*, Paris: OECD.

Organization for Economic Co-operation and Development (1987) *International Technology Licensing: Survey Results*, report no. 23, Paris: OECD.

Root, F.J. (1987) *Entry Strategies for International Markets*, Lexington, Mass.: Lexington Books, D.C. Heath and Co.

Rubin, P.H. (1978) 'The theory of the firm and the structure of the franchise contract', *Journal of Law and Economics*, 21: 223–33.

Sanghavi, N. (1990) *Retail Franchising in the 1990s*, London: Longman.

Thompson, R.S. and Wright, M. (1988) *Internal Organisation, Efficiency and Profit*, London: Philip Allen.

Welch, L.S. (1989) 'Diffusion of franchise system use in international operations', *International Marketing Review*, 6 (5): 7–19.

Williamson, O.E. (1983) 'Credible commitments: using hostages to support exchange', *American Economic Review*, 73.

Young, S. (1987) 'Business strategy and the internationalization of business: recent approaches', *Managerial and Business Economics*, 8: 31–40.

Young, S., Hamill, J., Wheeler, C. and Davies, J.R. (1989) *International Market Entry and Development: Strategies and Management*, Hemel Hempstead, Herts.: Harvester Wheatsheaf.

Part II

Organizational responses to foreign market environments

Jan Johanson and Lars Gunnar-Mattsson describe an alternative explanation for international marketing, one that is driven by networks. There is an important interaction in terms of the internationalization of the firm and of the environment which is encapsulated in their model and not found elsewhere. According then to this explanation the firm establishes and develops positions in relation to counterparts in foreign networks. They then proceed to describe a four-cell matrix against internationalization of the firm and internationalization of the market. Various aspects of the firm's international marketing strategies may then be explained within each specific context.

Ulf Andersson and Mats Forsgren also use a network approach but here it is to examine, with the use of a number of short case studies, the organizational relationship between multinational parent company and subsidiary and to explode a number of popularly held beliefs. They classify subsidiaries in terms of buyer and supplier relationships and examine also influences on the international exchange relationships in which they engage. The classification is not about stages of internationalization but the growing importance of exchange relationships with the corporate network. The authors use networks to assess multinational parental control over subsidiaries allowing for institutionalization and environmental factors.

Gilbert D. Harrell and Richard O. Kiefer revisit an article which they wrote over ten years ago on the use of market portfolios as a strategic planning tool for multinational corporations which is an important step towards dealing with world markets simultaneously. It also helps track movement in markets over time and enable management to reconfigure strategy against emerging patterns.

Part II

Organizational responses to foreign market environments

4 International marketing and internationalization processes

A network approach

Jan Johanson and Lars Gunnar-Mattsson

INTRODUCTION

Recent state-of-the-art presentations indicate that researchers in international marketing are less than happy with the situation. International marketing is a 'step-child of marketing' (Wind 1979), it has failed to develop a specific body of knowledge (Hampton and Van Gent 1984: 202), there is an absence of conceptual and theoretical frameworks to guide research (Cavusgil and Nevin 1981: 207), the literature on 'comparative marketing' is lagging behind that of other areas of marketing (Kaynak and Savitt 1984: 273). All these reviewers, not surprisingly agree that international marketing is an important subject for research, and increasingly so.

The modest aim of our paper is to discuss some of the critical problems in received international marketing research in relation to conceptual frameworks used by researchers. More specifically, we will examine potential contributions, in terms of problem recognition and research approaches, by looking at markets as networks of relationships between actors. We have no ambition to systematically present or assess the 'state of the art' in international marketing, but we believe that our analysis might also be relevant for many aspects of consumer goods marketing.

The title is meant to signify that we believe that important issues in international marketing can be fruitfully analysed as interdependent with internationalization processes in the firm and in the firm's environment.

We take the broad view that international marketing concerns the exchange of goods and services with actors from more than one country involved. International marketing therefore involves crossing national borders, operating in 'foreign' markets and dealing with interdependent activities in several nations. The individual firm can be more or less internationally interdependent and go through an internationalization process.

After this general introduction we will try to categorize some major aspects of international marketing research and the general conceptual frameworks that the studies build on. After that, admittedly very sketchy, background we will briefly describe out network model and the types of research issues it raises for marketing in general.

Next, international marketing and internationalization processes are interpreted within the network model and some of the research insights are mentioned. Finally, we discuss how the firm's and the environment's internationalization interact in analyses of international marketing problems.

MAJOR ASPECTS OF INTERNATIONAL MARKETING RESEARCH

Cavusgil and Nevin (1981: 197) organize their review of international marketing in four broad categories of studies:

- *the environment of international marketing* These studies include the impact of political, legal, cultural, economic, technological variables on international marketing activity;
- *area oriented studies* of markets in the sense that structure and behaviour of customers, distribution channels, competitors and facilitating institutions are described and analysed;
- *strategic international marketing management* This category of studies includes entry and expansion strategies, segmentation strategies, marketing-mix policies and relationships between headquarters and subsidiaries;
- *decision tools for international marketing* include both research methodology and studies of buyer behaviour.

We find that this way of structuring the subject areas is typical for the international marketing literature. There is a division between the general international institutional environment, the immediate business environment, the strategic, tactical and organizational behaviour of the individual firm and the analytical and descriptive background for analysis of the market. We might add that this is also typical for the general marketing management literature linked to the marketing mix model.

With reference to the definition of international marketing and to the above categorization, it is possible to list five major research areas:

1 Differences (and similarities) between markets.
2 Interdependencies between markets.
3 Foreign market entry strategies and expansion, including modes of entry and expansion.
4 Characteristics of the firm's marketing activities on foreign markets.
5 Interdependencies between activities on different markets and control of these activities.

Comparisons between markets

Comparisons between markets in different national, regional or cultural contexts are made in comparative marketing studies. These studies have to a large extent concentrated on consumer behaviour, distribution channels and different types of institutional arrangements on a macro level. Even if little research in the comparative marketing field has concerned industrial marketing, relevant material can be found in the comparative management or cross-cultural management literature and in industrial organization studies comprising several countries or internationally dispersed industries (de Jong 1981).

Comparisons, when made from an actor's point of view, often concern differences between foreign markets, and the home market. Variables measuring the distance in various respects (economic, psychological) between markets have been used to explain the internationalization processes by individual firms (Hornell *et al.* 1973). Comparison between markets has also been a major tool suggested in the literature on international market segmentation and market selection, and has obviously relevance for the analysis of the standardization-adaption issue. Finally differences and similarities influence the type of methodological problems encountered in international marketing research (Douglas and Craig 1983).

Interdependence between markets

Interdependence between markets exists if the behaviour of one market influences the behaviour or outcome of activities of another market. Studies on international oligopolistic competition (Knickerbocker 1973), on purchasing by international companies (Davis *et al.* 1974), on the effects of economic integration between countries, on the diffusion of innovations (Ray 1984), on the product cycle (Vernon 1979) and on transfer of technology (Frame 1983) give examples of such interdependencies that can be seen as aspects of internationalization of the environment. In a very general sense the literature on international economics and international politics is relevant. In a more narrow sense, the recent interest focused on the globalization of markets (Levitt 1983) fits into this category.

Foreign market entry and expansion strategy

This is a very important international marketing research issue that links marketing, international business, and corporate strategy-oriented studies. One aspect is the determination of which markets the firm enters. Another is by which organizational and inter-organizational arrangement that the entry takes place. A third aspect is the development over time of the firm's involvement on the foreign market. These three aspects are integrated in the process models that describe the firm's internationalization as a gradual, step-by-step commitment to sell and to manufacture internationally as part of a growth process (Johanson and Wiedersheim-Paul 1974; Johanson and Vahlne 1977). Focusing specifically on export behaviour; Bilkey (1978) conceptualized exporting as a learning sequence by which the firm went through stages of increasing commitment to foreign markets. The stage model has lately come under criticism. Reid (1983) argues that successive internationalization, going from low-commitment modes and selling in nearby markets to high-commitment modes such as manufacturing abroad and operating also in more distant markets is a too deterministic and general model. The firm's choice of entry and expansion modes are, according to Reid, more selective and context-specific and can be explained by heterogeneous resource patterns and market opportunities. Firms will therefore use multiple modes of international transfers. Reid suggests that a transaction cost approach is superior to the experential learning model. Hedlund and Kverneland (1983) also criticize the stages model. They conclude that 'experiences of Swedish firms in Japan suggest that establishment and growth strategies on foreign markets are changing towards more direct and rapid entry modes than those implies by theories of gradual and slow internationalization processes' (Hedlund and Kverneland 1983: 22).

The literature on foreign direct investments and on alternative modes for international resource transfers is of course very relevant in this context. A recent analysis of the links between international business theory and international marketing is Soldner (1984). Analysis of the advantages and disadvantages of internationalization (Rugman 1982) is of particular interest because the analysis can be linked to specific market characteristics, and not only to country-, industry- or company-specific advantages.

A quite different approach to entry strategies is taken on the marketing management literature that looks at selecting which countries to enter as a rational screening process. The following quotation from a recent textbook on international marketing research is typical:

> For companies entering international markets for the first time, a dual decision has to be made concerning the appropriate combination of countries and modes of entry to be used. This requires the collection of information to assess the investment climate and market potential in all countries to be considered, as well as the risk and costs associated with operations in these different environments.
>
> (Douglas and Craig 1982: 105)

They advocate the use of secondary data in the evaluation of which countries to enter (ibid.: 129).

Entry and expansion modes involve strategies concerning co-operative and competitive relations to other firms. The literature on inter-organizational co-operation, mergers and acquisitions therefore give important inputs to these aspects of international marketing (Goldberg 1983). Given that the firm sells on several markets, how does it behave on each of these markets? The majority of studies deal with adaptation

to each individual market versus standardization of behaviour across countries. Some of the classical, often reprinted and quoted articles analyse
this problem (Keegan 1970; Buzzell 1968). Obviously, the trade-off is
between the scale-economy and control offered by standardization, on
one side, and the benefits from adaptation to the specific environmental
conditions, on the other. Much of the writing on the standardization issues
deals, not surprisingly, with mass communication (see Cavusgil and Nevin
1981: 204, for an extensive list of references).

Most of the studies referred to here have the marketing mix model as
their conceptual background. Recently, a number of studies using an interaction approach have emerged. Hakansson (1982) reports on a large
research programme involving researchers in five European countries (the
IMP Group) and most of the analyses and results deal with firms' interactive behaviour on different European markets. Cunningham (1984) and
Ford (1979) are other interaction studies linked to international marketing
contexts and to the IMP programme. Baker and Parkinson (1984) also
report on some interaction studies, in their case of innovative behaviour,
on different national markets. Even if there is a growing number of international marketing studies using an interaction approach the marketing
mix approach still completely dominates the literature on international
marketing.

Interdependencies between the firm's behaviour on one market and
behaviour and outcome of activities on other markets are treated in some
of the entry/expansion strategy literature and is also a more or less explicit
background for the analyses of the adaptation–standardization issue.
Interdependencies between the various markets obviously can create
interdependencies between the firm's own activities, for example, in international oligopolies, or when customers operate internationally. Interdependencies call for co-ordination and co-ordination can also cause
interdependencies. The typical studies dealing with co-ordination take
the headquarters–subsidiary perspective, analysing the centralization–
decentralization issue. These studies either are limited to marketing activities (Picard 1977) or deal with the total corporation (Otterbeck 1982).
On the general level of the firm, Perlmutter's (1969) classical distinction
between ethnocentric, polycentric and geocentric attitudes in the multinational corporations adds a behavioural dimension to the analysis of the
firm's internationalization.

We draw the following conclusions from this short overview:

1 International marketing needs a broader conceptual framework than
   the 'marketing mix' approach that is predominant. We have seen how
   most of the international marketing issues deal with comparisons
   between socioeconomic-political systems, with interdependencies
   between markets, with corporate strategy issues involving various forms
   of co-operation and competition in interorganizational contexts, with

development processes and with interdependence and co-ordination between activities. To look, as the marketing-mix approach does, at the actor in international marketing as an autonomous, decision-making unit that decides upon and controls its marketing activities in order to influence a passive environment, disregards too much of the above. (It is not a very helpful solution to increase the number of 'Ps' by adding 'production' and 'probe', as suggested by Keegan 1984!) Therefore it is quite natural that much of the literature listed above is usually not labelled 'marketing' but international business, corporate strategy, organizational behaviour, cross-cultural management. We agree with Hans Thorelli's ecological view of international marketing (1980: 5). According to this, the company (and its resources), its marketing strategy and its market environment is regarded as an open interaction system. The firm must fit into specific contexts and is dependent on its interaction over time with its changing environment.

2 The 'non-marketing' literature that is of relevance for international marketing is, however, either mostly without explicit links to market and marketing concepts (such as the comparative management literature), is built on market concepts that are difficult to link to marketing activities (such as the traditional microeconomic theory) or is not conceptually 'rich' enough in its description of markets and marketing (such as the Williamsonian transaction cost approach). We need therefore a conceptual framework that includes rich 'market' and 'marketing' concepts and is more holistically, process- and resource-oriented than the marketing mix/marketing management framework.

3 The criticism directed against one of the few process-oriented international marketing models, the 'stage' or 'establishment chain' model, seems to be very relevant. At the same time we think that it is important to describe and explain longitudinal developments of firms in international markets.

At the beginning of this paper we referred to the lack of conceptual frameworks for international marketing that some of the recent state-of-the-art authors have mentioned. If we look at the 'typical' international marketing issues that have been touched upon in our list we can conclude that we need a framework that includes:

1 interaction between firms and their disaggregated environment;
2 processes, including time length and timing of these processes;
3 total company resources and activities; and
4 complementary interorganizational relationships.

The first point deals with the always difficult bridging of the analytical distance between macro and micro analysis. The second deals with several important issues: 'internationalization' is a process; interdependencies between firms make the length of time and the timing of activities and processes important; and the problems encountered in implementing plans and decisions make the process and time element important. The third point, that we must look not only at marketing activities but also at other activities, and not only at activities but also at resources of the firm, is important when we consider that much of the relevant non-marketing literature deals with total firm activity, and the need to co-ordinate activities between markets. The fourth point is linked to the importance of different types of entry and expansion modes and in general to the importance of interorganizational interdependencies.

The following section describes an attempt to develop a conceptual framework that includes the above dimensions.

MARKETS AS NETWORKS: A GENERAL DESCRIPTION

The network approach in the form described in this section has been developed by a group of Swedish researchers whose background is research on distribution (systems), internationalization of industrial firms (processes) and industrial purchasing and marketing behaviour (interaction) (Mattsson 1984 describes this background). The approach is developed in a general way in Hagg and Johanson (1982) and Hammarkvist *et al.* (1982). The section builds on those publications and on Johanson and Mattsson (1984).

The industrial system is composed of firms engaged in production, distribution and the use of goods and services. We describe this system as a network of relationships between the firms. There is a division of work in the network which means that the firms are dependent on each other and that their activities need to be co-ordinated. Co-ordination is not brought about through a central plan or an organizational hierarchy, nor does it take place through the price mechanism as in the traditional market model. Instead co-ordination takes place through interaction between firms in the network, where price is just one of several influencing conditions (cf. Lindblom 1977). The firms are free to choose counterparts and thus 'market forces' are at play. To gain access however, to external resources and make it possible to sell products, exchange relationships have to be established with other firms. Such relationships take time and effort to establish and develop, which constraints the firms' possibilities to change counterparts. The need for adjustments between the interdependent firms as to quantity and quality of goods and services exchanged and the timing of such exchanges call for more or less explicit co-ordination through joint planning, or through power exercised by one party over the other. Each firm in the network has relationships with customers, distributors, suppliers, and so on, as well as indirect relations via those customers, distributors, suppliers, etc., with the suppliers' suppliers, the customers' customers and the rest.

The networks are stable and changing. Individual business transactions between firms usually take place within the framework of established relationships. Evidently, some new relationships are established now and then and some old relationships are disrupted for some reason (e.g. competitive activities), but most exchange takes place within previously existing relationships. However, those existing relationships are changing all the time through activities in connection with transactions made within their framework. Efforts are made to maintain, develop and change the relationships.

In the relationships, bonds of various kinds are developed between the firms. We distinguish technical, planning, knowledge, social, economic and legal bonds. These bonds can be exemplified by, respectively, product and process adjustments, logistical co-ordination, knowledge about the counterpart, personal confidence and liking, special credit agreements, and long-term contracts.

We stress complementarity in the network. There are also important competitive relations. Other firms want to get access to specific exchange possibilities either as sellers or as buyers, and co-operating firms also have partly conflicting objectives.

The relationships imply that there are specific interfirm dependence relations which are of a different character from the general dependence relations to the market in the traditional market model. A firm has direct and specific dependence relations to those firms with which it has exchange relationships. It has indirect and specific dependence relations to those firms with which its direct counterparts have exchange relationships, that is the other firms operating in the network where it is engaged. Because of the network of relationships the firms operate in a complex and difficult-to-survey system of specific dependence relations. Getting established in a new market, that is a network which is new to the firm, it has to build relationships which are new to itself and its counterparts. Sometimes this is done by breaking old existing relationships and sometimes by adding a relationship to already existing ones. Initiatives can be taken both by the seller and by the buyer. A supplier can become established in a network which is new to the firm, because a buying firm takes the initiative.

This model of industrial markets implies that the firm's activities in industrial markets are cumulative processes where all the time relationships are established, maintained, developed and broken in order to give satisfactory short-term economic returns and create positions in the network, securing the long-term survival and development of the firm. Through the activities in the network the firm develops the relationships which secure access to important resources and the sale of its products and services.

Because of the cumulative nature of the market activities, the market position is an important concept. At each point in time the firm has certain positions in the network. They characterize its relations to other firms, are a result of earlier activities in the network both by the firm and other firms, and constitute the base which defines the development possibilities and constraints of the firm in the network (see Mattsson 1984, for an analysis of strategies to defend and change positions).

We distinguish between micro-positions and macro-positions. A micro-position refers to the relationship with a specific individual counterpart. A macro-position refers to the relations to a network as a whole or to a specific section of it. The micro-positions are characterized by:

- the role of the firm in relation to the other firms;
- its importance to the other firm; and
- the strength of the relationship with the other firm.

The macro-positions are characterized by:

- the identity of the other firms with which the firm has direct relationships and indirect relations in the network;
- the role of the firm in the network:
- the importance of the firm in the network; and
- the strength of the relationships with the other firms.

Thus the macro-position, while referring to the whole network, is not an aggregation of the micro-positions in the network. The macro-positions are also affected by the interdependencies in the whole network as well as by the complementarity of the micro-positions in the network (see Figure 4.1). Examples of the micro-position of firm A in relation to firm B are:

1 it is a secondary supplier of fine paper and of know-how about printing processes;
2 the sales volume is 100, A's share of B's purchases of fine paper is about 30 per cent and A is an important source of technical information;
3 the knowledge bonds are strong, but the social bonds are rather weak due to recent changes in personnel in both A and B.

Examples of the macro-position of firm A are:

1 lists exist of suppliers, customers, competitors and other firms in the network to whom the firm is directly or indirectly related;
2 it has the role as a full line distributor of fine paper in southern Sweden;
3 its market share is 50 per cent, which makes it the market leader;
4 it enjoys strong knowledge, planning and social bonds to its major customers and strong economic and legal bonds to its suppliers.

The positions describe the firm's relations to its industrial environment and thereby also important strategic possibilities and constraints of the firm. All the other firms in the network likewise have positions which they want to establish. Desired changes or defence of positions describe important aspects of the firm's strategy. The strategies of firms can be complementary to each other or competitive or a combination of both.

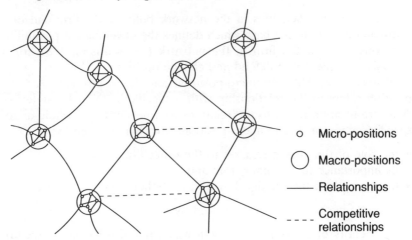

Figure 4.1 Illustration of macro- and micro-positions in a section of a network

Important dimensions of the network structure are related to the set of positions of the organizations that are established there. The degree of structuring of the network is the extent to which positions of the organizations are interdependent. In tightly structured networks the interdependence is high, the bonds are strong, and the positions of the firms are well defined. In loosely structured networks, the bonds are weak and the positions are less well defined.

The global industrial network can be partitioned in various ways. Delimitations can be made concerning geographical areas, products, techniques, and so on. We use the term 'net' for superficially defined sections of the total network. When the grouping is made according to national borders, we distinguish different 'national sets'. Correspondingly, we refer to 'production nets' when the grouping is made on the basis of product areas. A production net contains relationships between those firms whose activities together produce functions linked to a specific area. Thus it is possible to distinguish a heavy truck net including firms manufacturing whole or parts of heavy trucks, distributing, repairing and using heavy trucks. This heavy truck net differs from the corresponding 'industrial branch' as it also comprises firms with complementary activities whereas the industrial branch comprises firms with similar, mostly competing, activities. The firms in the net are linked to each other and have a specific dependence on each other.

Within the framework of a product area with its production nets, different national production nets can be distinguished. Thus, in the heavy truck field we can speak of a Swedish, a Danish, a West German, an Italian heavy truck net comprising the firms or operations in each country engaged in manufacture, distribution and use of heavy trucks – whole or parts – or services linked to heavy truck transport.

To sum up, we have described markets as networks of relationships between firms. The networks are stable and changing. Change and development processes in the networks are cumulative and take time. Individual firms have positions in the networks. Those positions are developed through activities in the network and define important possibilities and constraints for present and future activities.

Marketing activities in networks serve to establish, maintain, develop and sometimes break relationships, to determine exchange conditions and to handle the actual exchange. Thus important aspects of market analyses have to do with the present characteristics of the positions, the relations and their development patterns in relevant for the firm networks. Important marketing problems for management, and for researchers, are related to investments (since activities are cumulative), timing of activities (because of interdependencies in the networks), internal co-ordination of activities (since all the firm's resources are involved in the exchanges and since the micro-positions are interdependent), and co-operation with counterparts (since activities are complementary). For a conceptual analysis of investments in networks, see Johanson and Mattsson (1984). After this general description we turn to the meaning of internationalization in networks.

INTERNATIONALIZATION ACCORDING TO THE NETWORK APPROACH

The internationalization of the firm means, according to the network model, that the firm establishes and develops positions in relation counterparts in foreign networks. This can be done:

1 through establishment of positions in relations to counterparts in national nets that are new to the firm, i.e. international extension;
2 by developing the positions in those nets abroad where the firm already has positions, that is penetration;
3 by increasing co-ordination between positions in different national nets, that is international integration.

The firm's degree of internationalization exhibits the extent to which the firm has positions in different national nets, how strong those positions are, and how integrated they are. International integration is an aspect of internationalization which it seems motivated to add to the traditional extension and penetration concepts against the background of the specific dependence relations of the network model. Since position changes, by definition, internationalization according to the network model will analytically direct attention to the investments in internal and external assets used for exchange activities. Furthermore, the firm's positions before the internationalization process starts are of great interest, since they show what external assets the firm has access to, via relationships which might influence the internationalization.

The network model also has consequences for the meaning of internationalization of the market (network). A production net can be more or less internationalized. A high degree of internationalization of a production net implies that there are many and strong relationships between the different national sections of the global production net. A low degree of internationalization means that the national nets have few relationships with each other. Internationalization means that the number and strength of the relationships between the different parts of the global production network increase.

It can also be fruitful to distinguish between the internationalization of production nets, implying increased links between the national sections of the global production net, and the internationalization of national nets, implying that they are becoming increasingly interconnected with other national nets. The difference is a matter of perspective. In the former case attention is focused on the production net, in the latter on a national net. The distinction is interesting, because there may be important differences between the degree of internationalization of different national nets. In one country the production net may be highly internationalized whereas the corresponding net may not be very internationalized in another country. The distinction is also interesting because in some situations an internationalization of the global production net affects all the national sections of the global production net. In other situations only some specific national nets with their production nets are internationalized. This may be the case when two or more national economies are integrated.

AN APPLICATION OF THE NETWORK MODEL TO ANALYSES FOR INTERNATIONAL MARKETING

Against this background we can formulate some overriding research questions for international marketing research: how are the international marketing activities of the firm affected by the internationalization of its markets and how is this effect in turn dependent on the degree of internationalization of the firm? We shall discuss the question by distinguishing four different situations, characterized by, on the one hand, a low or a high degree of internationalization of the firm and, on the other, by a low or a high degree of internationalization of the market (the production net; Figure 4.2).

The early starter

This situation is characterized by the firm's having few and rather unimportant relationships with firms abroad, and the same holding for other firms in the production net. Competitors, customers, suppliers and other firms in the domestic market as well as in foreign markets have no important international relationships.

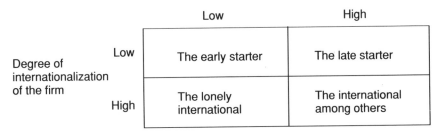

Figure 4.2 Four cases of international marketing situations

The firms which started their internationalization during the early twentieth century were usually in this situation. The studies of the internationalization of Swedish industrial firms, on which the Uppsala model of the internationalization process was based, have described this situation and its transition to the situation of the Lonely International. Similarly, government export-promotion policy studies of export behaviour and marketing of small and medium-sized firms and the need for development aid for their export behaviour seem in general implicitly to assume this type of situation. In it, the firm has little knowledge about foreign markets and it cannot count upon utilizing relationships in the domestic market to gain such knowledge. As ventures abroad demand resources for knowledge development and for qualitative and quantitative adjustments to counterparts in the foreign market, the size and resourcefulness of the firm can be assumed to play an important role. The strategy, often found in empirical studies, of starting internationalization in nearby markets using agents rather than subsidiaries can be interpreted as

- minimization of the need for knowledge development;
- minimization of the demands for adjustments;
- utilization of the positions in the market of already established firms.

The firm can utilize those investments in positions which the agent in the foreign market has made earlier and thereby reduce the need for investment and risk-taking.

An alternative strategy of firm acquisition or greenfield investment in subsidiaries would require a greater investment in the short run and might perhaps enhance the long-term possibilities for knowledge development and penetration in the market. This is a strategy which is possible mainly for firms which have already become large and resourceful before internationalization.

The importance of agents and other middlemen is reinforced by the presumptive buyers in the foreign market lacking experience of international operations. If those buyers happen to be conscious of foreign supply alternatives they would probably be somewhat reluctant. This means that the supplier must let some third party – an agent – guarantee the firm's delivery capability or itself invest in confidence-creating activities, for instance getting 'reference customers', keeping local stocks or building a service organization in the foreign market. This means further market investments.

Initiatives in the early internationalization of the firm are often taken by counterparts, that is distributors or users which already have positions in the foreign market. Then the counterpart uses its own market assets to establish a new firm within its own network. Whether the firm, with this introduction as a base, can develop its position in the market is very uncertain and may depend on the degree of structuring of the network and on the positions of the 'introducer'. If the 'introducer' is a leading distributor in a tightly structured network, it is probable that conditions are created for rapid penetration of the network, given that the adjustments to the network are made. An obstacle may be that the demands for quantities become too high for the production capacity of the firm. This may require increased engagement in the market through the establishment of production units. To reduce the risk of overcapacity, the parties may have to enter into long-term supply contracts, which is quite consistent with a tightly structured network.

In the Uppsala model of the firm's internationalization, the gradual involvement in the market via agent and sales subsidiary to manufacturing subsidiary is primarily a process by which market knowledge gives the base for stronger commitments. The network model analysis stresses the need for balance between internal resources and external demands and possibilities, and the consequent need to establish market positions which can match the production capacity that is supplied to the market through a production investment. The production investment can also be regarded as a means of improving the firm's position in the market by giving possibilities for the development of supplier relationships and thereby strengthening technical and planning bonds with the users (Johanson and Mattsson 1984).

As already discussed, the need for resource adjustment may become quite pressing in connection with a first step abroad. Such adjustments can be assumed to imply investments and it is important to minimize the resource adjustment need in connection with early steps abroad. This holds for quantitative resource adjustments in connection with capacity increases which the added market may demand. It also holds for qualitative resource adjustments which may be required due to the needs of the new market possibly deviating from those of the earlier one. Obviously, it may be possible to complement the resources through external sources. To the extent that such resource completions are made in the domestic market they probably imply the same type of problems. They mean commitments which may be difficult to fulfil if the foreign engagement is a failure. On the other hand they probably reduce risk reductions if they can be made in the actual market. However, it is not likely that a firm which has no experience of foreign operations would have the qualifications to organize resource completions in the actual market; that is, to establish positions through supplier relationships.

Another problem is that some resource adjustments can be made possible by giving up control over the operations in exchange for the flexibility needed to reduce risk-taking in connection with foreign ventures. Such ventures may be carried out if the old owner transfers control over the firm to someone able to complement the resources of the firm.

The lonely international

In what ways is the situation changed if the firm is highly internationalized while its market environment is not? To start with, in this situation the firm has experience of relationships with and in foreign countries. It has acquired knowledge and means to handle environments which differ with respect to culture, institutions, and so on. Therefore failures are less likely. The knowledge situation is also probably more favourable when establishing the firm in a new national net.

A second advantage is that the international firm probably has a wider repertoire of resource adjustments. The need for resource adjustments is likely to be more marginal and less difficult to handle. This holds for both quantitative and qualitative adjustments even if the former are perhaps more strongly affected by the larger size which follows internationalization rather than by the internationalization *per se*.

In particular, it is easier for the international firm to make various types of resource completions in the foreign markets. This is a special case of the general advantage of international firms, because of much greater resource combination possibilities. Note that resource combinations also include those external resources which the positions give access to.

Concerning the structuring of the national nets, it can be assumed that the international firm has fewer difficulties than others in entering a tightly structured net; Experience and resources give it a repertoire that allows it to make the necessary heavy investments. It has also better possibilities of taking over firms with positions in the structured net or of establishing relationships with such firms. It can also give the counterparts access to other nets. For instance, the international firm has greater possibilities than others to engaged in barter trade.

Initiatives to further internationalization do not come from other parties in the production nets, as the firm's suppliers, customers and competitors are less internationalized. On the contrary, the lonely international has the qualifications to promote internationalization of its production net and, consequently, the firms engaged in it. The firm's relationships with, and in, other national nets may function as a bridge to those nets for its suppliers and customers. Perhaps they have a similar effect on the competitors (Knickerbocker 1973).

firms which are internationalized before their competitors are frontrunners in the internationalization process and may enjoy advantages for that reason, in particular in tightly structured nets, by having developed market positions earlier than the competitors. A basic condition if the firm is to be able to exploit the advantages of being a lonely international is that it can co-ordinate activities in the different national nets. International integration is therefore an important feature in the development of the highly internationalized firm. However, this is probably less so when the environment of the firm is not internationalized than when it is internationalized. In that case, integration can be enforced.

The late starter

If the suppliers, customers and competitors of the firm are international, even the less-internationalized firm has a number of indirect relations to foreign networks. Relationships in the domestic market may be driving forces to establishments in foreign markets. The firm can be 'pulled out' by customers or suppliers, and in particular, by complementary suppliers, for example in big projects. Thus investments in the domestic market are assets which can be utilized when going abroad. In that case it is not necessary to go from the nearby market to more distant markets, and the step abroad can be rather large at the start. On the whole the internationalization process can proceed much more rapidly.

On the other hand, if the firm is embedded in a highly internationalized network its products can be spread internationally by its international customers. Volvo's Swedish subsuppliers to Swedish plants have their products spread internationally via Volvo's foreign sales without the need for the firms to establish themselves in those markets.

Is the market penetration process of the firm affected by the degree of internationalization of the production network where it is operating? The need for co-ordination is greater in a highly internationalized production net, which implies that establishment of sales subsidiaries should be made earlier if the firm is a late starter than if it is an early starter. The size of the firm is probably important. A small firm going abroad in an internationalized world probably has to be highly specialized and adjusted to solutions in specific sections of the production nets. Starting production abroad is probably a matter of what bonds to the customers are important. If joint planning with customers is essential, it may be necessary to start local production. Similarly, if technical development requires close contacts with the customers, it may be advantageous to manufacture locally. On the other hand, it may be easier to use relationships with customers in the domestic market for development purposes.

We can also hypothesize that the structuring of the production net is very important if the late starter is a small firm. In a loosely structured net a small firm can probably establish some relationships on which further penetration of the market can be based. This is less likely if the net is tightly structured.

The situation is different for large firms. As firms which have become large in the domestic market often are less specialized than small firms, their situation is often more complex than that of the small firm. One possibility is to get established in a foreign production net through acquisition or joint venture. Of course, this is associated with great risks to a firm without experience of foreign acquisitions or joint ventures, particularly if the other firms in the production net are internationalized.

In general, it is probably more difficult for a firm which has become large at home to find a niche in highly internationalized nets. It cannot, as the small firm can, adjust in a way which is necessary in such a net. Nor has it the same ability as the small firm to react to the initiatives of other firms, which is probably the main road to internationalization in a net where other firms are already international.

The late starter has a comparative disadvantage in having less market knowledge than its competitors. Furthermore, it is often difficult to establish new positions in a tightly structured net. The best distributors are already linked to competitors. Competitors can, more or less legally make the late newcomer unprofitable by predatory pricing.

In comparison with the early starter, the late starter probably has a less difficult task with regard to trust. The firms in the foreign markets already have experience of suppliers from abroad.

In a highly internationalized world firms are probably more specialized. Consequently a firm which is a late starter has to have greater abilities to adapt to customers or to influence the need specifications of the customers. However, the ability to influence a late starter is probably rather limited. The comparison between early and late starters can serve as an example of the importance of timing in international marketing.

The international among others

In this situation, both the firm and its environment are highly internationalized. A further internationalization of the firm only means marginal extensions and penetrations which, on the whole, do not imply any qualitative changes in the firm. It is, however, probable that international integration of the firm can lead to radical changes concerning internationalization.

Both with regard to extensions and penetration, the firm has possibilities of using positions in one net for bridging over to other nets. A necessary condition for such bridgings is that the lateral relations within the firm are quite strong. Some kind of international integration is required.

As extension takes place in a globally interdependent network, the driving forces and the obstacles to this extension are closely related to this interdependence. Models of global oligopolies fit in here. Establishments are made in those sections of the global production net which the competitors consider their main markets in order to discourage the competitor from making threatening competitive moves in other markets. In such a situation the establishment may meet some resistance, but it is difficult for the competitors to use predatory pricing.

For the 'early starter', penetration through production in a foreign market is mainly a result of the need to bring about a balance between internal resources and external demands and the possibilities in the specific market. For the 'international among others', the situation is affected by the firm's having operations in several markets as well as the markets being highly internationalized. The operations in one market may make it possible to utilize production capacity for sales in other markets. This may lead to production co-ordination by specialization and increased volumes of intrafirm, international trade. SKF in Europe is an example of such a development. When the markets are expending it is possible in that case to put off capacity increases in one market, while capacity increases are made in another market before the positions in that market motivated such expansion. The surplus capacity could be linked to the wider international network, but this requires strong international integration of the firm.

Establishment of sales subsidiaries is probably speeded up by high internationalization as the international knowledge level is higher and there is a stronger need to co-ordinate activities in different markets.

The need for co-ordination puts heavy demand on the organization. Competitors can utilize weaknesses in one market if they are not likely to meet counterattacks in markets where the firm is strong. Co-ordination gains in production and R&D are possible in a different way than if the internationalization of the firm and of the surrounding network is low. National differences are smaller, innovations are diffused more rapidly, indirect business relations via a third country become more important to utilize. The market investments in one country will probably be more important as the external resources which the relationships give access to are more dispersed internationally.

The advantages of being able to co-ordinate operations in international networks is still more evident when change takes place in the environment. Assuming that such changes spread from country to country, the international firm is likely to have better possibilities of discovering such changes and of taking advantage of them by adjusting and complementing resources. A third advantage may be that the international firm can dominate and influence the international diffusion process and thus affect the development. But this probably requires size as well.

CONCLUDING REMARKS

In the discussion of the four situations we focused our attention on the two internationalization characteristics: that of the firm and that of the environment. We discussed how various aspects of the firm's international marketing strategies and organization could be explained by each specific context. Both the internationalization of the firm and of its environment imply change processes and increasing interdependencies that influence, and are influenced by, marketing resources. Our analysis suggests a number of research ideas of a conceptual and empirical nature. We need empirical, conceptual and methodological studies of various types of industrial networks as to their structure in terms of positions and relationships and as regards structural change processes. Such studies would differ from typical industrial organization studies because the emphasis would be on relationships rather than on corporate units or plants. We also need descriptions of strategic developments at the firm level, taking into consideration the processes by which a firm's network positions undergo changes. Such studies would include both entry and further development processes. Also development over time of relationships between individual counterparts, and how these relationships are controlled, need to be described and explained.

The key issue, as we see it, is to be able to conceptualize and understand the cumulative nature of the marketing activities. Linked to this is the sequential developments in the market, the timing of activities, the balancing and development of different kinds of interdependent resources, and action preparedness. When is action appropriate? All this is not a matter of increasing the complexity of market models. It is rather a matter of finding new and better conceptual frameworks for describing markets and firms' behaviour on and relations to markets. Obviously, we consider the network approach promising, but must of course admit at the same time that we are only at the very beginning of its development. Many of the basic concepts are vague, only few empirical studies exist. There are also of course alternative conceptual frameworks that might be used to handle the problems that characterize international marketing. It is, however, easy for us to interpret empirical case studies that we have come into contact with, in the network model described here. In fact, the major empirical input to our framework comes from contacts with managers through research, consulting and teaching.

Our subject is international marketing. What we have done is not only to discuss paradigmatic issues in international marketing, but also as regards marketing in general. The debate among marketing academicians on such issues has increased somewhat during recent years (Dholakia and Arndt 1984). It is also interesting to note that most of the published literature on international marketing originated in North America. Of the more than 250 writings listed by Cavusgil and Nevin (1981), more than

90 per cent are written in the US or Canada. It might very well be that the institutional setting, academically and as regards business conditions, explains the relatively little interest shown in the US by the academic community in doing research on these phenomena and the research frameworks and methodologies used (cf. the analysis in Mattsson and Naert 1984, on the different marketing research behaviour in Europe). We believe that a positive development for research on international marketing lies ahead.

REFERENCES

Baker, M. and Parkinson, S.T. (1984) 'Research into organizational buying behaviour and industrial marketing: the Strathclyde experience', paper presented at the International Research Seminar on Industrial Marketing, Stockholm School of Economics, 29–31.

Bilkey, Warren J. (1978) 'An attempted integration of literature on the export behavior of firms', *Journal of International Business Studies*, Spring, 93–8.

Buzzell, R. 'Can you standardize multinational marketing?', *Harvard Business Review*, 46(6): 702.

Cavusgil, S.T. and Nevin, J.P. (1981) 'State-of-the-art in international marketing: an assessment', in B.M. Enis and K.J. Roering (eds) *Review of Marketing 1981*, Chicago: American Marketing Association, pp. 195–216.

Cunningham, M.T. (1984) 'Controlling the marketing purchase interface: resource deployment and organizational implications', paper presented at the International Research Seminar on Industrial Marketing, Stockholm School of Economics, August.

Davis, H.L., Eppen, G.D. and Mattsson, J.G. (1974) 'Critical factors in world wide purchasing', *Harvard Business Review*, 52: 81–90.

de Jong, H.W. (ed.) (1981) *The Structure of European Industry*, The Hague: Martinus Nijhoff.

Dholakia, N. and Arndt, J. (eds) (1984) *Changing the Course of Marketing: Alternative Paradigms for Widening Marketing Theory*, Greenwich, Conn.: JAI Press.

Douglas, S.P. and Craig, C.S. (1983) *International Marketing Research*, Englewood Cliffs, N.J.: Prentice-Hall.

Ford, I.D. (1979) 'Developing buyer–seller relationships in export marketing', *Organisation, Marked og Samfunn*, 16(5): 291–305.

Frame, J.P. (1983) *International Business and Global Technology*, Lexington, Mass.: Lexington Books.

Goldberg, W.H. (ed.) (1983) *Mergers, Motives, Modes, Methods*, Aldershot, Hants.: Gower.

Hagg, I. and Johanson, J. (ed.) (1982) *Foretag i natverk*, Stockholm: SNS.

Hakansson, H. (ed.) (1982) *International Marketing and Purchasing of Industrial Goods: An Interaction Approach*, Chichester, Sussex: John Wiley.

Hammarkvist, K.O., Hakansson, H. and Mattsson, L.G. (1982) *Marknadsforing for konkurrenskraft*, Malmo: Liber.

Hampton, G.M. and van Gent, A.P. (eds) (1984) *Marketing Aspects of International Business*, Boston, Mass.: Kluwer-Nijhoff.

Hedlund, G. and Kverneland, A. (1983) 'Are establishment and growth patterns for foreign markets changing? The case of Swedish investment in Japan', Stockholm School of Economics, Institute of International Business.

Holmlov, P.G. and Julander, C.R. (1984) *Reklam i satellitTV – Konsekvenser for svensk industri*, Stockholm: EFI.

Hornell, E., Vahlne, J.E. and Weidersheim-Paul, F. (1973) *Export och utland-setableringar*, Uppsala: Almqvist & Wiksell.

Johanson, J. and Mattsson, L.G. (1984) 'Marketing investments and market investments in industrial networks', paper presented at the International Research Seminar in Industrial Marketing, Stockholm School of Economics, August.

Johanson, J. and Vahlne, J.E. (1977) 'The internationalization process of the firm: a model of knowledge development and increasing foreign market commitments', *Journal of International Business*, 8: 23–32.

Johanson, J. and Wiedersheim-Paul, F. (1974) 'The internationalization of the firm: four Swedish case studies', *Journal of Management Studies*, 3: 305–22.

Kaynak, E. and Savitt, R. (eds) (1984) *Comparative Marketing Systems*, New York: Praeger.

Keegan, W.J. (1970) 'Five strategies for multinational marketing', *European Business*, 35–40.

Keegan, W.J. (1984) 'International marketing: past, present and future', in G.M. Hampton and A. van Gent (eds), *Marketing Aspects of International Business*, Boston, Mass.: Kluwer-Nijhoff, 1–14.

Knickerbocker, F.T. (1973) *Oligopolistic Reaction and Multinational Enterprise*, Cambridge, Mass.: Division of Research, Harvard Graduate School of Business Administration.

Levitt, T.H. (1983) 'The globalization of markets', *Harvard Business Review*, May–June, 92–102.

Lindblom, C.E. (1977) *Politics and Markets*, New York: Basic Books.

Mattsson, L.G. (1984) 'An application of a network approach to marketing: defending and changing market positions', in N. Dholakia and J. Arndt (eds) *Alternative Paradigms for Widening Marketing Theory*, Greenwich, Conn.: JAI Press.

Mattsson, L.G. and Naert, P. (1984) 'Research in marketing in Europe: some reflections on its settings, accomplishments and challenges', unpublished MS.

Otterbeck, L. (ed.) (1982) *The Management of Headquarters – Subsidiary Relationships in Multinational Corporations*, London: Gower.

Perlmutter, H.V. (1969) 'The tortuous evolution of the multinational corporation', *Columbia Journal of World Business*, 9–18.

Picard, Jacques (1977) 'How European companies control marketing decisions abroad', *Columbia Journal of World Business*, Summer, 12.

Ray, G.F. (1984) *The Diffusion of Mature Technologies*, Cambridge: Cambridge University Press.

Reid, S. (1983) 'Firm internationalization, transaction costs and strategic choice', *International Marketing Review*, Winter, 44–56.

Rugman, A.M. (ed.) (1982) *New Theories of the Multinational Enterprise*, London: Croom-Helm.

Soldner, H. (1984) 'International business theory and marketing theory: elements for international marketing theory building', in G. Hampton and A. van Gent (eds), *Marketing Aspects of International Business*, Boston, Mass.: Kluwer-Nijhoff, pp. 23–57.

Thorelli, H.B. (1980) 'International marketing: an ecological view', in H. Thorelli and H. Becker (eds), *International Marketing Strategy*, New York: Pergamon.

Vernon, R. (1979) 'The product life cycle hypothesis in a new international environment', *Oxford Bulletin of Economics and Statistics*, 41: 255–67.

Wind, Y. (1979) 'The *Journal of Marketing* at a crossroad', *Journal of Marketing*, 9–12.

5 Using networks to determine multinational parental control of subsidiaries

Ulf Andersson and Mats Forsgren

EXTERNAL VERSUS CORPORATE INTERESTS IN THE MULTINATIONAL CORPORATION

Ericsson, the Swedish telecommunications company, has a well-known product, the AXE system, which is marketed in many countries all over the globe. The system is highly advanced and complex and consists of different subsystems which can be combined in many ways for different applications. The development and production of AXE is today carried out in several subsidiaries, especially in those subsidiaries which have a status of being what the company call 'major local companies'. One reason for this is the pressure that local governments and state-owned telephone-companies have put on Ericsson to produce locally. The company also claims that the development and support of the system requires a larger amount of qualified technicians than can be found in Sweden.

The costs for research and development linked to the AXE system are enormous. It is therefore of the utmost importance for Ericsson to co-ordinate the different units in order to avoid the duplicating of resource investment in R&D and to reach large-scale economy in production and development. The ability to integrate R&D is assumed to be one of the most critical competitive forces among the main competitors in the telecommunications industry. But the driving forces behind product development are to a large extent local. Specific customers demand special adaptations of the AXE system which sometimes result in more or less customized R&D activities at the subsidiary level. From the subsidiary's point of view there can be a very good reason to start such an activity, especially for a large customer (which telephone companies usually are). From the perspective of Ericsson as a group, though, it is important whether or not the expected results of such an investment have a wider application to the group as a whole. In fact, the R&D activities in Ericsson are officially divided into two separate groups: standard development and market development.

Standard development means development of specific applications of the AXE system suited for all or many of the countries Ericsson is operating in. Market development means adaptation of existing standard applications or development of new applications particularly suited for a specific local market or a local customer. Standard development is carried out centrally as well as in the major local companies, while market development is an affair only at the subsidiary level (Karlsson and Olsson 1993).

The manager of Ericsson Telecom, the telecommunications business area, strives to increase the proportion of resources invested in standard development in order to take advantage of large-scale economies. This implies that a larger part of the proposals initiated at the subsidiary level for market development must be redefined as a request for standard development. But that is not altogether an easy task for the business area manager. One reason for this seems to be the way the research and development activities have been organised in Ericsson Telecom. Different proposals from local subsidiaries were transmitted to a specific central unit which operated as a link between the central R&D function and the local subsidiaries. If a proposal was defined as a request for standard development it was sent to the central R&D unit for further processing and for a decision about if and where in the organisation the proposed standard development should be carried out. If it was described as a demand for market development it was transmitted back to the local subsidiary for execution.

This organisation was considered to be too time-consuming, especially from the subsidiaries' point of view. Too much time elapsed from the customer's request until development of a standard application had started. The subsidiaries were therefore inclined to define proposals as market development instead of standard development in order to speed up the process. Partly because of that, different applications which could have been integrated into one standard application were instead developed for different markets. Ericsson Telecom more or less lost control of the market development process in the subsidiaries, and the development of systems for different regions drifted apart with an accompanying reduction in the proportion of standard development in the total R&D budget.

Ericsson Telecom therefore tried to support the standard development process by a change in the organisation. The process at the central level for handling proposals for standard development was shortened by combining the handling and decision-making units into just one unit. The units for standard development in the subsidiaries, mainly the major local companies, had been organisationally separated from the market development activities. In the new organisation the units for standard development and market development were placed in the same organisational unit in order to support communication and integration between these two activities at the subsidiary level (Karlsson and Olsson 1993).

So far, this change in the organisation has not been very successful in increasing the integration between the two different types of development processes or in increasing the proportion of standard development. One reason is probably that the conflict between the two types of development processes is too fundamental to be solved by a change in the formal organisation. It is rooted in different interests at the subsidiary and business area level, interests which are conditioned by the network context of the two levels. At the subsidiary level the relationships with local customers, suppliers and authorities constitute important parts of the context. These relationships are not only crucial for subsidiaries' business and survival, but also for the subsidiaries' formulation of what is important in the development of new applications. This explains a tendency to give higher priority to local than to corporate needs at the local level, irrespective of the type of organisation, especially if local relationships dominate over corporate relationships at this level (as they often do). At the business area level the network context is, of course, different. It includes relationships with the corporate level, other business areas and with all the other subsidiaries in Ericsson Telecom. In general, this is a context more applicable to standard development than to development suited for specific local customers.

The influence from the two contexts produces different results depending on the resource configuration in the company. In the Ericsson case, the resources for development are, for historical and other reasons, spread to several units, some at the central level and some at the subsidiary level. This gives the subsidiary context a direct influence on how some of the resources for development are used and will increase the difficulty for the business area level to integrate the R&D function and to initiate standard development projects.

The situation in Fatme, one of Ericsson's largest subsidiaries, is a good illustration of the general picture described above. Fatme is an Italian company that was established in the 1920s and has been in the Ericsson group ever since. It is defined as a major local company in the group, which means that is responsible for sales to ultimate consumers without interference from the headquarters. Italy is one of Ericsson's biggest markets and Fatme has always been very profitable. It also exports to some countries in Latin America and Africa.

Fatme has an important role in Ericsson's R&D function as a developer of standard applications as well as a developer of applications adapted to the Italian market. But these two activities have always been totally separated in Fatme, even if today in the new organisation they belong to the same formal organisational unit. Market development has always been very dominant and 75 per cent of the resources are spent on development of local applications. One important reason for that situation is that almost every request from one dominant customer, the Italian telephone state agency SIP, is defined and handled as a request for market development by Fatme. This is due to the old and strong commercial and social linkages between Fatme and SIP, an important and profitable relationship for both parties. From Fatme's point of view, it is more important to maintain and develop this relationship by servicing SIP's special needs than to initiate development of systems which are applicable to customers in other countries, even if that would be beneficial for its sister companies in the group (Karlsson and Olsson 1993).

The case shows that the different context produces not only differences in interests in the firm but also behaviour in the subsidiaries that is not in accordance with the overall strategy of the business area. In the case of Fatme, the well-established relationship with SIP had a profound influence on the propensity to give higher priority to market development activities than was desirable at the business area management level. It could also force through this policy because the profitability of the whole business in Fatme, a considerable proportion of the profitability of Ericsson Telecom, to a large extent resulted from this relationship.

Difference in interests does not always lead to difference in behaviour, as the following case will show. One of the divisions in a large international firm produces and markets saws and tools of different kinds, for instance hand saws, saw chains, spanners, files, and so on. The products are produced by special production units in several countries and are then sold mainly through the division's own sales subsidiaries, one in each of the main countries. The number of products is high and the inventory costs constitute a large part of the division's total cost through the whole process from manufacturing to selling to end-users. The divisional management together with the production units therefore decided to change the logistics of the whole process in order to reduce inventory costs. One important feature of this change was to strip off the product inventories at each sales subsidiary and concentrate the inventory at one central unit in Europe. As a consequence of this change the sales subsidiaries were no longer allowed to make complementary purchases from local suppliers.

This change was not in accordance with some of the sales companies' interests. They considered a complete assortment of goods, prompt deliveries and well-known brands to be the most important competitive forces in the local markets. Introducing central inventory handling would have negative effects on at least the first two forces and reduce their services to the different outlets. So they objected to the change.

The system was introduced without any severe difficulties despite the sales subsidiaries' view. They were too much dependent on deliveries from the division's own production units, and the system of relationship with local distributors and end-consumers was unable to supply the necessary power to back up the sales subsidiaries' interest. There were many small rather than few big customers and suppliers, none of them of special importance for the business and profitability in the local market. The configuration of resources and relationships on the subsidiary level produced differences in interests compared to the divisional level, but was not able to produce any difference in behaviour.

The cases above seem to indicate that interests and influence at the subsidiary level as well as at the divisional or corporate level have something to do with the extent to which the different units are embedded in different network contexts and with the type of dependencies in these contexts. An important dividing line seems to be between the corporate context in terms of sister units of different kinds and the context in terms of customers, suppliers, competitors and other actors in the market in which the focal unit is operating.

EXTERNAL VERSUS CORPORATE INFLUENCE

A common view is that the socio-cultural milieu has a major influence on how firms evolve and behave. At least in origin, all multinational corporations (MNCs) are 'locally grown'; they develop their roots in the soil in which they were planted. The deeper the roots, the stronger the traces of the economic, social and cultural characteristics of their home country, even if they have been multinational for many years (Dunning 1979; Porter 1990). This is not to argue a case for cultural determinism or even to argue that all MNCs of a given nationality are identical. Clearly, they are not. But they do tend to share some common feature. Such similarities can be regarded as a reflection of 'embeddedness ... [as] the contingent nature of economic action with respect to cognition, culture, social structure and political institutions' (Zukin and DiMaggio 1990:.15). Differences related to the country of origin have also been found in MNCs' modes of organisation and control (Franko 1976; Egelhoff 1984).

This argument is also valid for each unit in the MNC. They will also develop their roots in the soil in which they were planted. At the beginning of the internationalization process the subsidiary's operation is very much shaped by the role as a long arm to the parent company, including dependence on products and knowledge from the home country. But gradually the subsidiary develops and adapts its operations to the local counterparts and therefore becomes more and more locally embedded. Eventually the MNC may become many trees with many root systems rather than one many-branched tree with one root system.

One main issue in the literature about the MNC is management's need to find the right trade-off between local adaptation and global integration (see, e.g., Doz 1986; Porter 1986; Bartlett and Ghoshal 1989; Poynter and White 1991; Dicken 1992). But like a tree's root system, a business network develops over a long time and a subsidiary's role in such a network is formed from long-lasting interactions with customers, suppliers, regulators and competitors (Tichy *et al.* 1979, Håkansson and Johanson 1993). It is shaped by management as well as by history. If local adaptation can be analysed as mainly a question of management *decision*, local embeddedness cannot. While the former concept is often related to the degree of adaptation of products and services to the specific needs of customers in a certain country, the latter concept identifies the long-lasting structural consequences behind such an adaptation. The issue of global integration will therefore also be somewhat reformulated. It is not first of all a question of finding the right balance between local adaptation and global integration but rather of trying to reach an economy of scope and scale among subsidiaries which are embedded in different networks with different sets of interests not specifically suited to integration.

Institutionalization theory emphasises the isomorphic pulls of the environment in which the organisation operates (Meyer and Rowan 1977; DiMaggio and Powell 1983). But MNCs which straddle several organisational fields and are therefore subject to a variety of different and potentially contradicting isomorphic pulls have not been a major object of study by institutionalists. A general conclusion we can draw from the institutional model is that in cases where environmentally induced processes are incompatible with other institutionalised patterns or with structures shaped by technical criteria, the organisation responds by loose coupling across subunits. In some cases the coupling is so loose that some subunits are functionally isolated from the rest of the organisation (Westney 1993: 60–1).

Isomorphic pulls in MNCs must not lead us to assume that there is always tight coupling in relation to the external environment and loose coupling in the organisation. There are also forces which exert isomorphic pulls on a subunit from 'inside'. These forces are often described in terms of different administrative devices of integration, for instance task forces, or as integration on the individual level, for instance 'matrix in managers' minds' (Bartlett and Ghoshal 1989) or socialization. Even if these forces can be important as countervailing powers to isomorphic pulls from the external environment, we must analyse the basic structure of exchange relationships in terms of resource flows between the focal unit and units *outside* and *inside* the MNC. Sometimes these structures have developed over a long time and therefore have a profound influence on a subunit's behaviour. A few examples may clarify this point.

FURTRE, the Italian subsidiary of a Swedish telecommunications company, has its three most critical suppliers in Italy and these relationships go back between 15 and 30 years. FURTRE and its suppliers are mutually dependent on each other in developing new products and production processes. The output side is dominated by the state telephone company, the police and a military organisation in Italy. The importance of these customers for FURTRE's sales volume is profound, and FURTRE's products, production technology and organisation structure are highly adapted to the telephone company. The links to the parent company in Sweden or other sister companies are mainly administrative.

In Tyrol Pap, a very old company in Austria owned by a Swedish pulp and paper producer, the relationships with the rest of the company are also administrative. But contrary to FURTRE, Tyrol Pap's most important relationships are international. Two of the most critical suppliers are situated in North America, while the third is located in Sweden. The links to the suppliers are about 20 years old and are considered by the subsidiary to be difficult to replace. The main part of Tyrol Pap's production is exported. The subsidiary has very old links to three large customers in a neighbouring country, and over the years a considerable adaptation in terms of products and organisation structure between the parties can be observed.

In other cases the subsidiary's relationships with the rest of the corporation are more of an exchange type. Common examples are subsidiaries which are vertically integrated with the parent company or other corporate units. Sometimes they function more or less as long arms to the MNC for the local market, which is often the case for sales subsidiaries but also but subsidiaries with their own production. For instance, in a Danish assembling subsidiary, Danphone, the parts which are put together as final products and sold to local customers are bought exclusively from a corporate component supplier. Danphone's activities are very much adapted to this supplier while the supplier's operation is not adapted to Danphone. Three local customers buy no less than 90 per cent of the production and have done so for many years. Two of them are considered to have an important influence on the way Danphone designs its products. In comparison with FURTRE and Tyrol Pap, Danphone's network is a mixture of external and corporate relationships.

In other cases, there is a mixture of external and corporate embeddedness on the supply side as well as on the demand side. For instance, Kraft AG, a Swiss subsidiary which produces electrical components for high-voltage systems, has as its customers several other corporate units, many of them outside the local country. On the supply side the most critical supplier is a sister company located in Sweden. On both the supply side and customer side the dominant relationships are very old, and in particular the relationship with the corporate supplier is characterized by a very high degree of adaptation between the partners.

These examples how different structures of the network in which the subsidiary is embedded. Some subsidiaries' supplier and customer relationships are mainly external while other subsidiaries show different mixtures of external and corporate relationships. The relationships can also vary in importance and adaptation and be more or less international. If we want to understand what type of influence different units in MNCs are exposed to, we must start with a classification of the basic structures of the subsidiaries' relationships into some simple categories. In the next section such a classification is presented.

EXTERNAL AND CORPORATE EMBEDDEDNESS

At the heart of our concept of an MNC lies the assumption that its operations are spread over several different countries. The external environment is often implicitly treated as if it consists of a set of different national environments, one for each subunit. Or, as stated by one scholar: 'the

MNC presents an unusual case of a firm that belongs, with varying degrees of membership, to multiple national networks' (Kogut 1993). But with the network approach (see, e.g., Axelsson and Easton 1992) the external environment is first of all the set of exchange relationships in which they are embedded, whether these relationships cross borders or not. It is through these relationships that external actors can exert influence on the subunit. We call this a subsidiary's external embeddedness.

Correspondingly, by corporate embeddedness we mean exchange relationships between the sister units and the focal subunit; that is, interdependencies that go beyond the administrative links because of adherence to a common legal entity. Corporate embeddedness can also be more or less local but as the overwhelming majority of the sister units are located in other countries it is obvious that the non-local character dominates in most cases.

The embeddedness concept, external and corporate, has to do not only with the location of counterparts but also with the type of exchange relationships used as a mode to handle activity interdependencies. The stronger the specific activity interdependence between the subunit and other actors, the more they will be inclined to develop close relationships rather than conducting business through arm's-length relationships. Inversely, two actors who are engaged in a close relationship will tend to strengthen their specific interdependence over time in order to raise the joint productivity of their activities. We can assume that the closer a subsidiary's relationships, external or corporate, the higher the subsidiary's degree of embeddedness, because close relationships are more difficult to substitute. The root system is deep.

To sum up, a subsidiary's degree of external and corporate embeddedness can be estimated through:

- identifying the subsidiary's exchange relationships;
- specifying the closeness of the relationships (age, type of interdependence, relative importance, adaptation);
- identifying if the counterparts are external or corporate units.

There is of course an indefinite number of possible combinations of external/corporate as well as local/non-local embeddedness of subunits in MNCs, especially if we consider every possible type of relationship. Below eight typical situations are identified based on the subsidiary's customer and supplier relationships. These archetypes reflect the degree of external/corporate embeddedness and the extent to which the foreign subsidiary's relationships cross the border or not. The classification is influenced by the analysis of networks in 45 foreign subsidiaries belonging to Swedish international industrial firms.[1]

The degree of external and corporate embeddedness is related to the question of autonomy and influence in the MNC (Forsgren and Pahlberg 1992). External embeddedness mirrors the possible impact of non-corporate actors on the subsidiary's interests and behaviour. The higher the external embeddedness, the more circumscribed is the MNC management's possibility to control. Corporate embeddedness mirrors the extent to which the subsidiary is functionally part of the corporate system. The higher the corporate embeddedness, the higher the MNC management's possibility to control and impose rules of specific behaviour on the subsidiary. The basic reason for this is not only that the subsidiary is legally and hierarchically incorporated but also the MNC management's greater knowledge of and influence over the subsidiary's critical relationships. This is in accordance with looking upon the MNC as an interorganizational network (Ghoshal and Bartlett 1990, 1993).

Subsidiary embeddedness: a classification

Here we try to illustrate the different types of embeddedness to be found in MNCs. The classification reflects a subsidiary's different degrees of corporate embeddedness; it consists of four main groups: the external subsidiary; the semi-vertical subsidiary; the vertical subsidiary; and the integrated subsidiary. In each group we distinguish between local and international types of subsidiaries, depending on where the subsidiary's most critical counterparts are situated.

The external subsidiary

The exchange relationships are dominated by counterparts outside the MNC. The connections with other corporate units are therefore delimited to administrative and financial links. This structure characterises the multidomestic or conglomerate type of MNC with little integration within the MNC but with a varying degree of external embeddedness into a network of suppliers and customers. It is possible to distinguish between two different types of external subsidiaries. The first is labelled the external local subsidiary, where the exchange relationships are primarily with counterparts situated in the same country as the subsidiary (see Figure 5.1(a); see also the FURTRE case sited above, p. 77). The second type, the external international subsidiary is where the subsidiary's exchange relationships cross the country border (see Figure 5.1(b); see also the example of Tyrol Pap, page 77). This structure characterises MNCs where the international part of the firm has gone through an internationalisation of its own in combination with a successive declutching from the parent company. We have called this 'internationalisation of the second degree' (see, e.g., Forsgren and Pahlberg 1992). It also characterises MNCs which have been internationalised by acquisition of foreign firms with extensive international operations of their own.

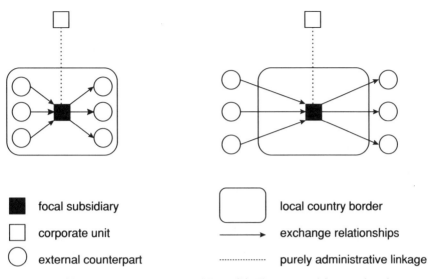

Figure 5.1 (a) The external local subsidiary (b) The external international subsidiary

The semi-vertical subsidiary

The exchange relationships in this category are predominantly external, but there are also exchange relationships with other corporate units which separate these subsidiaries from the external subsidiary above. Vertically integrated MNCs, in which integration is limited to certain semi-finished products or services while other important inflows originate from external companies, have this structure. The category comes in two different types depending on the configuration of its market, one local and one international. The semi-vertical local subsidiary is recognised by its locally situated external counterparts (see Figure 5.2(a)). The semi-vertical international subsidiary's situation differs from the former by the subsidiary's external relationships being international instead of local (see Figure 5.2(b)). For example, many subsidiaries within the car industry are assembly units which buy, for example, the motor from other corporate units but chassis and chariot from external suppliers located abroad. Normally these subsidiaries have a high degree of export.

The vertical subsidiary

Here the subsidiaries function mainly as long arms or outlets to the parent company's or other corporate units' production for the local market. The vertical integration dominates the subsidiary's input side, while the output side can have two directions: to local customers or to customers situated in a larger area where more than one country is involved, for example,

Figure 5.2 (a) The semi-vertical local subsidiary (b) The semi-vertical inter-national subsidiary

Key: As for Figure 5.1

Europe. For instance, within the car industry, Japanese companies have established subsidiaries in Europe to assemble components from their parent company in Japan into finished products. The product is sold in most European countries. The local type of this category can be exemplified by Danphone (see p. 78 above). These two types, the vertical local subsidiary and the vertical international subsidiary, are illustrated in Figures 5.3.

Figure 5.3 (a) The vertical local subsidiary (b) The vertical international subsidiary

Key: As for Figure 5.1

The integrated subsidiary

Some units are much more integrated into the corporate system than the subsidiaries in the vertical category because their output is also directed to counterparts within the MNC. The corporate flows are mutual, and the external counterparts are either local customers, as in Figure 5.4(a), or international, as in Figure 5.4(b). They are highly integrated systems in which economies of scale in production and marketing are the main

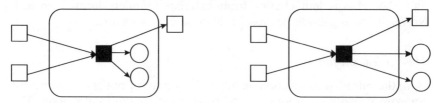

Figure 5.4 (a) The integrated local subsidiary (b) The integrated international subsidiary

Key: As for Figure 5.1

features. The Kraft AG case (p. 78) illustrates the situation of an integrated international subsidiary.

It must be pointed out that the classification does not depict different stages in a firm's internationalisation process. For instance, the vertical structure in Figures 5.3(a) and 5.3(b) can develop into the external structure (see Figures 5.1(a) and 5.1(b)). The different archetypes, rather, reflect production and transport technology, degree of local adaptation, competitive structure and company history. The classification from 1 to 4, though, depicts a growing importance of exchange relationships with the corporate network. For instance, an integrated subsidiary is more embedded in a corporate network than a semi-vertical subsidiary, which in turn is more corporately embedded than an external subsidiary.

We have argued above that the degree of embeddedness is not only a question of where the different counterparts are located but also of the structure of the counterparts and the degree of adaptation. We can state that the larger the specific supplier and customer in relative terms, the older the relationship, the higher the proximity and the more the counterparts have adapted to each other, the closer the relationship and therefore the more they can be expected to influence behaviour on each side.

This classification is limited to the supplier and customer relationships. But a business network does not only consist of actors in terms of suppliers and customers but also other types of counterparts, for instance regulating agencies, research institutes, business associations, trade unions, competitors, and so on. If the classification were also to include these relationships, in terms of external/corporate and local/international, it would consist of many more classes and be very difficult to survey. There is reason to assume, however, that there is a positive correlation between the structure of the supplier/customer relationships and the structure of other important relationships. For instance, if a subsidiary's business is mainly local and procures locally, a large number of other relationships will probably also have a local character. But there is no one-to-one correlation, and sometimes a specific relationship can counteract the external character of the supplier/customer relationships. For instance, if an external local subsidiary, according to the scheme above, has important relationships with other corporate units concerning product or process development, the subsidiary's business network is less external and local in character than the classification suggests.

CONCLUDING REMARKS

An MNCs corporate or divisional management exerts control over the subsidiaries in different countries through hierarchy and knowledge about the different units' business conditions. But corporate control always competes with influence from other interest groups in the subsidiaries' environment.

In this paper we have claimed that influence over the subsidiaries' behaviour can be analysed through the business networks in which the different subunits are embedded. These networks consist of activity interdependencies between the subsidiary and other actors on which influence can be based. As these activity interdependencies are of many different kinds, endless, dynamic and formed by the views of the involved actors rather than by some intrinsic technical imperative, the delimitation of the network is arbitrary (Håkansson and Johanson 1993). The aim of this paper has been to base a classification on a few simple network indicators which can be used to differentiate between subsidiaries in different 'control' situations. Implicit in this classification is the subsidiaries' own views about important customer and supplier relationships and to what extent the partners in these relationships belong to the same corporate system. The last criterion is due to the fact that we think that the hierarchy in an organisation matters even if it is only one possible mechanism for influence. Based on legitimacy the management is in a better position, *ceteris paribus*, to control corporate units than external units. But this control is exerted in a structure where other actors also have a say. Suppliers and customers are such important actors. The management will be in a different position if some suppliers or customers are corporate units than if the focal subsidiary is the only corporate unit in the network.

The degree of external embeddedness is of course a continuous variable. In the classification it has been reduced to four groups. The first group includes the subsidiaries in which the network of customers and suppliers are totally external. These subsidiaries are the least integrated in the corporation and have therefore probably the greatest autonomy in relation to corporate management. In the second group, the semi-vertical subsidiaries, the subsidiary network is mainly external but includes some form of supplier relationship with another corporate unit. The third group, the vertical subsidiaries, includes situations in which the subsidiary functions more as a long arm to other corporate units and are supplied more or less totally from the corporate system. Finally, in the fourth group, the integrated subsidiaries, the exchange relationships with the rest of the corporate system also include the customer side. In this situation the network is more corporate than external and the subsidiary autonomy is probably more circumscribed than in the other three classes. Within each class we can also identify to what extent the network is national or international.

The perspective behind the classification is that influence is highly dependent on exchange relationships. Actors in a network can affect each other through interdependencies in exchange relationships. To understand the behaviour of subsidiaries of an MNC and the possibility for the management to control we need some comprehension of the subsidiary network. The classification can be used as a first approximation of how the network is configured, where the basic indicator is the degree of corporate embeddedness of the subsidiary. In the first two groups the corporate embeddedness is non-existent or limited. In subsidiaries such as these the corporate management compete with external suppliers and customers for influence over the subsidiary. If the exchange relationships are dominated by a few relationships on which the subsidiary is highly dependent it is possible that the external actors influence the subsidiary more than the corporate management. The first group is similar to what has often been called the multinational organisation in which the management control consists mainly of financial control systems (see, e.g., Bartlett and Ghoshal 1989). In the second group the management control can be sustained by exchange relationships with other corporate units. But these relationships are limited to some of the important relationships on the supply side while the other relationships are external.

In the third and fourth groups the corporate embeddedness is higher. In the integrated subsidiary the exchange relationships with other corporate units dominate and the management can probably exert considerable influence over the subsidiary through these relationships. This situation has certain similarities with what is sometimes called the transnational company where the subsidiaries are interdependent and specialised (see, e.g., Bartlett and Ghoshal 1989). In the vertical subsidiary, the subsidiary is totally dependent on other corporate units on the supply side while dominant customers are external. This is a more 'balanced' type of situation in which the content of the relationships in terms of dependence and adaptation will determine which actors have the strongest influence over the subsidiary.

In a population of 45 foreign subsidiaries, all belonging to large international industrial Swedish firms within the engineering and forest industry, the three most important supplier and customer relationships have been investigated. Based on these relationships one can estimate that 14 of the subsidiaries were of the external type while 12 were semi-vertical, together almost 60 per cent (see note 1). Among the rest of the subsidiaries there were only a few – seven – which were of the integrated type. To the extent that supplier and customer relationships are representative of the network and the population is representative of foreign subsidiaries in Swedish industry, we can conclude that the degree of external embeddedness is rather high and that the integrated subsidiary, a form which is often discussed as a sort of 'ideal' type in literature about international business strategy, is an exception rather than a rule.

The data also show that international subsidiaries are less common when there is any form of corporate embeddedness. This underlines the impression that in Swedish industry the globally integrated firm is not an ordinary creature on the international scene. A common situation instead is MNCs with local subsidiaries highly dependent on external actors who compete with the corporate management for the influence over the subsidiaries' behaviour.

NOTE

1 The empirical material referred to on page 79 is collected within the MIN (Managing International Networks) project which started in 1990 at the Department of Business Studies at Uppsala University. The project investigates Swedish international industrial corporations foreign subsidiaries exchange relationships. The project was presented at the EIBA conference in Madrid 1990, at the Strategic Processes Research Conference in Oslo 1991 and at the IMP conference in Uppsala 1991 and Lyon 1992. The project is partly financed by the FA Institute – Institute for Research on Business and Worklife Issues. Project leaders are Professors Mats Forsgren and Jan Johanson and assistants are Ulf Andersson, Ulf Holm, Cecilia Pahlberg and Peter Thilenius.

REFERENCES

Axelsson, B. and Easton, G. (1992) *Industrial Networks: A New View of Reality*, London: Routledge.
Bartlett, C.A. and Ghoshal, S. (1989) *Managing Across Borders: The Transnational Solution*, Boston, Mass.: Harvard Business School Press.
Dicken, P. (1992) *Global Shift: The Internationalization of Economic Activity*, 2nd edn, London: Paul Chapman.
DiMaggio, P.J. and Powell, W.W. (1983) 'The iron cage revisited: institutional isomorphism and collective rationality in organizational fields', *American Sociological Review*, 48: 147–60.
Doz, Y. (1986) *Strategic Management in Multinational Companies*, Oxford: Pergamon Press.
Dunning, J.H. (1979) 'Explaining changing patterns of international production: in defence of the eclectic theory', *Oxford Bulletin of Economics and Statistics*, 41: 269–96.
Egelhoff, W.G. (1984) 'Patterns of Couhol in US, UK and European multinational corporations', *Journal of International Business Studies*, Fall, 78–83.
Forsgren, M. and Johanson, J. (1992) 'Managing in international multi-centre firms', in M. Forsgren and J. Johanson (eds), *Managing Networks in International Business*, Philadelphia: Gordon & Breach.
Forsgren, M. and Pahlberg, C. (1992) 'Subsidiary influence and autonomy in international firms', *Scandinavian International Business Review* 1(3): 41–51.
Franko, L.G. (1976) *The European Multinationals*, London: Harper & Row.
Ghoshal, S. and Bartlett, C.A. (1990) 'The multinational corporation as an inter-organisational network', *Academy of Management Review*, 15(4): 603–25.
Ghoshal, S. and Bartlett, C.A. (1993) 'The multinational corporation as an inter-organizational network', in S. Ghoshal and D.E. Westney (eds), *Organization Theory and the Multinational Corporation*, New York: St Martins Press.
Håkansson, H. and Johanson, J. (1993) 'Networks as a governance structure', in E. Grabher (ed.), *The Embedded Firm: On the Socioeconomics of Industrial Networks*, London: Routledge.
Karlsson, T. and Olsson, Å. (1993) *Integration och koordination av produkt utveckling i ett internationellt foretag: en fallstudie* (Integration and co-ordination of product development in an international company: a case study), Department of Business Studies, Uppsala University.
Kogut, B. (1993) 'Learning, or the importance of being inert: country imprinting and international competition', in S. Ghoshal, and D.E. Westney (eds), *Organization Theory and the Multinational Corporation*, New York: St Martins Press.

Meyer, J.W. and Rowan, B. (1977) 'Institutionalized organizations: formal structures as myth and ceremony', *American Journal of Sociology*, 83: 340–63.

Porter, M.E. (1986) 'Competition in global industries: a conceptual framework', in M.E. Porter (ed.), *Competition in Global Industries*, Boston, Mass.: Harvard Business School Press.

Porter, M.E. (1990) *The Competitive Advantage of Nations*, New York: The Free Press.

Poynter, T.A. and White, R.E. (1990) 'Organization for world-wide advantage', in C. Bartlett, Y. Doz and G. Hedlund (eds), *Managing the Global Firm*, London: Routledge.

Tichy, N.M., Tushman M.L. and Fombrun, C. (1979) 'Social network analysis for organizations', *Academy of Management Review*, 4: 507–19.

Westney, D.E. (1993) 'Institutionalization theory and the multinational corporation', in S. Ghoshal, and D.E. Westney (eds), *Organization Theory and the Multinational Corporation*, New York: St Martins Press.

Zukin, S. and DiMaggio, P.J. (eds) (1990) *Structure of Capital*, Cambridge: Cambridge University Press.

6 Multinational market portfolios in global strategy development

Gilbert D. Harrell and Richard O. Kiefer

Approximately a decade ago, we wrote an article on the use of market portfolios as a strategic planning tool for multinational corporations (Harrell and Kiefer 1981). A lot has happened in global strategic thinking since then. Still, market portfolios have a place. Because that article has been widely reproduced, we were asked to develop an updated version. This article describes the use of multinational strategic market portfolios in the light of recent additions to global strategic thinking. It includes the original concepts and data with reference to other tools and techniques. Two noteworthy developments which have occurred in the past decade should be addressed with regard to continued globalization of business competition. First, business has had more experience with portfolio planning techniques in general. Therefore, executives now have a better understanding of which techniques are appropriate as well as a recognition of those which have been inappropriately applied. Second, business planning is focusing more on issues of competitive strategy and numerous tools have been developed which can help executives better position their global operations once market portfolios have been developed. This paper describes how to apply the technique of multinational strategic portfolio market analysis, based on these developments.

Multinational business executives are facing complex strategic planning decisions at a time when rapid shifts in world markets are causing broad fluctuations in potential profitability. Planning on a country-by-country or even regional basis can result in spotty worldwide market performance. The problem of international strategic planning is particularly salient for industries in which major corporations are competing on a global scale – automotive, steel, energy, electronics, information processing, and so on.

Planning processes that focus simultaneously across a broad range of markets provide multinational businesses with tools to help balance risks, capital requirements, competitive economies of scale, and profitability to gain stronger long-term market positions. For example, by choosing well-balanced product and market strategic combinations systematically, Japanese car companies have reached world prominence in a few short years.

Fundamentally, strategic planning seeks to match markets with products and other corporate resources in order to strengthen a firm's competitive stance. It requires the involvement of executives from different functions, notably, marketing, production, finance, distribution, procurement and others. Together, these executives can focus their attention on both products and markets. However, there is a strong tendency to plan around either products or markets, but not both. The problem is one of perspective: the complexity of world business makes it difficult to comprehend either product strategies or market strategies, much less both at the same time. Adding to this complexity is the diversity of global competition – global firms, multinational firms, world regional companies, strong national firms and firms regionally focused within countries.

Several domestic planning tools can be used to aid global strategic planning, but most lose effectiveness when applied to international settings. They tend to focus on *products* as the principal unit of strategic endeavour. Yet, the great variation in market conditions around the world suggests that it is more appropriate to make decisions about *market* portfolios. For example, although Ford Tractor operations had experienced varying profitability, cash flow, and market share by product type (such as light versus heavy tractors), some of their greatest opportunities were due to wide potential profit variations across market areas.

Major corporations, including General Electric, Westinghouse, General Motors, Eastman Kodak, and Shell Oil Company, to name a few, use some type of business portfolio analysis in their domestic planning. A great deal has happened to change the nature of these techniques since Bruce Henderson of the Boston Consulting Group (BCG) first popularized product portfolios analysis based on business growth and market share matrices. The changes have addressed the severe limitations inherent in using growth and share as key variables, and in basing planning assumptions inordinately on the experience curve, a rationale offered for the share/growth matrix approach.

Business or product portfolio analysis can be viewed as an effort to sort opportunities according to a few strategic variables. Basing specific business decisions on general ideas such as the experience curve can be extremely dangerous. This is particularly true for international business because numerous variables in addition to the experience curve often determine cost and competitive success. Differences attributable to geographic diversity can be particular significant.

Most planners have employed procedures that differ from the BCG approach, substituting business growth with a more elaborate market attractiveness index and market share with a competitive strength index. Unfortunately, the unit of analysis is still too often a product or a product line – a strategic business unit more appropriate for domestic planning. In most cases the unit has comprised products, singularly or grouped – particularly if their prices are linked, competitors are similar, customer groups are alike and/or if they are similar regarding R&D and manufacturing.

In principle, the strategic business unit (SBU) is considered by some to be the optimum unit around which decisions can be based, such as a division, product line, technology or market. In each case the unit of analysis is plotted based on two axes, one representing opportunity (attractiveness, growth, etc.) and the other representing resources (business strength, competitive position, market share, etc.). However, there is growing concern that the use of SBUs can fragment organizations to the degree that their strengths are not levered across products, technologies or segments. In multinational businesses it is important to be able to bring the appropriate resources from all business areas to focus on relevant markets.

Many corporations have related the product portfolio to the product life-cycle concept. The portfolio matrices are broken into areas and each is given a designation. The number of cells generally varies from four to twenty depending on the number of categories used to divide each axis. In the most basic four-cell approach, highly attractive/lower strength products are in the introduction phase of the life cycle; highly attractive/higher strength products are in the growth phase; less attractive/higher strength are in the maturity phase: and less attractive/lower strength products are in the decline phase. In this way, companies' domestic operational programmes can be altered depending on the amount of growth or decline in product sales. Again, the focus is on product elements, and while domestic life cycles may tend to follow a pattern, international life cycles are more complex. For example, one of the many international patterns has been:

1 invention in, for example the United States;
2 heavy domestic production and sales of the product;
3 export to foreign countries;
4 stimulation of foreign production based on the US version;
5 foreign economics of scale and lower labour rates in the other nations' own market; and
6 export from foreign manufacture back into the US market.

Again, while the product life-cycle is helpful, a more functional picture of the international pattern can be drawn by looking at market development stages.

A review of how companies employ portfolio techniques indicates that portfolio analysis is described best, not as an approach, but as a class of approaches. The strategist should remain flexible in selecting the variables and units of analysis most suited to the problem at hand. While some companies stick rigidly to a doctrinaire formula to build portfolios, more often the techniques are being used to achieve insights rather than provide rigid 'formula-based' decisions. This is particularly true in international environments where the business variables are so complex that doctrinaire formula approaches (sometimes used in domestic business) are sure to find difficulty. One major area where multinational businesses have the greatest difficulty is in dealing with diverse geographic market segments, for example differences across subregions of the world and countries. The market portfolio is an important tool in these cases. For example, several automotive components companies and Eastman Kodak have used market portfolios successfully as part of their multinational market planning to help focus attention in diverse markets.

MARKET PORTFOLIOS

The conceptual simplicities of presenting the combinations of competitive strengths and market attractiveness provide a two-dimensional matrix useful for plotting products. More important to the international planner, each axis is a linear combination of factors which together can be used to define a country's attractiveness from a market view and determine the company's competitive strength in that country, as shown in Figure 6.1

Data on international markets, although much improved in recent years, are difficult to obtain for elaborate measures of country attractiveness. However, Ford Tractor extensively explored four basic elements – market size, market growth rate, government regulation, and economic and political stability.

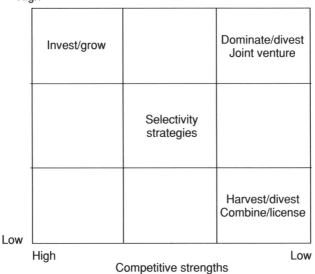

Figure 6.1 Matrix for plotting products' country attractiveness

Also, competitive strength must be defined within an international context. Unfortunately, no quantitative models exist. Ford Tractor executives suggested the following factors for this scale: market share, product fit, contribution margin, and market representation and market support. Manfred Perlitz used a similar process in 1985 based on extensive secondary data to develop a generic portfolio of countries by assessing risk and opportunity.

The country attractiveness and competitive strength scales are plotted to form a 3 × 3 matrix, as indicated in Figure 6.1. Those countries which fall in the upper left generally should receive funding for growth, while those in the lower right are prime areas to harvest or divest – or to ignore if no operations have been started. Those countries falling on the lower-left to upper-right diagonal will require selective funding strategies. The reasons for these generalizations will be clearer after a more complete discussion of the content of the two scales.

Country attractiveness scale development

Market size is measured according to projected average annual sales in units. Ford selected a three-year average to avoid anomalies resulting from short-term economic shifts and strike effects among major companies. This measure provides a good base on which to build growth projections, the second element of the scale. Market size, is obviously critical because minimum volumes are required to achieve the economies of scale necessary for entry, including technical assistance, training, and product and service information. Large volumes produce support for permanent local organizations and affiliated companies as well as justification for on-site manufacturing.

Market rate of growth is estimated as the ten-year compound percentage increase in sales. This is longer than most domestic time frames; however, the long-term frame is warranted.

Government regulation includes three subfactors: price control and regulations, homologation requirements, and regulations covering local content and compensatory exports. Homologation relates to non-tariff barriers, for example, local safety and product requirements and, in many cases, simple red tape designed to restrict foreign market entry. Local content and compensatory export laws require that end products contain components manufactured locally or that exports contain components of products made by the receiving country to offset imports. Governments play a significant role in determining the ease of market entry through safety and environmental regulations, price regulation and incentives, and production of local industry against foreign competition.

Economic and political factors include the inflation rate and trade balance. Ford has used sophisticated measures of political stability developed in conjunction with consulting groups and government agencies.

A single linear scale composed of the four factors was computed as follows:

country attractiveness = market size + 2 × market growth + [0.5 × price control/regulation + 0.25 × homologation requirements + 0.25 × local content and compensatory export requirements] + [0.35 × inflation + 0.35 × trade balance + 0.3 × political factors].

The weights represent the relative importance of each variable to Ford's strategic planning efforts. In order to standardize each of the analysis units, all estimates are transposed to ten-point scales, as Table 6.1 demonstrates. The above formula is then applied to provide a single number that falls on the linear country attractiveness scale. This number is then transformed to conform to another ten-point index for plotting.

Table 6.1 Country attractiveness scale weights

(1) Market size		(2) Market growth	
Units	*Rating*	*Amount (%)*	*Rating*
25,000	10	5 plus	10
22,500–24,999	9	4–4.9	9
20,000–22,499	8	3–3.9	8
—	—	—	—
—	—	—	—
—	—	—	—
5,000	1	Under 3	1

(3) Government regulations

(a) Price control		(b) Homologation		(c) Local content/ compensatory exports	
Type	*Rating*	*Type*	*Rating*	*Type*	*Rating*
None	10	None	10	None	10
Easy to comply	6	Easy	6	Easy to comply	6
Moderately		Moderate	4	Moderately easy	
easy to comply	4	Tough	2	to comply	4
Rigid controls	2			Rigid controls	2

(4) Economic and political stability

(a) Inflation		(b) Trade balance		(c) Political stability	
Amount (%)	*Rating*	*Amount (%)*	*Rating*	*Type*	*Rating*
7 and under	10	5 and over	10	Stable market	10
—	—	–0–4.9	9	Moderate	9
—	—	–5–0	8	Unstable	8
40 and over	1	—	—		
		—	—		
		–36	1		

Competitive strength scale development

Market share, critical in domestic profitability, is likely to be an important characteristic in international business, as well. It is a surrogate for several characteristics of strength. Because market share tends to vary considerably from country to country, this is a good discriminating factor. In domestic markets, many stable industries have only three or four major competitors. In international markets, they may have many more. In some cases, certain national manufacturers have strong market shares and brand loyalty, and are protected by non-tariff barriers. Thus, two market share factors are relevant to Ford in this case, the number of major competitors in the market and Ford's total market share.

Product fit represents an estimate of how closely the product fits a particular market need. In the tractor industry, Ford defines this broadly in terms of horsepower classes and more specifically in terms of unique product features which may or may not match country needs. The broad range of environmental differences and buyers' tastes and preferences makes product fit a key strategic factor. If the product is tailored closely to unique national needs, the firm may be able to forfeit economies of scale.

Contribution margin is a measure of profit per unit and profit as a percentage of net dealer cost. Low contribution margins often reflect limited price scope because of competition or government controls. They may also reflect an inefficiently operated local group. While this measure should be reflected in the other three elements, it does serve as a measure of ability to gain profit, an important competitive strength. Again, relatively broad fluctuations do exist across countries.

Market support includes the quantity and quality of company personnel located in the country, parts and technical service support, and advertising and sales promotion capability within the country, that is, it represents the general company image in a local environment. This is difficult to quantify, which is a major drawback.

Ford used all these factors to compute a single linear scale reflecting its competitive strength as follows:

competitive strength = [0.5 × absolute market share + 0.5 industry position] × 2 + product fit + [0.5 × profit per unit + 0.5 × profit percentage of net dealer cost] + market support.

Again, the weights reflect Ford executives' subjective estimates of the relative importance of each variable in defining the competitive strength required to excel in international markets. Table 6.2 provides examples of the ten-point scales used for this measure.

Strategic situations

In Figures 6.2 and 6.3 each European country and key countries from the rest of the world are located on the market matrices based on the ratings

Table 6.2 Competitive strength weights

(1) Market size

(a) Percentage of market		(b) Position	
Share	Rating	Rank	Rating
30+	20	1	10
27–21	9	2	8
—	—	3	6
—	—	4	4
—	—	5	2
4	1		

(2) Product fit

Because this scale suggests Ford's competitive product strategy, we decided not to publish it. In general, a ten-point subjective index was created to match product characteristics with key local product needs

(3) Contribution margin

Again, this is proprietary, but it reflects two factors

(a) Profit per unit		(b) Profit percentage of net dealer cost	
Amount	Rating	Amount (%)	Rating
$5,000 (example)	10	40 plus	10
—	—	—	—
—	—	—	—
$1—400	1	5	1

(4) Market support

(a) Market representative		(b) Market support	
Evaluation	Rating	Evaluation	Rating
Quantity and quality of Ford distributors and service are clearly 'best in country'	10	Ford market support in advertising promotion is clearly 'best in country'	10
Ford representation is equal to leading competitor's	8	Ford support is equal to leading competitor's	8
Ford representation is behind several leading competitors'	2	Ford support is behind several leading competitors'	2

assigned for country attractiveness and competitive strength. These examples show one way Ford can look at the world. Obviously, the picture is incomplete for all parts of the strategic plan, but it does offer strong implications for finance, production, research and development, and marketing, as well as for the overall corporate objective for each country.

Invest/grow countries call for corporate commitment to a strong market

Country attractiveness

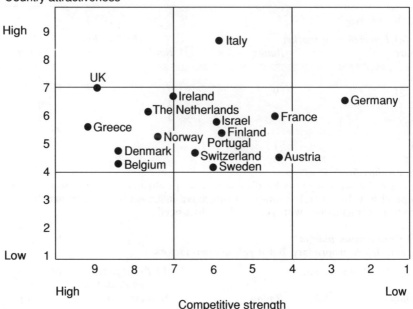

Figure 6.2 European matrix

position. A dominant share in a rapidly growing market will require substantial financial investments. Equally important are the investments in people at the country level to sustain a strong competitive position.

Research and development will be important to match products closely with specific market requirements. This will involve both the additions of new models and the expansion of options for more applications. The growth in models should be, where practical, in directions which will capitalize on the company's experience curve in mature markets. However, action is required so that unique product demands in these growth areas are not excluded. This is particularly important for firms from countries, in which the domestic market has lost its innovative posture.

Local production often is required for the sake of rapid delivery and service. Major competitors usually will be producing close to the market in these countries. Export strategies are likely to fail because of cost problems, or government pressure when the balance of trade considerations is involved.

Marketing support of all kinds should be expansive – number of personnel, advertising, quality of trade services, and support. All these investments will support growth. Personnel selection should focus on increasing realistic risk taking and the cutting of red tape. Doers are a necessity in these markets.

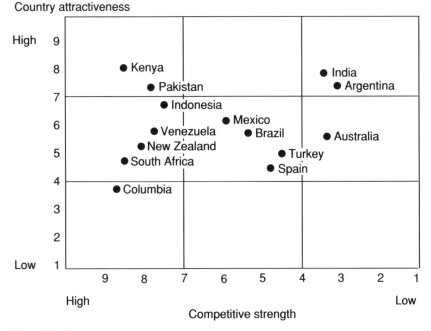

Figure 6.3 Key-country matrix

Harvest/divest/license/combine countries often call for strategies to harvest profits or sell the business. Generally, any cash they generate will be required to maintain share; therefore, share generally is given up for profit. Cash-flow timing becomes critical. Since the corporation's market share and competitive position are probably low, and the market is relatively small and the growth low, strategic plans should focus on harvesting near-term profits until the day the business is sold or abandoned.

Finance should concentrate on frequent cash flow calculations to ensure that variable costs are covered. Pricing policy will be keyed to short-term considerations. By increasing price and reducing the marketing costs, the firm generally can produce cash from those sales which do occur. Thus, market share will be sold off in the interest of maintaining margins. Exceptions to abandonment occur when several of these countries can be combined to give enough volume for a sizeable export or subsidiary business. In addition, licensing arrangements can be beneficial to the licensor as well as the local licensee.

Dominate/divest/joint venture countries (the upper right in Figures 6.2 and 6.3) present a particularly difficult strategic choice because the firm is competitively weak but the market is appealing. Movement towards dominance requires the presence of a buyer and cuts the company off from cash and profit opportunities.

The decision demands a careful analysis of cash requirements and cash availability, as well as most of the other factors pertinent to entering a new venture. This is a particularly good time to enter into joint ventures with firms which complement the organization. It would be wise, for example, to match a corporation with product design strength with one possessing distribution and marketing strength.

Selectively countries (centre and lower left) present another problem. In domestic situations, products falling into these two sections on the grid generally are perfect candidates for milking. They produce strong cash flows. This is only partially the case in international environments. In general, market share in these countries will be difficult to maintain even if the corporation is in a second or third ranking competitive position. Competition is extreme. Yet, these markets clearly suggest maintenance strategies that build flow or, if technological and other advantages can be transferred from invest/grow environments, strategies that build share. (The share-building domestic strategy generally is avoided because it can be destructive to the industry.) Unfortunately many international markets fail to reach the mature stability of traditional US markets, and such strategies are necessary.

The finance department should do frequent analyses to ensure that strategies are properly focused. Often, strategies require transfer of excess funds to other countries. Full product costing is usually required. Increasingly, strategists are applying value-based financial procedures in conjunction with portfolio techniques to determine where a multinational strategy will increase or decrease the value of the entire business. In this way, strategy adjustments can be evaluated based on the total business rather than one country or one situation at a time. The ultimate test of a strategy is whether it increases the value of an organization. More and more, this value is a reflection of the markets served, access to technology-intensive executive talent, and other assets not traditionally identified in the domestic organization. Because market portfolios provide a relatively comprehensive picture, they facilitate appropriate valuing methodologies.

Manufacturing will usually involve plants in or near the market. They will be maintained efficiently rather than expanded drastically. Profit can come from improved capacity utilization, thus marketing will be important here. Marketing will concentrate on strong reliability and adequate but not excessive margins. Much of the focus will be on current customers.

Research and development will be interested primarily in maintaining an efficient full line of products. Therefore, modular units and many options will make good use of inventory availability, in contrast to building many unique models.

In this area, any of the three primary strategies mentioned previously might also apply. For example, Ford in Mexico might set its share objective to move from 30 per cent to 50 per cent, that is, seek market dominance. For example, if Ford's current price is at a premium, it might drop down to the market leader and strengthen its dealership network. At the same time, a fuller product line would provide a larger potential customer base. In contrast, Ford in Japan might require the same or a completely different strategy, depending on management risk preferences and company condition.

Additional considerations

Variable selection

As an addition to market portfolio analysis, one of the most significant developments in competitive strategy for use by multinationals is the utilization of competitive structure analysis to help isolate factors which shape competitive advantage. (For an extensive discussion of structure analysis of industries, see Porter 1985.) Market portfolios should evaluate business strengths relative to the competition. However, to be effective one must consider variables which relate specifically to the competitive advantage of industry groups as well as to the company doing the planning. Thus, an important criterion for selecting variables for multinational portfolios is to measure those which help gauge the firm's competitive position relative to different classes of competitors. A single class can seriously distort findings in global settings. For example, a company's strength against multinationals might be different from strength against focused regional firms. Knowing this can help shape strategic initiatives and responses. Content analysis of recent literature (the list is too long to note here) and work with many firms suggests that the drivers of competitive advantage – the customer base, competitive environment, technology, manufacturing capability, distribution channels, financial characteristics, environmental forces and human resources – are all variables that should be considered in scale development.

Industry-structure analysis groups competitors into categories for analysis. Variables such as mobility barriers are particularly important in this context because they highlight the alternative strategic positions that a firm can use in particular markets.

Recent work focusing on competitive strategy such as industry-structure analysis can be used to identify market variables which segment companies according to characteristics useful for describing their competitive positioning. The following variables have been identified as particularly useful by one of the largest multinationals because these variables help define characteristics that describe the bases for competitive advantage. These variables are used to assess competitive strength for the company as well as each group of competitors. When market portfolios are plotted for each strategic company group, a clearer picture emerges of types of competition and their unique sources of competitive advantage in each country. Based on this analysis, for example, companies falling in low-cost positions with global sourcing might have market portfolios significantly different from technology leaders with higher-cost structures. When variables found useful for industry structure analysis are included as strength variables for market portfolios, markets will be evaluated according to salient competitive dimensions such as, manufacturing cost, technology leadership, geographic scope, raw material (procurement) control, home nation laws, product/service width and depth, and extensiveness of distribution.

GEOGRAPHICAL UNITS

Market portfolio analysis using cities as the unit of analysis has been used by at least two multinationals in efforts to refine plans. As an example, one automotive components supplier used the technique to evaluate the 24 cities that represent the vast majority of vehicle manufacturing. In turn, marketing resources were redeployed to maximum advantage. In another case, a photography company used the technique to evaluate their position in 'gateway cities' – those cities which have been historically most closely associated with major world cultures. The analysis helped explain what was required to adjust marketing practices to match cultural differences across a broad range of geographics historically tied to these cultural 'city' centres.

CONCLUSION

Business strategy is designed to match unique company resources with market opportunities to accomplish competitive advantage. Products or SBU portfolio analysis, market portfolios and industry structure analysis together provide a picture for multinational strategists. This article described the market portfolio technique.

Many organizations have adopted international market portfolios as a fundamental tool in multinational strategic management. Although most companies have traditionally focused on product strategies, many are finding new opportunities based on variances among countries. The strategic planning tool presented in this paper is one step towards dealing simultaneously with world markets.

Several suggestions are in order when applying such a tool. First, because the implications extend across several business functions, it is important to involve finance, production, research and development, distribution, human resources, and marketing in the development of the strategic options for each type of country as well as in measuring country attractiveness and competitive strength. Second, the approach should be recognized as only a tool and not a set of fixed rules. Often, the dynamics of international markets warrant special attention that runs counter to the strategies that match a particular portfolio category. Thus, the market portfolio provides only a part of the total picture. Also, although many of the calculations require subjective information, rigorous development of scales is useful. The better the information, whether objective or subjective, the closer the market portfolio plots will match actual conditions.

Finally, the process can aid executives in the analysis of current world market positions. It can also be used to plot the movement of markets over time, thus keeping track of environmental and competitive shifts for future projections. To the degree that patterns begin to emerge, the strategic planning organization can better track its successes and failures and learn about its capabilities in diverse international markets. Certainly, strategic management can benefit from a range of executive tools and global strategic market portfolios should be in most organizations' tool kit.

REFERENCES

Harrell, G.D. and Kiefer, R.O. (1981) 'Multinational strategic market portfolio', *MSU Business Topics*, Winter.
Porter, M.E. (1985) *Competitive Advantage*, New York: The Free Press.

Part III

International product management

It seemed entirely appropriate to invite Warren Keegan to share his ideas with us again on a topic on which he has been such a formative influence. Dr Keegan revisits his 1969 article that provoked such worldwide attention and became a marketing classic. In this new contribution, he reassesses the contribution of that earlier article and provides us with an update and a new improved matrix of communications – product mix strategic alternatives.

Rajan Saxena then discusses generic product strategies for a world market in which consumers are better educated than before, product life-cycles are shorter than before, trade buyers are less loyal than ever before, and international competition which exists in every market sector is very keen. The 'own label' range of products sold by grocery and department stores is becoming a global reality that has completely overthrown the status quo and highlighted a new reality, the shift of power away from producers to buyers.

Branding is still an important marketing tool whether a manufacturer's brand or an 'own label' brand. Branding is what creates a global identity, but the costs and the stakes are high. Similar segments do exist across countries, making international product segmentation possible, and meeting those needs puts companies ahead of their competitors, giving them the economies that keeps them competitive.

Quality and reassurance are what is sought from a brand name, yet is this the way for developing countries such as India to go? Dr Saxena raises this question himself with regard to the Indian tea industry and provides some answers pointing particularly to the need to build brand equity, not just for the product in question, but country source of origin, given that product quality and regularity of availability can be assured.

A quite different, but equally important, fact of life facing everyone trying to do business today, is that of international harmonization of product and quality standards. Where mandatory, there is no opportunity for differentiation. However, when few in an industry are, for example, able to boast a recognised quality accreditation standard, then this clearly differentiates one producer from the rest of the industry. Quality is increasingly becoming a requirement for doing business and so H. Michael Hayes takes us through the strategic considerations of ISO 9000 in a paper that was first published in *Business Horizons*. The international environment of the Triad, typified by Kenichi Ohmae as consisting of the USA, Japan and Europe, is the focus for a review of the three major quality awards. Behnam Nakhai and Jaoa S. Neves review the criteria and the measures for each of these three quality awards and place each along a quality-management continuum stretching from 1951 to 1992. Lastly, Joseph L.Orsini focuses on the role of marketing as part of the quality effort and outlines twelve areas of marketing expertise which can be instrumental in an organization's quality efforts.

7 Global product management: strategic alternatives

Warren J. Keegan

INTRODUCTION

In 1969, I published an article[1] that addressed the challenge of product management on a global scale. The article appeared at a time when the multinational corporation (MNC) was at its zenith. US companies were at the vanguard of the multinational era. The hallmark of the MNC was its focus upon adaptation to each national environment. The MNC also aimed to be efficient and creative, and my article addressed issues of efficiency and creativity in product planning by offering a model for choosing strategy alternatives and a rationale for the alternatives.

THREE STRATEGY ALTERNATIVES

The article became a marketing classic because it addressed important issues in a timeless way. The key variables identified in Table 7.1, product function or need satisfied, conditions of product use, and ability to buy product are as important today as they were in 1969. Three strategy alternatives were identified:

- *extension:* taking the home-country product, communication, price, channel strategy or management practice and extending it to the target market without change. Many companies begin their international expansion with this strategy;
- *adaptation:* taking the home-country product, communication, and so on, and adapting it to the conditions in the target market. Example: putting the steering wheel on the right side of the car for autos that are sold to customers in Japan, the UK, and other countries where the rule is to drive on the right-hand side of the road;
- *creation:* based on information from target markets, creating a new product designed to fill a need. Example: the Sony Walkman was created to fill a world need for portable, personal sound.

Since 1969, the power of strategy 1, dual extension, and strategy 2, product extension and communications adaptation, has been brilliantly

Table 7.1 Global product–communications mix strategic alternatives

Stategy	Product function or need satisfied	Conditions of product use	Ability to buy product (as percent of base case)	Product strategy	Communications strategy	Recommended pricing strategy	Relative cost of adjustment	Product examples
1	Same	Same	100	Extension	Extension	Extension	1	Fast food
2	Different	Same	100	Extension	Adaptation	Extension	2	Diamonds
3	Same	Different	100	Adaptation	Extension	Extension	3	Detergents Textbooks Movies Software and food
4	Different	Different	100	Adaptation	Adaptation	Extension	4	Greetings cards
5	Same	Different	25	Invention	Create	Create	5	Hand-powered washers
6	Same	Same	Limited Financial Resources	Extension	Extension	Create	6	Telephone digital switches

demonstrated by industry leaders. The importance of these strategies has grown as companies have recognized not only the cost savings of this approach to global markets, but also the fact that if it is creatively executed it offers greater value to the customer than any other approach. The reason is that this strategy forces a company to identify the basic needs and wants that are served by a product and figure out how to best serve these needs and wants and how to best communicate the product's advantages.

CASE EXAMPLES OF SUCCESSFUL APPLICATION

The Japanese success in automobiles is an example of the powerful competitive advantage offered by these strategy alternatives. Take, for instance, the world car. The Japanese first succeeded in designing a car that with minor variations was sold worldwide. The advantage of a single design is that it lowers costs while at the same time offering superior performance to the customer because of refinements in design that improve the manufacturability and performance of the product. Today, Ford is preparing to launch its first world car after failing to do so with the Escort. The challenge to Ford is that a standard car in Europe and Japan is a compact in the US. The same car fills a different need. This is a classic strategy 2 situation and the recommended product strategy is extension.

Leading companies in newly globalizing industries have adopted strategies 1 and 2 to achieve rapid global expansion. The US fast-food industry, for example, confounded skeptics who argued that food was so culturally linked that there was no opportunity for food companies to expand outside their home country. In fact, just as Hollywood movies appeal to global needs and wants for entertainment, American fast-food companies have demonstrated that by following strategy 1, or more frequently strategy 3 they can serve global needs. McDonald's follows strategy 1 in Russia, where it offers the basic US menu, and strategy 3 in France and Japan. In France McDonald's offers wine as a drink, and in Japan they have added rice to their menu.

Strategy 3 has been widely adopted. Software companies, the fastest-growing segment of the computer industry, are succeeding with it. The adaptation they make to their product to fit local use conditions is to translate the language of command structure and type fonts to the customer's native language and font. The basic product, the underlying software code for the application function whether it be word processing or a spread sheet, is identical.

Marine Optical is one of the fastest growing companies in the world in the eye-frame business. Marine's success in global markets is based on the company's ability to choose markets in which their product line can fill a need at a competitive advantage. Marine's strategy for its home market is to offer middle-market mid-priced eyeware with brand names that consumers respect and styling that appeals to US buyers. When Marine decided to go global, the company decided to 'stay in the box', as CEO Michael C. Ferrara puts it. Staying in the box for Marine Optical means simply that the company will continue to address the middle-market segment, offering superior service to customers with appealing product designs and middle-market pricing. This focus decision helped rule out the two largest eyeware markets in the world outside the US: Japan and Germany. Each is quite different than the US market in its styling, quality and price preferences. Ferrara did not see how Marine could compete in these markets with its existing product line, and the company did not want to reinvent itself for these new markets. So staying in the box meant finding markets that would accept the US product line, this is strategies 1 and 2.

Packaged food companies are often addressing the same need, but must adapt to different preferences in taste. For example, a company marketing ketchup globally must adapt the sweetness of its product to conform to tastes in different cultures. Soft-drink companies must also adapt to different preferences for sweetness.

ABILITY TO BUY

The original article focused upon product planning and communications strategy. Ability to buy was included in the model to introduce the case of a product need in a country at an early stage of development where there was a limited ability to purchase. The model suggested invention to meet the same need. This approach remains the best way to address a consumer market in a low-income country. The example in the article, the hand-powered washing machine, was based on an actual machine commissioned by Colgate Palmolive for low-income markets. This strategy has been little used because the economic incentive to develop lower-priced products does not exist in the high-income countries, and the creative talent to develop lower-priced products has not appeared in sufficient force in the lower-income countries.

Strategy 6 illustrates the case of an industrial market where the product offered in the high-income countries is an expression of the world's latest and greatest technology. In many cases, buyers in a lower- or middle-income country will not want to accept a product that is below current world-class, high-income country standards. For example, in high-income countries the standard telephone switch is digital. Over the past 25 years, the earlier electromechanical switches have been replaced. The now obsolete electromechanical switches are available at prices that are close to scrap-metal value. In spite of the fact that these switches are available, there is limited demand in lower-income countries for electromechanical switches because of the clear preference of buyers for the latest technology.

Companies addressing this type of market need to develop financing approaches to enable buyers to acquire the equipment they want. The best strategy for this situation is strategy 6, which extends or adapts the product and communications as needed, and links this with creative financing tied to high-income country aid or customer revenue which will be generated by the product or both. For example, China is rapidly expanding its telecommunications infrastructure by adding digital switch capacity. Switch manufacturing companies seeking to penetrate the Chinese market have been challenged to offer creative financing packages. Government export incentives are one source of financing.

Another source is to tie communications service revenue to financing the equipment sale. A company that is in both the switch and communications business has a special advantage because it can link its equipment sale to communications revenue generated in the target country market. As China develops economically and as it expands its telecommunications infrastructure, revenues from use of the network will expand dramatically and could easily finance equipment purchases.

CONCLUSION

The new frontier of marketing is global product management. This paper presents a framework for thinking about global strategy alternatives. The three basic strategy alternatives, extension, adaptation, and creation exist for each element of the marketing mix including price. As more and more industries globalize, companies that recognize the importance of global product management are leveraging their strengths and developing new skills as they pursue global customers.

NOTE

1 Warren J. Keegan 'Multinational product planning: strategic alternatives', *Journal of Marketing*, January 1969: 58–62.

8 Generic product strategies for the world market

*Rajan Saxena**

In an increasingly competitive and complex world market, products tend to have a short life. Three factors contribute to this, namely technology, shifting customer preferences and intensive competition within the industry. Consider the example of the electronics industry. One of the most important parts of our modern life is the telephone. Originally, the goal of any telephone company was to provide the customer with a simple, all-black, plastic moulded rotary dial telephone set, but the introduction of chip technology to the telephone industry changed the entire concept of the telephone. Today there are more than 1,000 versions of the telephone with options ranging from different colours, sizes, multiple lines and portability to answering machines and programmability. It is not uncommon to see a new model or a new set with additional features being marketed in a department store every third month. With every new model, earlier models become obsolete. To prevent an erosion in market share, firms have no other alternative but to adopt a leapfrog strategy and kill their existing products/models or else phase them out. In the business of telecommunications, optical fibres and computers hold promise for tomorrow's products. Looking back, therefore, in the telecommunications business, the old classical black telephone set continued well into the 1960s in the US market and into the mid-1980s in India and several other developing countries. Thus, it had a long life, but that is not the case with the modern telephone sets.

Illustrating this dimension of shortened product life-cycles, Sony's Chairman, Akio Morita, mentioned that Sony Corporation was considered the 'guinea pig' of the electronics industry, for according to him, Sony gave to the world some of its modern communication products, such as small solid-state transistorized radios, transistorized TV sets, portable stereo music systems, a small hand-held flat television called Watchman, a compact-disc player, Discman, and so on (Morita 1987). In the beginning, Sony's competitors waited one year to respond to its technological

* The author wishes to place on record sincere gratitude to his student, Ravi Sehgal, who did the research on tea marketing as part of his research thesis at Master of Management Studies level. The research data have been taken from his thesis.

development, but today Sony gets barely three months' head start on a new product.

Often, structural changes in the market or anticipated changes in consumer buying behaviour may motivate a firm to develop a new product. This may initially look to be a product ahead of its time, but a pioneer firm is able to sense this opportunity well before others. Continuing in his book, Akio Morita describes the process of the development of the Walkman. According to him, the idea of personal portable music systems first occurred to him when his daughter came home, ran upstairs even before greeting her mother and put the cassette in her stereo. He had seen in the streets of New York and Tokyo several people with big tape-recorders, players and radios perched on their shoulder, blaring out music. In fact, this was a common sight in all major cities of the world. Thus was born the Walkman – a product in response to the changing needs, preferences and life-styles of consumers. This eliminated the need to carry big tape-players or portable stereo music systems while travelling or on holiday. The Walkman was a success from the start. Soon, other versions of personal music systems came with features such as recording, tiny speakers, waterproof, sandproof and in different sizes, colours and prices. Perhaps the original Sony Walkman did not last even six months from the date of its introduction. Today, the Walkman has become a generic name describing all personal portable music systems made by any company.

Thus, we now live in a world characterized by a standardization of technologies leading to undifferentiated products with shorter lives, a world marked by intense rivalry among producers and manufacturers who are fighting a no-holds-barred war to get our attention and our wallet. While the intensity of interfirm rivalry at a global level is high and the world market size is large, it is interesting to observe how often the bargaining power or leverage of a manufacturing firm or a producing firm gets reduced by a handful of intermediary or buyer firms who source their products from different parts of the world. These firms market these products in their own name or that of their marketing organizations. Mondial International, for example, is a buying organization of the C&A chain of department stores in Europe. Mondial buys ready-made garments and apparel from different garment manufacturers in India, Hong Kong, Taiwan and Malaysia. It provides designs and fashions to these garment firms, buys from them at competitive prices and markets them in Europe under the C&A name. Likewise Sears, J.C. Penney and other leading department stores and designer fabric stores source their requirements from all over the world. Twinings & Company, a leading packager and blender, buys tea from India, Sri Lanka and other countries and markets them as Twinings Darjeeling Tea or Twinings English Breakfast Tea or pre-flavoured Ceylon tea, etc. This scenario, that is, a buying organization purchasing from different sources and selling under its brand name, is common in the ready-made garment business and also in commodities such as tea, coffee, cocoa, rubber and industrial products.

The bargaining power of a firm in international markets is also reduced by pirates who trade in duplicates. It is not uncommon to see this parallel trade in practically all leading brands and products. In countries of Africa and Asia where the copyright legislation may not be all that strong, it is not uncommon to come across a duplicate product looking identical to a leading brand and sometimes even having the same brand name.

In such a complex and competitive world, a firm has two alternative routes to enhance its leverage and command a higher market share:

1 brand marketing: enhancing and protecting brand equity;
2 generic product marketing: also termed consortia marketing.

BRAND MARKETING

Branding is the most powerful tool in the strategic armoury of US and European firms. It is a well-known fact that US companies spend billions of dollars to create and sustain their brands. Millions of dollars each year are spent not only on ensuring top-of-the-mind awareness, but in establishing their brand as the most preferred by the target customer group. Famous examples are Coke, Pepsi, McDonald's, IBM, Ford, Nescafé, Lux, Tide, Liptons, Brooke Bond, and so on. Invariably, each of them have several versions in order to satisfy needs of different market segments. For example, Coke Diet responds to the needs of health and a calorie-conscious consumer group whereas Coke Classic is for the cola drinker who does not necessarily bother about calories. In fact, of late, there has been a growing interest in brand marketing. For branding is seen as a central strategic input in differentiating the product from other 'me-toos'. In a way, it's a 'face in the crowd' strategy. Firms have established unique brand associations through the use of several techniques such as developing unique product features or attributes, for example the usage of herbs in cosmetics, name, packaging, aesthetic presentation styles, distribution channels and promotions. In fact, a combination of all these helps to create a brand image. US enterprises are known to create such imagery even though sometimes it may work against them. Remember the famous Coke controversy in the summer of 1984 and the subsequent launch of Coke Classic? 'The power of the brands, and the difficulty and expense of establishing them is indicated by what firms are willing to pay for them. For example, Kraft was purchased for nearly $13 billion, more than 600% over its book value' (Aaker 1991: 8). Recently Coke has offered to buy Parle's brands in India for US$1 billion (*Economic Times* 1993). Coke knows that perhaps it is the only way to penetrate the Indian market, where Parle has more than 60 per cent of the soft drinks market and its arch-rival, Pepsi has not been able to make any significant dent, despite it being available there for more than three years.

The $13 billion price for Kraft, or an offer of $1 billion for Parle's brands is much more than their balance sheets show. Such high prices are explained by the fact that today it is far more difficult and expensive to create a new brand. Advertising, distribution, selling and promotion costs are all moving increasingly upwards. Besides, in each product category there is a high degree of brand proliferation. Many a time more than a dozen brands are targeted or positioned in the same market segment, thus leading to a higher probability of new brand failure. The classical case is again of Pepsi in India, whose accumulated losses for the last three years have virtually wiped out its entire paid-up capital. In fact, shelf space in supermarkets and department stores is gradually being reduced and new brands face difficulty in finding a place. All this heralds increased competition for the customer's mind and wallet.

Yet branding is the most powerful way of creating a global identity. Perhaps this may become important as customer needs become homogenized the world over. As Theodore Levitt (1983) puts it, the most significant developments of the 1990s are the proletarianization of communication, transport and travel which has reduced the time between an event and its news. This is also going to lead to customers becoming aware of products and services available elsewhere in the world. They are then likely to demand the same products, thus creating a need for global products. Arguing the case for global products, Levitt further believes that firms geared to this new global reality will benefit from economies of scale in production, distribution, marketing and management (ibid.). This will ensure that such firms will be able to wipe out their competition as they will be globally competitive. This will happen because global firms identify similar segments across national boundaries that demand the same product and services. It is in this sense that product and services become undifferentiated commodities.

Further, the advantage of a global brand is that it communicates identical quality and value to customers all over the world, and hence commands a higher value, leading to a higher market share than local brands. In practice, nothing confirms this better than McDonald's, Coca-Cola, and Pepsi Cola, and even Revlon and designer wares such as those from Yves St Laurent. A global brand leads to higher brand loyalty as it communicates global quality and higher value to the customer. This is supported by market research conducted by the ad agency, BBDO, on brand parity among consumers throughout the world in 13 consumer product groups. They probed consumers on whether they felt that the brands they could choose from in a given product category were the same: 52 per cent found parity in cigarettes and 76 per cent found parity in credit cards. The agency found it higher for products like paper towels and dry soup as these emphasized performance. But in other consumables, such as cigarettes, coffee and beer, perceived parity was low as these are marketed through imagery (Aaker 1991: 10).

Thus, global branding seems to be the answer to the global market even though it is an expensive alternative. Could this be the route to globalization for firms from developing countries like India which have a sound industrial infrastructure and a buoyant and resilient economy? The experience of firms from Hong Kong, Taiwan, China, South Korea and India in the last decade provide us with an alternative global marketing strategy, namely the generic product strategy. Darjeeling tea, Sri Lankan (still sold as Ceylon) tea, Columbian coffee, ready-made garments from Hong Kong and China are all as well known in department stores and grocery stores in the US, Canada and Europe as Coke, Pepsi, McDonald's, Visa, MasterCard, Diners' and Sheraton are known in India, Dubai and China. Even in Japan there are a large number of small manufacturers who manufacture electronics and other consumer products and market the world over through large Japanese trading houses such as Matsushita, whose brand National has become a household name the world over. These distribution houses enjoy economies of scale in distribution. Since they buy at low cost and are able to distribute the product through their trade channels, they are able to pass to the customer the benefit of low price. This kind of interrelationship among Japanese firms has made them globally competitive.

GENERIC PRODUCT STRATEGIES

In short, manufacturers and producers of goods and services from developing countries find it economical to market their merchandise through a trading house or through an overseas buying organization. The reason for doing so is not just the cost involved in creating a brand identity but the size of most of these firms. They are relatively small when compared to their US or European counterparts. Hence, their bargaining power is low. Individually they do not enjoy economies of scale in production, distribution and marketing and hence are unable to command a higher price for their products. Often, the foreign buyer has a tendency to squeeze the profits of such small firms. The resultant effect is that not only does the supplier firm lose; even the home country loses on foreign exchange.

Besides the size of the firm, there is the problem of *inter se* domestic competition. In a bid to woo a foreign buyer it isn't uncommon to see domestic firms reducing their prices often to the point of affecting their long-term viability. This has been the experience in India with ready-made garments, leather goods, light engineering products such as handtools, and chemical products. In order to overcome such problems, the Government of India set up the State Trading Corporation and the Metals and Minerals Trading Corporation. The prime objective of these corporations was to market Indian products in 'hard currency' markets (i.e. North America and Europe) and also to develop new markets for Indian products. The government also set up the Trade Development Authority (TDA) to help small manufacturers export their products. For this purpose, the TDA organized meetings between foreign buyers and Indian firms. These meetings produced positive results and two major industries received a boost. These were the sports goods industry in Meerut, about 40 miles from Delhi, and light engineering goods in Jullandar in Punjab, again near Delhi. Likewise, the government set up export promotion councils to boost exports of several products where India had the ability to manufacture and market them. The Tea Board, the Apparel and Ready-made Garment Export Promotion Council and the Engineering Export Promotion Council are such bodies which have done an exceedingly good job. In all of these cases, the thrust had been to market the 'Made in India' label and to adopt a consortium approach to derive the benefits of economies of scale and a strong bargaining power in the international market.

But does this strategy work? What does the customer buy? A brand or a product? Does the label 'Made in' or 'Brought from the tea gardens of India' or 'Darjeeling tea' make any difference to customer choice? If it does, then the issue becomes – how does one create and manage equity in such products? Pilot research with 50 foreign tourists visiting India was conducted in March–April 1993. The product being researched was tea, where traditionally India has had a competitive advantage. Before I share the research findings, let's take a look at the global and Indian scenarios in the tea industry.

TEA INDUSTRY SCENARIO

It has been estimated that today the world market for tea is 1,110 million kg valued at $1.07 billion and growing at an annual rate of 2.5 per cent. The total world production of tea is 2,600 million kg produced in 25 countries. Following the break-up of the former Soviet Union, the industry faces uncertainty, for it was the single largest buyer. This has undoubtedly depressed tea prices in the world market. It should be noted that tea-producing countries such China, India, and Sri Lanka are also large consumers of tea.

India's share in world production of tea as of 1992 is approximately 28 per cent and in exports 18 per cent. China follows India very closely in exports, her share being nearly the same. The systematic development of tea agronomy and of processing and manufacturing technology over the past century have contributed significantly to the development of the tea industry in India. Different habitats, climatic conditions and agronomy in India has given the world some of the best teas, like Darjeeling and Assam. Each of these has a loyal set of customers the world over, including in India. For India, tea is a major export earning product. For the customer, what does it mean? Does he or she buy Indian tea or brands like Lipton, Brooke Bond, Twinings, and so on?

The following section presents the research findings of a survey of over 50 foreign buyers.

Customer survey findings

A closed-ended questionnaire was developed and pretested with an English and an American customer, who were visiting Bombay as tourists. This was done to ensure common understanding of the words and terms used in the questionnaire. In other words, to avoid any cultural bias and misunderstanding of words, the questionnaire was tested with these foreign tourists. The final questionnaire was personally administered randomly to over 50 foreign tourists at tourist spots and five star hotels in Bombay. The only care that was taken was to discover whether the tourist was either a regular or an occasional tea drinker. About 100 questionnaires were also sent to the UK, USA, Singapore, Germany and France to select customer groups but the response was poor. Personal contact therefore yielded us the desired response. When asked to recall brand names or types of tea bought, 76 per cent of foreign customers interviewed recalled well-known brands like Lipton, Tetley, Brooke Bond and Twinings. Together, these brands in fact account for 44 per cent of the global tea market, and Brooke Bond and Lipton account for 25 per cent. Another 18 per cent of consumers recalled both branded and unbranded tea and only 6 per cent recalled unbranded teas. Thus the recall for unbranded tea was low. This, as mentioned earlier, is explained by the dominance of shelf space in supermarkets and grocery stores by four major international brands. Incidentally, these firms are also the major buyers at the world auction. They are also the major blenders/packagers in the world market.

However, notwithstanding the fact that brands were recalled more frequently, research shows that for 70 per cent of consumers, tea means 'Produce of India'. For them, tea as a product is associated with the country name and in this case, India.

The attributes sought of tea by a consumer were taste (90 per cent), flavour (54 per cent), strength (44 per cent), consistency in quality (38 per cent), price and physical form, i.e. whether a tea bag, or leaves or tea dust and so on. *Branding was the last attribute looked for by consumers when buying tea.*

Asked to identify parity between branded and unbranded tea, the research shows divided opinions, with 50 per cent of consumers feeling the branded tea is better than unbranded because of perceived higher quality in the former. The other half believes that unbranded tea was high on aroma/flavour and hence superior to branded tea.

Since tea is bought for taste, flavour and aroma, brand/product loyalty seems to be in vogue. A Darjeeling tea-drinker is unlikely to change his preference. Likewise a Brooke Bond Red Label tea drinker is a customer who will not accept another brand of tea. Taste is critical. Hence, the research showed that 44 per cent of respondents had not changed their preference over their previous three purchases.

Sri Lanka has introduced flavoured tea to the world market. Flavours like orange, banana, raspberry, lemon, strawberry, and so on are being marketed by Liptons and others in the North American and European market. India has not yet introduced these flavours. We wanted to know if consumers had tried them and, if so, their preferences. The research showed that 76 per cent of respondents had tried flavoured tea and 84 per cent of them liked it.

On the price front, 72 per cent of the respondents were unaware of the retail price they paid in their country. Thus price awareness is low among tea buyers.

Research also showed that for 48 per cent of consumers, word-of-mouth or social channel was the most important source of awareness about various types and brands of tea. For another 32 per cent, in-store displays and shelf displays were the source of information. Advertisements seem to have a low impact, as only 18 per cent of respondents became aware of tea through this promotional tool.

Finally, those who did not buy unbranded tea, did not do so because of a lack of assurance of purity, poor taste and its non-availability.

Implications

This research brings to the fore important marketing implications: while tea as a product is strongly associated with India and Sri Lanka, it is brands that are commonly recalled by customers. They buy Indian Darjeeling tea but perhaps the one packed by Twinings, Tetley, Lipton or Brooke Bond. The hold of these companies on the tea market is so strong that none of the local Indian or Sri Lankan companies has been able to make a dent, even though they may have a reasonable market share in their own domestic market. As mentioned earlier, the bargaining power of these large buyers/intermediaries and blenders/packers is so high that none of the tea companies in India or Sri Lanka are able to get any foothold for their own brands in foreign supermarkets. Hence for them the strategy has been to sell tea in bulk. Darjeeling tea or Sri Lankan (Ceylon) tea has now become generic and enjoys high customer loyalty. But this loyalty does not appear to be for a brand. Rather, it is for the flavour and the taste. Surprisingly, imagery seems not to affect tea much, as reflected by the low percentage of customers who became aware of a brand/type of tea through an advertisement. It is the experience of others that has motivated a consumer to look for a particular type or brand of tea. Thus, it is for historical reasons and not because of brand image that

Brooke Bond, Lipton, Twinings or Tetley have a strong consumer pull. But the same companies perhaps find it hard to push Indonesian or Kenyan tea as compared to Indian or Sri Lankan tea. Hence, customer loyalty is to tea produced or grown in India or Sri Lanka.

CREATING EQUITY IN THE PRODUCT THROUGH THE GENERIC ROUTE

Generally, today one talks of brand equity, because brands are perceived as strong indicators of a company's worth. Brand equity represents a brand's assets and liabilities. It includes its name and symbol that add to or subtract from the value provided by the product or service to a firm and/or to that firm's customers. Brand/equity is created by the following:

- brand loyalty;
- awareness of brand name;
- perceived quality of the brand;
- brand associations;
- other proprietary brand assets, such as trademark logo, patents, channel relationships, and so on (Aaker 1991: 16).

Extending this concept of equity to a generic product like tea, it is imperative for countries such as India and Sri Lanka to consider different aspects of product extension in tea. Sri Lanka has already taken a step in this direction by offering flavoured tea; iced tea is also another step in the same direction. Tea companies may also examine the possibilities of offering ethnic flavours in their products. Fortunately for India and Sri Lanka, customers associate tea with these countries. Hence, name aware-ness, for example Darjeeling tea, is not a major constraint but these coun-tries will need a strategy to ensure consistency in quality, for the undoing of all these firms has been their failure to provide a quality product on a regular and consistent basis. Innovations in retail packing and tie-ups with large supermarket chains all over the world is yet another way by which they can offer higher value to the customer at a lower price. This might even help them overcome the bargaining power of large buyers, but will be possible only when the 'Made in' or 'Grown in' labels enjoy higher customer confidence.

The prerequisite for the success of this strategy is the producer firm's and the nation's credibility in the international market. While no nation or firm has a monopoly over a highly credible image, it takes a long time and substantial resources to build up this image. Nothing better illustrates this aspect of image-building than Japan, which swung the pendulum in its favour from a low-quality to a high-quality producing nation. Likewise, in the 1980s the Asian Tigers received a fillip to their image. India and other countries of Asia, Africa, Latin America and former East Europe will have to examine microscopically these successes and take lessons from them. Some of the most important lessons that emerge from Japan and the Asian Tigers' success are:

- adherence to the buyer's time schedule;
- ability to be in the market just when the buyer wants the product;
- conformance to quality and other specifications laid down by the buyer; and
- the interrelationships between producing firms and the large trading houses or buyer organizations.

Are the developing countries in Asia, Africa and former East Europe listening?

LIMITS TO GENERIC PRODUCT STRATEGY

It is not thought that generic product strategy will work in all market situations. Like all other marketing strategies, this, too, has limitations. This strategy works well only when there is loyalty to the product class and not the brand. For example, customer loyalty is visible for products like tea and coffee. But the same is not true for perfumes, cosmetics, soft drinks, cigarettes, and so on, so perhaps to promote the traditional Indian perfume, 'Attar' (once used by the great Mughal emperors and royalty), as perfume from India alone may not work. One of the Indian companies has now branded its perfume and is seeking to market it in the Middle East and Europe. A film actress and former beauty queen has been signed up to advertise the brand. So the generic strategy works in situations characterized by product loyalty.

Another important limitation of this strategy is that it encourages 'cherry-picking' behaviour on the part of buying organizations. It has often been observed that large international buyers often pick up fast-moving items from the vendor. This leads to building up an inventory of slow-moving products at the vendor's end. Many a time the vendor has to keep an inventory of fast-moving products also, because the buyer has either no warehouse space or may not have the money to pay for it. In either case, the vendor (supplier) has to work with large amounts of working capital, often available to him at high interest rates.

Further, it has been observed that at times the buying organization may adopt a 'loss leader strategy' to market these products. Sometime back, a leading chain of department stores in the US bought elegant looking silk shirts from India at almost the supplier's breakeven price. It merchandised these shirts in its stores at almost 100 per cent markup and offered to its customers another of its slow-moving items like a tie/scarf free or at a discounted price with every shirt bought. Though the store was able to make a profit and also sell off its slow-moving products, the supplier lost out on this order.

It has also been observed that at times, because of a lack of interest by the intermediary (in this case the buying organization), a product may not get accepted even though its quality might be good or better than others. At one stage Indian engineering products suffered in Europe solely for this reason. The Indian engineering industry, in collaboration with the Government of India, decided to showcase itself to the European and US customers (in this case, user firms). It invited senior and top executives from leading user firms in Europe and the US to visit India. They were taken around some of the leading Indian firms. This proved highly beneficial, as many of the foreign buyers confessed they did not know the competencies of these suppliers. Now that they had seen for themselves, many of them placed orders directly with these manufacturers. This strategy boosted Indian engineering exports. One of the sectors that received a shot in the arm as a result of this strategy was automobile components. Thus, if the relationship between the supplier firm and the buyer organization is one of conflict, the generic strategy will not work, for the cornerstone of this strategy is a good interrelationship between the two which should provide synergy to each of them.

The strategy may also not work if the country's credibility is low. This could be for several reasons, such as low concern for quality and productivity, non-adherence to delivery schedules and buyer specifications, political and economic instability, and even a lackadaisical stand on patents and copyrights or intellectual property.

Finally, this is a good entry strategy in a foreign market. In other words, when a firm from a developing country launches or introduces its product in a foreign market, the generic strategy delivers results. For it can piggy-back-ride on well-known brands. It can also encash any promotion that the home country government may be doing in that market. But once the product gets established or is in the late growth phase of its life-cycle, it is best advised to invest resources in creating brand awareness and building up brand traffic. In other words, it pays to invest in creating brand image when the product has become established, has a loyal set of customers, and competition from other firms (home and foreign) is just showing up. But once the product has reached the latter part of maturity and is entering the decline stage, a generic strategy may again be advisable. Radios and transistors from India are exported in sizeable quantity to African countries. Indian firms such as Bush have invested resources in building up a brand image for their radios and transistors there. The firm competes with others from India and from other countries such as Taiwan and Hong Kong. But in the developed countries where the demand for radios has almost entered a decline phase, it is quite common to see a buyer asking for a Taiwanese or Japanese radio or a transistor. Rarely does he shop for a brand. But the same is not true for portable stereo music or CD systems.

CONCLUSION

To sum up, a generic product strategy is a viable low-cost strategy for firms from developing countries wishing to globalize their operations; but to be effective they will have to pay attention to quality and ensure regular product availability in retail outlets worldwide. They must also invest resources in building their credibility and also that of the home country and the industry. The 'Made in' label has to be credible in order for the generic product strategy or consortia approach to work. This requires an extra effort at the macro level, i.e. the industry level, a task which the Confederation of Indian Industry has now set itself.

REFERENCES

Aaker, David (1991) *Managing Brand Equity*, New York: The Free Press.
Economic Times (Bombay) (1993) August issues.
Levitt, Theodore (1983) 'The globalization of markets', *Harvard Business Review*, May–June: 92.
Morita, Akio(1987) *Made in Japan*, London: Collins.

9   ISO 9000: the new strategic consideration

H. Michael Hayes

In the lexicon of quality, a new word – ISO 9000 – has surfaced. It is not, as some have facetiously suggested, a new soap that reaches 9,000 parts of the body. Nor is it a new superfast film for 35 mm cameras. And it is not, as has been seriously suggested, a plot on the part of the European Union (EU) to erect another trade barrier against US goods and services. It is a new set of standards, promulgated by the International Organization for Standardization, that is likely to have more impact on quality practices around the world than any other single quality concept.

For some firms, legal requirements or the mandates by large customers may leave little choice as to the adoption of ISO 9000. For others, however, there is considerable flexibility with respect to adoption (*per se*), timing, and functional responsibility. The impact to date of ISO 9000 has been felt most directly by those in manufacturing and general management. For those in marketing, however, the growing interest in ISO 9000 will significantly affect customer relations and the pursuit of competitive advantage. It will also change the organizational context within which marketing works to represent customer views on quality.

This paper provides a brief background on ISO 9000, describes the current trends with respect to it, and develops its implications for managers, with particular emphasis on those for marketing.

BACKGROUND

Few things are as high as quality on the agenda of corporate America. The Malcolm Baldrige Award has become practically a household word. There is renewed interest in the Deming system. Many firms are adopting the Motorola Six Sigma approach. Classes in Total Quality Management (TQM) are increasingly popular. Major firms, such as Ford and Xerox, are certifying their suppliers who meet specified quality standards. 'The Quality Imperative' was the title of *Business Week*'s 25 October 1991 bonus issue.

This heightened interest is not without reservation. Many managers are concerned that the interest in quality may be another fad, embraced today only to be discarded tomorrow. The proliferating approaches to quality raise concerns as to the 'right' approach. In any event, there are questions about the payoff from increased attention to quality. Is improved quality likely to be a source of competitive advantage? Or will it simply be yet another requirement uniformly imposed on all businesses?

In 1990 and 1991, managers in the US began to hear of a new approach to quality. First promulgated in 1987 by the International Organization for Standardization (ISO), four years later ISO 9000 was well on its way to becoming the *de facto* – and in some instances, the *de jure* – approach to quality in Europe. A similar move is now under way in the United States, not just for firms doing business in Europe, but also for firms with a strictly domestic orientation.

For American firms, this raises a number of questions. At the most fundamental level, under what circumstances should firms pursue registration to ISO 9000, and when? More specifically, how does ISO 9000 relate to other quality systems, and what is an appropriate role for marketing in an activity that has long been the province of manufacturing? Finally, how does a firm get started with ISO 9000?

THE INTERNATIONAL ORGANIZATION FOR STANDARDIZATION AND ISO 9000

Headquartered in Geneva, Switzerland, the ISO is the specialized international agency for global business standards. Currently made up of the national standards bodies of 91 countries, its object is to promote the development of standardization and related world activities with a view toward facilitating the international exchange of goods and services. The American National Standards Institute (ANSI) is the member body representing the US to the ISO.

In 1987, the ISO published five international standards designed to guide internal quality management programs and facilitate external quality assurance purposes. Briefly described in boxes throughout the paper, ISO 9000 stipulates the quality system requirements necessary to ensure meeting stipulated requirements in varying situations. The rationale for these standards is stated in ISO 9000:

> Most organizations – industrial, commercial, or government – produce a product or service intended to satisfy a user's need or requirements. Such requirements are often incorporated in 'specifications'. However, technical specifications may not in themselves guarantee that a customer's requirements will be consistently met, if there happen to be any deficiencies in the specification or in the organizational system to design and produce the product or service. Consequently, this has led to the development of quality system standards and guidelines that complement relevant product or service requirements given in the technical

specification. . . . The series of International Standards (ISO 9000 to ISO 9004, inclusive) embodies a rationalization of the many and various national approaches in this sphere.

Essentially, then, and in contrast with the Baldrige competition or other major approaches to quality that are discretionary with a supplier, ISO 9000 is discretionary with the purchaser in two significant ways:

- it provides purchasers with a way to specify that a supplier shall have a quality assurance process *without having to design the process*;
- it provides a way for a purchaser to have third-party certification of a supplier's conformance with the standards, at the supplier's expense.

The five standards that collectively make up ISO 9000 are described in Table 9.1. ISO 9000 sets the stage for the rest of the series. Purchasers use ISO 9001, 9002, and 9003 to specify the exact nature of the quality assurance process. ISO 9004 provides general guidelines to the firm as it designs its quality assurance process.

For the purchaser, supplier compliance with ISO 9000 can be assured in one of three ways:

- the purchaser can rely on the supplier's self-certification;
- the purchaser can audit the supplier for compliance with the requirements of the standard;
- the purchaser can require that the supplier have its quality system registered to the selected standard through an audit conducted by an accredited independent third party, usually a designated certifying body in Europe or registrar in the United States.

CURRENT STATUS

As of February 1993, the EU and 56 other countries had adopted the ISO 9000 series, either exactly or with minor modifications. In the US, the series was adopted in 1987 through the joint efforts of ANSI and the American Society for Quality Control (ASQC) as ANSI/ASQC Q90. In the EU, the series was adopted as EN29000. Although each country has established a slightly different nomenclature for the standard, the common reference is ISO 9000, the terminology that is used throughout this article.

Adopting ISO 9000 in Europe has had two principal driving forces. EU directives (or laws) mandate compliance with the standard for a number of products; at present, these include medical devices, construction products, industrial safety equipment, telecommunications terminal equipment, gas appliances, and commercial scales. For a host of other products – and increasingly for services – European firms outside the mandatory sector have started to give preference to ISO 9000-certified suppliers. As more suppliers are achieving certification, purchasers are now moving from preference to requirement.

Table 9.1 ISO 9000: international standards for quality management

Standard	Effect
ISO 9000 Quality Management and Assurance Standards – Guide- lines for Selection and Use	This is the road map for the series. Its purpose is to provide the user with guidelines for selection and use of ISO 9001, 9002, 9003, and 9004.
ISO 9001 Model for Quality Assurance in Design, Development, Production, Installation, and Servicing	This standard is for use when conformance to specified requirements is to be assured by the supplier during several stages, including design, development, production, installation and servicing.
ISO 9002 Model for Quality Assurance in Production and Installation	This standard is for use when conformance to specified requirements is to be assured by the supplier during production and installation.
ISO 9003 Model for Quality Assurance in Final Inspection and Testing	This standard is for use when conformance to specified requirements is to be assured by the supplier solely at final inspection and test.
ISO 9004 Quality Management and Quality System Elements – Guidelines	This standard describes a basic set of elements by which quality management systems can be developed and implemented. There is heavy emphasis on 'meeting company and customer needs'.

Source: ISO 9000: 1987 (E)

Initially viewed as just a requirement for doing business in Europe, it is now becoming clear that ISO 9000 will be required in the US as well. Large and small firms alike have already registered US plants to ISO 9000 to satisfy the requirements of European customers. These firms in turn are requiring their suppliers to be registered as well. GE's plastics business, for instance, has mandated compliance to some 340 suppliers. Although initially driven by requirements of the European market, it is unlikely that firms will specify different quality approaches to their suppliers – one for Europe and one for the United States. For most multinational corporations (MNCs), ISO 9000 is likely to become the specified quality requirement, regardless of country of manufacture or sale.

Specification of compliance with ISO 9000 is not, however, limited to MNCs. W.W. Grainger, the large US industrial wholesaler, operates entirely in the United States. Nevertheless, it is pursuing registration to ISO 9000 and is encouraging its more than 1,000 suppliers to do so as well (see box).

The Grainger Experience

With 337 branches, W.W. Grainger of Chicago sells over $2 billion of main-
tenance, repair and operating (MRO) supply items to thousands of industrial and commercial firms. According to Dennis Jensen, Director of Quality
Development:

> We deal with hundreds of suppliers, large and small, and we have long
> had an aggressive approach to improving their quality. ISO 9000 is
> another tool to help this effort – maybe something like 20 percent of an
> overall quality effort. For some firms, registration may impose an exces-
> sive financial burden. Hence, we are not mandating compliance. In most
> cases, however, we see the cost of ISO 9000 compliance offset to a large
> extent by cost reduction. At least that's the experience we're familiar
> with.
>
> Within Grainger, we are also seeking registration. This may be a first,
> as we are a multisite service organization and ISO 9000 was initially
> designed for single-site manufacturing companies. Our feeling is that we
> cannot encourage the requirement without meeting it ourselves.
>
> Our experience suggests that ISO 9000 will be the *de facto* quality
> requirement for most US firms within the next three to five years.

Source: Personal interview with author

Government agencies are also moving to adopt the standards. The US
Food and Drug Administration is incorporating ISO 9001 into its Good
Manufacturing Practices for medical devices. The Department of Defense
plans to replace its MIL-Q-9858A and MIL-I-45208A quality system stan-
dards with ISO 9000. Other agencies considering its use include the
Federal Aviation Administration and the National Aeronautics and Space
Administration.

For regulated products in Europe – that is, those for with EU law
mandates compliance – the certifying body must be approved by government or quasi-government agencies and designated as a notified body. For
non-regulated products, requirements for compliance may be specified by
the purchasing organization, but in practice certification by notified bodies
is required.

In the United States, there is no legal requirement for compliance with
ISO 9000, nor are there legal requirements for qualification of registrars.
Hence, its requirement and approval of a registrar are at the discretion
of the purchasing organization. There is, however, a substantial move
toward accreditation of registrars by the Registration Accreditation Board
(RAB), an affiliate of the ASQC. Currently US accreditation of registrars
is not recognized in Europe, but negotiations are under way between the
US and the EU for mutual recognition. Until an agreement is reached,

US firms planning to do business in Europe are advised to seek registration by a European notified body or its American subcontractor.

Europe currently leads the world in the number of firms that have been registered to ISO 9000. More than 20,000 companies have been registered in the UK alone. France and Germany are estimated to have registered between 500 and 1,000 firms. After a relatively slow start, the pace of registration in North America has accelerated rapidly. According to Mark Morrow, Director of CEEM Information Services, the number of certificates of registration in the US has grown from just a handful in early 1992 to close to 1,600 in mid-1993, and almost 500 certificates have been awarded in Canada. Finally, it is estimated that some 1,000 firms in the Far East have been registered.

In short, the evidence strongly indicates a move toward ISO 9000 in the US and the rest of the world similar to the one in Europe. There are, of course, concerns. The cost of compliance, for instance, is substantial and may impose undue burdens on small firms. Leaders in quality make the point that ISO 9000 is not synonymous with total quality and that their suppliers must do far more than what is required by ISO 9000 to qualify for their business. The certification process is both bureaucratic and subject to abuse, or at least to misuse.

On the other hand, the general experience has been favorable. Of some 2,300 UK firms that qualified for ISO 9000, as surveyed by Pera International, 89 percent reported improvements in operational efficiency, 76 percent reported obtaining a marketing benefit, and 48 percent reported an improvement in profitability. This parallels much of the Wilkerson experience profiled here. Wilkerson's president, Dick Angelo, said, 'ISO is just one part of a quality organization, but it fits the kind of company we want to be.'

KEY QUESTIONS

Although ISO 9000 has become a hot topic for articles, seminars, and consultants, it is still largely unknown or misunderstood. In a recent survey by Grant Thornton of 254 companies with sales between $10 million and $500 million, 48 percent of the senior executives polled indicated they had never heard of ISO 9000 (Miller 1993). According to Tierney (1993), 'One thing is clear about ISO 9000: it's one of the most misunderstood global business issues ever.' Against this backdrop there are four key questions that management should ask.

Under what circumstance should we seek registration, and when?

For firms doing business in Europe, there is little choice. For all intents and purposes, products affected by EU directives will have to be in compliance with ISO 9000 on a phase-in timetable over the next two to

The Wilkerson Experience

Founded in 1948, the Wilkerson Corporation, located in Englewood, Colorado, has become a leading manufacturer of compressed-air treatment and control products. Despite its relatively small size (in the neighborhood of $40 million in annual sales) and its location far from either coast, it has been a winner of the 'E Award' for excellence in export service and the President's 'E Star Award' for continued superior performance in foreign marketing. On 21 May 1992, the corporation received its certificate of registration to ISO 9002. Why and how did Wilkerson become one of the earliest registrants in Colorado? Says Richard Angelo, President:

> We had started with Crosby in 1987. All our managers attended the Crosby School in Florida or Chicago and we started our own approach to quality. The question was, 'What next?' We looked at the criteria for the Baldrige [Award], but concluded it was very expensive. Then in early 1990, our European distributor were starting to ask, 'Where are you on ISO 9000?
>
> At that time we hadn't heard of ISO 9000 in the US. Our investigation led us to conclude that it would become a competitive advantage in Europe and might well become a requirement. In the fall of 1990 we decided to go for certification.
>
> We invited UL reps (affiliated with the British Standards Institute) to visit us in March 1991. Because of our work with the Crosby approach, they told us we were not too far from meeting ISO requirements. From March 1991 until February 1992, we worked on writing work instructions and processes, training employees, and establishing in-house assessing and auditing. Our manager of QA was in charge and we did it without outside training or consultants.
>
> The biggest cost was the time of our in-house people, which we estimate at about $485,000. Generally we were able to divert people to this effort without any negative impact on the organization except in the last month. Then it was coming down to the wire and, with the auditors coming in, we diverted so many people to completing the effort that we went slightly into the red.
>
> The audit lasted three days. At the end of each day we had a 30-minute meeting with the auditors. If they had seen a breakdown, the process would have stopped right then. As it was, they found only minor items and we passed. We were the 66th company in the US to be registered, and we were told that only two of five companies passed on first trial.
>
> We think customers will view our registration to mean that we're a well-run company with good cost control, and that we're easier to deal with. We can't prove that registration has gotten us business, but in Europe we think it tilted a couple of large accounts our way. Plus, we have won Grainger's 'key supplier' award two years in a row, and feel that winning it the second year was a result of our ISO 9000 work.

Overall, we're pleased with our ISO 9000 experience. To remain registered will require continued improvement and senior management involvement. I'm personally committed to this and to our quality effort. For instance, I chair our quality review committee, which meets once a month, and every year I'm the cook at our annual quality barbecue.

It's important to recognize that ISO 9000 is not the total quality story. For instance, it doesn't require customer input – something we feel is critical. Also, the ISO 9000 picture is dynamic. Because of the nature of our business we went for ISO 9002 certification. Since then, we have found that customers tend to feel ISO 9001 registration is superior. This isn't really the case, but we are going back for registration to ISO 9001.

Seeking ISO 9000 registration did not replace Wilkerson's quality efforts; rather, it complemented them. According to Pete Santeusanio, vice president of marketing and international sales:

Our approach to quality is now a three-pronged one, consisting of our TQM program, statistical process control, and ISO 9000. Some see ISO 9000 as mostly a manufacturing program, but at Wilkerson, we in marketing are very much involved, particularly in contract reviews, product development; customer service activities, and warranty work.

As far as competitive advantage is concerned, Dick is right. We can't prove that being registered got us an order, but we're convinced that it gives us an edge over competitors who are not registered. Once they are registered, however, we will not have that edge. As we look to the future, this means we will have to continue to go beyond just meeting customer minimum requirements for competitive advantage.

Source: Personal interviews with author

---

four years. For products not covered by EU directives, an increasing number of purchasers are specifying that their suppliers must also be in compliance with ISO 9000. There will be exceptions, of course, particularly in the case of small or specialty suppliers. But when compliance is not mandated there is little question – as in the case of Wilkerson – that registered suppliers will have an advantage over those that are not.

Although the imperative to seek ISO 9000 registration to do business in the US has not been as great as in Europe, the view of those experienced with ISO 9000 is that it will become the *de facto* approach to quality in the United States in three to five years. There will be exceptions, of course. Sole suppliers with proprietary technology or small firms for whom compliance might be too costly may be granted exceptions. For most firms, however, the main question will be when, not whether, to pursue registration. Generally this question will be answered in the context of customer preferences, competitor actions, and the firm's own cost-benefit ratio. An additional consideration is the potential of ISO 9000 to simplify the firm's response to its customers' quality requirements. As John Stott, marketing manager At Cobe Labs, said:

> We welcome ISO 9000. Meeting one standard for an approach to quality will be a tremendous improvement over the current situation, in which each customer specifies unique requirements for a quality system. With ISO 9000, one approach should satisfy most of our customers and slight modifications or extensions of our ISO 9000 approach should satisfy the rest.

The increasing likelihood that purchasers will require registration, and the fact that registering before one's competitors has the potential to provide competitive advantage, improve costs, and simplify the quality picture, argue for early registration.

How does ISO 9000 relate to other quality systems?

A major criticism of ISO 9000 has been that it is not a total quality system and that its adoption will not ensure leading-edge quality. This criticism has some merit, but it misses two important points. First, leading-edge quality systems are fundamentally concerned with competitive advantage, whereas ISO 9000 is fundamentally concerned with providing purchasers with a standardized way to require that *all* suppliers have in place good quality assurance systems. Second, firms that go beyond just compliance with ISO 9001, 9002, and 9003, and follow the guidelines in ISO 9004, may well put into place much of what is found in leading-edge quality systems.

In this context, ISO 9000 should be viewed from two perspectives. If the firm already has quality assurance systems in place, compliance with any of the ISO 9000 standards provides additional assurance as to the ongoing integrity of these systems and, through the use of third-party audits, provides purchasers with assurance that the systems are indeed working as anticipated. For the firm that has no quality assurance system in place, compliance alone with ISO 9001, 9002, or 9003 will ensure a basic, workable quality system. That is, it will need to have in place the quality elements listed in the box and will be audited for its integrity.

Examination of the quality elements will confirm the point that compliance with ISO 9001, 9002, or 9003 does not require a total quality system. For instance, it does not require consideration of a host of soft issues, such as responsiveness to customer requests, accuracy of quotations, or internal relations. Nor does it specify the processes and procedures necessary to meet its requirements. Further, it does not specify the use of statistical methods or the nature of text procedures. In sum, the purpose of compliance is to meet well-specified product characteristics and customer requirements. It does not address competitive advantage. Hence, ISO 9001,

---

ISO 9000: the quality elements

The ISO 9001 standard includes 21 elements that must be addressed in developing a quality system, as listed below:

- management responsibility
- quality system
- contract review
- design control
- document control
- purchasing
- purchaser supplied product
- product identification and traceability
- process control
- inspection and testing
- inspection, measuring, and test equipment
- inspection and test status
- control of non-conforming product
- corrective action
- handling, storage, packaging, and delivery
- quality records
- internal quality audits
- control of production
- after-sales servicing
- training
- statistical techniques

ISO 9002 and 9003 require compliance either with the above elements to a lesser degree, or to a smaller list of elements.

9002, and 9003 are starting points, to be tailored and augmented to individual firm requirements.

Because firms register to ISO 9001, 9002, or 9003, it is easy to overlook ISO 9004. But it is this part of the standard that, if followed, will provide the basic for the pursuit of competitive advantage. Though not as detailed as the Baldrige requirements or those of other total quality approaches, ISO 9004 nevertheless provides a comprehensive outline for establishing organizational goals, focusing on the customer, and generally putting into place a system that goes far beyond passively meeting specified requirements. Of particular interest to marketers is that portion of ISO 9004 that deals with anticipating and meeting customer requirements.

Where does marketing fit into the ISO 9000 picture?

Despite the emergence of total quality systems, the tendency of most firms has been to regard quality principally as a manufacturing concern. The

ISO 9004: Quality-related items

SECTION 7.1 – MARKETING REQUIREMENTS

The marketing function should take the lead in establishing quality requirements for the product. It should:

a. determine the need for a product or service.
b. accurately define the market demand and sector, because doing so is important in determining the grade, quantity, price, and timing estimates for the product or service.
c. accurately determine customer requirements by a review of contract or market needs; actions include reassessment of any unstated expectations or biases held by customers.
d. communicate all customer requirements clearly and accurately within the company.

SECTION 7.2 – PRODUCT BRIEF

The marketing function should provide the company with a formal statement or outline of product requirements; e.g. a product brief. The product brief translates customer requirements and expectations into a preliminary set of specifications as the basis for subsequent design work. Among the elements that may be included in the product brief are the following requirements.

a. performance characteristics (e.g., environmental and usage conditions and reliability)
b. sensory characteristics (e.g., style, color, taste, smell)
c. installation configuration or fit
d. applicable standards and statutory regulations
e packaging
f. quality assurance/verification

SECTION 7.3 – CUSTOMER FEEDBACK INFORMATION

The marketing function should establish an information monitoring and feedback system on a continuous basis. All information pertinent to the quality of a product or service should be analyzed, collated, interpreted, and communicated in accordance with defined procedures. such information will help to determine the nature and extent of product or service problems in relation to customer experience and expectations. In addition, feedback information may provide clues to possible design changes as well as appropriate management action.

SECTION 16.3 – MARKET REPORTING AND PRODUCT SUPERVISION

An early warning system may be established for reporting instances of product failure or shortcomings to ensure rapid corrective action as appropriate, particularly for newly introduced products.

A feedback system regarding performance in use should exist to monitor the quality characteristics of the product throughout its life cycle. This system should be designed to analyze, as a continuing operation, the degree to which the product or service satisfies customer expectations on quality, including safety and reliability.

Information on complaints, the occurrence and modes of failure, customer needs and expectations, or any problem encountered in use should be made available for design review and corrective action in the supply and/or use of the item.

Source: ISO 9004 1987 (E)

original Deming emphasis was on the use of statistics; the original Crosby emphasis was on meeting requirements. Most quality assurance managers report to the manager of manufacturing. In this context, and as has been previously noted, ISO 9001, 9002, and 9003 are also passive with regard to customer requirements. Their focus is on meeting those requirements rather than addressing how requirements are specified. As one quality manager wryly observed, 'With ISO 9000, a manufacturer of concrete life jackets could be registered as long as there were systems in place to assure they were well made' (Henkoff 1993). Without involvement of marketing in the quality process, it is unlikely that this concern will be addressed.

The final standard in the series, ISO 9004, recognizes this concern. Its introduction paraphrases the marketing concept by stating, in part, that to be successful a company must offer products or services that meet a well-defined need, use, or purpose as well as satisfy customers' expectations. It identifies the need for marketing and market research, and it recognizes that sales and distribution are part of the quality loop. Section 7 of *Quality in Marketing* (see box) elaborates a very specific role for the marketing function that, if followed, should do much to ensure that customer requirements are extensively researched and well understood.

Use of the ISO 9004 guidelines, however, is discretionary with the firm rather than mandated by the purchaser. Companies with comprehensive TQM systems and competent marketing organizations are likely to have in place customer-oriented processes along the lines suggested by ISO 9004. If not, management must require them. Otherwise, registration to ISO 9001, 9002, or 9003 will likely fail to capitalize on the potential of ISO 9000 and may, in fact, result in analogs to concrete life jackets.

This is not an easy task. As asserted by O'Neal and LaFief (1992), 'Many marketing managers have limited understanding of marketing's key responsibilities for quality.' This limited understanding may explain such instances as the Fidelity experience, in which the original approach to quality was 'to turn it into a marketing campaign with logos, buttons, and mugs' ('Gurus of quality' 1990), or a survey that found that most marketing managers do not really understand the concept of quality or its effects on profitability (Cravens *et al.* 1988). It may also explain the results of another survey indicating that only one-third of some 500 US manufacturing and service companies believe that their total quality programs were having a significant impact on their competitiveness ('The cracks in quality' 1992).

For both general and marketing management, the foregoing emphasizes that marketing must be involved in the quality process. There are four fundamental requirements. First, renewed effort must be devoted by those in marketing to become more skilled at determining customer wants and needs in the context of total quality. In particular, they will have to become more skilled at what has been called the 'dual concept of marketing' – making sure that their enthusiasm for the firm's current products and services does not interfere with their ability to listen creatively to customers' wants and needs.

Second, those in marketing must measure the satisfaction of customers on an ongoing basis. This measurement should be based, as Gale (1990) argues, on key product/service attributes customers use to make purchase decisions. More particularly, they must measure the firm's customer satisfaction performance relative to its competitors, with input from both its own customers and those of its competitors.

Third, those in marketing need to learn and apply quality and productivity improvement processes. As Cravens *et al.* (1988) argue, marketers, must become full-fledged members of the quality team, leading or cooperating, as may be appropriate.

Fourth, those in marketing will have to accept that their own activities contribute to perceptions of quality. As Takeuchi and Quelch (1983) argue, marketers must be active in contributing to perceptions of quality. How the sales force interacts with customers, how the firm otherwise promotes its products, and how customer complaints are handled all determine customers' perception of quality.

How does one get started with ISO 9000?

A major benefit of ISO 9000 is that the required processes and procedures are developed internally by those who will be implementing them. The Wilkerson experience highlighted on p. 128 indicates that firms with a total quality system in place are well positioned to develop these processes and procedures without external assistance. Other firms will require extensive external help, and training will be an important factor. Digital Equipment Corporation, for instance, with more than 100 registered sites, found that plants committed to training achieved registration in six to nine months, compared to as much as 22 months for those with no training programs. Today a growing number of consultants, including

Digital, are available to provide training or other assistance. In either case, selecting a registrar is key. In addition to auditing the final system, the registrar can also provide valuable advice, as in the case of Wilkerson, at the start of the process.

For firms doing business in Europe, registrar selection is straightforward. The registrar must be a 'notified body' or, in the US, an organization that has an agreement with a notified body to represent it in the United States. Technically, notified bodies are equal, regardless of the EU country. In practice, there is evidence of customer preferences. German firms, for instance, appear to prefer German registrars.

In the United States, the picture is not as clear. The process by which quality registrars are accredited is currently in a state of flux. According to Hagigh (1992), large numbers of registrars have surfaced, many of whom have no credentials or proof that they are competent to perform quality system audits.

Efforts are under way to improve the accreditation process. There is now an American National Accreditation Program for Registrars of Quality Systems. ANSI, in conjunction with the Registrar Accreditation Board (RAB), is now seeking recognition of its program by European accreditation bodies.

It is expected that the registrar situation will improve as accreditation processes develop and as a result of negotiations between the US and the EU. Even for appropriately accredited registrars, however, customer preference will still be the key to selection.

CONCLUSION

For many managers, the concern will persist that ISO 9000 is a fad that will go away, as have so many other fads that once attracted management interest. However, two aspects of ISO 9000 suggest otherwise. First, it is unique in that it is purchaser-driven; purchasers can control its destiny through the specification of compliance and their requirement of proof of compliance. This purchaser discretion and the interest of purchasers in quality improvement suggest a high degree of permanency. Second, it is not a set of procedures to be transplanted from one organization to another, essentially intact, to be characterized by many in the organization as the procedure of the month. (Remember quality circles?) Rather, it requires each organization to design its own system, using ISO 9000 only as a set of guiding principles; thus it is likely to result in ownership by those involved in its design.

Two additional points should be made. First, ISO 9000 does not take the place of technical specifications with regard to functional requirements, physical dimensions, and so on. In most cases, firms will have to comply with technical specifications and ISO 9000. Second, whereas the initial focus of ISO 9000 was on produce manufacturers, drafts of guidelines for software and service corporations have been developed; the formal extension of ISO 9000 to these areas is expected shortly.

In summary, if ISO 9000 becomes the *de facto* approach to quality, as appears likely, firms will have two options. They may elect simply to be registered to ISO 9001, 9002 or 9003, as their customers specify. Quality will improve but competitive advantage will not necessarily result. Or they may use ISO 9000 as a point of departure for a customer-led quality effort, one in which marketing is a full-fledged participant. It will be interesting to see which option prevails.

REFERENCES

'The Cracks in quality' (1992) *The Economist*, 18 April, 67–8.

Cravens, David W., Holland, Charles W., Lamb, Charles W. Jr and Moncrieff, William C., III 'Marketing's role in product and service quality', *Industrial Marketing Management*, May, 285–304.

Gale, Bradley T. (1990) 'The role of marketing in total quality management', paper presented at the Quest for Excellence II conference, Washington, D.C.

'Gurus of quality are gaining clout' (1990) *Wall Street Journal*, 27 November B1.

Hagigh, Sara E. (1992) 'Obtaining EC product approvals after 1992: what American manufacturers need to know', *Business America*, 24 February, 30–3.

Henoff, Ronald (1993) 'The hot new seal of quality', *Fortune*, 28 June, 116–20.

ISO 900: International Standards for Quality Management (1991), Geneva: International Organization for Standardization.

Miller, Cyndee (1993) 'U.S. Firms lag in meeting quality standards', *Marketing News*, 15 February, 1, 6.

O'Neal, Charles R. and LaFief, William C. (1992) 'Marketing's lead role in total quality', *Industrial Marketing Management*, May, 133–43.

Takeuchi, Hirotaka and Quelch, John A. (1983) 'Quality is more than making a good produce', *Harvard Business Review*, July–August, 139–45.

Tierney, Robin (1993) 'ISO 9000 unmasked', *World Trade*, April, 46–50.

10 The Deming, Baldrige and European Quality Awards

Behnam Nakhai and Jaoa S. Neves

Increasing global competition has resulted in renewed interest in quality and has led many firms to seek guidance in implementing their quality programs. Meanwhile, several national and regional quality awards have been established to promote quality and serve as models of total quality management (TQM). The Deming Application Prize, Malcolm Baldrige National Quality Award, and European Quality Award (EQA) will be compared in terms of their application categories, criteria and areas of examination, and the underlying values and concepts embodied in their respective frameworks.

QUALITY MANAGEMENT IN THE CHANGING INTERNATIONAL ENVIRONMENT

Kenichi Ohmae identified an emerging group of customers in a global triad comprising the United States, Japan, and Western Europe. He argued that for a multinational firm to survive in the world economy, it must be present and remain competitive in these three markets.[1] The approximately 600 million customers of these markets have increasingly similar educational backgrounds, income levels, life-styles, and aspirations. In view of recent quality management initiatives, one might add that in these three markets similar concepts, standards, and quality movements have evolved. In fact, in addition to the Japanese and American quality awards, the European Foundation for Quality Management (EFQM) in conjunction with the European Commission has recently launched the EQA. Now, a multinational firm can be recognized for the quality of its operations in the three main world markets.[2] The Deming Price, Baldrige Award, and EQA are playing a key role in the quality revolution in these three markets and will effectively raise quality performance standards and expectations throughout the world.

THE DEMING PRIZE

The Deming Prize was established in Japan by the Union of Japanese Scientists and Engineers (JUSE) in 1951. This award is named in honor of W. Edwards Deming, an American statistician and proponent of quality control techniques who is recognized as the father of the worldwide quality movement. The prize has three award categories: the Deming Prize for the Individual Person, the Deming Application Prizes, and the Quality Control Award for Factory.[3, 4] The Deming Application Prizes are awarded to private or public organizations and are subdivided into small enterprises, divisions of large corporations, and overseas companies.

The Deming Prize was established to ensure that good results are achieved through successful implementation of companywide quality control activities.[5, 6] Its framework is centered on the implementation of a set of principles and techniques, such as process analysis, statistical methods, and quality circles. The Deming Prize evaluates the operations of a firm against ten criteria (see Table 10.1) but, unlike the Baldrige Award and EQA, all criteria have equal scoring weights. The Deming Prize introduced examination characteristics such as visiting teams and scoring methods, the award ceremony, and the obligation of the winners to disseminate the quality techniques they have developed. These features inspired similar characteristics in the Baldrige Award and EQA.

In the past few years, several studies have been conducted that compare the characteristics of the Deming Prize with the Baldrige Award framework.[7-11] The most striking difference is in the purpose of the Deming Prize: 'To award prizes to those companies that are recognized as having successfully applied companywide quality control based on statistical

Table 10.1 The Deming, Baldrige and European quality awards criteria

Deming Prize	Baldrige Award	European Quality Award
1 Company policy and planning	1 Leadership	1 Leadership
2 Organization and its management	2 Information and analysis	2 Policy and strategy
3 Quality control education and dissemination	3 Strategic quality planning	3 People management
4 Collection, transmission, and utilization of information on quality	4 Human resource development and management	4 Resources
5 Analysis	5 Management of process quality	5 Processes
6 Standardization	6 Quality and operational results	6 customer satisfaction
7 Control	7 Customer focus and satisfaction	7 People satisfaction
8 Quality assurance		8 Impact on society
9 Effects		9 Business results
10 Future plans		

quality control and are likely to keep up with it in the future.'[12] Therefore, most Deming Prize criteria are confined to the application of statistical techniques. Even criteria such as company policy and planning, results, or future plans, which are considered in a broader context in the Baldrige Award and EQA, are primarily concerned with quality assurance activities and quality results, especially the elimination of defects. Human resource development, customer satisfaction, impact on society, and business results are criteria that are outside the realm of the Deming Prize. The application and interpretation of the Deming Prize criteria by JUSE examiners have been described as highly qualified and sophisticated.[13] For instance, the guidelines for the judges include the consideration of aspects such as cost, productivity, delivery, safety, and environment. These dimensions, however, are not as explicitly measured as in the Baldridge Award or EQA frameworks.

THE BALDRIGE AWARD

The Baldrige Award was established in 1987 to 'promote quality awareness, understand the requirements for quality excellence, and share information about successful quality strategies and the benefits.'[14] There are three eligibility categories – manufacturing, service, and small firms – with a maximum of two awards given in each category. Any for-profit, domestic, or foreign organization located in the United States that is incorporated or a partnership can apply, and the applicant can be a whole firm or an eligible business unit. Unlike with the Deming Prize, public or non-for-profit organizations and overseas firms are not eligible. Many informative articles on the Baldrige Award have been published.[15-17]

The award is based on seven examination criteria (see Table 10.1) that are subdivided into 28 items of examination with 91 areas. The rationale for the seven criteria is based on senior executive leadership – the driver – being the foundation on which a quality organization is built and quality results are obtained. According to this framework, information and analysis, quality planning, human resource management, and process quality management – the system – are companywide efforts that lead to measurable quality and operational results – the measures of progress – which in turn affect customer satisfaction relative to competitors, customer retention, and market share gain – the goals (see Figure 10.1).

The Baldrige Award is competitive. Unlike the other two awards, there is no category in which all applicants that satisfy a given level of performance receive a quality prize. Since its inception, the Baldrige Award framework has evolved to embrace a set of core values and concepts that go far beyond mere management of quality control activities. In fact, those core values embody what one can safely consider the principles of quality management. Therefore, for the first time in the United States, there is a cohesive and convergent set of principles that most professionals agree con-

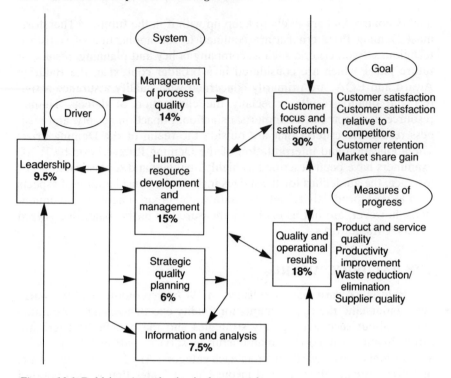

Figure 10.1 Baldrige Award criteria framework

stitute the tenets of TQM. According to these principles, the role of quality data collection and analysis as the basis for managerial decisions is paramount. Furthermore, quality efforts should not concentrate only on the elimination of defects but also encompass creative activities that will influence customer satisfaction – the positive side of quality.[18] Another key principle is that results should be quantifiable, measured, and benchmarked.

THE EUROPEAN QUALITY AWARD

In 1988, responding to the quick success of the Baldrige Award, 14 large European multinational corporations formed the EFQM to promote TQM principles in Western European countries. In 1991, EFQM, with the support of the European Organization for Quality and the European Commission, established two types of quality awards for firms: the European Quality Prize, given to firms that meet the award criteria, and the EQA, presented to the most accomplished applicant.[19, 20] In 1992, four European Quality Prizes and an EQA were granted for the first time.

Firms with a 'history of significant commitment to Western Europe' that are public or private, small or large, and manufacturing or service, are eligible to apply, albeit competing in one category.[21] Similar to the other awards, government agencies, not-for-profit organizations, and trade and professional associations are excluded.

The rationale for the European model is that customer satisfaction, people (or employee) satisfaction, and impact on society – the results – are achieved through leadership driving policy and strategy, people management, resources, and processes – the enablers – leading ultimately to excellence in business results (see Figure 10.2).

Some of the evaluating criteria for the EQA reflect further investigation of what constitutes quality management. In addition to criteria that are similar to those in the Baldrige Award – leadership, people management, policy and strategy, resources, processes, and customer satisfaction – three EQA criteria – people satisfaction, impact on society, and business results – introduce new elements that merit attention.

People satisfaction refers to how the employees feel about their organization, and some of the aspects addressed in this category include the working environment, perception of management style, career planning and development, and job security. The human-resource-development criterion of the Baldrige Award and the people-management criterion of the EQA are similar. The Baldrige Award's framework-enhanced human resource management, however, should ultimately result in better products and improved customer satisfaction. The EQA, on the other hand, incorporates employee satisfaction as an independent component of the quality system and as a measure of excellence in management.

The EQA's impact-on-society criterion focuses on the perceptions of the company by the community at large and the company's approach to the quality of life, the environment, and the preservation of global resources. Aspects such as charity: involvement in the community's education, sports, and leisure; and the effects of employment instability, energy conservation, and ecology are a few examples of areas that are not addressed by the other two quality awards.

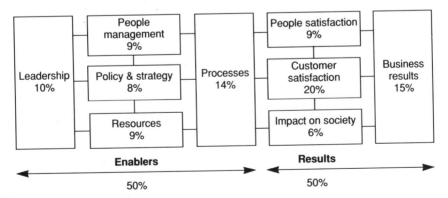

Figure 10.2 The European Quality Award model

The business-results criterion explicitly addresses the financial performance of the firm and its market competitiveness and the firm's ability to satisfy shareholders' expectations. Additionally, a host of non-financial areas of performance, such as order-processing time, new-product design lead time, and time to break even, are also considered in the evaluation.

The European model represents a radically broader guideline for addressing total quality issues. In fact, the EQA criteria seem to extend the central concepts of TQM in a myriad of aspects that pertain more to the general performance of an organization, including performance within its social and ecological environment.

THE QUALITY MANAGEMENT CONTINUUM

It is apparent that the three quality awards are part of a continuum that helps describe the notion of quality management today (see Table 10.2). While the overall approach of the Deming Prize is the control of processes that ensure the quality of goods and services, the Baldrige Award places the highest emphasis on customer satisfaction to achieve competitiveness.

Table 10.2 The quality management continuum, 1951–92

	Deming Prize (1951)	Baldrige Award (1987)	European Quality Award (1992)
Overall approach	Management of quality	Quality of management	Quality of corporate citizenship
Definition of quality	Conformance to specifications	Customer-driven quality	Customer, people, and community perceptions
Purpose	Promote quality assurance through statistical quality control techniques	Promote competitiveness through total quality management	Promote European identity through excellence in total management
Scope	Essentially national (Japan)	National (United States)	Regional (Western Europe)
Types of organizations	Essentially manufacturing companies, private or public	Manufacturing, service, and small business	Essentially large manufacturing companies, private or public
Key contributions	Dissemination of companywide quality control/total quality control, continuous improvement, relations with suppliers	Customer satisfaction, competitive comparisons and benchmarking, self-appraisal model	Relations with the community, customer satisfaction, employee satisfaction, financial and nonfinancial results

The EQA, on the other hand, broadens the notion of quality even further, and includes corporate social responsibility as an important criterion for excellence in management.

The three awards seem to place a different focus on the definition of quality: the Deming Prize views quality as defined by the producers, the Baldrige Award clearly indicates that quality is defined by the customer, and the EQA takes the view that the customer as well as the employees and the community at large all contribute to the definition of quality.

The purpose of the three awards can best be understood by looking at the organizations that created and developed them. The Deming Prize, which focuses on the application of statistical quality control techniques, originated from JUSE, a professional society of engineers responsible for the quality control activities of manufacturing firms. JUSE's primary purpose is to improve and disseminate among colleagues current, revolutionary quality assurance techniques. The impact of a few solid ideas combined with dogged application and improvement changed the entire Japanese management approach.

The Baldrige Award was promoted by the US Department of Commerce under a climate of intense industrial competition. With the co-operation of ASQC and the National Institute of Standards and Technology, the Baldrige Award has become an instrument of industrial policy and has acquired a public and formal status. Consequently, it has grown very rapidly and has gained substantial national and international prestige. Today, the Baldrige Award is a catalyst for many organizations – public and private, educational and professional; national, state, and local government – that are searching for a model of TQM to guide them in their pursuit of greater competitiveness.

The EQA was developed by a group of European multinational corporations. Since its inception, the EFQM has had a policy of supporting the evolution of the European Common Market and the emergence of a new Western European management identity. Hence, it is not surprising that dimensions such as the community's perception of the company and employee satisfaction are included in the European TQM model as measures of quality performance.

These three awards are making major contributions to the definition and practice of TQM. The Deming Prize serves as a symbol for companywide quality efforts, the pursuit of continuous improvement, and the extension of quality management to the suppliers of the firm. The Baldrige Award focuses firms on customer satisfaction, and has popularized terms such as competitive comparisons and benchmarking. Also, the Baldrige Award office has distributed hundreds of thousands of copies of the award's guidelines as a self-appraisal model for TQM programs. The EQA brings a host of new ideas – impact on the community, employee satisfaction, and financial and non-financial results – some of which will need further refinement. EQA's broad definition of quality might prove to be difficult to assess. There is a risk of diffusing the energies of managers over too many aspects that are out of their direct control. In addition, some of the dimensions proposed are difficult to measure and might have to rely exclusively on subjective opinions.

It might be too early to ascertain the full influence of these quality awards on the TQM movement that is sweeping industry worldwide. The trend to grant awards for quality has brought tremendous attention to quality issues and has helped to better understand the meaning, dimensions, and requirements of quality. TQM is rapidly extending to all sectors of the economy, especially government, health care, and education. The emerging quality management paradigm has proven to be richer than the traditional profit-maximizing model and is becoming the dominant management philosophy in many organizations.

NOTES

1 Kenichi Ohmae, *Triad Power: The Coming Shape of Global Competition*, New York: The Free Press, 1985.
2 Other countries, such as Canada, Mexico, and Australia, have launched similar initiatives.
3 Union of Japanese Scientists and Engineers, *The Deming Prize Guide for Overseas Companies*, Tokyo, 1986.
4 Union of Japanese Scientists and Engineers, *The Deming Prize Guide for Overseas Companies*, Tokyo, 1990.
5 Kaoru Ishikawa, 'How to apply companywide quality control in foreign countries', *Quality Progress*, September 1989, 70–4.
6 Union of Japanese Scientists and Engineers, *The Deming Prize Guide for Overseas Companies*, Tokyo, 1986.
7 David Bush and Kevin Dooley, 'The Deming Prize and Baldrige Award: how they compare', *Quality Progress*, January 1989, 28–30.
8 Robert E. Cole, 'Comparing the Baldrige and the Deming', *Journal for Quality and Participation*, 14(4) (1991): 94–104.
9 Kevin J. Dooley, David Bush, John C. Anderson, and Manus Rungtusanatham, 'The United States' Baldrige Award and Japan's Deming Prize: two guidelines for total quality control', *Engineering Management Journal*, 2(3) (September 1990), 9–16.
10 Howard S. Gitlow, *A Comparison of the Japanese School of Quality and the Deming School of Quality*, Coral Gables, Fla: University of Miami Institute for the Study of Quality in Manufacturing and Service, 1989.
11 Curt W. Reinmann, 'Baldrige Award, Deming Prize: a clear distinction', *Quality Progress*, April 1989, 10–11.
12 Union of Japanese Scientists and Engineers, *The Deming Prize Guide for Overseas Companies*, Tokyo, 1990.
13 Bush and Dooley, 'The Deming Prize and Baldrige Award: how they compare'.
14 National Institute of Standards and Technology, *1993 Application Guidelines for the Malcolm Baldrige National Quality Award*, Washington, D.C. U.S. Department of Commerce, 1993.
15 Neil J. DeCarlo and W. Kent Sterret, 'History of the Malcolm Baldrige National Quality Award', *Quality Progress*, March 1990, 21–7.
16 David A. Garvin, 'How the Baldrige Award really works', *Harvard Business Review*, November–December 1991, 80–93.

17 *Inside the Baldrige Award Guidelines*, a collection of articles that appeared in *Quality Progress* from June through December 1992, Milwaukee, Wis: ASQC Quality Press 1993.

18 National Institute of Standards and Technology, *1993 Application Guidelines for the Malcolm Baldrige National Quality Award*, p. 10.

19 *Total Quality Management, The European Model for Self-Appraisal: Guidelines for Identifying and Addressing Total Quality Issues*, Eindhoven, Netherlands: European Foundation for Quality Management, 1992.

20 *The European Quality Award 1993 Application Brochure*, Eindhoven, Netherlands: European Foundation for Quality Management, 1993.

21 Ibid., p. 7.

11 Make marketing part of the quality effort

Joseph L. Orsini

As this decade progresses, it is becoming increasingly clear that economic conditions dictate the involvement of all fields in improving quality. One field largely ignored by the quality movement so far is the marketing discipline; similarly, the marketing discipline has been largely unaware of the technical aspects of the quality movement.

This mutual state of unawareness has historical roots. During the first half of the twentieth century, marketing defined its domain as 'marketing begins at the factory gate' while quality defined it as 'conformance to design specifications'. Marketing's concern with distribution issues and quality's focus on design specifications provided little common ground between the two disciplines.

Beginning in the 1950s, however, the quality discipline began to define quality as 'conformance to customers' requirements', and the marketing discipline began to see itself as having input into product design. Thus began the convergence of the disciplines.

Recently, the marketing discipline has been obviously, albeit narrowly, involved in quality-related issues. When Buick placed fifth in the J.D. Powers Initial Quality survey, there was nationwide advertising of the fact.[1] when the Cadillac Motor Car Division won the Malcolm Baldrige National Quality Award in 1990, it prominently displayed its accomplishment on television. But is marketing's involvement in quality limited to advertising?

Perhaps the firmest support for the inclusion of marketing in the quality process might be found in the ISO 9000 quality standards management guide. As stated in ISO 9004:[2]

- **Section 7.1. Marketing Requirements:** The marketing function should take the lead in establishing quality requirements for the product ...
- **Section 7.2. Product Brief:** The marketing function should provide the company with a formal statement or outline of product requirements: e.g., a product brief ...
- **Section 7.3. Customer Feedback Information:** The marketing function should establish an information monitoring and feedback system on a continuous basis ...

The older definition of quality (conformance to design specifications) did not make it mandatory for the quality discipline to address customer considerations in the design process. But the newer definition (meeting customer needs) is bringing the marketing discipline into the quality effort.

The inclusion of the marketing discipline in quality management does require elaboration. This is especially true for those who do not fully understand marketing's role in activities beyond advertising and sales. Marketing potentially has an even greater role to play in the quality process than the ISO 9000 standards indicate. Both quality and marketing publications have pointed to this increased role.[3] While there is general agreement on the need for greater marketing participation in the quality process, there has been little definitive discussion on the expertise that marketing staff possess and how this expertise can be applied to quality efforts.

AREAS OF MARKETING EXPERTISE

Just as quality is more than statistical process control, marketing is more than advertising and selling. While the boundaries of any discipline are difficult to define precisely, there are several broad areas of marketing expertise:

- *Advertising:* management, design, and implementation of paid impersonal communication messages and channels and channels for the presentation and promotion of ideas, goods, and services;
- *Competitive assessment:* comparison of the marketing aspects of the company's offering (including the product or service) with that of the competition;
- *Consumer behavior:* understanding the cognitive and behavioral aspects of organizational and individual consumers regarding their purchases and use of marketed offerings;
- *Distribution planning:* determination of methods of physical movement and context of buyer-seller transaction exchanges for marketed goods and services;
- *Environmental assessment:* evaluation of present and future uncontrollable economic and social factors affecting marketing processes;
- *Market assessment:* activity related to the understanding of present and future market needs and of segment (group) differences within the market;
- *Personal selling:* management and performance of personal presentations to prospective buyers for the purpose of making sales;
- *Pricing:* determination of offering price based on cost, value, or competition;
- *Product planning:* participation in the development of new or improved offerings (products, services, and ideas) from consumer-need assessment through distribution;

- *Promotion:* paid non-advertising methods of influence on the attitudes and behavior of existing and potential buyers;
- *Publicity:* unpaid and impersonal communication related to influencing attitudes and behavior;
- *Research methods:* management and implementation of procedures to gather and analyze socioeconomic information for management decisions.

While no one person will be highly skilled in all these areas, an organization with a large marketing staff might have expertise in all of them. Marketing consultants with these skills are also available.

It should be noted that the marketing discipline assumes a managerial role in several of these areas. Advertising, distribution planning, personal selling, and marketing research are marketing managerial functions typically found in companies. In these areas, the quality discipline can help marketing managers by using quality improvement processes to improve marketing functions, such as personal selling.[4]

The 12 areas of marketing expertise can be very useful in an organization's quality efforts. It would therefore be useful to have a framework that would indicate where marketing expertise could be of maximum benefit to quality implementation. The Baldrige Award produces this framework.

THE BALDRIGE AWARD

The Baldrige Award produces both an incentive and implementation guide for US companies wanting to improve the quality of their products and services. The award criteria are broken into seven categories: each category has a maximum number of points possible, which shows the importance of that category to the overall quality effort. The seven categories are subdivided into examination items, which focus on major management requirements. The award categories, items, and point values are shown in Table 11.1.

One area of potential marketing contribution, as indicated by the ISO 9004 requirements, is category 7, Customer focus and satisfaction, which is worth 30 per cent of the total number of points. The marketing discipline has a history of involvement in the study of customer satisfaction. For example, in 1977, the first of a dozen conferences devoted to that topic was held, and a customer satisfaction journal. *Journal of Consumer Satisfaction, Dissatisfaction, and Complaining Behavior*, was established in 1988. Evidence of the recent mutual interest in customer satisfaction by both marketing and quality disciplines is the inception of a joint conference by the American Marketing Association and ASQC in 1989. The sixth annual Customer Satisfaction and Quality Measurement Conference was held this year.

Table 11.1 Baldrige Award categories, items and scores

1.0 Leadership (95 points)
    1.1 Senior executive leadership
    1.2 Management for quality
    1.3 Public responsibility and corporate citizenship

2.0 Information and analysis (75 points)
    2.1 Scope and management of quality and performance
        Data and information
    2.2 Competitive comparisons and benchmarking
    2.3 Analysis and uses of company level data

3.0 Strategic quality planning (60 points)
    3.1 Strategic quality and company performance
        Planning process
    3.2 Quality and performance plans

4.0 Human resource development and management (150 points)
    4.1 Human resource planning and management
    4.2 Employee involvement
    4.3 Employee education and training
    4.4 Employee performance and recognition
    4.5 Employee well-being and satisfaction

5.0 Management of process quality (140 points)
    5.1 Design and introduction of quality products and services
    5.2 Process management: product and service production and delivery processes
    5.3 Process management: business and support service processes
    5.4 Supplier quality
    5.5 Quality assessment

6.0 Quality and operational results (180 points)
    6.1 Product and service quality results
    6.2 Company operational results
    6.3 Business and support service results
    6.4 Supplier quality results

7.0 Customer focus and satisfaction (300 points)
    7.1 Customer expectations: current and future
    7.2 Customer relationship management
    7.3 Commitment to customers
    7.4 Customer satisfaction determination
    7.5 Customer satisfaction results
    7.6 Customer satisfaction comparison

Source: 1994 Award Criteria, Gaithersburg, MD, National Institute of Standards and Technology, p. 13.

Review of the Baldrige Award criteria reveals additional areas of potential marketing involvement, such as item 5.1, Design and introduction of quality products and services.[5] While item 5.1 and category 7 are obvious areas of potential involvement, it would be useful to have a tool that would indicate other not-so-obvious areas in which marketing staff could

Table 11.2 Potential use of marketing expertise in the Baldrige Award

Baldrige Award category/item	Marketing areas of expertise											
	Advertising	Competitive assessment	Consumer behavior	Distribution planning	Environmental assessment	Market assessment	Personal selling	Pricing	Product Planning	Promotion	Publicity	Research methods
1.0 Leadership												
1.1					*	*					*	
1.2	*											**
1.3			*							*	*	*
2.0 Information and analysis												
2.1		*	**		**	**				*		**
2.2		**	**		*							**
2.3			**									**
3.0 Strategic quality planning												
3.1		**	**		**	**			*			**
3.2		*			*				*			**
4.0 Human resource development and management												
4.1												*
4.2			*				**					
4.3							**					**
4.4												
4.5						*						**
5.0 Management of process quality												
5.1	**	**	**	**	*	**	**	**	**			**
5.2				*					**			*
5.3	**			**			**		**			**
5.4									**			
5.5	**			**			**		*			**
6.0 Quality and operational results												
6.1		**				**			**			**
6.2			*	*	*	*			**			
6.3	*	**	*	**			**	**	*			**
6.4		*				**						
7.0 Customer focus and satisfaction												
7.1	*	**	**	**	**	**	**	**	**			**
7.2	*	**	**	*	**	**	**	*	**	**	**	**
7.3	**	*	**	**	**	**	**		*	*	*	**
7.4	*	**	**	*		**	**	*			*	*
7.5			**			**	**					**
7.6	*	**	**		*	**	**	*	*			**

Notes * = Modest potential use
** = High potential use

use their expertise. Table 11.2 provides such a tool. It contains a subjective estimation of how the areas of marketing expertise are applicable to the Baldrige Award criteria.

In Table 11.2, the award items in which marketing expertise might play a strong role are indicated by a double asterisk; items with a more modest role are noted with a single asterisk. For example, in item 1.3, Public responsibility and corporate citizenship, advertising expertise plays only a modest role, while environmental-assessment expertise plays a more important role.

In addition to the information presented in Table 11.2, quality managers might find it worthwhile to estimate a priority for inducing the involvement potential of the various areas of marketing expertise in the quality process. Educating the marketing discipline in quality concepts will take resources and time. Prioritization of applicable marketing expertise is done for the same reasons prioritization is done for any quality improvement process.

Charts indicating the approximate level of marketing potential applicability to quality processes can be constructed by adding up the number of asterisks across each award category. Table 11.3 shows a Pareto analysis of the potential areas of marketing involvement in the quality field, based on the award categories in Table 11.2. This can also be done for the types of marketing expertise. Table 11.4 shows a Pareto analysis of the areas of marketing expertise useful to quality efforts, based on the evaluation in Table 11.2.

If a company has employees possessing particular types of marketing expertise, it should take advantage of their expertise. It is far more beneficial to use in-house personnel in quality planning than to hire external consultants. This will broaden marketing's understanding of and participation in the quality effort.

GENERAL TRENDS IDENTIFIED

The results of the analyses in Tables 11.2, 11.3, and 11.4 can be summarized as follows:

- marketing has at least some potential for involvement in all categories of the Baldrige Award;
- there is substantial variation in the level of marketing involvement potential among the award items;
- all areas of marketing expertise have at least some potential for involvement in quality processes;
- there is substantial variation in involvement potential among the areas of marketing expertise;
- customer satisfaction and quality management are categories with the highest potential for marketing contributions;

Table 11.3 A Pareto analysis of the Baldrige Award categories

Category	No.[a]
Customer focus and satisfaction	89
Management of process quality	44
Quality and operational results	28
Information and analysis	19
Strategic quality planning	16
Leadership	12
Human resource development and management	12
Total	220

Note: [a] Based on the number of asterisks for each item in Table 11.2.

Table 11.4 A Pareto analysis of marketing expertise

Marketing expertise	No.[a]
Research methods	45
Consumer behavior	26
Market assessment	23
Competitive assessment	22
Personal selling	21
Product planning	21
Distribution planning	17
Environmental assessment	16
Advertising	14
Pricing	7
Publicity	5
Promotion	3
Total	220

Note: [a] Based on the number of asterisks for each area of expertise in Table 11.2.

- marketing expertise in marketing research, consumer behavior, personal selling, product design, market assessment, and competitive assessment are the areas with the highest potential contribution to award items.

This summary of the potential involvement of the marketing discipline in quality processes has, by choice, been in general terms. The participation level will be different for each company. For example, the role of marketing might be less prominent in manufacturers of industrial products than in manufacturers of consumer products. (It is no coincidence that the Baldrige Award's entrance into television advertising occurred when Cadillac won the award.) For service industries in general, however, the level of marketing participation might well be greater than in consumer product industries. This is particularly relevant to consumer services, since service intangibility results in a greater necessity for quality measurement to be accomplished through customers.

NOTES

1 PR News Wire Association, 5 Sept 1990.
2 ISO 9004–1987, *Quality Management and Quality Systems Elements – Guidelines*, Geneva: International Organization for Standardization, 1987.
3 Some of these publications include J.M. Juran, *Juran on Leadership for Quality* (New York: The Free Press, 1989); Paul E. Psek, 'Defining quality at the marketing/development interface', *Quality Progress*, June 1987, 28–36; David W. Cravens, Charles W. Holland, Charles W. Lamb, and William C. Moncrief III, 'Marketing's role in product and service quality', *Industrial Marketing Management*, 17 (1988): 285–304; and Joseph L. Orsini, 'Quality function deployment: marketing participation in product/service design', Proceedings of the American Marketing Association Winter Educators' Conference, 1991.
4 Cas Welch and Pete Geissler, *Bringing Quality to Sales* (Milwaukee, Wis.: ASQC Quality Press, 1992).
5 John R. Hauser and Don Clausing, 'The House of Quality', *Harvard Business Review*, May–June 1988, 63–73.

Part IV

International advertising

The contributions in this section are internationally diverse. Douglas West reviews the performance or evolution of British multinational advertising agencies and some of their recent problems, starting first with the early advantages which British multinational agencies possessed relative to their US counterparts and moving on to try to pinpoint the nature of the uniqueness which the British have been able to internalise and deploy so successfully. The chapter concludes with structural challenges being faced globally by the industry as a whole.

A quite different departure is being able to incorporate a chapter from an advertising practitioner based in a Muslim country. Traditionally, we have been blinkered into accepting a view of the world in terms of what does and does not work in the home country, for which we may assume the USA. In a refreshing departure, Nükhet Vardar takes Turkey, which lies across two continents, Europe and Asia, as the base for her chapter: 'Media burst in a Eurasian country: a blessing or a burden?'.

The third contribution in this section is by Ursula Gruber who, rather uniquely, has an agency which specialises in the transposition of advertising campaigns, reviewing all aspects of copy for their suitability for transference. Four illustrations of campaign messages that have been successfully transferred across languages and cultures are offered to highlight the complexity of the task and minimise the common belief that it is mainly a matter of luck.

Part IV

International advertising

12 British multinational agencies
Recent problems and the challenges of structural change

Douglas C. West

INTRODUCTION

The chapter examines the new challenges that have confronted top British multinational agencies (MNAs). Modifying Caves (1982b: 1) definition of a multinational enterprise, an MNA is defined as an agency that controls and manages offices located in at least two countries. United States-based advertising agencies dominated the top end of the world MNA business by the 1960s (West 1988). 'Madison Avenue' became synonymous with advertising in virtually every other country outside the old communist bloc. The position had changed dramatically in Britain 20 years later. By the mid-1980s, the United States MNA supremacy of the British advertising market, with agencies such as J. Walter Thompson, Young & Rubicam and McCann-Erickson, had been checked and eroded by a small group of highly creative and financially adept local agencies. In addition, several London-based agencies had entered the United States market in pursuit of their own multinational ambitions, in particular Saatchi & Saatchi and WPP.

However, the continued success of British agencies has faltered since the late 1980s, and changes in the marketing environment on both sides of the Atlantic have added to their problems. This chapter reviews the strengths and weaknesses of British MNAs in the 1990s within the framework of the multinational enterprise literature and structural change in the advertising industry of Western economies.

BRITISH AND UNITED STATES MNA COMPETITION

The major element in the process of Americanization of the British advertising market in the postwar period was acquisition. United States MNAs purchased 32 British agencies between 1957–67 (O'Connor and Crichton 1967: 13). The three main agency purchases came a little later

I would like to thank Stanley Paliwoda and Stephen King for their detailed comments and suggestions. Any inaccuracies and mistakes are entirely my responsibility.

with Colman, Prentis and Varley (CPV) by Kenyon & Eckhardt in 1969, and the London Press Exchange (LPE) by Leo Burnett, also in 1969, and Masius by D'Arcy-MacManus in 1974. Somewhat ironically, CPV, the LPE and Masius had all stretched their resources to the limit in attempting to build international networks, and it was this which left them vulnerable to takeovers. None had succeeded in the key element of establishing a successful home-based US network. They subsequently found that without a successful United States branch they could not win American advertisers or fully service British companies advertising there. By 1970 just six United States MNAs controlled 42 per cent of British above-the-line billings.

The United States MNA global expansion began to lose momentum in the 1970s and early 1980s. Outside of the then communist bloc, United States' MNAs were operating in every country except Curaçao, Egypt, Malta, Morocco, Paraguay and Turkey (Anderson 1984). Their absence from these countries was largely a function of market size and risk. Just at the time when most United States' MNAs were reaching maturity, several local agencies in Europe were reasserting their position. In Britain a small group of local agencies had begun to challenge the giant United States agencies. Later to be dubbed the 'new wave', agencies such as Saatchi & Saatchi, Boase Massimi Pollitt and Collett Dickenson Pearce and, more recently, Butterfield Day Devito Hockney and Still Price Court D'Souza, had began to make their marks on the local British market and often internationally. In the wake of this local resurgence the United States' MNA share of the British domestic market had significantly declined from 42 per cent in 1970, to 34 per cent in 1980 and 19 per cent by 1987. Furthermore, several new British MNAs were formed in the 1980s, principally Saatchi & Saatchi and, a newcomer, Wire & Plastic Products (WPP).

Saatchi & Saatchi's example played a strategic role in stimulating other British agencies to go MNA. Founded in 1970, by 1974 Saatchi & Saatchi had purchased three British agencies (Kleinman 1987). The agency then merged with the publicly quoted Compton UK. Advertising for the Conservative Party campaign in 1978–9 had raised Saatchi & Saatchi's image amongst the public and business communities in Britain. Thereafter, it embarked on an ambitious domestic acquisition programme funded by rights issues. It was financially adept, as well as creative, and quickly gained a reputation for savvy financial management practices such as retaining the full media payment from their clients until the media owner finally demanded it. This enabled the agency to keep the interest. A foreign agency network was developed in the early 1980s, again by acquisition. Its most notable United States purchases were Compton Communications in 1982, Dancer, Fitzgerald Sample in 1986 (bought by one of its subsidiary agencies, Dorland) and Ted Bates, also in 1986 (now part of the Spielvogel Bates network). By 1987, Saatchi & Saatchi was placed second in worldwide billings behind Young & Rubicam and the third agency in the United States.

Smaller networks were completed by other British MNAs in the wake of Saatchi & Saatchi's success and appeal to the London Stock Market. This encouraged other agencies to seek flotations in the 1980s. Wight Collins Rutherford Scott merged with the French Groupe Belier in 1986 and completed a global grouping two years later with the purchase of the Ball partnership of Asia and Australasia. The London-based Lopex Group purchased the United States agency Warwick Baker & Fiore, and Gold Greenless Trott purchased GSD & M, Joey Reiman and Martin Williams agencies. Boase Massimi Pollit also formed a modest MNA network in 1986, as did Lowe Howard-Spink, which subsequently merged with Inter-public. Lastly, Wire & Plastic Products (WPP) notes special mention as the world's biggest advertising organization of the 1990s (see Table 12.1).

WPP made supermarket trolleys when Martin Sorrell purchased a signif-icant interest in the company in 1985. Sorrell was Saatchi & Saatchi's financial director at the time and had helped engineer the early United States acquisitions (*The Financial Times*, 29 June 1987). As a publicly quoted company, WPP acquired a group of design houses in the United States and Britain in 1986 initially using investment from Saatchi & Saatchi and the City of London. Shortly after leaving Saatchi & Saatchi, Sorrell mounted an audacious hostile takeover bid for the enormous J. Walter Thompson Group in 1987. WPP paid $566 million for Thompson's, seen by many Wall Street observers as precariously high. The City of London, however, had confidence in Sorrell's ambitions and offered funds. A WPP

Table 12.1 Top ten world advertising organizations, 1992

Rank	Advertising organization	Billing ($m)
1	WPP Group (UK)	
	Ogilvy & Mather; J. Walter Thompson; Scali, McCabe, Sloves.	18,955
2	Interpublic Group (US)	
	Lintas; Lowe Group; McCann-Erickson.	13,343
3	Omnicom Group (US)	
	BBDO Worldwide; DDB Needham Worldwide; TBWA.	13,226
4	Saatchi & Saatchi (UK)	
	Saatchi & Saatchi Advertising Worldwide; Backer Spielvogel Bates Worldwide; CME KHBB.	11,575
5	Dentsu (Japan)	10,477
6	Young & Rubicam (US)	7,879
7	Euro RSCG (France)	6,888
8	Foote, Cone & Belding Communications (US)	5,198
9	Hakuhodo (Japan)	5,078
10	Grey Advertising	4,916

Source: Advertising Age, 14 April 1993

rights issue raised £270 million and £260 million through long-term debts. J. Walter Thompson was purchased for cash: the most respected of leading United States MNAs' had fallen into British hands in 1987. In an equally audacious hostile takeover, Sorrell purchased the Ogilvy & Mather world-wide network in 1989.

By the late 1980s, five British agencies held positions in the top ten of the local market as opposed to only three in 1980. By 1989, WPP, with its purchase of J. Walter Thompson and Ogilvy & Mather, was placed first in worldwide billings. The British challenge had been, initially, highly successful. This chapter continues by examining the problems faced by British MNAs from the late 1980s onwards.

BRITISH MNA PROBLEMS

Since Lowe Howard-Spink merged with Interpublic and WCRS with the French Groupe Belier, only four British agencies now remain in the world top 50, namely Lopex, Gold Greenless Trott, and the main two: WPP and Saatchi & Saatchi. WPP and Saatchi & Saatchi experiences since the late 1980s have been turbulent.

J. Walter Thompson USA experienced several account problems shortly after WPP's takeover (*Advertising Age*, 10 Dec. 1990: 2, 8). It should be noted that virtually every one of the account losses and problems had its roots prior to the WPP takeover, including the relationship with LGFE (see below). The takeover did not help, but the impression given by the trade press that United States clients were lining up to leave is far from true. Difficulties began for JWT when it lost the media buying portion of Bally's, Health & Tennis, a $60 million account, leading to the dismissal of one-third of the Los Angeles office. Additionally, the office lost its largest client, 20th Century Fox Film Corporation, so it ended 1990 with $100 million in billings, just half the size it was in 1989. Most importantly, WPP's ambitious takeover of Ogilvy & Mather for $864 million in 1989 to form the world's number one agency group, proved to be an over-payment. Sorrel was subsequently forced to take a $425 million write-off from the acquisition. Furthermore, while Ogilvy & Mather's worldwide billings remained relatively healthy, the New York office suffered the loss of several major accounts, including American Express and Campbell Soup. The office subsequently received a major fillip in 1992 with the award of the $15 to $20 million Ford subsidiary Jaguar Cars account, said to be quite a coup for Chair-CEO Charlotte Beers, who had just joined the agency in April 1992 (*Advertising Age*, 20 July 1992: 4).

Several smaller acquisitions were made in advertising and sales promo-tions by WPP. One agency, Lord, Geller, Federico, Einstein (LGFE), proved to be a particularly unfortunate one (*Advertising Age*, 9 July 1990: 1, 42). Six LGFE executives quit the company to form Lord Einstein O'Neill & Partners (financed by Young & Rubicam). Several major LGFE accounts moved across to the new agency and WPP promptly entered into litigation. WPP was awarded $7 million in damages, but the fallout of the legal fight included the withdrawal of the $138 million IBM account from both agencies and with it much of LGFE's prestige. WPP eventually decided to merge LGFE with Brouillard Communications in 1990.

Martin Sorrell originally faced a daunting task of making the payments due to bankers given that advertising agencies, in general, were no longer 'in fashion' with the City since the crash of October 1987 (*Advertising Age*, 8 Feb. 1993: 45). Options for WPP ranged from asset disposals to new stock offerings depending on the improvement in profit and cash flow. Despite the problems, the money has since been raised because, whilst the 'gloss' has been removed from agency stock, there is still widespread confidence in British MNA management. WPP underwent a financial restructuring in 1993 and much of the earlier pressure has now subsided.

In Saatchi & Saatchi's case, despite the success of the 1980s, the agency reported pre-tax losses in 1990 of $41.6 million and about $15 million in 1991. Part of its problems included reducing high overheads in both the advertising networks and in the parent company, paying off the accumulated debt from its acquisitions against the backdrop of a declining advertising market, and in the cost of attempting to establish a stand-alone Tokyo office. On this last point, most observers agree that it is not possible for Western agencies to succeed in Japan without a link with a large Japanese agency. Its Backer Spielvogel Bates network underwent a particularly troubled period, losing $200 million in billings between 1989 and 1991, including the $90 million Miller Lite account (*Advertising Age*, 24 June 1991: 1, 59). Internationally Saatchi & Saatchi set itself a goal to operate as a single global unit to enable it to pick up more business from

Table 12.2 Top ten agencies in the local UK and US markets, 1992

Rank	UK market	Billings (£m)	US market	Billings ($m)
1	Saatchi & Saatchi (UK)	379	Young & Rubicam (US)	3,466
2	J. Walter Thompson (UK)	348	DDB Needham (US)	2,945
3	D'Arcy Masius Benton & Bowles (US)	176	FCB (US)	2,646
4	Ogilvy & Mather (UK)	175	D'Arcy Masius Benton & Bowles (US)	2,598
5	BMP DDB Needham (US)	144	BBDO (US)	2,564
6	Lowe Howard Spink (US)	137	Saatchi & Saatchi (UK)	2,503
7	BSB Dorland (UK)	135	J. Walter Thompson (UK)	2,163
8	Abbott Mead Vickers BBDO (US)	128	Leo Burnett (US)	2,104
9	McCann-Erickson (US)	114	Ogilvy & Mather (UK)	2,017
10	Publicis (France)	102	Grey (US)	1,904

Sources Campaign, 5 March 1993; *Advertising Age*, 14 April 1993

Table 12.3 Advertising as percentage of GDP in the UK and the US, 1992

Year	UK (%)	US (%)
1985	1.11	1.41
1986	1.18	1.44
1987	1.22	1.43
1988	1.28	1.42
1989	1.29	1.38
1990	1.20	1.34
1991	1.09	1.25

Source: Advertising Association, *Advertising Statistics Yearbook, 1993*, Henley: Advertising Association, 1993

clients that the network already handled in one region by winning their accounts in other parts of the world. Its major clients continue to include Procter & Gamble, British Airways, Sara Lee and Toyota.

It appears that both WPP and Saatchi & Saatchi will improve their position, prophets of doom being greatly overrated, and their agencies remain firmly at the top end of the business on both sides of the Atlantic (see Table 12.2). However, further major expansions are unlikely in the short run. As Table 12.3 shows, the advertising slump in the United States since 1989 and in Britain since 1990 has taken its toll (see *Advertising Age*, 20 July 1992: 4, for a discussion of the effects of recession on British agencies). Additionally, the mega-market mergers of the 1980s have consolidated and eliminated many well-known brand names across a number of industries and there is a new source of MNAs to compete with: France. French MNAs such as Publicis, Euro RSCG, FCA and BDDP are the 'new kids on the block' and now account for a 10 per cent share of the world's top 50 advertising organizations (see Table 12.4). It should be noted in relation to this, that the largest single agency in the world is the Japanese Dentsu, and that, on the whole, Japan's creative reputation

Table 12.4 Market shares of world's top 50 advertising organizations, 1992

Country	No. in top 50	Total billings	% of total
US	22	63,620	47
UK	4	31,984	23
Japan	15	25,800	19
France	4	13,388	10
Italy, South Korea, Switzerland & Australia	5	1,804	1
Total	50	136,596	100

Source: Collated from *Advertising Age*, 14 April 1993

is excellent. Well over 90 per cent of its business comes from its domestic market, where account conflicts are not viewed as a problem. Consequently, Japanese advertising agencies have few multinational ambitions and, so far, do not pose a threat to other MNAs.

Aside from the particular business problems mentioned above, the major British MNAs, along with much of the rest of the agency business, faced adverse structural changes in the late 1980s and early 1990s, which have yet be fully appreciated by many observers of the advertising industry (see Shergill 1993) which will be assessed later. This chapter continues by examining the nature of the early advantages of British MNAs in the context of the multinational enterprise literature.

EARLY ADVANTAGES OF BRITISH MNAS

Monopoly advantage

According to Kindleberger (1969), Caves (1971) and Hymer (1975), in deciding whether or not to undertake a foreign direct investment (FDI) a potential multinational enterprise must have an advantage. This is a prerequisite because the potential multinational enterprise will be at a cost disadvantage when operating at a distance. Obviously the local market must be imperfect or the potential multinational enterprise could simply export the advantage. Additionally the advantage must be transferable abroad, but not available to locals. As the advantage is firm-specific this theory is generally known as 'monopoly advantage'. This is a useful framework to adopt to evaluate the advantages held by British MNAs in the 1980s.

British MNAs in the 1980s possessed one significant firm-specific monopoly advantage: as public companies they had access to the capital of the City of London and, linked to this, they enjoyed much more favourable accounting rules for 'goodwill' compared to the United States. It is worth mentioning at the outset that price competition did not exist as a serious factor. Agencies on both sides of the Atlantic earned the bulk of their income by media commission at standard rates. However, the system has come under significant threat in the last few years with increasing numbers of advertisers demanding commission rebates and the paying of fees instead. Nevertheless, the British did not, as a group, undercut United States prices either locally or in America.

Returning to the key advantage – their access to capital to counter United States MNAs size advantages – Saatchi & Saatchi began the process in that they demonstrated to the City that agencies were *bona fide* businesses. In the get-rich-quick atmosphere of the 1980s, City funds were readily made available for British agency multinational ambitions. The traditional United States ownership advantage of size was therefore challenged by the City of London enabling smaller British agencies to purchase larger American ones. Financiers were convinced that British MNAs offered the requisite management skills for success.

The advertising environment was another aspect of British advantage. The British advertising market did not provide a consistent period of growth upon which to base a well-supported MNA network until the mid-1970s. However, the tide began to turn in favour of British agencies from the mid-1970s with positive macro advertising conditions. Despite the recession of the early 1980s, British consumer expenditure remained buoyant in real terms and advertising reaped the benefits. British advertising agencies initially prospered in this environment. Between 1980 and 1984 the turnover of the top 50 British agencies rose by four-fifths, pretax profits by 85 per cent and shareholders' funds by 72 per cent (Phillips 1986). United States MNAs based in London also benefited from the upswing, but several British agencies were able to make the most of the opportunity by going public.

Another important ownership advantage has been the trends in world FDI investment. The almost uninterrupted growth in international trade from 1945 to 1970 was dominated by the United States. However, in 1980–5 the American percentage of FDI fell to 22. The difference was made up by the Europeans increasing their share to 63 per cent and the Japanese to 13 (United Nations 1988). British FDI had been solidly aimed at the United States, accounting for two-thirds of all the United States takeovers by 1987. British investors spent the equivalent of just under 5 per cent of British GNP on FDI in the United States. The strategic advantage of a bridge into the United States market for British MNAs was consequently more easily achievable in the 1980s than previously.

The British MNAs' advantage in the changing trend in FDI flows in the 1980s was different to the previous American one in the 1950s and 1960s. It provided access to capital, rather than the patronage of large advertisers. British agencies were never able to exploit the indigenous British-based multinational advertiser in the same way that United States MNAs had. The pioneering United States MNAs all came to Britain to service the accounts of their large domestic advertisers who were going multinational. However, British-based multinational enterprises (MNEs) generally treated each country separately and used a local agency. Only a few small British MNA networks had European and/or Commonwealth focuses. Entrance to the important United States market was not accelerated as British advertisers preferred United States agencies abroad.

British agencies could match United States MNAs organizational experience by the 1980s. As was often the case with American multinationals of all kinds (Wilkins 1974), United States service MNAs' were familiar with extending themselves domestically owing to the geographically vast land mass. Consequently, when they went over borders they already had the administrative and organizational skills to cope. A new office or acquisition in London became like a new one in Detroit or Los Angeles and this gave United States MNAs an organizational skills advantage. British agencies had had little experience of significant domestic expansions, until the early 1960s. The Brunning Group floated itself in the early 1960s and developed a chain of regional offices in virtually every major city in Britain. But most importantly, Saatchi & Saatchi established an enormous domestic network before it went MNA and thus benefited from the experience of managing branch offices. However, one problem in linking MNAs to multinational organizational theory that must be borne in mind is that (unlike most MNEs) they are service companies with a very wide range of both local and international clients. To take the example of J. Walter Thompson, JWT has one form of organization and management for highly centralized MNEs like Ford and Rolex, another with a rather decentralized MNE such as Nestlé, and a whole range of different ones for its local clients all over the world.

A final ownership advantage of some potential significance held by British agencies was the 'perception of creativity' issue. To put it simply, there was a widespread perception amongst practitioners and advertisers on both sides of the Atlantic that British agencies were more 'creative' than their United States counterparts in the 1980s. Many observers of the United States advertising industry argued that creative standards declined during the 1973–4 recession. Advertisers opted for less risky hard-sell approaches. Furthermore, United States agencies suffered much more than the British from entrepreneurial cowboy research companies with highly mechanistic 'testing techniques'. This was just at the time when British agencies were learning from the examples of America's finest copywriters of the 1960s, such as Bill Bernbach (best known for the marvellous 'Think Small' Volkswagen campaign). The 'new wave' of British agencies, as they were dubbed in the 1980s, exemplified this process by winning numerous international awards for advertising.

Observers seeking an explanation of the British creative 'mystique' have offered several explanations. For one thing, there are more creative start-ups in Britain than the United States because barriers to entry are lower. Media independents are more common in Britain than the United States, and this reduces the heavy capital requirement for agencies in media planning and buying. Additionally, the evidence suggests that large clients are more willing to take risks in committing their business to small British agencies than their counterparts in the United States. Thus, more young creative hot-shots have developed in Britain compared with the United States.

At a deeper level, Carey (1975) has argued that European and North American communication is grounded in two different metaphors. He hypothesized that American communication is largely a transportation view: transmitting messages at a distance for the purpose of control, of which advertising is a part. The use of 'transportation' terminology is a kind of metaphor for the history of the development of North America where transport was the key to the continent's expansion and power. By contrast, he termed European communication as 'myth and ritual': communication of a shared culture which is created, modified and transformed. This is a richer process, more closely linked to European traditions of structuralism and semiotics. Lannon and Cooper (1983) have also argued that culture defines the difference between British and United States advertising. They commented that 'the understated humour, the highly visual (in contrast to verbal) content and the apparent absence of advertising "sell" are all linked very closely with features of specifically English life, and thus readily understandable to English consumers. In turn they are drawn from the written and oral traditions of England, updated by our media' (Lannon and Cooper 1983: 200). Empirical evidence comparing the work practices and creative output of British and United States agencies offers less support for the concept of the British creative mystique than the general discussions of the topic amongst practitioners and in the trade press. West has shown that agency personalities, processes and philosophies are extremely similar on both sides of the Atlantic (1993a) and likewise with work practices (1993b). Top British agencies offered similar services and equal skills and expertise in working with clients as did top United States agencies. Knowledge could not be monopolized by any agency. Staff moved between agencies frequently and in significant numbers, and any new creative approaches or developments in one country or agency could be readily seen and adopted by another.

Research by Weinberger and Spotts (1989a), which compared British and United States advertising creativity in the use of humour, has also provided some interesting results. They examined whether or not British and United States advertising executives differed in their views about the use of humour in advertising and the frequency and situation of the use of humour. (The research was limited in that it relied on mean scores of executive opinions – often there were significant differences in the scores, but the rankings of the issues by both groups were identical. This implies that the scales may have been viewed differently by both groups, rather than the importance of the issues concerned.) Overall they found both British and United States advertisers favoured the use of humour in advertising, but that the British groups were more positive about the range of objectives that humour could achieve as well as the breadth of media in which humour could be effectively used. Their analysis showed that the perception that United States advertising is dominated by a hard-sell orientation, while British advertising is soft sell, was not fully supported. Whilst a higher proportion of British commercials were humorous, the majority of ads from both countries did not use humour. However, their wider study of the information content of British and United States ads (Weinberger and Spotts 1989b) concluded that British ads had significantly lower information content than similar United States ones.

However, it is unlikely that most United States clients would agree that American advertising standards have declined or that they view hard-sell approaches as bad. It is doubtful that in a sample of an evening's TV commercials and a day's press advertisements anyone would see a huge difference between the United States and Britain. Furthermore, it is far from clear that the British style of 'creativity' in advertising would work in the United States. In addition, the British made inroads into the American market by acquisition of domestic agencies and staff. Equally, United States MNAs in London have demonstrated exemplary creative flair in British advertising using local staff for clients aiming at the local market. Nevertheless, the issue cannot be easily dismissed. The perception of superior British creative flair in the 1980s gave an added cachet to British multinational ambitions, particularly Saatchi & Saatchi, and probably helped British agencies to maintain more clients and attract more new business than might otherwise have been the case.

Internalization advantages

Refiners of the monopoly advantage theory have focused on the early work of Coase (1937) on internalization. Coase set the ground rules. His argument was that, given transaction costs, firms will exist and 'tend to expand until the cost of organizing an extra transaction within the firm becomes equal to the cost of carrying out the same transaction by means of an exchange in the open market' (Coase 1937: 395) Internalization theory is concerned with transaction costs and is firm-specific. There is general agreement in the literature that a firm-specific monopoly advantage is not a prerequisite for FDI. In the FDI literature it is argued that an important aspect of going MNE are savings in the costs of coordinating markets: transaction costs. Arrow (1975) argued that internalization of production often leads to higher profits and maximizes efficiency because it gives sellers full information about the buyer's demand and minimizes resale. Johnson (1970) argued that knowledge was central to internalization. Knowledge has high co-ordination costs and is imperfect. Buckley and Casson (1976) added the idea that FDI arose when firms internalized market imperfections in intermediate products like entrepreneurship and technical skills. Williamson (1979) added a market hierarchy approach stressing that MNEs can reduce their risks in world trade because it is easier for them to police contractual agreements by being located around the world. The concept of internationalization advantages is a useful one for considering British MNA success in the 1980s.

Up until the 1980s, an important spin-off from the failure of British agencies to enter the American market was that the United States' MNAs were better able to defend their domestic market. Much of the potential for the British entrance into the United States market was stifled by the American MNA toehold in Britain. The ownership advantage of the

United States agencies expanding with their clients indirectly spawned an internalization advantage.

The internalization advantage was directly recognized by United States agencies and acted upon. A major impetus here was the long-established agency/client conflict rule of 'exclusivity'. Agencies are unable to service the business of directly competitive accounts (for example, chocolate manufacturers) or sometimes indirectly competitive (for example, Rowntrees would not use an agency advertising petfood because Mars make petfood). Internalization abroad offers top agencies market growth when unable to gain new business that conflicts with their current portfolio. Coca-Cola and General Foods were two well-known advertisers using exclusivity clauses. The result was that some agencies were blocked in expanding their business by one advertiser. Exclusivity could, of course, be operated internationally where an office in one part of an organization might be blocked from taking any advertising in a category because another office in the same organization had a particularly important account. For example, J. Walter Thompson's London office was unable to handle a car account during the 1950s and 1960s (West, 1987). Ford had placed its business with most of Thompson's international offices during the time, but London failed to win any of it until the late 1960s (apparently because of its close ties to General Motors in the interwar years). However, this was not so common and the international route did normally offer a way out of domestic exclusivity.

One option for 'stay-at-home' agencies was to form a group. Marion Harper's Interpublic of the 1960s was the first major United States agency group consisting of McCann-Erickson and Erwin Wasey, and Brunnings and Saatchi & Saatchi were the first major British groups in the 1960s and 1970s. Each agency within the network had a separate identity, enabling the group to handle conflicting accounts that would never have stayed together in one agency. Internalization for market growth was a key incentive. Anderson (1984: 90) observed 'an almost frantic rush by major American agencies to get a foothold in markets around the globe'. Terpstra and Yu also found that United States MNAs reacted 'oligopolistically in investing abroad' (1988: 42). The successful British MNAs of the 1980s acted like the latecomers they were, and purchased their international networks with a mixture of offensive and defensive motives. Offensively they were entering new markets and expanding their client base. Defensively, they were holding on to domestic business that might have sought an international network with the globalization of markets and mergers of the 1980s. Additionally, internalization enabled British MNAs to control the entire income from international advertising. Arrow (1975) argued that internalization often leads to higher profits and maximizes efficiency because it gives sellers full information about buyers' demands and minimizes resale. British MNAs did not have to share their profits with associate agencies abroad.

Finally, the synergistic benefits of internalization for agencies need to be briefly mentioned. According to one observer: the MNA 'found that the whole is stronger than the sum of its parts. The interaction of different types of talent in different countries started to contribute everywhere. The cross fertilization of ideas, the exchange of people, the exposure to new situations all helped to build a stronger whole' (Anderson 1984: 93). British agencies did not start out internalizing to benefit from synergy, but it was an important advantage compared to locals who were confined to the home market. For example, WPP's acquisition of J. Walter Thompson and Ogilvy & Mather has enabled the group to form media partnerships and foster cross-referrals of clients among nonadvertising businesses, such as research, design and graphics (*Advertising Age*, 22 May 1989: 1, 72). The following section examines the problems of the growth of direct marketing, growing retail power and the changing attitudes of clients and consumers.

LATER STRUCTURAL PROBLEMS FACING BRITISH MNAS

Direct marketing

WPP is well placed in the direct marketing business, as evidenced by the success of Ogilvy & Mather Direct, which is the top United States agency in the direct marketing business. Nevertheless, direct marketing's growth is undoubtedly adversely affecting all full-service advertising agencies in the United States and Britain. Despite the fact that about 40% of direct mail is left unopened, it is still sufficiently cost-effective enough to divert millions of dollars away from the major media (*Time*, 26 November 1990: 62–70). Traditionally, direct mail has been viewed as 'junk mail' – a downmarket activity for catalogue companies, charities and business-to-business marketers with little or no focus. This is no longer the case owing to database marketing, which has enabled selective targeting and consumers receiving more relevant information and offers. Databases are currently being generated at a pace. It has been reliably estimated that about half of United States consumer marketers are currently compiling them. In Britain the Royal Mail estimates that direct mail expenditures doubled to around £1 billion between 1987 and 1990 (*Campaign*, 11 June 1993: 6). In the United States, direct marketing billings reached $4.1 billion in 1991 which represented a growth rate of over 13 per cent, outstripping gains of both general advertising and sales promotions (*Advertising Age*, June 8 1992: 29–30). Databases are being used extensively by consumer goods and service marketers. Among high-spending advertisers, direct mail is increasingly seen as a vital part of the marketing mix. In Britain the top 3,000 advertisers (6 per cent of all companies) account for nearly two-fifths of direct mail spending, according to a survey by the Direct Mail Information Service. Virtually every time a customer pays by cheque or credit card, enters a sweepstake, asks for a rebate or orders anything by

mail or telephone (especially with toll-free numbers), he/she will probably enter a database.

Many leading marketing companies have used database marketing with
considerable success, for example Burger King, MCI, British Airways,
Mazda and Gillette. Car companies regularly use lists resulting from callers
responding to TV commercials and print advertisements (*Advertising Age*,
22 June 1992: 3). They are then mailed brochures and personalized videos.
Prospects spend 15 minutes or longer examining the brand rather than 30
seconds of TV imagery. Local car dealers are supplied with the names and
phone numbers of people who call in. This helps dealer–company relationships. Furthermore, it is well known that it costs far more to find new customers than to continue selling to loyal ones. Thus, database marketing may
seem more expensive than mass media advertising on a cost per person basis,
but in the long run it may be cheaper if it achieves core-customer loyalty.
Given that few markets are expanding, this may be of paramount importance. Highly specific database marketing has become a major marketing
success in the computer-oriented 1990s which has severely dented the role
of advertising agencies and curtailed numerous advertising budgets.

Retail power

Retail power in consumer markets has been growing since the 1960s with
increasing concentration of business and own-label brands (Jones 1985).
UPC scanners have accelerated this shift in power away from consumer
marketers. Instantaneous scanner data has enabled retailers to calculate
quickly Direct Product Profitability (DPP). DPP compares brands and
pack sizes within their category and assesses how they impact shelf space,
handling and inventory. Consumer marketers often sell against retailers
who know more about brand profitability than they do.

To get shelf space, consumer marketers must divert funds from media
to the trade promotions in the form of 'slotting allowances' – paying to
have a brand placed on the shelves. Additionally, they are placing an
increasing emphasis on consumer coupons to get the trade to 'stock up'
on a brand and trade promotions that offer bulk-buy discounts to retailers
that can be extremely lucrative. Furthermore, the data revolution has
enabled, and perhaps diverted, mass marketers to worry about sales at
particular stores rather than national share. Retail advertising has not been
large enough to fill the gap in brand advertising as companies have
diverted advertising funds to trade promotions. Again, one of the primary
losers in this process has been advertising agencies.

Clients

It has become a widespread phenomenon in the 1990s that many clients
have decided to examine the 'effectiveness' of different creative

approaches. This has partly been driven by the fact that many leveraged companies need to justify advertising expenditures to shareholders and lenders. However, it is also because the growth of direct marketing has offered the opportunity for advertisers to track advertising responses by toll-free numbers. Database marketing has enabled advertisers to get some sense of the impact of the activities in a more precise way. On the other hand, traditional mass-marketing objectives, such as building an 'image', are hard to measure and of debatable value even if achieved. Measurement techniques for 'images' are complex and costly to undertake. Databases also allow marketers to test promotions that reward loyal customers and entice users of competitive brands.

Another issue is the fact that many clients are in positions of market maturity. The North American and British markets have a large number of brands that have been around for between 20 and 70 years. The level of brand equity built up is so high that it has enabled many of these brands to reduce their media expenditures with hardly a flicker in brand awareness or image. In a recent study of 45 top major packaged-goods manufacturers, companies focusing on promotions fared no worse in their brand awareness/image indexes than companies maintaining media advertising (Johnson 1992).

This trend has accelerated in the late 1980s and early 1990s as agencies have struggled to find a clear role for themselves in the market place (*The Economist* 1990). Too many clients, especially in the United States, regard advertising as a necessary evil and are doubting the value of all advertising agencies in their marketing mix. Given that creativity often seems to flourish best in small agencies, clients are also increasingly questioning whether creativity is worth more than the convenience of dealing with large agencies. This was spectacularly demonstrated when in 1992 Coca-Cola shifted much of its advertising out of its long-standing agency, McCann-Erickson, to the Creative Artists Agency, a Hollywood production company.

Turning to international advertising, clients are questioning whether the gains from the economies of scale from global marketing outweigh the potential lost revenue from failing to discriminate between international customers. According to the *The Economist* (1990) international clients are faced with three options:

1 use one multinational agency or several local ones;
2 use one advertising campaign or adapt it;
3 buy all advertising services (creative, media, PR, direct marketing and sales promotions) from one group or several local ones.

To these three may be added another popular option adopted by clients, which is to cut down the number of 'club' agencies. They often finish with two, three or four big MNAs more or less worldwide, plus quite a large number of small local agencies in various countries (often for historical or almost personal reasons).

In general, the more positive clients are about the centralized options, the better for global agencies. Over the past 20 years the trend is definitely towards global alignment, although Levitt's (1983) proposition, that all markets will globalize, has failed to materialize. Even Saatchi & Saatchi, the agency that pioneered global advertising's virtues, has recently, and wisely, begun to 'soft-pedal' global campaigns as its sole *raison d'être* and has fostered a more realistic view, instead, that the global campaign is an 'extra'. After all, the number of truly global brands, that is brands which mean the same to everyone internationally, are few and far between, and are probably best epitomized by Coca-Cola and Gillette. Even United States markets lack homogeneity, as evidenced by the advertising of such products as pick-up trucks, advertised functionally to Southern farmers and symbolically to East Coast yuppies (*The Economist* 1990). However, global agencies have benefited from client reorganization, which has seen a change in focus from countries to products. This has been especially so in the Pan-European market place, where companies such as Mars have been busy renaming and restructuring their products across Europe. Overall, advertising agencies are no longer central and at the front of branding, and many of their traditional roles are being questioned by clients. The end result has been declining budgets and account losses for many agencies, aside from the impact of the recession.

Consumers

The overwhelming evidence suggests that there will be no consumer spending spree in the foreseeable future (*Business Week* 1990: 204; *Campaign* 7 May 1993: 24–5). Debt, negative equity (particularly in Britain) and the threat of unemployment are the key issues which have moved consumers a long way from the 'charge it' slogan of the 1980s. Average American and British real disposable incomes rose by only a few per cent in the 1980s, but the credit boom fuelled consumer spending, and personal debt mushroomed (as did corporate debt). Consumers enjoyed the decade, with better standards of living in all areas and greater travel experiences, but there will be no going back to the same spending patterns.

The 1990s have proved to be a watershed era compared to the 1980s, replacing consumer concerns for 'prestige' with 'value' and 'prudence' (*Time* 8 April 1991: 58–63). In a way, changes in consumer attitudes are mirroring those of advertisers. While the recession is an important factor, consumers are questioning the role of brands in much the same way as clients are questioning the role of agencies. For 1990s consumers, 'upscale' is out and 'downscale' is in and flaunting money is frowned upon. In place of materialism people are spending more time with family and friends, rest, recreation and 'good deeds' (ibid.). For the first time in many years it has become socially acceptable to be frugal. Peer group heroes commonly boast about bargains and cheap purchases. Many up-scale consumers regularly shop at discount stores: not sacrificing brands, but instead changing the outlets where they traditionally shop. People have been awakened to many personal issues such as the plight of a homeless neighbour or the loss of a job. Middle-aged 'baby boomers' now have older families and more financial responsibilities. Consumers are reconciled to the position that their income growth will be slower in the 1990s and that jobs will be less secure and career changes probably more frequent. Instead of spending, consumers are concentrating more on managing spending. The 1990s consumer believes that most brands are at parity and that value is the main quest. Furthermore, they no longer believe that advertised brand names denote who they are, despite the continued prominence of brand names in the market place. Ironically, marketers have fed this belief with price discounts and coupons which have led to a constant expectation of a 'sale.' Few people now buy brands without checking prices at rival retailers. Consumers now have a 'gritty' realism that the advertising dreams of the 1980s can no longer be fulfilled. Rather than prestige and image, advertisers have turned to durability, classic design, warranties and good workmanship: rarely the basis for highly creative advertising of the kind most favoured by agencies.

Creativity

Turning to creativity, the perception that London leads the world in creativity has significantly changed in the late 1980s and early 1990s. Again, as with the apparent superiority of British advertising in the 1980s, it is a topic to be viewed with some scepticism. Nevertheless, many observers have argued that much of British advertising has fallen into a malaise with tired repeated commercials, cynical appeals and play-safe print ads. British public approval of the advertising industry has recently shown signs of wavering (*Campaign* 26 March 1993: 13). Furthermore, due to the growing importance of continental Europe, it appears that London will no longer be the European centre of advertising (*Advertising Age* 22 April 1991: 1, 20). After the tumble that British MNAs took in the stock market crash of October 1987, entire agencies vanished from London. By contrast, Paris is doing extremely well and, although not seen as having reached London's level of creativity, it has a more dynamic reputation for media buying and in-store promotions. This has given the French MNAs an edge with the 1990s client who is often more concerned with these issues than with creative strategy. Furthermore, with reunification, Germany is expected to overtake Britain as Europe's largest advertising market. However, more time may be required before sound judgements can be made on this issue owing to the fact that the British recession predated those of France and Germany by over a year.

CONCLUSION

The pace of growth of United States MNAs slowed in the 1970s and local agencies began to reassert their position. The locals took full advantage of favourable FDI flows in the 1980s and the welcome reception of the City of London to flotations and rights issues in the wake of Saatchi & Saatchi's demonstration that British agencies could perform against the best international competition. British MNAs' ease in raising capital facilitated their spectacular entrance into the American domestic market from the early 1980s. They enjoyed an exemplary creative reputation, especially Saatchi & Saatchi. The motives of the British were transactional in terms of defending their home market and expanding abroad. A new entrepreneurial culture arose seeking major United States expansion, compared to previous acceptance of the inevitability of American dominance. This was essentially an *ownership* advantage throughout, rather than a managerial one. The size of the United States advertising market means that management inevitably stabilizes in New York for most MNAs. It may get increasingly harder to locate the management of an MNA centrally as MNE clients are increasingly headquartered outside of the United States, but it has not quite happened yet.

A period of consolidation is likely for the next few years as British MNAs pay down their debts, restructure and cope with the declining advertising market and the structural changes occurring. Their expansionary phase has been replaced by a period of retrenchment, aggravated by a series of factors beyond their control, such as a more sober assessment of their potential by the London Stock Market since October 1987. In addition, they have faced a new wave of competition from French MNAs. Structurally, British MNAs, along with most other agencies, have been adversely affected by a double threat: the increasing role of direct marketing, which has cut into already dwindling advertising budgets, and growing retail power. Clients want measured results, and are actively seeking to replace the long-standing commission system with fees, often based on sales effectiveness. Multinational advertisers are questioning the benefits of larger agencies over smaller creative shops which can produce advertising for adaption and/or translation abroad. Consumers still seek brand values, but have become cynical of brand image and the reality of brand differences. Finally, the British 'creative mystique', always more a perception than a reality, is now looking a little tarnished, according to many influential observers.

Getting a 'true' perspective on the impact of the recession and these structural changes is a difficult task, however. Most observers view their own times as apocryphal, though historically they rarely are. At the end of every recession there is an element of 'never again will the boom-style spending come again', but often it does. To prove the subjective nature of the issue, it should be noted that at the time of writing there is a huge boom underway in most of the Asia-Pacific region and in some parts of Latin America. Nevertheless, the structural changes underway do present many challenges for agencies, and agencies will inevitably react to the changes and get involved in a wider range of communications methods rather than just advertisements.

For the future, the proportion spent on major media advertising from all advertising and promotional expenditures will probably continue to decline over the 1990s and retail power will increase further. For many companies, advertising's role will shift to providing database leads where the 'real' selling will begin, rather than brand awareness or image. However, by the turn of the century, above-the-line advertising may enter a resurgence as brand equity will inevitably have been reduced by then and the potential for direct marketing solely to rebuild brand equity will be minimal. The irony is that many clients 'want the impossible' from their agencies. They want the security of brand equity (an intangible attribute) and on the other hand they want tangible advertising effectiveness. In response to this, British MNAs will continue to diversify their interests in sales promotions and direct marketing while building on the core function of creativity. There is little that they or any other agency can do to affect consumer or client attitudes on spending and advertising budgets respectively, and these will be the key elements which affect their future prosperity.

REFERENCES

Advertising Age, various issues.
Anderson, M.H. (1984) *Madison Avenue in Asia: Politics and Transnational Advertising*, Rutherford, N.J.: Fairleigh Dickinson University Press.
Arrow, K.J. (1975) 'Vertical integration and communication', *Bell Journal of Economics*, 5: 173–83.
Buckley P.J. and Casson, M.C. (1976) *The Future of the Multinational Enterprise*, London: Macmillan.
Business Week, 10 December 1990.
Campaign, various issues.
Carey, J.W. (1945) 'Communication and Culture', *Communications Research*, 2: 173–91.
Casson, M.C. (1982) 'Transaction costs and the theory of the multinational enterprise', *New Theories of the Multinational Enterprise*, ed. A.M. Rugman, New York: St Martin's Press.
Caves, R.E. (1971) 'International corporations: the industrial economics of foreign investment', *Economica*, 38: 1–27.
Caves, R.E. (1982a) *Multinational Enterprise and Economic Analysis*, Cambridge: Cambridge University Press.
Coase, R.H. (1937) 'The nature of the firm', *Economica*, 4: 386–405.
The Economist, 'The party's over', 9 June 1990.
The Financial Times, various issues.
Hymer, S. (1975), The International Operations of National Firms, Cambridge: Mass.
Johnson, H.G. (1970) 'The efficiency and welfare implications of the international

corporation', in *The International Corporation*, ed. C.P. Kindleberger, Mambridge, Mass.: MIT Press, ch. 2.

Johnson, T. (1992) 'Seventeen years of brand loyalty trends: what do they tell us', *Proceedings PMAA Conference*, 3 March, Chicago, cited by Shergil (1993).

Jones, J.P. (1985) 'Is total advertising going up or down', *International Journal of Advertising*, 4: 47–64.

Kindleberger, C. P. (1969) *American Business Abroad: Six Essays on Direct Investment*, New Haven, Conn.: Yale University Press.

Kleinman, P. (1987) *Saatchi & Saatchi: The Inside Story*, Lincolnwood, Ill.: NTC Business Books.

Lannon, J. and Cooper, P. (1983) 'Humanistic advertising: a holistic cultural perspective', *International Journal of Advertising*, 2: 195–213.

Levitt, T. (1983) 'The globalization of markets', *Business History Review*, May–June, 92-102.

O'Connor, J. and Crichton, J. (1967) *Fifty Years of Advertising – What Next?*, London: IPA.

Phillips W. (ed.) (1986) *The Advertising Agency Review*, London; cited by W. Phillips; 'The agency business: on top in the eighties', *Admap*, September, 1986, 34–5.

Shergil, S. (1993) 'The changing US media and marketing environment: implications for media advertising expenditures in the 1990s', *International Journal of Advertising*, 12: 95–115.

Terpstra, V. and Yu, C.-M. (1988) 'Determinants of foreign investment of U.S. advertising agencies', *Journal of International Business Studies*, 19: 33–46.

Time, various issues.

United Nations Centre on Transnational Corporations (1988) *Trends and Issues in Foreign Direct Investment and Related Flows*, New York: United Nations.

Weinberger, M.G. and Spotts, H.E. (1989a) 'Humor in U.S. versus U.K. TV commercials: a comparison', *Journal of Advertising*, 18: 39–44.

Weinberger, M.G. and Spotts, H.E. (1989b) 'A situational view of information content in TV advertising in the U.S. and the U.K.', *Journal of Marketing*, 53: 89–94.

West, D.C. (1987d) 'From T-square to T-plan: the London Office of the J. Walter Thompson Advertising Agency, 1919–70', *Business History*, 2, 199–217.

West, D.C. (1988) 'Multinational competition in the British advertising agency business, 1936–87', *Business History Review*, 62, 467–501.

West, D.C. (1993a) 'Cross-national creative personalities, processes and agency philosophies', *Journal of Advertising Research*, 33: 200–13.

West, D.C. (1993b) 'Restricted creativity: advertising agency work practices in the US, Canada and the UK', *Journal of Creative Behavior*, 27: 200–13.

Wilkins, I.M. (1974) *The Maturing of the Multinational Enterprise: American Business Abroad from 1914 to 1970*, Cambridge, Mass.: Harvard University Press.

Williamson, O.E. (1979) 'Transaction cost economics, the governance of contractual relations', *Journal of Law and Economics*, 22: 233–61.

13 Media burst in a Euroasian country
A blessing or a burden?

Nükhet Vardar

Turkey, with a population of 56.5 million people in 1990 and a land of 779,452 sq. km, lies across two continents, bridging Europe and Asia (see Figure 13.1). Turkey's geographic location, culture, people, history, political climate, socio-economic and economic conditions all carry traces of both European and Asian elements, but these European and Asian elements' weights change according to circumstances. Therefore Turkey sometimes looks more Western and at other times more Eastern. Its rich past and promising future are the two key elements which make Turkey such an exciting and a lively country to live in. Before concentrating on the media scene, let us first examine Turkey as a country, putting figures to facts.

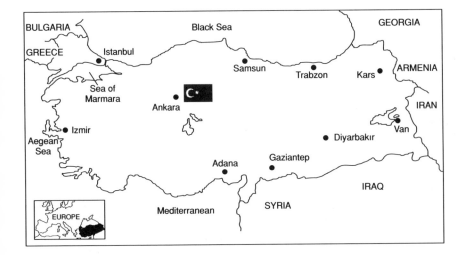

Figure 13.1 Map of Turkey

AN OVERVIEW OF TURKEY

The land

The mainland, Anatolia or Asia Minor, lies in Asia, accounting for 97 per cent of the total area, adding up to 755,688 sq. km. The European side, called Thrace, covers 23,764 sq. km (1993: 15). The whole country is roughly three times the size of the UK.

Turkey is a huge peninsula surrounded by the Black Sea on the north, the Aegean Sea and the Sea of Marmara to the west and the Mediterranean to the south. Turkey has a special importance in international shipping trade due to two crucial straits: one is the Bosphorous, linking the Black Sea to the Sea of Marmara; the other is the Dardanelles, connecting the Sea of Marmara to the Aegean. Turkey's neighbours in Europe are Bulgaria and Greece on the north-west corner. In Asia from north-east to the south, in a clockwise direction, are located Georgia, Armenia, Iran, Iraq and Syria. The country is more mountainous in the east, with long and harsh winter days and hot, dry summers. Animal husbandry is the main source of living. However, in the west the climate is milder and the land more fertile.

The population

The general census results reported Turkey's population as 56,473,035 in 1990 (Institute of Statistics 1991: 4). According to the State Institute of Statistics' estimations, the population is expected to reach 59.9 million in 1993. The annual growth rate of the population is 2.2 per cent (ibid.: 4). This high rate of population increase is often cited as a major impediment to Turkey's development.

Urban population is 33.3 million, constituting 59 per cent of the total population, whereas rural population is 23.1, accounting for 41 per cent (ibid.: 7). The rate of increase in the urban population is again alarmingly high, at 43 per cent, whereas the rural population is shrinking. This poses another big problem for the country. As more and more people migrate to large cities for better jobs, better housing, better sanitary conditions, existing problems are carried over to larger cities creating a snowball effect. Large municipalities feel the strain and react by putting extra pressure on their existing means in regard to infrastructure, transportation, housing, sanitary and health conditions, job opportunities, social security and the like.

Not all the figures regarding the Turkish population are that gloomy. According to 1985 figures, the 0–14 age group makes up 37.5 per cent of the total population (ibid.: 13). Therefore, Turkey is definitely a very young country. Although it means more schools, more jobs, more of everything, this fact also sets the pace for the country's development plans.

The language, religion and the flag

The official language is Turkish; 98 per cent of Turks are Muslims; the Turkish flag is on red background with a vertical white crescent and a five-pointed star.

The government

The capital is Ankara, situated right in the heart of the country. There are 76 provinces headed by state-appointed governors and locally elected municipal heads. The administration system is a parliamentary democracy. The Turkish Republic was founded by Mustafa Kemal Atatürk on 29 October 1923. Electors vote for members of the parliament every five years to elect their own local representatives; the members of parliament in turn elect the president as the head of state.

The literacy rate

In 1985, the total population's literacy rate was 77 per cent, split between the sexes at 87 per cent for men and 68 per cent for women (ibid.: 5). This total literacy rate is estimated to have risen to around 85–90 per cent in 1993.

Education

Five years of primary school education is compulsory in Turkey. Secondary and high school training takes a further six years. University education is another four years. Table 13.1 gives cumulative figures regarding primary, secondary, high schools, higher education institutions and universities. These figures indicate that in 1990 the number of schools had increased 12-fold over the previous 66 years. The number of staff and enrolments multiplied by nearly 31 times during this period. However, the ratio of students to staff did not change much: it was 30 in 1924 and it went down only to 28 in 66 years. Therefore it is possible to say that physical needs could not keep up with the demand of students and the supply of teachers.

Table 13.1 Education statistics, Turkey 1923–4 and 1989–90

Academic year:	1989–90	1923–4
Number of schools	58,742	4,998
Number of staff	366,421	11,854
Number of students	10,283,184	352,001
Ratio of students to staff	28.1	29.7

Source: Institute of Statistics 1991: 76–8, 80, 88

Also, as the increase in the number of staff equalled the boom in the number of students, Turkish schools could not greatly advance the quality of training at all levels of their schooling system.

Tourism

State statistical indicators give the estimated tourist figure for 1990 as 5.4 million (ibid.: 273). Business sources forecast that 7.5 million people would visit Turkey in 1992, bringing in around $4 billion in revenue. Tourism revenue for 1993 is projected to be $6 billion. Over the last few years tourists pouring in from Eastern European countries in particular have contributed to Turkey's tourism boom. In addition Turkey with its less-spoilt coastline, cultural and historical heritage remains a favorite spot in Europe.

General economic indicators

Although Turkey enjoyed a high GNP growth rate in 1990 and 1992, growth stagnated somewhat in 1991, signalling a short-term recession (Table 13.2). The 1993 target is a rate of 5.0 per cent (TOBB 1993: 6). After 1990, GNP per capita surpassed the $2,000 limit and continues to be around $2600 since then.

Table 13.2 Turkey's GNP, 1990–2

	GNP at constant prices (%)	GNP per capita ($)[c]
1990	9.2[a]	2,675.0
1991	0.5[b]	2,570.7
1992	5.9[b]	2,622.3

[a] *Source:* Institute of Statistics 1991: 415
[b] *Source: The Financial Times Survey,* 7 May 1993: 4
[c] *Source:* TOBB 1993: 18

Contributions of each sector to GNP indicate that every year for the last 30 years Turkey has obtained less of its GNP from agricultural products and more from industrial goods. Agricultural products' share was halved, industrial goods' contribution was nearly doubled and services' input was increased by 15 per cent between 1960 and 1990.

Table 13.3 shows each sector's share in Turkey's GNP and each sector's rate of annual growth in 1990.

Although agricultural products have got the least share in the total GNP, it still continues to surpass industry goods and services when it comes to annual rate of growth. Rate of inflation has been a sore problem for years for the Turkish economy. Both in wholesale and consumer prices, 1980

Table 13.3 Sectorial share in Turkey's GNP and annual growth rate, 1990 (%)

	Agriculture	*Industry*	*Services*
Share in GNP in 1990 (at constant prices)	17.7	28.7	53.9
Rate of annual growth in 1990 (at constant prices)	11.5	9.1	8.5

Source: Institute of Statistics 1991: 417, 419

was the worst year, when the inflation rate was well above 100 per cent. With the help of tight monetary policies, it was pulled back to 30+ per cent in 1981. However, once again in 1988, inflation reached 74 per cent. This reoccurring battle with inflation remains to be won. Consumer price index (taking 1987 as the base year) is cited as 60.3 per cent in 1990 (Institute of Statistics 1991: 356), 66.0 per cent in 1991, and 70.1 per cent in 1992 (*FT* Survey 7 May 1993: 4). The latest twelve-month inflation figure announced by the State Statistics Institute at the end of July 1993 is 73 per cent (*Hürriyet* August 5, 1993: 7).

Finally foreign trade figures in Turkey are shown in Table 13.4. In 1990, imports were increased by 41 per cent in value over 1989 figures. This rate of annual growth was 11 per cent for exports. The ratio of exports to imports (in value) remained at around 64 per cent in 1992, up from 58 per cent in 1990.

Table 13.4 Turkish foreign trade, 1990–2

	1990	*1991*	*1992*
Exports ($bn)	13.0	13.6	14.7
Imports ($bn)	22.3	21.0	22.9
Trade deficit ($bn)	(9.3)	(7.4)	(8.2)

Source: TOBB 1993: 75

LOOKING INTO THE FUTURE

Before concentrating on the recent state of the Turkish media, a few new and promising projects lying ahead for Turkey are included in this section. These are the kind of strategic plans and tasks which will bring into the country a long-term vision and a distinct outlook.

The Turkish Industrialists and Businessmen's Association (TUSIAD) published a useful reference book in 1991, covering Turkey's future strategies on the threshold of the twenty-first century. In this source, factors which hinder Turkey's socio-economic development are diagnosed as:

- high inflation rate;
- weaknesses in the education system, coupled with high population growth rate;
- lack of firmly-based publicity;
- insufficient degree of expertise in industry (TUSIAD 1991: 1.88).

TUSIAD suggests that all these factors dictate that Turkey needs to act courageously, even making daring attempts at times.

TUSIAD reviews the Turkish economy from 1920s to date and splits this span of more than seventy years into four periods. The first was the Republic's proclamation days when there was virtually no industrial activity; the second period was the 1950s during which industrialisation was underlined. The third was the liberalisation era in the 1980s, and the fourth period is the 1990s, carrying us over to the twenty-first century. This general overview is summarised in Figure 13.2. Similarly, Figure 13.3 clearly outlines the stages that the Turkish economy has passed through, mainly concentrating on the third and fourth periods. Within the last decade, from the 1980s to the 1990s, Turkey has moved from rehearsing liberalisation scenarios to aiming to gain a competitive edge on an international scale, hence taking a huge step towards globalisation. The

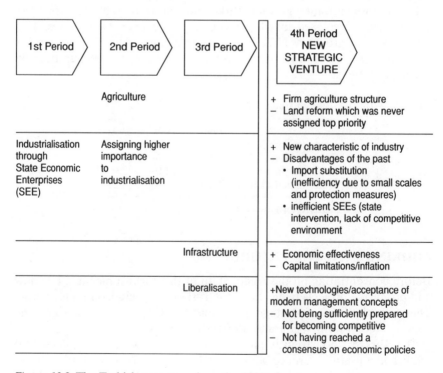

Figure 13.2 The Turkish economy since the 1920s
Source: TUSIAD 1991: 1.64

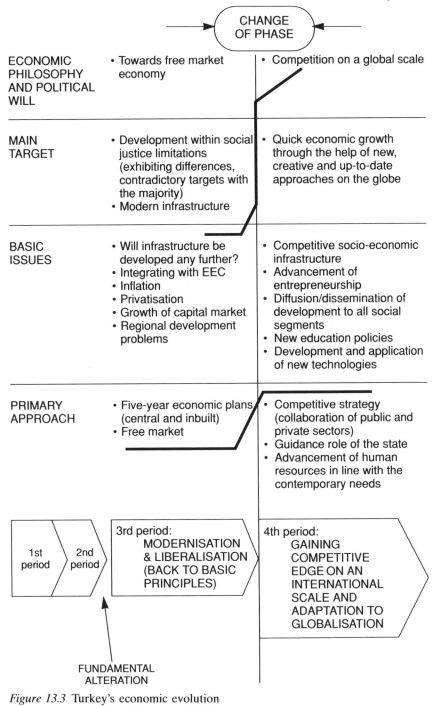

Figure 13.3 Turkey's economic evolution
Source: TUSIAD 1991: 1.29

economic philosophy, main target, basic issues and primary approach inherent in each period is lucidly put forward in Figure 13.3.

Within the frame of reference of these targets, Turkey has become actively engaged in some long-term, large-scale projects which will help the Turkish economy in accomplishing its fourth-period objectives. Here, five such projects are mentioned, all of which were embarked with a long-term investment vision.

Welcoming signals to foreign investors

After 1986, the number of foreign investors and their degree of involvement showed signs of increase. Today some 70 foreign countries have investment links with Turkey (Gözlem Survey May 10, 1993: 2). Opening the doors first to foreign banks, tourism companies and hotel chains was a wise decision, as these initial investors also voluntarily produced good publicity for Turkey, motivating other investors to follow them. Foreign companies consider the skilled and less-expensive labour force, the country's central location, foreign investment incentives, its advanced banking system and the market potential as Turkey's major advantages. End of 1992 figures indicate that there are 2,330 foreign firms in Turkey, with a total investment amounting to $1.820 billion (TOBB 1993: 96). Service companies dominate the area of foreign investors in Turkey, followed by manufacturing companies. In terms of investment, manufacturing companies lead with $1.3 billion, followed by service firms with $493.1 million investment. On a country basis, French companies lead with $353.8 million, followed by $272.9 million from Dutch and $203.5 million from Swiss firms. US companies have $197.6 million-worth of investment in Turkey (TOBB 1993: 98).

The GAP project

The Southeastern Anatolian Project (GAP) was started in the mid-1980s, with the aim of harnessing the Tigris and Euphrates rivers to irrigate 1.7 million hectares of land and build 19 hydroelectric power plants, 22 dams and numerous irrigation schemes (*FT* Survey 7 May 1993: 4; *FT* Survey 24 July 1992: 4). This part of the world is known historically as 'Upper Mesopotamia' and has a reputation as the 'Fertile Crescent'. The area included in the project is half the size of Belgium, with a population of 5.2 million. The project is calculated to provide 3.3 million jobs nationwide, doubling the per capita income of the region. The entire project is planned to be completed by the year 2005, at a total cost of $32 billion. In July 1992, Atatürk Dam was opened, costing $2.3 billion. This dam is the most important element of the project and is the world's ninth largest dam.

Other projects with a vision:

Turkey is busy trying to complete its infrastructure as quickly as possible. After two bridges across the Bosphorous, the first underground metro is being built in Istanbul at present. Similarly, a 430 km, $4 billion high-speed train project, connecting Ankara and Istanbul's Asian side is underway. This will be complemented with another $4 billion Istanbul Bosphorous rail tunnel, crossing to the European side (*FT* Survey 7 May 1993: 4).

Turksat 1B was finally launched on 11 August 1994, after an eight-month delay from its original timescale. It has 16 transmitters with a capacity for 22 broadcasting channels. It is the first satellite to reach 25 countries in Europe and Asia. There are plans to launch another – Turksat 1C – in July 1996. Turksat will give a service to 60 million people of Turkey, relaying data, telephone calls and television programmes to the two million Turkish guest-workers in Europe and 57 million people in Azerbaijan and Central Asia (*Independent* 1 June 1993: 26).

Istanbul's Olympic bid

Another long-term, large-scale project that Turkey happily let itself in for was bidding for the year 2000 Olympics. Istanbul was among the final contenders but Sydney was announced to be the winning city on 23 September 1993. Being in a central location, minimising time differences with most countries, its mild climate, authentic setting all seemed to be in favour of this historic city. Its advertising campaign was carried out by Young & Rubicam/Reklamevi. Input on design work was supplied by Stang & Newdow and Copeland Hirthler with Y&R coordination (*The Financial Times*, Survey 24 June 1993: 3). Istanbul, generating 40 per cent of the country's taxable wealth and GNP was given fair odds in this competition (*The Economist*, 24 October 1992: 52). However, Turkey is determined not to give up this challenging project until it wins, and Istanbul is getting ready to apply for the Olympics in 2004.

Central Asian Turkic states

'The star of Turkey is rising' (*Independent* 1 June 1993: 26) this sums up the extent of new horizons for Turkey in its relations with Central Asian Turkic states. These Turkic states have emerged from the break-up of the former Soviet Union. Azerbaijan, Kazakhstan, Uzbekistan, Turkmenistan and Kyrgyzystan already have established links with Turkey. These relations cover a wide range. More than 8,400 Turkic students are in Turkish schools on an exchange programme. Turkey has donated 2,500-line telephone exchanges to each of the republics. In addition, $875 million Turkish Eximbank export credit guarantees are authorised to the republics

(*Independent* 1 June 1993: 26). Already 200 Turkish companies or foreign companies' Turkish operations are in these Turkic states. Multinational companies (MNCs) in particular consider their Turkish partners as a potential liason between their MNCs and the new Turkic states. Although ethnic roots and the language are not exactly the same, the Turkic states have far more similarities, due to the Muslim religion, historic ties, cultural links, customs and traditions, with Turkey than with any other Western country.

All these states are rich in natural resources, such as oil, natural gas and minerals. In addition cotton is produced. Their problems are mostly to do with lack of infrastructure, poor sanitary conditions, economic and political instability. Therefore Turkey needs to evaluate all these pluses and minuses and choose for itself a role in this part of the world. All these expansion projects for Turkey have one thing in common: they all cry out that Turkey has big ideals and big dreams. Furthermore, it has the motivation and drive to realise these plans. These signs proclaim that Turkey is determined to elevate itself to an upper level. It is getting ready to compete in international arenas. It is at times like this that Turkey's western side becomes more pronounced and more vivid.

Now we will take a closer look at what is happening in the Turkish media scene. The Turkish media demonstrates yet another quite remarkable side of the country.

TTHE MEDIA SCENE IN TURKEY

Important milestones for the Turkish media were 1968 and 1984 and 1990. In 1968 state TV started its broadcasts and in 1984 switched to coloured transmissions. Meanwhile, between 1968 and 1990 six channels were introduced, all belonging to the State Radio and Television (TRT, 1990). Of these six channels, five are nationwide. GAP is the South East Anatolia's regional channel, taking its name from the GAP project. Five of these channels accept advertising; only the Open University channel does not. TRT 5 or TRT- INT broadcasts to Europe and Central Asia, reaching 200 million people. Until 1990 no private channel was on air because private radio and TV operations were banned by the Constitution (article no. 133).

The rise of Star

In May 1990, although private television companies were still outlawed, Star TV, through a company called Magic Box based in Germany, started transmissions with the help of satellites. At the beginning, reception was poor and the technical reach of the channel was very low nationwide. Then municipalities become involved, and some municipal heads helped to instal dish antennae at appropriate high locations in their municipalities so that their and possibly neighbouring municipalities' households could get clear signals. Just as Star's limited advertising revenues began to show serious signs of trouble, thanks to municipalities' collaboration Star's technical reach increased to an acceptable level. Then big advertisers started to sign annual contracts with Star.

Star versus the TRT

As the first private channel, Star was lenient in its general attitude. At that time TRT only accepted payments five days in advance, Star only three days prior to broadcasting. Every commercial had to be viewed by a Censor Board at the TRT and was aired if it passed. The Board could and did ask for alterations prior to airing. Eroticism was often objected to. Advertising of alcoholic drinks, tobacco and over-the-counter medicines was totally banned. On the other hand, Star was more tolerant to eroticism and even exploited it to a certain extent, knowing that viewers have been deprived of it by the state TV. Alcoholic drinks were also advertised. Similary, whilst TRT only accepted 15-, 20-, 30-, 45- and 60-second commercials, Star had no limitations on the duration of the commercials to be aired.

Another major difference between TRT and Star was their approach to negotiations. Like other countries, prices were fixed at the state TV, whilst private ones were open to negotiations. Fixed versus negotiable rates in each European country in 1992 by medium is summarised by Stern (1993: 77). Star channel's end of year advertising revenue made up 2 per cent of the total TV revenues collected in Turkey in 1990 (Table 13.5). In 1990, TV's share in total advertising expenditure was 48 per cent, against 43 per cent of newspapers and 8 per cent magazine advertising. The Turkish media scene in 1990 was totally different from 1991. However, even in 1990, there were clear signs that the media would never be a dull topic in Turkey again.

Increase in alternatives and a yearn for research

As channels increased in number, advertisers and advertising agencies becme more confused by the day. Formerly all media buying decisions were made on a routine basis. All of sudden it started to consist of a twofold phase: first planning and then buying. In 1989, seeing the early signs of a need, AGB formed a local partnership and started its Establishment Survey in Istanbul as AGB-Anadolu AS. At the beginning of 1990, AGB peoplemeter data were available, collected from 110 households (nearly 550 people) living in Istanbul. Naturally these costly data were received with scepticism by both advertisers and agencies. It was a new method and people had every right to react to it. This new tool was proving to them that their 'tried and tested ways' had been wrong all

Table 13.5 Advertising expenditure in Turkey, 1990–3 (bn Turkish lira)

	1990 Expenditure	1990 % share	1991 Expenditure	1991 % share	Annual increase (%)	1992 Expenditure	1992 % share	Annual increase	Jan-June 1993 Expenditure	Jan-June 1993 % share
Total TV	568.3	47.9	1,266.8	49.4	2.3x	4,430.7	55.7	3.5x	4,764.0	55.6
TRT1(Jan 1968)	516.6		641.3		24.1%	471.4		(26.5)%	138.2	
TRT2(Oct. 1986)	35.3		52.9		49.9%	72.8		37.6%	60.2	
TRT3(Oct. 1989)	4.2		2.7		(35.7%)	16.6		6.2x	2.4	
TRT4(July 1990)	—		0.4		—	0.8		2x	—	
TRT5(Feb. 1990)	—		4.4		—	6.9		56.8%	20.3	
GAP(Oct. 1989)	0.6		3.3		5.5x	5.6		69.7%	1.3	
I.Star(May 1990)	11.6		561.8		48.4x	1,611.5		2.9x	1,154.4	
Teleon(Feb. 1992)	—		—		—	541.7		—	161.4	
Show TV(March 1992)	—		—		—	1,490.1		—	1,816.2	
Kanal6(Oct. 1992)	—		—		—	187.3		—	1,292.5	
HBB(Dec. 1992)	—		—		—	26.8		—	117.1	
Newspapers	512.6	43.2	1,073.4	41.8	2.1x	2,789.8	35.1	2.6x	2,941.7	34.4
Magazines	96.6	8.1	216.2	8.4	2.2x	683.3	8.6	3.2x	833.2	9.7
Radio	8.7	0.7	9.0	0.4	—	23.2	0.3	2.6x	4.8	0.1
Cinema	nm	—	nm	—	—	21.7	0.3	—	19.6	0.2
GRAND TOTAL	1,186.2	100.0	2,565.4	100.0	2.2x	7,948.7	100.0	3.1x	8,563.3	100.0

Notes
nm = not measurable
Dates in parentheses indicate the launch date of private channels (TRT, 1990)
Source: Deniz Reklam Etüdleri Monthly Advertising Expenditures, 1990–2; Bileşim Monthly Advertising Expenditures 1991, 1993.

along and no one could keep silent about that. Thanks to international advertisers and agencies, AGB data's denial period did not last long. AGB-Anadolu increased its panel first to 170 households, then to 220 and again to 440, aggregating two findings from other cities (Ankara and Izmir) into their data by August 1993. At the end of 1993, AGB plans to have 600 peoplemeters installed in seven cities of Turkey, with a target of reaching 1,000 households by the end of 1994.

From the very first day AGB-Anadolu AS and Star TV got on very well. After all, both symbolized new techniques, new ways in handling accustomed issues.

Star's expansion in 1991 and its reflections

In 1991, Star channel flourished beyond all expectations and changed its name to Interstar. It increased its advertising revenues by 48 times from rate card prices. (High discounts and free spots were given to all allocated budgets. In addition, one of the partners of Star channel also owned a holding company and their banks' and insurance company's advertising was aired repeatedly. All this free give-away advertising air time, which was not actually sold, was reflected in the calculations from declared rate card prices.) Even after making deductions for these free spots, Star's revenue boom in 1991 could not be ignored.

In 1991, TV's total advertising share was increased by 1.5 per cent against 1990, up to 49.4 per cent. Newspapers' share went down by 1.4 per cent, to 41.8 per cent in 1991. On the magazine side, there was a slight upward trend from 8.1 per cent in 1990, to 8.4 per cent in 1991 (Table: 13.7).

1992, or the year for new TV channels

From the early months, 1992 saw an upsurge in the number of new private TV channels launched in Turkey. First Teleon, sister channel of I.Star, came to life in February 1992. Then another channel, Show TV, was launched in March 1992, broadcasting from France through satellite, followed by the introduction of Kanal 6, based in England, in October 1992, and HBB in December 1992. There were other regional and smaller channels which joined in. Again from rate card prices, total TV advertising expenditures increased 3.5 times in 1992 over 1991 figures. Apart from HBB, all these channels have chosen foreign countries as their headquarters in order to find a way around Turkish law banning private TV and radio broadcasting. This boom in private channels in 1992, following a long silence in 1990 and 1991, was mainly due to many entrepreneurs waiting for the uncertainty to end. The entire sector was confident that a new law liberalising state TV and radio would be passed in 1992, at the latest by June 1992 (Price 1992: 42). (The new law finally passed through the Parliament in spring 1994, mainly accepting the articles of the European Broadcasting Directive. In addition, under this Act a Supreme Court was elected by the Parliament; it has announced new sanctions which come into effect from 1 December 1994. These rules and regulations are as yet too new to be able to comment on them.)

Private channels' influence on state TV

Meanwhile, from 1990, through 1991 and especially in 1992, TRT became more and more flexible in every respect. For one thing, TRT has not really increased its prices since February 1992, but only made slight adjustments. However, all the private channels regularly put up their prices by on average 30 per cent, every three to four months from 1992 onwards. Roughly speaking, on a rate card basis the most premium-priced advertising slot on a private TV channel is now three times more expensive than the TRT's highest-priced air time in July 1993. The Censor Board now takes a less restricted view; and most recently TRT answered agencies' long-standing request by announcing that its Istanbul office will start accepting material from now on. (Previously all material and payments had to be sent to Ankara, the capital, where TRT is located. As Istanbul is the centre of agency business, the distance put an extra strain on agencies' already tight schedules.) This last move has a greater symbolic significance than a functional one: in a way, TRT has finally accepted that the hub of the communication world has become Istanbul, where all private channels are based, and is trying to overcome its own shortcomings.

The good side of a bad experience

In April 1992 AGB and Interstar relations became soured. Due to the increased number of available channels, Interstar's viewership ratings started to decrease. I.Star's share dropped to 25 per cent in April 1992 from 49 per cent in December 1991. In mid-April, I.Star announced that 'the other private channel', namely Show TV, had got hold of AGB household addresses. Therefore AGB data were suspended for four weeks, during which time new households were chosen and peoplemeters were installed once again. This distruption in the AGB data caused great confusion among advertisers and agencies. Without AGB data, how could they do their media plans? These were the same people who had serious reservations about the same data only two years back. However, during this time, all parties had become dependent on the data. Once again the power of information and research was proven, and this time we were witnessing the Euro side of Turkey. After this mishap, AGB and I.Star could not mend the bridges once again. I.Star contacted Nielsen as an alternative source. The relationship with AGB gradually deteriorated and was

What's next?!..

I.Star's advertisement

Show TV's advertisement

You have not heard of Levent Kirca*, 'cause you never watch him on I.Star!

L. Kirca's programme does not appear on AGB's mostly watched programmes list.

But we at I.Star are proud to have L. Kirca on our channel.

*Well-known, very popular Turkish comedian

Daha neler!..

LEVENT KIRCA'YI
TANIMIYORSUNUZ . . . .
ÇÜNKÜ HIÇ
İZLEMIYORSUNUZ . . . .

Evet, ülke çapındaki bu sanatçı Show TV güdümlü AGB verilerine göre hiç izlenmiyor.

interstar, YENIDEN OLACAK O KADAR TELEVIZYONU kadrosuyla birlikte olmaktan onur duyar

TELEBAROMETRE

Show TV Sunar . . .

AGB'nin televizyon araştması

6 Mart Cumartesi (%)
(prime-time)

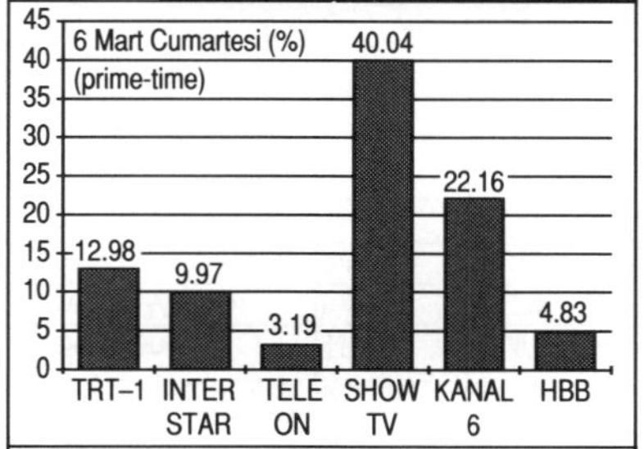

	%
	40.04
	22.16
	4.83
	3.19
	9.97
	-12.98

TRT-1 INTER STAR TELE ON SHOW TV KANAL 6 HBB

Geçen Cumartesi en çok izlenen televizyon programları

Program	Kanal	İzlenme Oranı
1– Banker Bilo	Show TV	23.82
2– Seç Bakalım	Kanal 6	13.00
3– Saklambaç	Show TV	12.95
4– Hz. Ömer'in Adaleti	Kanal 6	10.63
5– Süpermarket	Kanal 6	9.01
6– 20:00 Haberleri	TRT–1	8.80
7– Çarkıfelek	Show TV	8.65
8– 3 Asagi 5 Yukarı	Kanal 6	8.34
9– Gecenin Rengi	Kanal 6	7.72
10– Aksam Haberleri	Show TV	7.27

Figure 13.4 Simultaneous press advertisements for competing TV channels

Source: *Milliyet*, 16 March 1993

I.Star's advertisement

WELCOME TO NIELSEN

Welcome to real research, healthy, trustworthy viewership ratings.

GOODBYE to AGB

Goodbye to biased research and to distorted results.

The world's largest research firm, Nielsen, is in Turkey for TV viewership measurement research

HOŞGELDİN NIELSEN

Hoşgeldin gerçek araştırmacılık,

Hoşgeldin sağlıklı ve güvenilir izlenme verileri,

GÜLE GÜLE AGB,

Güle güle bağımlı ve taraflı araştırmacılık,

Güle güle güdümlü sonuçlar

Dünyanın en en büyük araştırma şirketi Nielsen, Televizyon İzleme Ölçüm Araştırması İçin Türkiye'de.

Show TV's advertisement

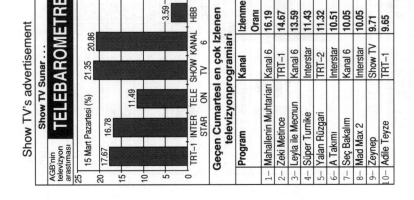

Show TV Sunar . . .

TELEBAROMETRE

AGB'nin televizyon araştırması

15 Mart Pazartesi (%) 17.67 16.78 21.35 20.86 11.49 3.59

TRT–1 INTER STAR TELE ON SHOW TV KANAL 6 HBB

Geçen Cumartesi en çok İzlenen televizyonprogramları

	Program	Kanal	İzlenme Oranı
1–	Mahallenin Muhtarları	Kanal 6	16.19
2–	Zeki Metince	TRT–1	14.67
3–	Leyla ile Mecnun	Kanal 6	13.59
4–	Süper Turnike	Interstar	11.43
5–	Yalan Rüzgarı	TRT–2	11.32
6–	A Takımı	Interstar	10.51
7–	Seç Bakalım	Kanal 6	10.05
8–	Mad Max 2	Interstar	10.05
9–	Zeynep	Show TV	9.71
10–	Adile Teyze	TRT–1	9.65

The ad gives the daily viewership ratings of the most-watched programmes. Show TV's share is again leading with 21.4%

Figure 13.5 Viewer research competition

Source: *Milliyet*, 22 March 1993

eventually reflected in the newspapers in March 1993 (Figures 13.4 and 13.5). These complementary advertisements appeared for two weeks in the same newspapers on the same days but in different corners! Now Nielsen data are expected to be produced in January 1994. Until then I.Star is destined to wait for the new source's ratings.

This time, press groups versus TV channels

At the end of 1992, based on rate card prices, newspapers' share in total advertising was down to 35 per cent. (This ratio was 43 per cent in 1990 and 42 per cent in 1991.) The first six months' cumulative findings of 1993 shows that newspaper's share have slipped further down, to 34 per cent. The TV/press (newspapers + magazines) split since 1990 is shown in Table 13.8. By late autumn 1992, private TV channels ceased fire. They had been in the battlefield too long and had planned their autumn 1992 programmes over the summer. Therefore they had to wait to see the ratings. However, at this point, newspapers were panic-stricken. Total newspaper advertising share was sliding. All the talk was about private channels. They had to be back in the agenda. Therefore they started running an advertising campaign in late 1992. The theme of this campaign was 'the power of press'. A similar campaign was also run in March 1993 by Cenajans-Grey, with six complementary designs. Two of these are shown in Figures 13.6 and 13.7.

In October 1992 the three best-selling newspapers in Turkey were (Price 1993: 27): *Sahah* with 760,000 copies; *Hürriyet* with 644,968 copies; and *Milliyet* which in 1991 was selling 447,658 copies (Price 1992: 42).

The encylopedia promotion

At this point *Sabah* launched a 12-month, 24-volume encyclopedia promotion that lasted until September 1993. This promotion campaign was also supported by competitive TV advertising. Sabah was giving away a black-and-white version of *Larousse* in Turkish. Every month readers received two volumes of the encylopedia in return for 30 coupons.

Then *Hürriyet* started offering its readers the *Children's Encyclopedia Britannica*. *Milliyet* was the last to join but capitalized most on this

Table 13.6 TV and press shares in Turkey's advertising, 1990–3

Share (%)	1990	1991	1992	Jan.–June 1993
TV	48	49	56	56
Press	51	50	44	44

Source: Vardar 1993 a: 5

EXHIBIT:3

Is anyone annoyed
by press advertising
between the lines?

yazıların arasına reklam girdi diye öfkelenen var mı?

Yok tabii...

Tam tersine,

uygun bir sayfa düzenlemesiyle yayınlanan reklamlar,

okuyucu için çok daha sempatik ve etkileyicidir.

Basın reklamları bu yönden de avantajlıdır.

ÖNCE BASIN SONRA TELEVİZYON

Of course not . . . On the contrary, ads make
the page layout more attractive and easier to read.
Press ads have got this advantage, too.
FIRST PRESS, THEN TELEVISION

Figure 13.6 Press advertising campaign

Source: Hürriyet, 5 March 1993

EXHIBIT:4

Why are TV ads debated with the help of press ads?

TV reklamlarının tartışmaları neden basın reklamlarıyla yapılır?

Basın reklamlarında
doğruları ve yanlışları
tüm ayrıntılarıyla
kamuoyuna söyleme olanağı vardır.
Basın reklamları bu yönden de avantajlıdır.

ÖNCE BASIN SONRA TELEVİZYON

In press ads, you can put down
all rights and wrongs in detail.
Press ads have this advantage, too.
FIRST PRESS, THEN TELEVISION.

Figure 13.7 Press advertising campaign

Source: Ekonomik Bülten, 15–21 March 1993

promotion. *Milliyet* chose to give away a more recent edition of *Larousse* in hard cover and in full colour.

These three newspapers' circulation figures reached their peak in February 1993, levelling off in the summer months. All three promotions lasted until September 1993. Everyone is anxious to see the anticipated net additions to the circulation figures after the promotions are over. The crucial question is, will purchasing a different newspaper for twelve or eleven months because of a promotion lead to the alteration of reading habits? Following September 1993, Turkish readers again exhibited promotion-driven newspaper-buying habits. As the contents of the newspaper become increasingly similar, the promotional offers were the only point of differentiation, influencing customers' choice of title. To this day, newspapers are continuing their concentrated consumer promotions. August 1993 net sales figures point out that, apart from *Milliyet*, *Sabah* and *Hürriyet* are more or less back to square one in spite of the promotion.

During this encylopedia promotion from December 1992 to February 1993, *Hürriyet* and *Sabah* bundled various fast moving consumer goods with their newspapers, such as toothpaste, detergent, ready made soup, bouillon, chocolate mousse mix. Ariel detergent and Colgate toothpaste have proven to be the most popular give-aways; both given by *Sabah*, daily net sales sky-rocketed to 2.3–2.5 million.

Then in March 1993, due to apparent costs of such an activity, all three made a gentlemen's agreement to put an end to any sort of extra promotional activity until the beginning of September 1993. This restriction on promotion also extended to their TV advertising. All three made competitive plans beyond September 1993 with the savings made from this wise agreement.

European press, also operating under severe competitive pressures from electronic media, have reached the conclusion that the answer is in forming the right concepts (Suddeutsche Zeitung 1993: 25). Yet in another Mediterranean country two Greek daily newspapers, *Elefterotipia* with 80,000 circulation and *Apoyevmatini* with 50,000 circulation, are also in encylopedia promotion (*Hürriyet* 2 June 1993: 17).

Table 13.7 Effect of encyclopedia promotion on newspaper sales

	Week February 1993 (average net sales)	1-10 August 1993 (average net sales)
Sabah	1,153,356	809,256
Milliyet	1,136,354	874,129
Hürriyet	1,051,182	706,291

Source: Yaysat-Birleşik Dağıtım Distribution Company.

Magazines

Share of magazine advertising in total advertising expenditure of Turkey has been rising slightly from 8.1 per cent in 1990 to 8.4 per cent in 1991 and to 8.6 per cent in 1992. The first six months' results for 1993 indicated magazines' share as 9.7 per cent. Especially after 1991, new magazines were being added to newsstands every month. Turkey has just started discovering specialised magazines and the market is now being segmented. With this segmentation idea, in addition to women's and men's magazines, auto magazines and jet-set magazines, travel magazines were introduced to the market one after another. One development which took everyone by total surprise was the launch of travel magazine *Atlas*, by the Hürriyet Group. In April 1993, *Atlas* was introduced with an estimated 20,000 sales. After its third printing in April, demand was still not exhausted. In August 1993, *Atlas* printed 60,000 copies. No one could even imagine such an immense potential for a travel magazine in Turkey. The result: Medi Group launched *Globe* in September 1993.

In addition, over the last few years, magazines have chosen joint ventures with various international magazine groups. This also had a positive effect on the quality of printing and on magazine content. One other expansion regarding magazines in Turkey was the collaboration between TV production houses and magazine groups. Early in 1993 these were a few TV programmes that were produced under the same name and content of well-known weekly current affairs magazines. This new venture of the Turkish media sets an example for TV activities merging with that of press.

Radio

Similar to cinema, radio has long been a latent medium in Turkey. The main reason behind this was again the state monopoly over radio broadcasting. TRT has nationwide and regional radio channels covering the entire country. Up until 1992, private radio entrepreneurs also waited for the liberalisation law to pass through before investing. However this long wait has proved to be futile and since private TV channels were operating, even although illegal, private radio stations also started becoming active in May 1992.

First I.Star's Metro FM was launched, broadcasting pop music, shortly followed by Super FM, playing Turkish music. Other TV channels also set up their stations: Show TV's Show Radyo and Kanal 6's Radyotek came to life. In addition, one time publisher Karacan Family launched Number 1 FM (Price 1993: 26). To start with, they were only transmitting to Istanbul. At one stage, as you travelled from one part of the city to the other, the radio channel you were tuned into automatically altered. For example, near Taksim Square, you could not listen to anything but

Power FM. However, as you went towards Esentepe, Energy FM dominated your wave length. In short, it was total chaos. Gradually most of these channels spread to other major cities, mostly in the west and the southern part of the country. Then this year on All Fool's Day, radios were all shut down by the Ministry of Transportation, stating that due to heavy interference these 'pirate' radios were adversely affecting air and sea traffic communications which could easily lead to tragic accidents. On 1 April 1993, the number of radio stations active in Turkey added up to 700. Many radio station owners had started this business without sufficient information, thinking that once the initial investment is made, the business means hiring one or two DJs talking Turkish with a bad American accent. The lesson learned was quite costly, but worth it. This relentless example of risk-taking with little or no information could not be explained by any Western business standard. However, now radio station owners are making more detailed plans regarding their near future.

Confusion over advertising expenditures in Turkey

Turkey's advertising expenditures, summarised in Table 13.5 between 1990 and 1993 are actually inflated figures. They are inflated because:

- press and TV advertising is calculated from rate card prices. However, in the absence of existing annual contracts, special prices are negotiated for each budget. In other words, there is not a single client advertising from listed media prices;
- often magazines' own advertising appears in newspapers belonging to the same press group. These ads are also included in advertising spending calculations;
- similarly, TV channels advertise other sister companies' business either free of charge or for incremental values. These ads are again calculated from rate card prices;
- added to all these escalating factors, the country suffers from a general inflation rate of approximately 65–70 per cent.

These problems regarding advertising expenditure totals are also cited in Vardar (1993b: 7–8) and in Gungor (1993: 2).

Use of the US dollar or total seconds advertised on TV as measurement units are suggested methods to overcome this problem. These measures only help in eliminating the price inflation factor from advertising expenditures. They do not help in seeding out extra or free advertising air time or space allocated to a given brand. In Table 13.8 Turkey's advertising expenditure is given in US$. In $ terms, total advertising expenditure added up to $1.151 billion in 1992, with a 87.3 per cent increase over 1991 totals.

The Turkish advertising sector is fully aware that the issue of collecting and circulating realistic figures regarding such fundamental statistics needs to be dealt with without delay.

Table 13.8 Advertising expenditure in Turkey, 1990-3 (US$)

	1990 Expenditure	1991 Annual change (%)	1991 Expenditure	1992 Annual change (%)	1992 Expenditure	Jan.–June 1993 Expenditure
Total TV	213,646,616	42.1%	303,643,337	2.1×	642,246,378	464,327,485
TRT1	194,210,526	(20.9)	153,715,244	(55.6)	68,318,841	13,469,786
TRT2	13,270,677	(59.0)	12,679,770	(16.8)	10,550,725	5,867,446
TRT3	1,578,947	—	647,172	3.7×	2,405,797	233,918
TRT4	—		95,877	20.9%	115,942	—
TRT5	—	3.5×	1,054,650	(5.2)	1,000,000	1,978,558
GAP	225,564	30.9×	790,988	2.6%	811,594	126,706
Interstar	4,360,902		134,659,636	73.4%	233,500,725	112,514,619
Teleon				—	78,507,246	15,730,994
Show TV				—	215,956,522	177,017,544
Kanal 6				—	27,144,928	125,974,659
HBB				—	3,884,058	11,413,255
Newspapers	192,706,767	33.5%	257,286,673	57.2%	404,318,841	286,715,400
Magazines	36,315,789	42.7%	51,821,668	91.1%	99,028,986	81,208,578
Radio	3,270,677	(34.0)	2,157,239	55.9	3,362,319	467,836
Cinema	nm		nm		3,144,928	1,910,331
GRAND TOTAL	445,939,849	37.9%	614,908,917	87.3	1,151,985,507	834,629,630.

Notes
nm: not measurable.
Exchange rates adopted: $1.00 = 2,600 TL (1990); $1.00 = 4,172 TL (1991); $1.00 = 6,900 TL (1992); $1.00 = 10,260 TL (Jan.–June 1993)
Sources: Deniz Reklam Etüdleri Monthly Advertising Expenditures 1990, 1992. Biles[cd]im Monthly Advertising Expenditures 1991, 1993.

Potential areas of research

Earlier we mentioned that AGB is already active in the country. Nielsen has formed a strategic partnership with a Turkish research firm – Zet. Similarly GfK-PEVA, Piar-Gallup, Dap/Yankelovich, IRI/Panel have established partnerships in Turkey. As media options increased in Turkey, media research started to become more sought after, because both advertisers and agencies felt the need to base their decisions on a rationale more than ever. This new demand also encouraged international research companies to set up new offices or tighten their existing links (Vardar 1993c: 9).

Although TV viewership data are collected by AGB, newspaper and magazine groups have contracted research firms, mainly gathering information on reader profiles and readership coefficients. The next move in press readership survey should be towards a single source to guarantee the supply of uninterrupted and consistent data. Another area for potential business will be on radio listenerships in the near future.

Despite all its shortcomings, market research is finally being considered as a basic decision-making tool by all parties involved. It is perceived as a 'must' today. Over the last three years advertisers, agencies and the Turkish media have come a long way. International advertisers and research firms have added a great deal to the Turkish experience. However, international experience is not a one-way process. The beauty of international research lies in the ability to apply internationally accepted norms to different but equally interesting business environments (Vardar 1993c: 10).

The choice of being Euro, Asian or Euroasian

Turkey is definitely experiencing a media burst, just like many other countries. Media and democracy are still being questioned worldwide (Keave 1991 and Sahin 1991: 38–77). The pendulum swings from deregulation to state censorship. However, the solution lies somewhere along the oscillation. Similarly, Turkey's encounter with increased media alternatives has proved to be quite a unique experience because, just like other countries, it has got specific characteristics. Therefore, Turkey has to and will find its own unique solutions to its Euroasian problems.

As for the question of whether this media burst is a blessing or a burden, that has no definite, clear-cut answer. The outcome actually depends upon the people, and the choice is theirs. The media burst can easily become a burden or a blessing, and we have seen examples of this in the Turkish media scene. The people involved at all levels, either as consumers or advertisers or media owners or media sellers, should approach the situation with a critical eye and a questioning mind. This includes not believing everything, gathering sound information and basing decisions on hard facts. Then, not a single obstruction will be left and the country will be enjoying the blessing of choice in media, in trade, in farsighted projects, in trained personnel. Above all, the Turkish people will then succeed in merging their European vision with their rich Asian heritage, with the skill and precision of a craftsman.

REFERENCES

Bileşim AS Monthly Advertising Expenditures, 1991 and 1993 (in Turkish).

Deniz Reklam Etüdleri Monthly Advertising Expenditures, 1990 and 1992 (in Turkish).

The Economist (1992) 'Byzantium was quieter', 24 October: 52.

The Financial Times Survey (1992) 'Turkey's South East Anatolian project', 24 July.

The Financial Times Survey (1993) 'Turkey', 4 May.

The Financial Times Survey (1993) 'Istanbul and the Olympics', 24 June.

Gözlem (1993) 'Foreign relations 93 – ideal country for foreign investment' (in Turkish), 10 May.

Güngör, T. (1993) 'Will all private channels survive?', *Dünya*, 18 February: 2 (in Turkish),:

Hürriyet (1993) 'Greek newspapers also engaged in encylopedia promotion', 2 June: 17 (in Turkish).

Hürriyet (1993) 'Annual inflation month by month', 5 August: 7 (in Turkish).

Independent (1993) 'Turkey and Central Asia', 1 June: 26–29.

Institute of Statistics (1991) *Statistical Indicators 1923–1990*, Prime Minister, Republic of Turkey, December.

Intermedia (1993) *Turkey '93 Almanac*

Keane, J. (1991) *The Media and Democracy*, Turkish Trans. Dr Haluk Şahin, Istanbul: Ayrinti Yayinlari.

Price, B. (1992) 'At the start of a boom', *Media International*, March, 42–3.

Price, B. (1993) 'Is Turkey really looking east?', *Media International*, April, 26–27.

Stern Marketing Series (1993) *Europe 1993: Media*, January.

Süddeutsche Zeitung (1993) *Daily Newspaper Advertising in Europe*, ed., M. Böckler, München: Süddeutsche Zeitung.

Şahin, H. (1991) *New Communication Environment, Democracy and Freedom of Press* (Basin konseyi bilimsel araştirmasi, Istanbul (in Turkish).

TOBB (Turkish Union Chamber of Commerce and Industry) (1993) Economic Report 1992, 48th General Assembly, no. 263, Ankara (in Turkish).

TRT (Turkish Radio and Television) (1990) *TRT from Past to Present 1927–1990*, Ankara (in Turkish).

TUSIAD (Turkish Industrialists and Businessmen's Association) (1991) *Turkey Towards the 21st Century: Competitive Strategy with a Future Outlook*, vols. I and II, March (in Turkish).

Vardar, N. (1993a) 'Advertising sector saying farewell to 1992', *Marketing Türkiye*, 1 January, Year 2, no. 41: 3–5 (in Turkish).

Vardar, N. (1993b) 'Figures do not lie! If people do not make them . . .', *Araştirmaci* 1 February, 7–8 (in Turkish).

Vardar, N. (1993c) 'Market research in Turkey', *ESOMAR Newsbrief*, July/August, 8–10.

14 The role of multilingual copy adaptation in international advertising

Ursula Grüber

THE INTERNATIONAL CAMPAIGN: A STRATEGIC CHOICE

Developments over the last decade have proved beyond doubt that advertising can indeed cross boundaries effectively. Frontiers which once seemed impermeable to advertising as we know it in a free market economy have opened up at an almost breathless rate. Advertising campaigns which once would have run only in a few selected markets are today being created from a central source to reach targets simultaneously in the United States, Latin America, the European Union, the countries of Central and Eastern Europe and a vastly extended Asian region. International advertising in the twenty-first century will no longer be addressing the issue of whether to go global, but how best to do it.

The practice of transposing a single, unified message into a multiplicity of languages has become an advantageous option for advertisers and advertising agencies. Press campaigns, TV spots, outdoor advertising, direct marketing campaigns, corporate brochures, product leaflets, merchandising material and packaging copy are increasingly generated from a single creative source. The motivating factors are varied: the need to communicate consistent brand values across world markets, the growing importance of corporate communications, new opportunities on the evolving European scene, the universality of many products and services, converging consumer needs, the consolidation of creative expertise, and, last but not least, cost savings in terms of research and execution.

Centralised, multilingual communications are no longer the exclusive domain of large international groups. Many smaller-scale national marketers are today 'thinking global' from the earliest stages of expansion, creating brand names, logos, advertising, marketing and merchandising material that are designed from the very first to 'travel' as and when their business expands beyond national borders.

Thinking internationally in tomorrow's market place means transcending the merely geographic. Any global strategy must be underpinned by a capacity to promote products in a culturally relevant manner. To assume that domestic brand values can cross national boundaries virtually unaided, simply because they are strong on their home ground, is a recipe for disaster.

Internationally sophisticated advertisers are aware of the potential impact of even the smallest label or instruction leaflet – let alone advertising copy – on consumers outside the home country. Who hasn't puzzled over an incomprehensible set of instructions for a foreign-made appliance? Or smiled at a clumsily worded item of packaging or merchandising material? Inevitably, such lapses can tarnish a company's international reputation. Even the humblest piece of marketing copy reflects well or badly on the company image, depending on the degree of care exercised in its transposition.

MULTILINGUAL COPY ADAPTATION: AN EFFECTIVE SOLUTION

Given the strategic importance of the multilingual campaign, it is essential to manage it with optimal effectiveness. For the global campaigner, effective management can be measured against three criteria. These are:

- consistency: the concept and the message must be faithfully reconstituted in each national market;
- flexibility: variations arising from cultural differences, local market factors or linguistic particularities must be handled with intelligence and sound, professional judgement;
- control: transposition of the original copy into the target languages must be centrally supervised by a single entity to prevent any drift in content, style or tone of voice.

Twenty years ago a professional service was created and pioneered to help advertisers and their agencies to meet these criteria. Known in the industry as 'multilingual copy adaptation', it is a full-fledged discipline used with success by international advertising networks, national advertising agencies, large corporations, manufacturers, service companies, governmental bodies, private associations, banks – in fact, by every type of organisation with an international image to build or maintain.

Multilingual copy adaptation is a discipline in its own right, not to be confused with translation. It works on the fundamental principle that adapting a foreign-language campaign is a task for advertising professionals working in unison to defend and promote a client's creative message. This message cannot be entrusted to linguists and translators whose experience of advertising may be limited to what they incidentally see in magazines or on TV, along with millions of fellow consumers. It should not be farmed out to local advertising agencies or agency network members who are not fully committed to the original concept and creative strategy, or who do not have full command of the original language. Nor should it be left to local managers and distributors in the target markets, whose time and copywriting capacities will necessarily be limited. In short, copy adaptation is a specialist skill which must be handled with the same professional rigour as the original creative research and execution.

THE METHODOLOGY OF MULTILINGUAL COPY ADAPTATION

Multilingual copy adaptation offers a working methodology designed to ensure maximum effectiveness for a transnational campaign – whether global, pan-European or involving only one or two foreign languages. It is based on an international network of professional copywriters with sound advertising experience. These copywriters live in their native country and write only in their mother tongue. In the case of highly technical copy, copywriters are assisted if necessary by technical back-up experts who can provide specific terminology and industry insights.

Effective adaptation implies centralised control. After all, the principal aim of global marketing is to project a consistent image and message across all markets. Every measure should therefore be taken to ensure that there is no 'slippage' between the original copy and the foreign language versions. The copywriters of the adaptation team are therefore briefed, supervised and quality-controlled by a centralised staff of project co-ordinators working in close liaison with the client.

But all adaptation projects should begin with a strong, global concept. In other words, adaptation begins at home – in the planning stage of the campaign. This is the right time for the advertiser or advertising agency to check out the creative framework of the campaign to ensure that it will adapt effectively to the various target countries. By consulting with the adaptation specialists before the creative work gets fully underway, costly mistakes can be avoided. Visuals, layout, headlines, taglines and body copy all need to have true adaptation potential, and only an advertising professional who is fully conversant with the local market and the local language can spot an eventual problem. The adaptation specialists can help the creative team to tailor the 'master' copy to local requirements.

International marketers would also be wise to have brand names, product names, catalogue models – even the names of colours and finishes – vetted by adaptation consultants for their acceptability in foreign markets.

Once the original creative research and execution are completed, the foreign language adaptation can get under way. The skill of the adaptors lies in their ability to respect the basic structure and message of the campaign while moulding it to local sensibilities. The campaign should be recognisable from country to country, yet never smack of translation or imitation. It should be able to stand by itself as an example of professional, masterful, creative copywriting, conveying all the freshness and impact of the original copy.

In adapting a campaign, it is important to differentiate between the elements which constitute its basic framework (the 'constants'), and those which can be adjusted to fit local requirements (the 'variables').

The 'constants' of an international campaign include the following:

- a basic concept;
- a strong creative idea;
- a style;
- a tone of voice;
- a sum of information on the product, the service or the company concerned;
- design and graphic features: logotype, typography, use of colour, etc.

These components of the campaign together constitute a coherent system which must be consistently respected in subsequent language versions.

On the other hand, the international campaign may need to adjust to certain specifics which will vary from country to country. Among the 'variables' that the adaptor must contend with and resolve, the following are the commonest:

- local legislation;
- specific market contexts;
- the positioning of the product in the local market;
- awareness level in the local market;
- methods of distribution;
- local purchasing patterns;
- socio-cultural differences;
- language usage.

PREPARING THE GROUND FOR A FOREIGN LANGUAGE CAMPAIGN

Campaigns for certain international giants like Coca Cola, Marlboro and Levi's convey such universal selling propositions and promote values so widely shared or emulated that the local 'variables' are minimal. This kind of 'consumer convergence' can also be seen in sectors such as the computer industry and in various service sectors – travel and tourism, for example. But despite the trends, the forward-looking campaign planner will maintain a strict vigilance when planning to cross national boundaries.

A few examples will illustrate this point. France Telecom regularly runs outdoor campaigns in major French cities to encourage foreign tourists to phone home. These campaigns are printed in various languages, including of course English. In preparation for the summer season, France Telecom's advertising agency consulted its adaptation specialists for an outdoor campaign promoting bargain long-distance rates among European, American and Japanese tourists. Each poster featured an easily recognisable national 'type' – a bowler-hatted Englishman, a tulip-bearing Dutch girl, a native American in Indian headdress and a Japanese *samurai* – the visual being accompanied by a humorous headline. The first three posters were duly adapted (the native American headline requiring careful copy adaptation for obvious cultural reasons). The Japanese *samurai*, however, with its allusion to '*hara kiri*', was, after checking with the adaptation team in Tokyo, declared out of bounds. For the Japanese, *hara kiri* is never, in any circumstances, a joking matter. The image of France Telecom and of French tourism undoubtedly benefited from the decision not to run this advertisement.

International marketer Timberland systematically checks out copy destined for European markets before proceeding to the adaptation stage. Advertisements created by the agency Mullen of Boston are scrutinised by the adaptation team for possible pitfalls. For example, a headline such as 'Boat shoes should go with a black sky. Not a blue blazer' may seem to be a perfectly translatable teaser, but what if blue blazers trigger a completely different connotation for the French or Spanish consumer? As it happens, there's no problem, but the advertiser is right to take precautions. Another headline from Timberland reads: 'Our name is mud'. The visual shows a Timberland boot well muddied – and loving every minute of it (Figure 14.1). Before proceeding to adapt this advertisement, research was carried out to ensure that an appropriate equivalent could be found in French. The result brought in an equally humorous and equivocal line: '*Vous pouvez nous traîner dans la boue*'.

Lamy, the German manufacturer of writing instruments, runs advertisements whose headlines are 'penned' in a bold, handsome script. For its pan-European campaign, the German headlines are adapted into a number of languages. However, Lamy's advertising agency, Leonhardt & Kern, has taken the adaptation process a step further by having the adaptation team provide samples of handwriting from the target countries. From the wide spectrum of styles collected, the agency's art director has distilled a script to suit each market. Many direct marketers might take a leaf from Lamy's book when producing 'handwritten' letters for their international mailshots. No matter how skilfully adapted the message, the impact is lost if the target cannot easily read or relate to the script selected.

All these examples show the importance of thinking ahead, before a single word of foreign copy is written. Another essential precaution is to provide the adaptation team with sufficient back-up material. Before assigning copy for adaptation, it is safe to assume that you cannot provide too much information. A typical back-up package includes a full briefing, copy strategy, a complete layout and any available printed material in the languages involved. Optional but useful extras include literature from the competition, samples of the product, copies of previous campaigns, and so on. Too often it is assumed that the only tool an adaptor needs is a

Figure 14.1 Timberland's England headline, created by Mullen of Boston and adapted by Ursula Grüber Communication Internationale

bilingual dictionary. It is probably the tool this specialist needs least. What is far more important is to provide maximum access to relevant, up-to-the-minute information on the brand, product or service being promoted.

Schott, Europe's leading manufacturer of special glass, not only does all the above but even arranges information sessions at headquarters in Mainz, Germany, where their foreign language copywriters can familiarise themselves with Schott production facilities and products – a constructive approach which gives their promotional literature added impact and quality.

THE VALUE OF INTERACTION

The advertiser or advertising agency calling on adaptation specialists for the first time may be surprised by the degree of teamwork undertaken on behalf of his campaign, whether for two or twenty-two languages. But the reason is simple. The methodology underlying multilingual copy adaptation is based on interaction.

At the first level, there is the interaction between professional copywriters and technical specialists who assist the writers with sector-specific terminology and information.

At the second level, there is interaction between copywriters in different countries working simultaneously on the same campaign. This interaction can be particularly intense and productive when many languages are involved. For example, an Agfa campaign with 12 headlines to be adapted

Figure 14.2 One message right across Europe: multilingual copy adaption helps to consolidate an international image

into 14 languages will mean involving teams of creatives in 14 countries for local brainstorming sessions (Figure 14.2). The results will be checked for their compatibility with the brief and transmitted to each team. Ideas from one country may trigger new ideas in another. The central co-ordination unit will progressively distil the best from each country and prepare a shortlist of proposals for the client, accompanied by a recommendation for each language.

However, not all adaptation work is so complex. Sometimes a strapline or slogan proves to be directly translatable. Compare this strapline from the German silverware manufacturer Wilkens: '*Silbernes für Ihre Esskultur*' with its Dutch equivalent: '*Zilver voor uw eetkultuur*' (Figure 14.3). Almost no adaptation required here. However, every language has its 'difficult' words which adaptors come to greet as a permanent challenge. The French word '*maîtrise*', for example, which translates literally as 'mastery', is a powerful, contemporary-sounding, extremely versatile word. In English it has a more literary ring and lacks impact in an industrial or high-tech context. Take the original French strapline for Thomson Broadcast, manufacturers of digital broadcasting equipment: '*La maîtrise numérique*' (digital mastery). The adapted version, 'State of the digital art', addresses this problem straight on and repackages the original content in a dynamic new form (Figure 14.4).

At the third level, there is interaction between the adaptation team and the client's local representative. Liaison between the adaptors and the subsidiaries provides an added assurance of success for the campaign. Many

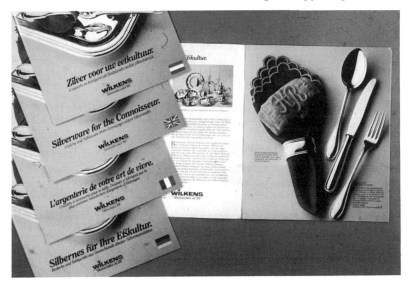

Figure 14.3 This German title finds its close counterpart in Dutch – but required greater adaptation in French and English

companies or agencies appoint a person in each country with whom the adaptation team may liaise. This contact may be a marketing, sales or product manager, or in some cases the local distributor or dealer. This system has multiple benefits for the advertiser, the adaptation team and the campaign. The adaptor in each country can consult with the local manager on technical questions specific to the product. By obtaining local approval of the finished copy the adaptor and the client can be sure that company terminology has been rigorously respected. This is of paramount importance in sectors where terminology tends to vary from company to company. Which cosmetic companies, for example, are using 'nail enamel' and which 'nail lacquer'? 'Moisturising' or 'hydrating'? 'Blush' or 'blusher'? Each company has its preferences. In the case of, say, computer software or photographic equipment, company terminology tends to be even more complex. By giving each subsidiary the opportunity to provide information to the adaptor, discuss the copy and give its seal of approval, the international marketer ensures goodwill for the global concept at local level and the assurance that each country has a marketing tool which serves its needs effectively.

But this does not imply decentralisation of the campaign or loss of control. The adaptation team will measure the proposed copy against the components of the brief, and any divergence requested locally will be reported back to central co-ordination and discussed with the client.

The adaptor's task is by no means finished when the finalised language versions are completed and approved. All typeset copy should be

Figure 14.4 Thomson Broadcast's English slogan after research and adaptation

submitted to the adaptation team for close scrutiny. Even in cases where the printer has been able to work directly from the copywriter's disk, it is advisable to submit proofs to the adaptation team. They will not only spot errors more easily than non-native readers, but can also advise on line breaks for headlines and other graphic considerations. At the same time, the proofs should be read by the client's local management. This provides double security and the assurance that no mistakes are made in local addresses, telephone numbers, and so on.

THE TECHNICAL STAGES OF MULTILINGUAL COPY ADAPTATION

The 'route plan' in Figure 14.5 shows a typical itinerary for a multilingual adaptation project. In the case below, the client is an international advertiser in the high-tech sector, with a corporate brochure to be adapted into six languages. Because the content of the brochure is fairly technical, the adaptors in each country are assisted by technical experts within the adaptation network who provide them with necessary terminology. After the copy has been adapted into the target languages, it is sent to the client's subsidiaries. Local management discusses any points directly with the local copywriters before approving the copy.

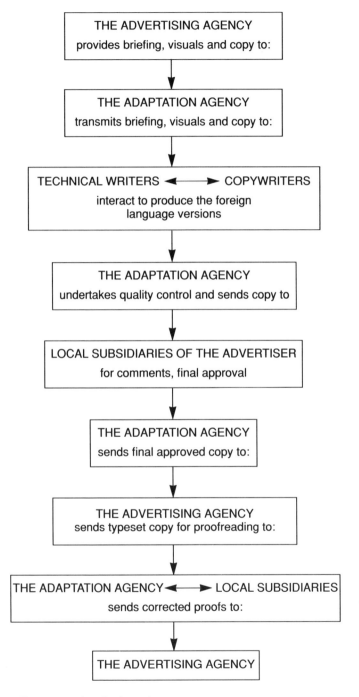

Figure 14.5 The transnational adaptation route

SOME DO'S AND DON'TS FOR SUCCESSFUL COPY ADAPTATION

Above all, multilingual copy adaptation is an interactive discipline, characterised by close synergy between the international communicator and the adaptation team. Concluding this overview of the adaptation process, here are some operational guidelines designed to assist the international marketer in preparing a transnational campaign.

Think international from the outset

- Make sure your concept can stand its ground in all your target countries. By consulting the adaptation specialist at an early stage you can avoid making a costly commitment to an unadaptable creative idea.
- Remember that a truly international campaign must have a basic framework: a concept, a strong creative idea, an argument, product features (if applicable), the same graphic treatment (visual, logo, typography, colour code).
- Take account of the variable elements as defined by local conditions: local legislation, market characteristics, the positioning of the product in the local market, sociocultural differences, and so on.
- Ensure that the name of your product or brand has no negative connotations in foreign markets and that it can be pronounced with ease.
- Create a layout that projects a sense of unity across the various target countries: the same positioning of visuals, headline and logo, the same colour code . . .
- In creating your copy, avoid local references and use any play on words judiciously.
- Refrain from using visuals which are too local in character and with which other countries will have difficulty identifying.
- Remember that the same copy content will vary in length from language to language. Compared with English, Latin languages require 20 to 25 per cent more space, and German and Scandinavian languages 25 to 30 per cent more.

Select your adaptation partners as carefully as you would your creative team

- Ensure that your adaptation partners are using authentic professionals with the experience and talent for the job: direct marketing specialists for mailshots, creative copywriters for press advertisements and brochures, journalist-copywriters for corporate newsletters, technical experts for providing specific terminology . . .
- Expect your adaptation partner to use writers who live in the country where the copy is going. Expatriate writers tend to become 'rusty' in

their own language through living abroad too long. In addition, they may be out of touch with new trends in their home country.

- Choose adaptation partners who treat your below-the-line material with the same professional care as your prestige press campaign. An uninspired eight-page brochure or three lines of poorly worded packaging copy can do long-term damage to your corporate or brand image.

Plan the adaptation as meticulously as the original creative phase

- Brief the adaptation team thoroughly. Whenever possible, provide the original creative strategy, relevant local market data, layout, visuals, existing literature in the languages concerned.
- Provide clear, finalised copy. Remember that each author's change is inevitably multiplied by the number of languages involved and leads to extra costs and time.
- Arrange for subsidiaries or agents in the local markets to approve the final copy. This ensures that the terminology used is acceptable to the marketing and sales teams, and helps create a climate of goodwill towards a campaign that originated outside their own country.
- Arrange to have the adaptation team proofread the typeset copy. They are best qualified to spot incorrect word breaks, missing accents, and so on.

A FINAL WORD ...

Multilingual copy adaptation is neither a translation nor a new creation. It is not the purpose of adaptation to re-invent the advertising message. Its mission is to relocate this message in the target markets with maximum consistency.

The brand values that will make the most impact in tomorrow's markets are those that succeed in travelling wisely – and well.

NOTE

A set of guidelines, *Some Do's and Don'ts for Advertising Successfully Beyond the Language Barrier*, is available on request in English, French or German from Ursula Grüber Communication Internationale SA, 83 rue Saint-Honoré, 75001 Paris. Tel: (33 1) 42 33 57 61. Fax: (33 1) 42 21 41 14.

Part V

International distribution

The topic of logistics is greatly neglected, yet there are few areas such as this, where economies can be made and efficiencies achieved now that the globalization of business has been widely recognized. Add to this cheaper communications from television and satellite, communications to transportation, the removal of barriers to trade and foreign investment, the need to achieve economies of scale in business, the degree of innovation in logistics, and the value density of the product in question, that is its value in relation to in weight and volume. These factors all shape logistics strategy, discussed in James Cooper's contribution. Corporate strategy alternatives are also discussed, as is the challenge of reconfiguring organisations to secure effective logistics management.

Therese A. Maskulka and G. Scott Erickson, in the second contribution in this Part, examine the retailing sector, which has been experiencing substantial international expansion over the last ten years. They offer a Retail Entry Model (REM) focused on control decisions rather than the traditional market entry mode decision, and create a classification of retailers. However, the application of this decision is to where to keep operational control. Based on Dunning's eclectic theory and Levitt's globalization, the REM seeks to evaluate the circumstances of the firm and the market it is entering, then render a recommendation on an appropriate control strategy.

Part V

International distribution

15 Logistics strategies for global businesses

James Cooper

INTRODUCTION

Over the past few years, there has been a sustained trend towards the globalisation of businesses. The driving forces behind this trend are several. Ohmae (1985), for example, points to the spread of similar lifestyle preferences among the young around the world, which creates ever-wider markets for products such as trainers and personal stereos. He calls this the 'Californianisation' of the young. Upstream of the market, in manufacturing, there are also important factors which drive the process of globalisation. Increasingly, it is too expensive to duplicate best manufacturing practice in each of an organisation's major markets (Porter 1986). Manufacturing facilities have therefore become more focused, both by product specialisation and geographical location.

Inevitably, as the process of globalisation continues, the character of companies must change. The following quotation from Levitt (1983) captures this point:

> The multinational and the global corporation are not the same thing. The multinational corporation operates in a number of countries and adjusts its products and prices in each – at high relative costs. The global corporation operates with result certainty – at low relative costs – as if the entire world (for major regions of it) were a single entity; it sells the same things in the say way everywhere.

Considerable discussion has arisen on how far global standardisation can go. Whereas Levitt refers to products being sold in the same way everywhere, others, such as Kotler (1985), Douglas and Wind (1987) and Jain (1989), have identified significant barriers to the standardisation of marketing in many industries. Similarly Piore (1987) and Bartlett and Ghoshal (1989) point to the rejection of standardisation in many products by a large and growing group of consumers.

Just as standardisation can be related to both the *processes* and *contents* of marketing (Raffée and Kreutzer 1989), it is a similar story for logistics. Theatre operations in logistics, for example, are highly variable throughout the world and the priorities for management in, say, Europe will differ significantly from those elsewhere (Cooper *et al.* 1991).

As a consequence, managing logistics at a global level represents a challenge of considerable complexity and it seems fair to say that many companies have yet to get to grips with the challenge of managing global pipelines (Braithwaite and Christopher 1991). Indeed, among some US managers, there seems to be a dichotomy in their thinking about global logistics. According to a survey carried out by Zinn and Grosse (1990), US managers did not expect much globalisation of logistics channels, yet simultaneously held the view that manufacturing facilities would become more centralised.

It therefore seems timely to review the process of business globalisations and to consider the implications for logistics with the aim of bringing more clarity to our understanding of both the strategic and the management issues. In particular, we need to embrace the point that global logistics management implies the making of choices between options, with respect to both content and process. There is no one standardised model for all companies to follow. Each company must cater for the particular business environment in which it operates.

This examination of global logistics begins with a brief overview of the globalisation of company operations, to provide a working context. The discussion then moves on to assess the development of global logistics strategy, taking a bottom-up approach. To begin with, the impact of product-market characteristics on strategy formulation is assessed, followed by an evaluation of logistics strategy at the level of the business unit or company. Finally, the paper considers the implications of global logistics strategies for management, notably the critical success factors that apply and the need for organisational change.

THE GLOBALISATION OF COMPANY OPERATIONS

Julius (1990) has estimated that trade between subsidiaries of the same company accounts for more than half of all trade between OECD countries. Of all US exports, one-third is to the overseas subsidiaries of US firms. Another third of US exports is accounted for by foreign manufacturers sending goods back to their home countries. Not all of this represents the activities of fully global businesses; many will be more restricted in scope. None the less, the figures do illustrate the importance in world trade of companies which are already global or some way towards achieving global status.

A further important point is that these trade flows are not only larger than in the past(as a result of global economic growth) but they are also qualitatively different than before. Trade used to be based on relatively fixed locations with raw materials sourced from where they were found or grown, production taking place in the industrialised centres of Europe and North America. Now the process is much more 'footloose' than it once was. Industrial components can be sourced from a variety of alternative locations and the assembly even of advanced products is less tied to established centres; for example, the Shanghai Aviation Industrial Corporation (SAIC) assembles civilian aircraft in China on behalf of McDonnell Douglas (Rosenthal 1989).

A number of key, but interdependent, factors have been responsible for reshaping the activities of major companies, including:

- the globalisation of markets;
- cheaper communications;
- removal of barriers to trade and foreign investment;
- achieving economies of scale in business;
- innovation in logistics.

Each of these factors is very briefly reviewed in turn below, both to expand on the trends outlined above in the Introduction section and to provide examples from companies which are either partly or fully globalised.

The globalisation of markets

This represents a phenomenon which is different from the simple growth in world trade. Rather, it means that the same products (or variants tailored to local tastes) are sold in more countries than ever before.

Probably the archetypal global product is Coca-Cola, which is sold in just about every country. Hamburgers from McDonald's are not far behind. But the list is not exclusively American. Other products with a strong global reach include: Benetton clothing (Italy), Sony consumer electronics (Japan), Rolls-Royce aero engines (UK) and Mercedes-Benz cars (Germany).

Some of these products represent useful illustration of the limits to standardisation in global marketing. Mercedes-Benz cars, for example, will not be sold with left-hand drive in all export markets; several, such as Japan, Australia and the UK, specify the steering wheel on the right of the car. Benetton, in its clothes range, balances standardisation with some local adaptation. Others, such as Pizza Hut, 'protects the core elements of its brand by copyrighting its individual product brand names e.g. Perfect Pizza. It also ensures standardisation across markets by operating a strict specification of product ingredients. However the concept is adapted to suit local needs. For example some elements of the menu (such as desserts) will vary, as will store design and even the way products are served to the customer' (Segal-Horn and Davison 1992). These examples seem to point to a clear enough message on the issue of standardisation in global marketing; namely, marketing is consumer-oriented and if consumers prefer a non-standard product, then companies must oblige to achieve or maintain success.

Cheaper communications

The process of market globalisation is inextricably linked with cheaper communications of various kinds. For example, the spread of television allows advertisements for goods to be directed at previously untapped markets. In this way, people can be persuaded that they have unrealised wants or needs that can only be satisfied by the purchase of a particular product. The spread of satellite television, which spans national boundaries, can only have contributed to the development of global markets, particularly in consumer products.

Furthermore, communications in the transport field are crucial to this process of globalisation. Cheaper transport through technical developments such as containerisation now make it economic to serve new markets or source from new locations. Also, communications, in the form of information systems designed to control the flow of goods, are now becoming a vitally important consideration. Developments such as Electronic Data Interchange (EDI) are fast reducing transaction costs and so make global trading more attractive to an increasing number of companies.

The removal of barriers to trade and foreign investment

This also underpins many changes in operations by major companies. The General Agreement on Tariffs and Trade (GATT) has had an important influence on world trade, which has been stimulated by the application of the most favoured nation (MFN) rule 'under which a government has to extend trade benefits granted to one country to all other GATT members and GATT's simple concept that protection against imports should be achieved by means of non-discriminating tariffs' (Dullforce 1991).

In the area of foreign investment there have also been major changes. Take, for example, the case of Ford in Spain. In the early 1970s the Spanish car market was heavily protected. Tariffs on imports were very high at 81 per cent on cars and 30 per cent on components. Moreover, there was a requirement that cars built in Spain had to have 95 per cent local content. Finally, no foreign company was allowed more than 50 per cent ownership of a company operating in Spain and this conflicted with Ford's policy of 100 per cent ownership of foreign subsidiaries (Dicken 1986). But, because the Spanish government was keen to establish a strong local motor industry and increase car exports, these conditions were relaxed. The pay-off for Spain was 19,000 new jobs and opportunities for export. With the further establishment of General Motors and SEAT (now owned by Volkswagen), Spain is now a major producer of cars in Europe.

Economies of scale

Achieving economies of scale in business has been an important parallel development in line with the above changes, not least in manufacturing. If economies of scale exist that extend beyond the size of national markets, then there is a potential cost advantage to companies through centralised production (Lee 1986). In other words, it will be worthwhile making in one location, to serve a number of national markets, rather than to have national manufacturing units.

This has long been the strategy of companies such as Procter & Gamble (P&G) in Europe. Toothpaste, for example, is made in Germany for sale throughout Europe. Furthermore, such focused production appears to be on the increase. Unilever, a major competitor of P&G, has recently changed its strategy from making most of the product range at plants in its main country markets to a series of specialised factories located at strategic centres in Europe (Cooper *et al.* 1991).

A vital point about single sourcing of production is that it distances many final customers from production, as shown in Figure 15.1. For the multinational company (MNC) operating a host-market production strategy, customers and production are in close proximity. As Figure 15.1 shows, this is less true for the global or transnational company (TNC) practising single-source production; it follows that there are major implications for logistics management in this transition from multinational to global operations.

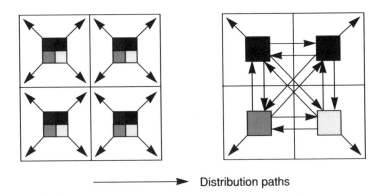

Distribution paths

Figure 15.1 Alternatives for international production and distribution (a) Host-market production (multinational companies) (b) Single-source production (Transnational companies)

Source: Adapted from Dicken 1986

Innovation in logistics

Innovation in logistics has played a key role in making sure that global companies can still react effectively to local market demands, even when their production facilities are distant. The application of the principle of 'postponement' is an important case in point (Zinn and Bowersox 1988). This allows for some activities normally associated with production to be performed downstream in the supply chain, delaying the point in time when goods become dedicated to particular markets or customers. Take, for example, the case of Caterpillar in its production of lift-trucks. In order to save on production costs the company moved manufacturing off-shore from the United States. But lift-trucks come with a variety of options and it would be excessively costly to stockpile lift-trucks fitted with a host of option permutations at a USA warehouse so that any one customer order can be rapidly filled from stock. Much better to ship across part-finished lift-trucks and to finish assembly, using the required options, at the warehouse. The important point here is that the warehouse has become an extension of the assembly line, allowing Caterpillar to maintain (or even improve) levels of service at an acceptable cost.

Logistics strategy is therefore a consideration of growing importance for Caterpillar and companies like it. Yet the precise formulation of a logistics strategy for any one company depends crucially upon a number of key product variables. In the following section we examine these variables and consider how global companies can thereby reconfigure their logistics operations in order to gain or sustain competitive advantage.

PRODUCT VARIABLES AND GLOBAL LOGISTICS STRATEGY

One of the key product variables in determining global logistics strategy is value density; namely, the value of a product in relation to its weight and volume. The general rule is that the lower the value density, the more localised the logistics system. Many *commodity* products, such as cement, have low value densities, which means they are usually shipped to local catchment areas (subject to supplies of raw materials being available close to market). By contrast, products with a high value density, such as precious stones and expensive perfumes, are distributed around the world from a relatively few points of supply. The 'logistics reach' of a product can therefore be represented as having a direct relationship with value density. Yet, as Figure 15.2 shows, it is extremely important to consider both the standard of customer service and the cost of logistics services when assessing the logistics reach for a product of any given value density. A desire to improve levels of customer service or increasing logistics services costs will tend to reduce the logistics reach of products (e.g. from r_2 to r_1) for a product of constant value density v_1.

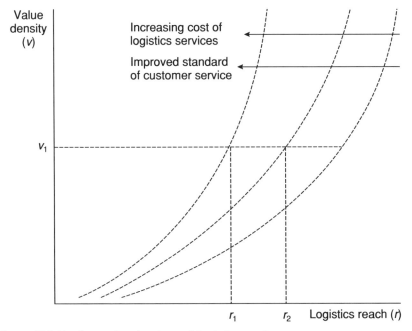

Figure 15.2 Product value density and logistics reach

This is an important consideration for a number of consumer products which are sold to a global market, but which have relatively low value densities. Many soft drinks are a case in point. Each bottling plant serves a well-defined area around it, and the radius of operation is largely determined by both customer service and the cost of logistics services for delivery to customers (the radius of operation varies according to local conditions, but in Europe it is about 150 miles).

The configuration of the bottling plant network is therefore highly dependent upon logistics reach. It follows that a change in logistics reach as a result of, say, changes in transport costs, will impact upon the bottling plant network. There must be continuous monitoring of the costs of production, as measured against the costs of distribution, to ensure that no imbalance develops in the network. Over the long term it must be a key logistics objective to maintain a production network that is neither too dense nor too sparse, when judged against the twin criteria of customer service and supply chain economics.

However, it would be wrong to construct a logistics network for a global product entirely on the basis of a primary product characteristic such as value density. In many product markets (not least soft drinks), brand or technical superiority (or both) are also vital considerations, especially when they are key factors in securing market share.

Take the healthcare sector, for example. Two of Johnson & Johnson's healthcare products have high value densities, yet the logistics strategy for Vistakon contact lenses is entirely different from the strategy appropriate to Ethicon sutures. This is because Vistakon operates in a highly competitive market place where product price is an extremely important driver. By contrast, Ethicon sutures hold 80 per cent of the market, so price is relatively unimportant next to high levels of customer service which deter the entry of rivals with competing products.

Accordingly, the logistics strategy for Vistakon is focused upon the centralisation of production and inventory in the USA with world-wide distribution taking place from this single location. For a non-standard, high-value product such as Vistakon, this strategy makes a great deal of sense, since economies of scale in production can be enjoyed, together with savings in inventory from centralisation. World-wide airfreight charges for a product with such a high-value density can readily be accommodated within this strategy.

The logistics strategy for Ethicon sutures is entirely different, given its dominant position within the market place. Customer service, rather than cost, becomes the driver, so the logistics strategy is geared to high-quality delivery in each operational theatre; neither production nor inventory is centralised, given the need to provide unfailing supply to demanding customers.

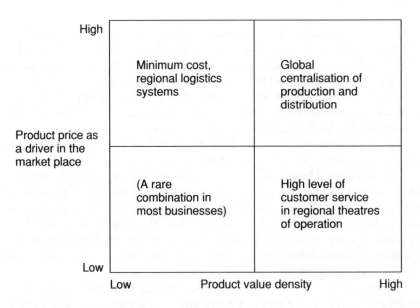

Figure 15.3 Product-market factors and priorities in logistics strategy formulation

Source: Adapted from *Reconfiguring European Logistics Systems*, a report for the Council of Logistics Management, jointly prepared by Cranfield School of Management and Anderson Consulting, 1993.

The different priorities in formulating logistics strategies for products in the healthcare market are summarised in Figure 15.3. It emphasises the importance of secondary product characteristics (namely, price as a driver in the market-place) as well as primary product characteristics (namely, product value density) when framing logistics strategy.

Clearly, it is important for management to appreciate that the position of a product in the Figure 15.3 matrix is not always static. Priorities in logistics strategy must therefore change as market conditions change. For example, products at an early stage of their life-cycle will often enjoy high profits that encourage rival companies to offer competing products. So while product price may not initially be a driver in the market, it will often become one eventually. As a result, the logistics strategy in the beginning (when competing products are not a threat) might emphasise very short lead times, with cost being a lesser consideration. Later, the strategy may well focus on cost-efficiency through centralised inventory and consolidation in transport movements.

There are, however, a number of other secondary product characteristics which can play an important role in configuring logistics systems to best advantage. In a number of cases these can be related to the principle of postponement, the application of which can lead to superior systems in logistics, not least because inventory levels can be cut, and problems associated with uncertainty of demand in particular markets can be considerably reduced. Postponement in a global context can be very readily related to 'yes' or 'no' answers to three questions that relate to secondary product characteristics. These question are:

Brand: Is it global?
Formulation: Is it common to all markets or different between
                     countries/customers?
Peripherals: Are labels, packaging and instruction manuals common
                     to all markets?

Starting from the perspective of global brands only, there can be only four different combinations of answers to these questions, as indicated in Table 15.1, using illustrations from consumer markets. These combinations underpin four strategy options in logistics which are based upon different kinds of postponement in the supply chain.

The postponement option which applies furthest upstream the supply chain is Bundled Manufacturing (see Figure 15.4). This is where the product formulation differs by market, either because of customer preference or varying technical standards. In the case of Bundled Manufacturing, the postponement aim is to retain product commonality for as long as possible in the production process. Only at the last possible opportunity should the product be configured to meet the needs of a particular market. This approach is exactly that taken by Sony in its Welsh factory, where they make television sets for Europe. The company began

Table 15.1 Logistics strategies for global products in consumer markets

1. Global logistics strategy	Unicentric	Bundled Manufacturing	Deferred Assembly	Deferred Packaging
	Fully centralised production and distribution	Design product so that customisation can take place at latest possible stage of production process	Final configuration of product at theatre warehouse	Labelling and packing at theatre warehouse
2. Product variables				
Brand: Is it global?	Yes	Yes	Yes	Yes
Formulation: Is it common to all markets?	Yes	No	No	Yes
Peripherals (labels etc.): are they common to all markets?	Yes	Yes	No	No
3. Potential strategy benefits (In addition to the benefits of postponed commitment of production to particular customers or markets)	Economies of scale in production and distribution	Rationalisation of components range simplifies inbound logistics and contributes to improved quality	Economies of scale in production and distribution, savings in inventory with high levels of customer service	Economies of scale in production, savings in inventory with high levels of customer service
4. Examples	Marlboro duty free cigarettes	Sony television (countries have different colour systems, electrical standards)	Compaq computers (countries have different keyboard requirements, especially for language instruction manual symbols such as the umlaut and cedilla). Instruction manuals must also be in appropriate language	Wash & Go Shampoo (Note: economies of scale in the bottling process limit the extent to which deferred packaging can be applied for products of this kind)

production by making different product ranges for countries, according to the local broadcasting and technical standards. Each product range had a very different manufacturing specification. Sony succeeded in simplifying production through the introduction of a 'Eurochassis', which was a base design for all European television sets. Only at a late stage in the production process was the Eurochassis tailored specifically for, say, the French or German markets (Ferguson 1989). Key benefits, alongside not having to commit production to specific countries until a late stage, were the rationalisation of the range of components required for television manufacture, the simplification of inbound logistics planning and improved product quality.

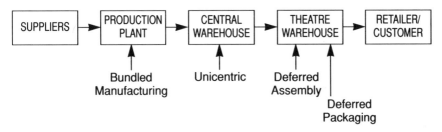

Figure 15.4 Postponement points in the supply chain

The Unicentric postponement option takes effect downstream from the manufacturing plant. Under this option global branding, together with common labels and peripherals, mean that the decision to allocate products to particular customers in world markets can be postponed until the product reaches a central warehouse; there is no need to earmark particular batches in production for given customers on account of their unique branding, formulation or packaging requirements.

Further downstream in the supply chain come the Deferred Assembly and Deferred Packaging options, both of which take place at theatre warehouses serving regions of the world or specific countries. Deferred Assembly means that it is the final configuration of the product itself which happens at theatre warehouses rather than at production plants.

The Caterpillar example, discussed earlier, shows the application of Deferred Assembly in an industrial market. A common application in consumer/business markets is for computers, as identified in Table 15.1, where different combinations of monitor, base unit and keyboard can be brought together at a late stage in the supply chain.

Lastly, Deferred Packaging can be a useful strategy when the brand and product formulation are common to all markets, but where packaging/labelling are country- or customer-specific. Again this is an operation that can take place at a theatre warehouse, close to several customers with different packaging/labelling requirements, so that production need only be committed to particular customers at an advanced stage in the supply chain.

It is, however, important to point out that the logistics strategies identified in Table 15.1 represent an *upper bound* to producers of global products. This is because not all products readily lend themselves to global logistics strategies and many activities will need to remain more localised. The following factors will favour some degree of localisation in logistics:

- products with a relatively low value;
- limited economies of scale in production;
- need to produce in local markets as a result of political considerations;
- uneven development of global markets, with some regions taking much more product than others.

None the less the four strategy options (Bundled Manufacturing, Unicentric, Deferred Assembly and Deferred Packaging) do represent distinct and realistic opportunities for companies, as the examples cited in Table 15.1 testify.

Moreover, this approach of defining strategic logistics options based on combinations of secondary product characteristics gives an opportunity to compare and contrast the results with Zinn and Bowersox (1988). In their key work in the area of postponement, they identify five different postponement types (labelling, packaging, assembly, manufacturing and time), rather than the four which arise from making all possible combinations of secondary product characteristics (see Table 15.1).

In broad terms, assembly and manufacturing postponement differ mainly in the degree of warehouse assembly which occurs; they therefore relate closely to the Deferred Assembly option as defined above. Similarly, the labelling and packaging postponement types are strongly linked and correspond to Deferred Packaging. The fifth of Zinn and Bowersox's postponement types (namely, time postponement) mean that 'products are shipped to customers only following order receipt, resulting in centralised inventories'. This compares with distribution in anticipation of orders', where products are shipped to warehouses on the basis of forecasts. Clearly, this postponement and the Unicentric option identified in this paper are strongly related.

This leaves one option in postponement strategy (Bundled Manufacturing) which has no obvious equivalent in the Zinn and Bowersox paper; each of their postponement types apply downstream of the production plant. It would seem, from the experience of companies such as Sony, that Bundled Manufacturing, resulting in the redesign of products and the consequent rationalisation of components required in manufacture, can contribute to significantly reduced costs. Yet the bigger prize will often be a valuable improvement in product quality as logistics complexity is reduced on the inbound side of manufacturing. At a time when Total Quality Management is paramount in the thinking of management at all levels, superior logistics performance through Bundled Manufacturing must be an attractive postponement option for those companies who sell complex, but non-standardised, products to different markets.

COMPANY STRATEGY IN GLOBAL LOGISTICS

The discussion so far as focused on the characteristics of finished products and their market place. Clearly, several key characteristics (namely, value density, product price as a driver in the market place, and the commonality of branding, formulation and peripherals) are closely linked to the formulation of logistics strategy for finished products from the point of manufacture, to the point of final consumption.

However, it is important also to consider logistics upstream of production to gain a complete picture of the logistics options for companies operating at a global level. For example, the sourcing of raw materials or components represents a major consideration when decisions are made on developing new markets or relocating production. The formulation of global logistics strategy must therefore take full account of production processes as well as product-market characteristics.

At this point, it is important to recognise that some companies will have not just one logistics strategy, but several. This is most often the case where business units of the same company manage product groups with varying logistics needs. Yet there are some companies which are less differentiated than others with respect to logistics strategy. As a result, it is possible to give them some overall classification according to their global logistics strategy.

Analysis of the strategic development of a variety of global companies suggests that there are five distinct clusters, one of which can be unsustainable beyond the short term. These are summarised in Figure 15.5, which also indicates the global logistics requirements of companies. The unsustainable logistics cluster is evident for companies which can be called *invaders*. Classic examples of invaders in the recent past are Japanese companies such as Sony and Nissan. They established plants to serve local markets in the 1970s (Sony) and 1980s (Nissan) mainly on an assembly basis, using components sourced from Japan. However, with the diminishing political acceptability of 'screwdriver' operations (which often competed (which often competed with local industry), the invaders began to seek local suppliers. (See Poynter 1985 for a full discussion of the role of government intervention and the responses of multinationals.)

In many respects Sony now acts as a *settler* rather than an invader; for example, CD players are sourced from a variety of countries and the finished product is sold in many countries. So, for example, Sony now operates in Europe much as an indigenous company would do. Its logistics requirements have changed accordingly. Several car companies from Japan, such as Nissan, Toyota and Honda, have followed the same pattern.

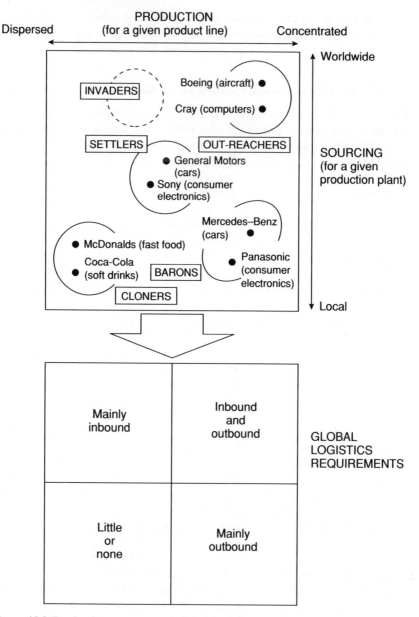

Figure 15.5 Production process and global logistics requirements

Yet it is always important to bear in mind the extent to which inbound logistics will be constrained by primary product characteristics. While high-value components may be sourced over long distances, it will usually make more sense to locate suppliers of relatively low-value and bulky components, such as plastic mouldings, seats and seat covers, close to the assembly plant. Indeed, components such as plastic mouldings, seats and seat covers close to the assembly plant. Indeed, such a pattern of supply can be observed around the new Nissan plant at Sunderland, in the north of England (Hudson and Sadler 1992).[1]

Cloners are companies which, because of sourcing and production needs, have limited logistics requirements on a global scale. Coca-Cola, for example, sources most of its inputs for soft drinks on a local basis (e.g. cans, water). Generally only the concentrate will be imported. Likewise, distribution of the finished product will be localised. Most logistics requirements for the cloners are therefore highly localised, with the operation in any one location bearing strong similarities to operations elsewhere in the world.

Some companies tend to concentrate their operations and sourcing, despite selling in global markets. These *barons*, which include Mercedes-Benz, seem to feel happier when manufacturing operations are close to home, although there are signs that Mercedes-Benz will soon be manufacturing outside Germany, not least because of high labour costs which are hampering competitiveness. Another German car company, BMW, is in a similar position and its plans to manufacture in North Carolina, USA, are well advanced.

Lastly, there are the *outreachers*: global companies which manufacture in perhaps just one location (e.g. Cray computers in Minneapolis, USA), but which source from around the world. Companies of this kind, which sell in global markets, therefore have extensive inbound and outbound logistics requirements.

It follows from the above discussion that global companies often need to pursue very different logistics strategies from one another, depending upon a variety of factors relating both to procurement and production processes. In turn, this has a major impact upon how they should approach the management of their logistics systems. The following section considers the key issues that arise.

MANAGING GLOBAL LOGISTICS SYSTEMS

There is no doubt that the successful management of all kinds of global logistics systems depends, in turn, on the successful management of information. Crucially, in the context of global logistics, the 'expansion of the information network makes possible a degree of control which could not be envisioned only a short time ago' (Schary and Coakley 1991). Networking, together with electronic data interchange (EDI), frequently represents the foundations upon which global operations are built (Runyan 1989).

Just as global companies vary in their logistics requirements, information needs are also different, not just between companies but very frequently within them as well. Reck (1989) identifies many companies having to operate in 'mixed mode' when managing information systems (IS). Financial systems may require an 'imperialistic' approach, in which a system is effectively imposed on all business units, whereas sales and marketing may be better advised to adopt a 'multidomestic' approach to reflect the national focus of operations. Yet, as Cooper and Browne (1992) point out, global companies often need to integrate their own information systems with those of global customers, a point emphasised by Morris (1991) when outlining the global strategy of Univar, the chemicals company.

Clearly IS management represents a critical success factor for all kinds of global company and one which is increasing in importance. There are, however, three other critical success factors which are strongly linked to the cluster classification of global logistics strategies summarised in Figure 15.5. These are:

- diffusion of best practice, which principally applies to cloners;
- partnershipping, particularly with logistics service providers, which is critical to the success of many outreachers;
- flexibility in switching between different global logistics systems especially those of invaders, settlers and barons (see Figure 15.6).

Diffusion of best practice is a critical success factor for cloners because logistics operations, although localised, are extensively replicated around the world. It is therefore important for any logistics breakthrough in one

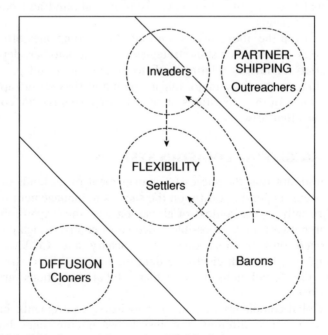

Figure 15.6 Critical success factors in global logistics

location to be recognised and then adopted by all the operational centres.

Generally, it will be insufficient to expect best practice in one location to be leveraged effectively and rapidly by management in other locations without some intervention by head office. In effect, there has to be a 'change management' team which acts as a catalyst for spreading best practice through the organisation.

This process is not, however, without its dangers. One of the greatest is to think in terms of 'transferring' rather than 'translating' best practice between operational centres. Transferring has connotations of taking a logistical innovation and implementing it without modification somewhere else. Costly failure can be the result since theatres of operation may only be slightly different, but these differences may be crucial to local success. It follows that translation of ideas between different theatres should be the preferred approach since this implies taking account of local conditions when bringing in best practice.

Outreachers, by their very nature, have a heavy reliance on both inbound and outbound logistics. Moreover, because production often relies on a highly skilled and specialised workforce, the scope for relocating manufacturing facilities may be limited. A production site will therefore be considered as having a fixed location for at least the medium term.

These factor point to relatively stable networks for inbound and outbound logistics, focused on the production centre. Yet, because of the extensive reach of the networks, it is most unlikely that outreachers will want to undertake many of the operations themselves. Invariably they find it preferable to outsource their global logistics services.

Service quality will be a crucial consideration. For example, on-time deliveries for inbound logistics will be one of the highest operational priorities because production delays will be extremely expensive in the making of high value products, which is typical of outreachers. Every step must therefore be taken to ensure a first-class logistics service. A key consideration will often be the development of a partnership in logistics which is predicated upon a relationship rather than a series of single transactions (Bowersox 1990) between the outreacher and the provider of global logistics services. A consequence of this must be for outreachers to form relationships on a more restricted basis than before. In effect, outreachers must work with fewer carriers (say) and in a more involved way (Copacino and Britt 1991). Managers of outreach companies need new skills in forgeing such essential relationships; amongst other things, they must reach new high standards in the art of negotiating and be capable of recognising and developing win–win opportunities. In addition, as noted by Rinehart (1992), a high degree of commitment to the formation of relationships is a vital factor in the successful negotiation of partnerships in logistics.

Fortunately for outreachers seeking partnerships, recent years have seen the genesis of freight mega-carriers on a global scale (Sparks and Mathe

1991; Browne 1992), whose growth will depend both upon information systems and scale of operation acting as a barrier to entry. But, at the same time, it would be wrong to suggest that the future prospects for forgeing effective relationships between outreachers and these larger carriers is straightforward. For example, many companies (including outreachers) would like to see their logistics partners almost as extensions to their businesses. This may seem an attainable goal when few significant relationships have been developed. But as Bowersox (1990) acutely observes: 'cultural absorption admittedly gets tricky when a service provider is simultaneously engaged in multiple alliances'.

Flexibility in switching between global logistics systems is arguably the most interesting of the critical success factors in global logistics. This factor applies principally to companies which fall into the classification of invaders, settlers or barons (see Figures 15.5 and 15.6). A key point about these global companies is their propensity to switch between classification, notably from invader to settler or from baron to settler. This is an entirely different set of circumstances from either the cloners or the outreachers and demands a special critical success factor, namely the ability to switch smoothly from one global logistics classification to another – in other words, flexibility.

So far, the ultimate requirement has been for companies to join the settler classification, for reasons ranging from political pressures to high operating costs (see p. 229). Yet the settler classification may soon require a great deal of flexibility by companies operating *within* it. Up until now, the emphasis in many manufacturing operations has been the achievement of economies of scale which has tended to emphasise the management of ever-lengthening supply lines (Fawcett and Birou 1992). Yet the increasing need to revamp international distribution channels (Anderson 1985) may in future be driven by flexible manufacturing rather than economies of scale. To date, the quest for economies of scale has introduced an element of inflexibility into global logistics systems (Braithwaite and Christopher 1991). But the literature increasingly speaks of new technologies which can overturn these prevailing economies of production (*Economist* 1986; Fife 1991; Goldhar and Lei 1991). Developments such a numerically controlled (NC) manufacturing, computer-integrated manufacturing (CIM), flexible manufacturing systems (FMS) and cellular manufacturing systems promise much once their current costs can be reduced, as seems likely.

Already, Nissan has been able to develop a car model which is profitable on a production run of only 20,000 units (Hamel and Prahalad 1991); Japanese companies are well to the fore in achieving economic flexibility in manufacturing (De Mayer *et al.* 1991). Furthermore, *The Economist* (1986) foresees the disbursement of production towards smaller manufacturing units and the diminished importance of labour costs – an important consideration when global companies want to retreat from low-wage countries.

Flexible manufacturing as a reality, rather than as a prospect, will inevitably transform the logistics requirements of global companies, not least the settlers. In particular, future settlement would mean manufacturing taking place in more, rather than fewer, locations. (An early example of this trend is in newspapers, where new technology has promoted the decentralisation of printing processes.)

The wider development of flexible manufacturing certainly has its attractions. Shorter supply lines to market raise for more companies the possibility of making to order, rather than making to stock. Also in many cases there would be a reduced dependence upon transport, resulting in a number of environmental and pollution benefits.

New ways of manufacturing, rather than new technologies in transport or the penetration of new markets for products, may therefore be the next big challenge in global logistics. Unquestionably, companies that succeed best in facing this challenge will be those that have flexibility built into both their logistics systems and their management.

THE CHALLENGE OF ORGANISATION CHANGE

The globalisation of markets, together with intensifying competition, new methods of manufacturing and changing relationships with both suppliers and customers, represents a considerable challenge to logistics managers with global responsibilities. As this paper has attempted to illustrate, global logistics management is a complex, fast-changing environment in which to work, and demands ever more sophisticated strategies. But as Bartlett and Ghoshal (1990) have accurately observed, many companies are organisationally incapable of carrying out these strategies. The issue of how to reconfigure organisations to secure effective logistics management is now a growing preoccupation in many boardrooms.

At the heart of the issue is a change in what the new organisation configurations should be expected to deliver. Bartlett and Ghoshal (1990) summarise it as follows:

> The critical strategic requirement is not to devise the most ingenious and well coordinated plan but to build the most viable strategic process; the key organisational task is not to design the most elegant structure but to capture individual capabilities and motivate the entire organisation to respond cooperatively to a complicated and dynamic environment.

For logistics managers, *process* is a vitally important word in the reconfiguration of organisations. All too frequently, within traditional, functionally based organisations, responsibilities for logistics have remained fragmented. Reporting structures which are focused on major functional areas such as production and marketing, create divides between each area and limit the effectiveness of overall supply-chain management.

Increasingly, however, companies such as Hewlett-Packard have moved towards a process-oriented approach which helps to bridge these divides (Marr 1991). This approach puts the emphasis on processes such as financial and information control, new product development and order fulfilment (the latter essentially being a synonym for logistics, but with the virtue of suggesting a strong customer orientation in the logistics process). Crucially, important linkages *between* processes can foster changes in organisation to the benefit of logistics management. Schary and Coakley (1991), for example, point to ways in which the development of information technology is reshaping logistics organisation. In a similar vein, Rockart and Short (1989) agree that information technology provides a new approach to the long-standing management problem of effectively managing interdependence – by which they mean linkages between areas of functional, product and geographical responsibility.

In a growing number of companies, the need to manage interdependence is expressed in the development of networking. Central to the idea of networks is that they encourage managers to evaluate problems from the perspective of what is right both for the customer and the company, rather than from the often conflicting viewpoints of business functions or departments (Charan 1991). The importance of networking to logistics, where effective management greatly depends on the breakdown of sectional interests within the organisation, and where customer service is paramount, is clear here.

Yet it is essential to realise that many senior managers, long used to working within highly formalised organisational structures, are likely to find themselves culturally challenged by networking and will need help, understanding and time to adapt. Also there must be a recognition that new career paths will be needed for those just entering management.

In this respect, Unilever has successfully adopted a programme of short- and long-term overseas assignments for managers along with careful and systematic proselytisation of Unilever's strategic vision and organisational values (Bartlett and Ghoshal 1989) to contribute to effective networking on a global scale.

Increasingly, however, the cultural challenge has become wider in scope as management paradigms which are not rooted in Western culture are seen to bring successful results. In particular, it is important to consider the extent to which the adoption of Japanese management styles (albeit in some modified form) can make a significant contribution to competitive advantage in Western-based companies. For example, Berkowitz and Mohan (1987), in their study of the steel industry, noted that US steel companies were more highly integrated than their Japanese rivals. But they also found that 'the unique nature of Japan's procurement and logistical system created significant economies of scale by virtue of industry-wide cooperation and learning, and through buyer-supplier arrangements that offered all the benefits of vertical integration without its disadvantages'.

The need for organisational change is, of course, based upon much wider considerations than logistics alone. Much of the general management literature of the late 1980s focuses on organisational change as one of the major issues facing businesses of all kinds (see, for example, Bower 1986; Miles and Snow 1986; Drucker 1988; Kanter 1989), and many questions still have to be resolved.

New organisational forms are by no means easy to introduce, especially when they represent a radical departure from long-established paradigms. Yet, for global businesses in particular, the need for change can no longer be denied. As companies re-invent their own organisations, many of them – perhaps for the first time – have the important opportunity to redefine logistics management roles. For global companies, where logistics is highly complex and where management flexibility is often a key requirement, this opportunity is not one to be missed.

NOTE

1 Hudson and Sadler (1992) also point to a significant different in logistics system development, with respect to the USA and Western Europe, in the case of component supplies to the Japanese automotive industry. A key factor was the extent of outsourcing, which was generally in Western Europe (typically around 50–60 per cent) compared with Chrysler, Ford and General Motors operations in North America (averaging around 35–40 per cent). Thus 'whereas the Japanese vehicle assemblers openly encouraged parts suppliers to follow them into production in the USA, there was from the outset greater potential opportunity and incentive for Japanese vehicle builders ... to work with the existing West European automotive components base'.

REFERENCES

Anderson, D.L. (1985) 'International logistics strategies for the 1980s' in M. Christopher (ed.), *Strategies for International Logistics*, a monograph edition of the *International Journal of Physical Distribution and Materials Management*, 15(4).

Bartlett, C.A. and Ghoshal, S.J. (1989) *Managing Across Borders*, London: Century Business Press.

Bartlett, C.A. and Ghoshal S. (1990) 'Matrix management: not a structure, a frame of mind!', *Harvard Business Review*, July–August: 138–45.

Berkowitz, M. and Mohan, K. (1987) 'The role of global procurement in the value chain of Japanese steel', *Columbia Journal of World Business*, Winter: 97–110.

Bowes, J. (1986) *When Markets Quake: The Management Challenge of Restructuring Industry*, Boston, Mass.: HBS Press.

Bowersox, D. 91990) 'The strategic benefits of logistics alliances', *Harvard Business Review*, July/August: 36–42.

Braithwaite, A. and Christopher, M. (1991) 'Managing the global pipeline', *International Journal of Logistics Management*, 2(2): 55–62.

Browne, M. (1992) 'Freight mega-carriers in the 1990s: the strategic importance of information technology in the race for global scale', *International Information Systems*, April 1(2): 59–76.

238   *International distribution*

Charan, R. (1991) 'How organisations reshape organisations – for results', *Harvard Business Review*, September–October: 104–15.

Cooper, J. and Browne, M. (1992) 'Logistics strategies for global industries: the consequences for transport and information technology", paper presented to the 6th World Conference on Transport Research, Lyon, June/July.

Cooper, J., Browne, M. and Peters, M. (1991) *European Logistics: Markets Management and Strategy*, Oxford: Blackwell Publishers.

Copacino, W.C. and Britt, F.F. (1991) 'Perspectives on global logistics', *International Journal of Logistics Management*, 2(1): 35–41.

Council of Logistics Management (1993) *Reconfiguring European Logistics*, Oak Brook, Ill.: Andersen Consulting and Cranfield School of Management.

De Meyer, A., Nakane, J., Miller J.G. and Ferdows, K. (1989) 'Flexibility: the next competitive battle. The manufacturing futures survey', *Strategic Management Journal*, 10(2): 135–44.

Dicken, P. (1986) *Global Shift: Industrial Change in a Turbulent World*, London: Harper & Row.

Douglas, S. and Wind, Y. (1987) 'The myth of globalisation', *Columbia Journal of World Business*, 31(4): 18–29.

Drucker, P.F. (1988) 'The coming of the new organisation', *Harvard Business Review*, 66(1): 45–53.

Dullforce, W. (1991), 'The final showdown', *The Financial Times*, 1 November.

The Economist(1986) 'Beyond robots', 5 July: 57.

Fawcett, S.E. and Birou, L.M. (1992) 'Explaining the interface between global and JIT sourcing' *International Journal of Physical Distribution and Materials Management*, 22(1): 3–14.

Ferguson, A. (1989) 'Britain's best factories', *Management Today*, November: 69–96.

Fife, W.J. (1991) 'Why flexible manufacturing systems are here to stay', *AACE Transactions* F4(1)–F4(4).

Goldhar, J.D. and Lei, D. (1991) 'The shape of twenty-first century global manufacturing', *Journal of Business Strategy*, March/April: 37–42.

Hudson, R. and Sadler, D. (1992) 'Just-in-time production and the European automotive components industry', *International Journal of Physical Distribution and Logistics Management*, 22(2).

Jain, S. (1989) 'Standardisation of international marketing strategies: some research hypotheses', *Journal of Marketing*, 53, January: 70–9.

Julius, D.-A. (1990) *Global Companies and Public Policy*, London: Royal Institute of International Affairs.

Kanter, R.M. (1989) *When Giants Learn to Dance*, New York: Simon & Schuster.

Kotler, P. (1985) 'Global standardisation – courting danger', Panel Discussion, 23rd American Marketing Association Conference, Washington, D.C.

Lee, W.J. (1986) 'Global economies of scale: the case for a world manufacturing strategy', *Industrial Management*, 10(9), October, 28–32.

Levitt, T. (1983) 'The globalisation of markets', *Harvard Business Review*, May–June: 92–102.

Marr, C.J. (1991) 'How to achieve global logistics coordination', *Competitive Global Logistics Symposium*, Cambridge, 7–10 April.

Miles, R.E. and Snow, C.C. (1986) 'Organisations: a new concept for new forms', *Californian Management Review*, 28(3): 62–73.

Morris, G.D.L. (1991) 'Univar: poised for global reach', *Chemical Week*, 148(13): 26–7.

Ohmae, K. (1985) *Triad Power – The Coming Shape of Global Competition*, New York: The Free Press.

Piore, M. (1987) 'Corporate reform in American manufacturing and the challenge to economic theory', Working Paper, Sloan School of Management, Massachusetts Institute of Technology.

Porter, M. (1986) *Competition in Global Industries*, Cambridge, Mass.: Harvard Business School Press.

Poynter, T.A. (1985) *International Enterprises and Government Intervention*, London: Croom Helm.

Raffée, H. and Kreutzer, R.T. (1989) 'Organisational dimensions of global marketing', *European Journal of Marketing*, 23(5): 43–57.

Reck, R.H. (1989) 'The shock of going global', *Datamation*, 1 August: 67–8.

Rinehart, L.M. (1992) 'Global logistics partnership negotiation', *International Journal of Physical Distribution and Logistics Management*, 22(1): 27–34.

Rockart, J.F. and Short, J.E. (1989) 'IT in the 1990s: managing organizational interdependence', *Sloan Management Review*, Winter: 7–17.

Rosenthal, T.M. (1989) 'McDonnell Douglas in China', *Global Trade*, February, 109(2): 22–4.

Runyan, L. (1989) 'Global IS strategies', *Datamation*, 1 December: 71–8.

Schary, P.B. and Coakley, J. (1991) 'Logistics organisation and the information system', *International Journal of Logistics Management*, 2(2): 22–9.

Segal-Horn, S. and Davidson, H. (1992) 'Global markets: the global consumer and international retailing', *Journal of Global Marketing*, 5(3): 31–61.

Sparks, D. and Mathe, H. (1991) 'Survival of the quickest: the challenge of the international express market in Europe', in Hervé Mathe (ed.) *Managing Services Across Borders* volume 8 in 'Research in Operations and Service Management' series, Eurolog Press.

Zinn, W. and Bowersox, D.J. (1988) 'Planning physical distribution with the principle of postponement', *Journal of Business Logistics*, 9(2): 117–35.

Zinn, W. and Grosse, R.E. (1990) 'Barriers to globalisation: is global distribution possible?', *International Journal of Logistics Management*, 1(1): 13–18.

16 A retail entry model for the operational control decisions of international retailers

Therese A. Maskulka and G. Scott Erickson

INTRODUCTION

The growing internationalization of their industry has prodded more and more retailers into making cross-border expansions. The form of these expansions (entry method) *and* the locus of control for the resulting operations should be a critical part of the fundamental strategic decisions made by these firms. Traditional globalization and entry theory tend to view these decisions as one. In this paper, the authors seek to isolate the control decision from the entry decision and develop a Retail Entry Model which can aid retailers in making such a decision.

As a means of providing an initial evaluation of the suitability of the model, we then make qualitative assessments of the control decisions made by a number of high-profile European retailers expanding into the United States during the past decade. Based on information contained in trade publications, we evaluate the circumstances facing each retailer, predict the control decision the model would recommend, and compare it to the actual control decision of the firm. Some subjective appraisals about the strategic fit of the decisions are also advanced.

ENTRY MODELS AND RETAILING

The Retail Entry Model (REM) flows from two distinct trains of thought in the literature: entry strategy and globalization. From Root's (1982) categorization to Dunning's (1981) eclectic theory, the form and reasoning behind entry decisions have fascinated internationalists. Pellegrini (1991) recently used Dunning's model in attempting to explain Direct Foreign Investment (DFI) decisions by retailers while focusing on some of the unique characteristics of international retail expansions (the physical presence required by traditional stores, for example).

We chose to apply this framework, specifically the structure suggested by Hill, *et al.* (1990), not to entry decisions but to control decisions. In traditional entry theory, the two decisions are generally treated as one. The firm will choose the high-investment DFI strategy if it seeks high control, the low-investment export strategy if is seeks low control. In retailing the relationship between the two decisions is not nearly so well-defined. Merger and acquisition (M&A) activity has yielded low-control strategies (Ito Yokado, Grand Metropolitan, and KBB have done little to influence the day-to-day operational decisions of 7–11, Pearle Optical, and FAO Schwartz, respectively) while licensing sometimes sees rigorous operational guidance (McDonald's franchisees).

As a result, REM applies the eclectic structure not to the relatively similar entry strategies found in retailing but to the control strategies. Control decisions have been a topic of interest since Levitt's (1983) globalization work. Applied to retailing by Salmon and Tordjman (1989) and Treadgold (1990–1), the global vs. multinational debate has always implicitly assumed a certain maturation of the firm. The experienced, seasoned retailer, for example, would be far more likely to use a consistent, global approach in all markets. The inexperienced, cautious retailer would tend to a diverse, multinational strategy. Quelch and Hoff (1986) questioned whether global marketing was appropriate for all firms: we follow their lead by questioning whether global control of the operation is the end goal for all international retailers. Indeed, we believe the control decision to be a strategic one which can be guided by the following model.

A RETAIL ENTRY MODEL

Figure 16.1 summarizes the relationship between Dunning's labels, the specific variables used by HHK and Pellegrini, and the key questions we have used within REM which we believe cut to the core of the retail control location decision. Strategic variables refer to those ownership-specific items of eclectic models suggesting the attractiveness of international expansion. Scale economies, world-wide concentration of the industry, or specific global strategic objectives are traditionally thought to encourage a firm to favor DFI and global control.

In retailing, the strategic variables will focus on where the competitive advantage of the retailer is found. A singular distribution system (Benetton), unique selling format (IKEA), or other part of the marketing mix benefiting from economies of scale or duplication in multiple markets will demand a great deal of home market control. If the firm's competitive advantage lies in some other area, perhaps a talent for recognizing potential in retailing ideas and funding such ventures (Vendex' backing of Dillard's and Barnes & Noble) or skill in adapting to local conditions (Ahold's various supermarket holdings), some control of the retailing operation may be better left within the host country. As pictured in Figure 16.2, the decision between global or multinational control (or a transnational mixture) will flow from this recognition of the source of competitive advantage.

Ownership-specific advantages	**Strategic variables**		Competitive advantage open to standardization, or based more on flexibility and adaptation?
	HHK:	Scale economies Global concentration Global strategic objectives	
	Pellegrini:	Organizational advantage Unicity of products Scale economies	
Location-specific advantages	**Environmental variables**		Will offering appeal to this market?
	HHK:	Political risk Cultural considerations Extent of demand Ferocity of competiition	Is market sizable?
	Pellegrini:	Cultural proximity Market size Competitors' moves	How established is competition?
Internation-alization advantages	**Transaction-specific (know-how) variables**		Competitive know-how from home or host?
	HHK:	Dissemination risk of firm-specific knowledge and know-how	How can it best be protected?
	Pellegrini:	Appropriability of market failure which gives competitive advantage	

Figure 16.1 Derivation of a retail entry model

Environmental or location-specific variables were originally thought to contribute to the decision of where to locate. Political risk, cultural differences, extent of demand, and ferocity of competition clearly make some markets more attractive than others, and are now also recognized as determinants of how to enter a market. When included in REM, they can be used to gauge the source of control as well. From this perspective, the appeal of the retailing concept to the target market, the size of the target market, and the intensity of competition all serve to inform the retailer whether to use global, home-market control or multinational, host-market control. The more likely the appeal of the foreign package to a sizable domestic market, the more likely the firm will be to adopt the global strategy. If substantial tinkering is necessary to make the offering palatable to local markets, the low-control strategy is more appropriate. Political risk may also arise, but since we are dealing only with entry into the US in our coming discussion, that topic is best postponed.

Finally, transaction-specific or internalization variables focus on the source of the firm's competitive advantage and whether it can be protected (or internalized) by the firm. The better a firm can protect its

Strategic variables
Competitive advantage
Standardization (G)
vs.
Flexibility (M)
Environmental variables
Market attractiveness:
Cultural similarity (G)
(accept offering)
vs.
Cultural dissimilarity (M)
Market sizable (G)
vs.
Market limited (M)
Untapped by competition (G)
vs.
Aggressively defended (M)
Know-How variables
Know-how source:
Home firm (G)
vs.
Host firm (M)
Protectability
(reinforces above)
Decision
Home control (GG
Mix (G/M)
Host control (MM)

Figure 16.2 A retail entry model

technologies or business know-how from competitors, the more inclined it will be to share the ideas with partners rather than take entry upon itself in all markets. Hence, in the REM, the direction of know-how flow and the difficulty of protecting it determine the source of control. A successful retailer must have unique operating ideas in order to gain and hold its position. An IKEA or Benetton, for example, undoubtedly pass on specific techniques to their stores worldwide. In such a situation, the know-how flow is unambiguously from home to host location.

A number of European retailers, however, have purchased pieces of US retailers in recent years with the explicit aim of acquiring some successful manner of doing business (Maskulka *et al.* 1991). By transferring this know-how from subsidiary back to the European parent, such firms clearly reverse the flow, going from host to home entity. To illustrate, Grand Metropolitan purchased Burger King with the express purpose of converting European restaurants to the Burger King format (Murrow 1989). The source of the know-how signals the preferred source of operational control.

Protecting know-how in retailing is extremely difficult, given the transparent operational techniques. In these models, the harder it may be to guard proprietary knowledge, the higher the degree of control generally required. In the context of this model, however, the control may lie with either the home or the host location, depending on the source of the know-how. The more difficult it may be to internalize this know-how, the more control should fall to the source of the know-how. Hence, the degree of difficulty in maintaining command over the proprietary idea will reinforce the decision made concerning the source of the knowledge. Hard-to-contain host know-how will demand even more host control, as hard-to-contain home know-how will demand even more home control.

Reviewing these variables should provide a retailer with cross-border aspirations with a structured way of analyzing operational control decisions. The nature of the firm's competitive advantage, the likelihood of achieving the necessary market share, and the source of operational know-how should influence the choice of control location: home (global approach), host (local or multinational), or mixed (transnational).

AN APPLICATION

As an initial application of this model, the authors selected a sample of European retailers who have made moves into the US retailing market during the past decade. We collected a comprehensive file of trade literature on these retailers, reviewing publications such as *Ad Age*, *Business Week*, *Forbes*, *Fortune*, *The Economist*, *Chain Store Age Executive*, *Stores*, and the *Wall Street Journal* from 1989–92, supplementing as necessary from earlier dates. Electronic data bases were also used, and a number of reports by investment firms were consequently included. We have also subsequently reviewed these firms, updating the information where appropriate.

Based on this secondary data, we were able to determine the control location used at entry by these retailers as well as enough background information to apply the REM to see if its recommendation agreed with the actual entry/control strategy. This process was highly subjective and so is meant only as an illustrative application. Future research should focus on more quantitative uses and evaluations of this model.

The results are, however, illuminating. After grouping the retailers by breadth of product offerings, we organized the results into the tables seen in Figures 16.3, 16.4, and 16.5. Home country retailers are listed first, with host country affiliates (if named differently) included directly underneath and indented.

Host control	Mix	Home control

Ahold
  Bilo
  Giant
  First National
  Tops
	Marks & Spencer
	  Kings
	
	Grand Metropolitan
	  Burger King	

Tengelmann
A&P
	Allied Lyons
	  Dunkin' Donuts
	  Mr Donut	

Delhaize le Lion
  Food Lion
	Marks & Spencer
	  D'Aillard's
		MARKS & SPENCER
		  D'AILLARD'S

Sainsbury Shaw's	Carrefour	CARREFOUR
Promodes Red Food	Auchan	AUCHAN

Docks de France
  Jiffy Food
  Lil' Champ
	Euromarche
	  Biggs
		EUROMARCHE
		  BIGGS

Figure 16.3 Mass retailers

Note: Control locus recommended by REM is represented by normal type; actual controls locus, when different, is represented in capitals.

Host control	Mix	Home control
Vendex Dillard's	Conran's	SuperClub
	GiB	Ikea

Bergner's
  Carson Pirie
  Scott
	Scotty's
	  Central Hardware
	  Handy Andy	

	Dixon's Silo	

	Otto Versand
	  Spiegel
	  Honeybee
	  Eddie Bauer	

	Printemps	PRINTEMPS

Figure 16.4 Specialized retailers

Host control	Mix	Home control

KBB
  FAO Schwartz
	Marks & Spencer
	  Brooks Brothers
		Benetton

Grand Metropolitan Pearle Vision	Laura Ashley	The Body Shop

Vendex
  Barnes & Noble
  (B. Dalton)
	Ratner's
	Kay Jewelers (?)
	
	Majestic
	  Liquor Barn
		MAJESTIC
		  LIQUOR BARN

W.H. Smith Wee Three Wall to Wall		
GUCCI	Gucci	

Figure 16.5 Targeted retailers

The horizontal categories follow the home control (global), mix (transnational), and host control (multinational) distinctions discussed earlier. The more the home country controls retailing operations, the more global the approach. The more the host country controls retailing operations, the more multinational the approach. Transnational strategies involve some mix of control.

The categories which separate the figures parallel Pellegrini's groupings of mass retailers (Figure 16.3), specialized retailers (Figure 16.4), and targeted retailers (Figure 16.5), though we define the categories a bit differently. Pellegrini's mass retailers tend to have broad product lines and appeal to most consumers – supermarkets and hypermarkets, for example. We also included restaurants within this category, more for the broad range of consumers attracted than for product lines.

Pellegrini's specialized retailers have fairly broad product lines but limit themselves to particular categories such as furniture and electronics. Again, we differ a bit by including some retailers with broad appeal who in some way limit their anticipated target consumer. Department stores, for example, seemed to better fit this category because those included here seek a more specialized clientele than mass retailers such as Wal-Mart or Ames.

Pellegrini's targeted retailers have narrow product lines and appeal to specific consumer groups. These are the niche players, generally having smaller stores and limited target consumers. We follow this definition.

Each figure illustrates both actual control locations and those recommended by the REM. In most cases, the actual and the recommended are the same. In those situations in which they disagree, we have highlighted the actual control decision by printing the company's name in capital letters. The corresponding recommended locus of control is printed normally.

A discussion of our use of the REM to make these designations follows, with particular attention paid to those firms which we feel may have made an incorrect strategic decision. As a result of this analysis, our intention is to draw some qualitative conclusions about the usefulness of the REM in planning and evaluating entry/control decisions.

DISCUSSION

Mass retailers

The mass retailers can be divided into three general business groups: the supermarkets, the hypermarkets, and the restaurants. The supermarkets have invariably followed a merger/acquisition entry method with a strong host control strategy, with the glaring exception of Marks & Spencer's initial foray onto the North American continent through its D'Aillard's venture.

Such strategies appear to make good sense for this business group. The strategic variables of the REM suggest a strong case for localization. The US industry has a number of regionally strong competitors, but no national concentration of players because of the need for local appeal. An important part of the grocery business is offering the product lines desired by the community, and although standardization of distribution and advertising benefits competitors, it seems that after a certain critical size is reached, the benefits of standardization are generally fully accrued and difficult to extend further. Strategic variables argue for strong local control.

Environmental variables tell a similar, though not as emphatic, a tale. The market is massive, but competition is also intense, so market share is hard to gain. A supermarket's competitive advantage is more likely to come from some local characteristic rather than a 'new' idea from outside the region which has no local attraction. As a result, it is unlikely that an entrant will offer something innovative which appeals to the local culture. Unless something truly revolutionary occurs in the grocery industry, the prudent strategy is again to steer the US units toward a more cautious local control strategy.

Know-how variables mirror these conclusions. Operating ideas which have made these US firms successes appear to come more often from host than from home sources and are extremely difficult to keep within the firm. A&P and Food Lion, for example, are portrayed in the trade press as being much more dependent on current CEOs Woods and Smith for their strength in the 1980s than from anything done by Tengelmann or Delhaize (Saporito 1990, Sheeline 1988)). Indeed, Tengelmann still sends

EU managers to the US to train in A&P subsidiaries and Delhaize has little more than a financial presence in Food Lion. Ahold, Docks de France, Promodes and Sainsbury appear to take similarly low-key roles in their subsidiaries.

The major exception to this pattern is found in Marks & Spencer's acquisitions, D'Aillard's and King's, especially the former. The highly successful UK retailer bought several Canadian/Western New York stores in the mid-1970s and attempted to convert them to its specific format. These units (D'Aillard's in the US) lost money in 10 of their first 14 years in operation and early 1990s' earnings predictions were similarly poor though finally looking up (*The Economist* 1993). The M&S trademark, close ties with suppliers, private labeling, and freshly prepared foods were found to be difficult to transfer to the North American market. The experience 'convinced executives that simply exporting their British formula to the US wouldn't work' (Maremont 1988). Further, '[a] team of executives evaluated the situation and concluded that the Canadian approach of copying the British formula had been a mistake' (Weiner 1989).

As a result, the newer King's venture has included some M&S guidance, but 'initial plans call for using 16-unit King's as a kind of test market to learn the tastes of US consumers' (Freedman and Marcom 1988). One could speculate that unless the firm finds that M&S has something to offer which differentiates King's from the competition, it should leave the formula alone. If it finds that it can add to King's appeal, perhaps through its expertise in setting up supplier systems and constructing strong relations within them, it should use the more transnational, mix approach.

In short, M&S' initial attempts at expansion onto the North American continent via a home control strategy have been termed failures. The more recent expansion has so far included a mixture of home and host operating ideas which should prove more successful.

The experiences of the hypermarkets (Carrefour, Auchan, Biggs) have been similar. Hypermarkets are designed to appeal to grocery buyers while incorporating the lines found in discount retailers. This combination can then provide single-stop shopping within one huge store. As a result, the strategic variables indicated an idea unique (at the time) to US retailing which would benefit from standardization, i.e., home control. The environmental variables, however, were very much the same as those facing grocers, though national discounters, such as Wal-Mart and K-Mart, are found in the US and pose significant additional competition. The environmental variables would argue for a more local approach.

The operational uniqueness of hypermarkets is found in their sheer size and convenience, and they were a new addition to the US markets in which they initially appeared. Their competitive advantages flowed from the EU parents, further evidence for a home-control strategy. Clearly, they needed some home control, given their innovative concepts. On the other hand, other factors suggested that for mass retailers in the US, some form of host control of operations was also necessary, given the maturity of the huge market and the intensity of the competition. Hence, a mix strategy seems to have been appropriate.

The initial entries, however, were made with established operational systems and essentially no real concern for local market characteristics, a home control strategy (*Chain Store Age Executive* 1988). Each hypermarket subsequently discovered that its operational system was not sufficiently unique or appealing to draw customers unless its units made some concessions to host preferences. As the partners loosened their structure and allowed the individual units to compete as local market conditions dictated (more advertising, different products emphasized, etc.), these units began to experience more success.

After some revision and consolidation (including the purchase of Biggs), Carrefour at least is now seeing better results. Its decade-long strong returns through its financial stake in the more locally oriented Costco reinforce the notion that a more localized initial US strategy might have engendered more immediate positive returns.

Finally, the restaurants seem to have a different orientation. The US market is similarly fragmented, saturated and competitively daunting, but the two major acquisitions (Burger King and Mister Donut/Dunkin' Donuts) have both been moderately successful. From the standpoint of the environmental variables noted for the other mass retailers, some localization is obviously necessary. Further, Grand Met purchased Burger King specifically to expand the operational system back to the EU, so the know-how flow is seemingly host to home, again suggesting a great deal of local control.

The success of a large restaurant chain, however, is invariably found in its ability to deliver consistency throughout different markets. Whatever its competitive advantage, the restaurant must deliver it as expected to customers, regardless of where they consume. As such, the financial and managerial strength and consistency added to these chains by Grand Met and Allied Lyons should not be underestimated. Indeed, one of the initial successes of Grand Met's Burger King strategy was getting all the franchisees back in line with some confidence in corporate management. From a strategic variables perspective, some home control is clearly recommended. As a result, the mix choice, embodying some home and some host control, appears appropriate.

Specialized retailers

The specialized retailers face a number of the same variables as the mass retailers. Generally, however, they are even more fragmented and more regionalized, suggesting some local control for most; but because specialty markets are not necessarily as developed, opportunities may be available to fill new niches if a retailing idea is unique enough. Hence, distinctive home know-how may be applicable to a particularly attractive segment lacking overwhelming competition. All in all, we should expect more opportunities for entry with home control in this segment, given the right set of circumstances.

The department store ventures in the US by European retailers have been a mixed bag. Dillard's, of which Vendex has owned up to 51 per cent, is an often-cited retailing success story, while Bergner's is in Chapter 11 and Printemps closed up 17 months after opening.

The department-store industry control decision would appear to boil down to the location of the competitive advantage of the retailing concept. In terms of the strategic variables, the industry is increasingly concentrated, but is still largely fragmented, even within the US. As a result, the competitive advantage often flows from ability to customize to local tastes. On the other hand, Dillard's is renowned for turning around new acquisitions by employing their proven operational methods. So some standardization is possible; the question is the source of that standardization and its degree.

Environmental variables show a huge market, extremely strong and entrenched local competition, and often pronounced cultural differences in what is expected from a department store. A hard nut to crack, calling for some local input. Know-how variables seem to be the determining factor, recognizing the source of the competitive advantage. Dillard's know-how is unambiguously from host to home, with Vendex contributing little but capital and actually transferring Dillard's POS control systems back to its own operating units in Europe. Given a competitive advantage embodied in flexibility, a tough market, and host-centered know-how, the recommended strategy is clearly host (local) control.

Bergner's situation is similar. The Swiss group purchased the well-known Chicago retailer Carson Pirie Scott, but contributed a mountain of debt rather than capital. Bergner's problems appear to be more of a finance crisis than a strategic mistake. Given the local status of the store and the inability of Bergner's to contribute in any way except financially (and even then negatively), the host-control strategy was probably appropriate; it just didn't work out.

Printemps also had some problems with a financier, being tied to a development in Colorado backed by one of the spectacular failures of the S&L crisis. However, the store's quick closing reflects a more basic failure in transferring the French retailer's name and operating techniques to Denver without concessions to local tastes, including such commonsense items as location. In this industry, it appears that even though the know-how flow is clearly from home to host, the cultural question is important enough to demand some mix of home/host control for success. The REM would suggest a mix approach for a venture such as Printemps. (Interestingly, the similarly upscale Galeries Lafayette appears to be having similar problems with a home control approach in New York City, where it recently underwent a major management shakeup.)

The non-department stores within this group are all dedicated to particular fields: Conran's and IKEA to home furnishings, Dixon's to home electronics and appliances, GIB to hardware, SuperClub to audio/video software, and Otto Versand to mail order. Each is particularly dependent on appeal to local tastes and know-how flow, but the opportunities for new retailing ideas which will appeal across cultures are much greater for these more specialized retailers. The competitive advantage seems to be open to repetition. Niche positioning strategies are available, allowing entry into unsaturated segments without the same level of competition found in mass retailing. And a unique retailing idea may very well occur and come from the parent firm. So all three variables could point to a home control strategy.

IKEA and SuperClub, for example, both have unique operating strategies which come purely from the parent organization and which have been more or less proven across cultures in Europe (showing some cross-cultural appeal within their given niches). Hence their chances for success without altering their strategy to local tastes seem much higher than for the other organizations we discussed. Indeed, IKEA is an often-cited success story of how an international retailer can duplicate operational success in different cultural environments with only minor concessions to the local market (Kelly 1987; Solomon 1991).

The remaining firms listed in Figure 16.3 could have similar cross-cultural appeal, but have also taken something specific in terms of operations from their US subsidiaries, be it product lines (Conran's), management techniques (Dixon's), or simply name recognition (GIB, Otto Versand). In the specialty retail market, the more specialized the operational concept, the more it seems to be dependent on know-how flow for determining the locus of control. If it is truly unique (and therefore subject to standardization across cultures), and if a noncompetitive market segment exists for the idea, then it should be carried out through a pure home or pure host strategy. If it needs some input from both sides, the mix approach is a better fit.

Targeted retailers

This conclusion is reinforced further by a look at the targeted retailers. As with the move from mass to specialty retailers, we see increasing fragmentation by market type, but also increasing opportunities for national chains as retailers seek to dominate very narrow segments. From a strategic-variable point of view, home control appears even more attractive for firms in this grouping. And the environmental and know-how flow variables offer further opportunities to bring in a new retailing idea which flanks established competition – provided it is culturally appealing. All in all, the chances for successful home control appear greatest in this segment. Again, however, the decision should be based on particular circumstances.

Benetton and The Body Shop have highly unique, focused operating techniques which have been successfully transferred across a number of borders. The Body Shop in particular epitomizes the successful international retailer, having a singular, duplicable operational system, a definite cultural appeal in a time of environmental awareness, and no current need for input from local operators. The company's biggest problem at present is opening stores fast enough to fend off copycats (Zinn 1991). FAO Schwartz and Pearle, on the other hand, have highly unique, focused operations which have been successful in the US and appear to be good bets to transfer abroad. In all four situations, the markets are extremely fragmented and extremely competitive, but have been proven vulnerable to unique niche retailing strategies. The critical decision on control flows from where the unique strategy originated, home or host, and whether that strategy/competitive advantage can be duplicated elsewhere.

The 'problem' retailers are especially enlightening in this regard. Majestic attempted to translate a British strategy to the Western US by converting liquor supermarkets to low-cost wine merchants. A number of difficulties, including duplicating supplier relationships, existing customer expectations, and a heavy debt burden conspired to doom initial efforts (Gabb 1989). The know-how flow was home to host, but the competitive advantage was found in local conditions in the UK and was not transferable to the new destination. More local control and adaptation might have saved the transition.

At the other end of the spectrum are found the US retailing efforts of Gucci. The Italian firm's competitive advantage is found in its association with high quality goods, a strong central brand image. Its initial US efforts, however, were so hodgepodge (both retail and as a supplier) that the name lost much of its meaning. Gucci appears to have given too much freedom to local operators, diluting its upscale appeal. The company realized this in the late 1980s and took steps to reassert home control, buying back all its US retail franchises (Rossant and Rothman 1990).

Other residents of this category have followed recommended strategies, by discretely managing locally well-known subsidiaries (Vendex/B. Dalton, W.H. Smith), by entering with a pure strategy and then adapting to local conditions (Laura Ashley), or by acquiring a dissimilar subsidiary with the explicit goal of melding the two organizations together (M&S/Brooks Brothers).

One acquisition which has not yet had sufficient time to prove itself success or failure is Ratner's purchase of Kay Jewelers. What would the REM suggest about Ratner's attempts to turn around the financially troubled Kay? Ratner's past success in the UK has been based on a low-cost strategy which is evidently also based on low quality (Gerald Ratner's own infamous remark about selling 'total crap'). Given a fragmented market with some national competition, our reading of REM suggests that Ratner's must offer something more unique to set itself apart from other

US jewelers. If the only thing the parent can offer Kay is a low-price strategy, without some specific, transferable operational guidelines on how to achieve it through lower costs, then Ratner's should make sure that some local control continues in its subsidiary. A pure global strategy would be a very dangerous move for Ratner's and Kay, because the circumstances do not appear to favor home control. And, indeed, in spite of publicized intentions to convert Kay's to the Ratner's formula (home control), little seems to have changed in Kay's US shops (still host control?), hence our question mark in the diagram.

CONCLUSIONS

This paper focuses on an important decision made by retailers with international expansion plans: should the firm keep operational control in the home office, shift it to the host country, or utilize some mixture of the two strategies? The Retail Entry Model (REM) is put forward as a structured method of analyzing this decision. Based on both eclectic entry model theory and Levitt's global marketing tradition, the REM seeks to evaluate the circumstances of the firm and the market it is entering, then render a recommendation on an appropriate control strategy.

By applying this model to a four-year survey of secondary information on European retailers entering the US during the 1980s, we were able to evaluate actual control decisions against those recommended by the model. Most firms follow the recommended strategy, and most seem to be doing fine. If not, ready explanations exist for their current problems – explanations not implying a basic strategic mistake. Those firms not following the recommended strategy appear to be having more than their share of problems. Not all these problems are solely due to a mistake in locus of control, of course, but the mechanism seems a useful predictor, albeit from a *post hoc* perspective in this exercise.

Future work with this model will involve more rigorous and more quantitative testing of its conclusions within specific retail industries. Examinations of other country-to-country movements (US to the EU, to and from Japan, and so on) should also be interesting, especially if combined with more formal statistical procedures. Any or all should add to our understanding of the choices faced by retailers seeking international expansion.

REFERENCES

Chain Store Age Executive (1988) 'Hypermarkets: Successful at Last?', January 15–8.
Dunning, J.H. (1981) *International Production and the Multinational Enterprise*, London: George Allen & Unwin.
The Economist (1993) 'Store of Value', 26 June, 63.
Freedman, A. and Marcom, J. Jr. (1988) 'Marks & Spencer, expanding boldly in

US, adds groceries to its list', *Wall Street Journal*, 18 August, 26.

Gabb, A., (1989) 'Not so Majestic', *Management Today*, May, 104–8.

Hill, C.W.L., Hwang, P. and Kim, W.C. (1990) 'An eclectic theory of the choice of international entry model', *Strategic Management Journal*, 11: 117–29.

Kelley, B. (1987) 'The new wave from Europe', *Sales & Marketing Management*, November, 45–50.

Levitt, T. (1983) 'The globalization of markets', *Harvard Business Review*, May/June, 92–102.

Maremont, M. (1988) 'Marks & Spencer pays a premium for pinstripes', *Business Week*, 18 April, 67.

Maskulka, T.A., Erickson, G.S. and Ryans, J.K. Jr. (1991) 'EC retail foreign investment in the U.S.: motivations and implications', in Robert L. King (ed.) *Retailing: Reflections, Insights, and Forecasts*, Richmond, Va: Academy of Marketing Sciences, 187–91.

Murrow, D. (1989) 'BK eyes Europe battle', *Advertising Age*, 14 August, 50.

Pellegrini, L. (1991) 'The internationalization of retailing and 1992 Europe', *Journal of Marketing Channels*, 1(2): 3–27.

Quelch, J.A. and Hoff, E.J. (1986) 'Customizing global markets', *Harvard Business Review*, May/June, 59–68.

Root, F.R. (1982) *Foreign Market Entry Strategies*, New York: AMACOM.

Rossant, J. and Rothman, A. (1990) 'Can Maurizio Gucci bring the glamour back?', *Business Week*, 5 February, 83–4.

Salmon, W.J. and Tordjman, A. (1989) 'The internationalisation of retailing', *International Journal of Retailing*, 4(2), 3–16.

Saporito, B. (1990) 'A&P: grandma turns a killer', *Fortune*, April, 207–14.

Sheeline, W.E. (1988) 'Making them rich down home', *Fortune*, 15 August, 51–5.

Solomon, B. (1991) 'A Swedish company corners the business: worldwide', *Management Review*, April, 10–13.

Treadgold, A. (1990/91) 'The emerging internationalisation of retailing: present status and future challenges', *Irish Marketing Review*, 5(2), 11–27.

Weiner, S. (1989) 'Low marks, Few sparks', *Forbes*, 18 September, 146–7.

Zinn, L. (1991) 'Whales, human rights, rain forests – and the heady smell of profits', *Business Week*, 15 July, 114–15.

Part VI
Pricing

Pricing is the most conspicuous of the marketing tools, but the one which should be used last of all. Only those who have no other means to compete should consider low pricing. Consider how the communist countries of Eastern Europe used what was often termed 'disaster pricing' to move their goods.

Former British Prime Minister Sir Edward Heath, in a speech at the University of Calgary, revealed how in his early days as President of the Board of Trade he had to meet the frequent challenges of the Soviet Ambassador that Britain was not doing enough to maximize trade with the Soviet Union and could do much, much more. Sir Edward countered directly that there were few goods that British companies or British consumers wanted to buy, and invited the Soviet Ambassador to name but one example. 'Watches!' was the Ambassador's reply. 'They are cheaper and go faster!'

Pricing is a very important topic, and here we have three important contributions. The first, by Robert A. Garda, deals with 'Tactical Pricing' which shows how pricing can be controlled. Tactical pricing, Garda compares to guerrilla manoeuvring that achieves the day's victory and yields an immediate payoff while being invisible to competitors. The tactic creates uncertainty in the market for others as they cannot even second-guess the final price which won the bid, given that there may well have been discounts that will never be fully revealed.

Ralf Leszinski assesses what falling trade barriers mean for prices and pricing policies within the European Union, where price harmonization poses a challenge to the unwary alongside exchange rate risks. There is an opportunity to turn these threats into opportunities that will lead to corporate restructuring, as keen competition will ensure that low market prices prevail. Monitoring and adjusting prices is difficult. There are questions as to the speed with which it should be done, at what level, and how close do you need to be to the market to do this? Leszinski explores all these issues.

Lastly, Clive Sims, Adam Phillips and Trevor Richards' article 'Developing a Global Pricing Strategy', which was an ESOMAR prize-winning paper, is reproduced here. The paper looks at the effects of pricing on the market for whisky in different countries, and describes how United Distillers set out to understand the effect of price in its various markets and how this understanding of portfolio optimization was incorporated into the management decision process.

17 Tactical pricing

Robert A. Garda

Pricing is a bit like the weather. People complain about it; they worry about it; and in the end, they feel there is not much they can do about it. But, unlike the weather, pricing can in fact be controlled. It can be managed. And it can be a powerful profit tool for business. Consider the following two examples:

- The general manager of a $165-million electrical equipment manufacturer believed his salesforce was leaving too much money on the table with its winning bids. The company tracked bids only on lost orders, which caused it to put downward pressure on prices. By analyzing successful bids, the general manager discovered that the company's average 'winning' price quote was a full 7 per cent below competition. Further, his research with key established customers revealed that, because of switching costs, it was necessary only to match the competitive bid to secure these orders.

    A system to track all bids – both won and lost – and to encourage less-aggressive price-cutting with existing customers was implemented. The result one year later: a 5 percentage point gain in return on sales and increased profits of $8 million annually.

- Executives of a specialty chemical manufacturer disagreed over whether to target small-company customers for a sales push. While large customers brought in volume, smaller customers were believed to be more profitable because they paid higher invoice prices. However, sales were reported at the invoice level only, and the final 'pocket price' paid by any given customer was not tracked.

    It was discovered that despite higher invoice prices, smaller, customers were actually paying a lower final 'pocket price' because they were taking advantage of off-invoice incentives such as cash discounts, year-end rebates, free cases, and freight allowances – all intended for larger customers. (Figure 17.1 depicts the pocket price 'waterfall' for the company.)

    Armed with this information, management cut back on off-invoice programs. The effective average price to smaller customers was increased by 9 per cent without changing list or invoice prices. And because of the strength of the sales organization, no large customers and only a few smaller customers were lost due to the changes.

These examples demonstrate that tactical pricing – the transaction-by-transaction control of pricing decisions – is one of the great unused profit levers available to management. Astute pricing tactics can yield nearly immediate and sustainable increases of 5 and even 10 percentage points in return on sales, without large price increases or significant lost sales volume.[1]

After nearly two decades of emphasizing cost reduction and productivity improvements as the means to increase profits, companies are reaching the point of diminishing returns. Many competitors, like the companies discussed in the examples above, are turning to the flip side of cost – price – for the next wave of performance enhancement.

TACTICAL VERSUS STRATEGIC PRICING

Tactical pricing is the day-to-day management of pricing. In contrast, strategic pricing defines a company's long-term price/value image in the market. Put another way, strategy is the grand battle plan designed to win the war over time, while tactical pricing is the guerrilla maneuvering that achieves the day's victory. And while strategic pricing decisions can net long-term competitive advantage, tactical pricing often yields a bigger immediate payoff.

Tactical pricing goes beyond traditional quantity and functional discounting to consider the unique customer- and order-specific costs of each transaction. Its goal: to optimize the frequently competing selling objectives of winning orders, maximizing order profitability, building long-term account potential, and assuring competitive positioning in the market place.

Tactical pricing can help a company:

- shift the mix of orders toward more profitable products;
- reduce the amount of money left on the table in winning situations;
- gain share by selectively cutting price with specific customers – where doing so will not lead to a price war;
- appear to exert upward pressure on industry prices in order to misdirect and confuse competitors.

Myths and misunderstandings

Despite the potential profit impact, tactical pricing remains largely misunderstood, undermanaged, and virtually ignored in many companies.

For starters, poor pricing practices and missed opportunities are difficult to detect. As was true in the first example, involving the electrical

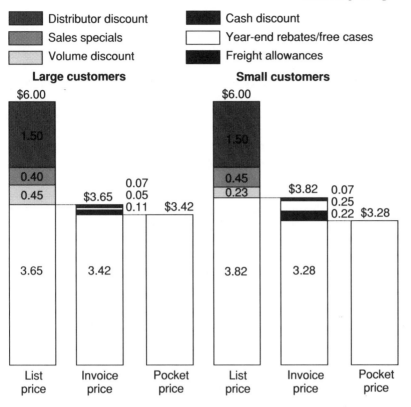

Figure 17.1 The pocket price 'waterfall'

Note: All prices are in dollars per pound

equipment manufacturer, few companies track competitive prices. They know their own 'won' and 'lost' bids, of course. But for wins, they generally do not know how much lower they were then competitors.

In losses, they may only know that their price was too high, without any specifics as to the competitive price range or significant nonprice factors. Unfortunately, both scenarios promote downward price pressure and contribute to a constant, though vague, sense that the company's prices are too high.

Those companies that do track competitive bids usually track a composite of their own won and lost bids against the competitors' winning bids. This comparison always makes the competition appear to be lower in price. It is, in effect, comparing apples with oranges; the only relevant comparison is your win prices and the competitors' win prices – the true market price.

In addition, as was illustrated in the second example, the specialty chemical company, few companies track picket price: the final cash-in-the-pocket price paid after all allowances, discounts, and deals. As a result, they have only a fuzzy picture of any one order's true profitability or where they really stand versus competitors' pricing.

Others believe that price is simply not manageable; they reason that price is set by the market at the point where supply and demand meet. However, the economic reality of nearly all markets is not a price point but a price band – a range of prices bid, accepted, and paid after all discounts and markdowns. The essence of tactical pricing is knowing where to price within the band in order to optimize a particular transaction.

Still others believe (erroneously, in many cases) that price differentiation among customers is illegal *per se*. They adhere to a printed price sheet and discount schedule for fear of Federal Trade Commission (FTC) prosecution.

It is a little-known fact that the Robinson–Patman Act dictates that price needs to be the same only for the same product sold to two customers who compete with each other. When these conditions do not exist, as would be the case in many industrial and business-to-business situations, pricing flexibility abounds.

Finally, the fact is that many companies have gotten along fine in the past with across-the-board increases and have not had to worry about transaction pricing. Thanks to increased competition, changing market dynamics, and cost pressure, those days are gone.

The combined, bottom-line results of these myths, misunderstandings, and information gaps are large sums of money left on the table in winning bid situations, volume orders lost because of a lack of selective price flexibility, and profit erosion caused by a weak product mix or inaccurate cost information.

THREE KEY ELEMENTS

Effective tactical pricing requires close attention to three principal elements: price level, timing, and method of communication.

Determining price level

This is the target point within the price band for a given transaction and involves a clear understanding of where you stand, not just in relation to the competitors' quotes, but also in relation to such customer-specific characteristics as price visibility and price sensitivity.

Price visibility is the ability of a competitor to 'see' your price 'through' a given customer. A high-visibility customer is one who will make your price known to your competitors. High-visibility situations can be used to misdirect competitors about costs and pricing strategy.

In such a case, a company may want to price high, even if it occasionally means lost business, in order to give competitors the impression of upward price pressure. On the other hand, with a low-visibility customer, price can be selectively lowered to discreetly build volume.

Price sensitivity (the customer's sensitivity to variation in price) is also related to switching costs – the cost to the customer of obtaining a new supplier – and to the length and strength of the relationship between the customer and the supplier. When price sensitivity is low, price should be set at, or even above, the competitive quote. Conversely, high sensitivity demands lower prices.

For example, a mechanical equipment supplier had a static share of a declining market and a pricing structure that was well known to competitors. Taking a fresh look at customers, management segmented the market on the basis of price sensitivity and visibility. Prices were raised for selected high-visibility customers, giving competitors the impression of upward price pressure. At the same time, the company gained share with low-visibility/high-sensitivity customers by selectively cutting price.

For low-visibility/low-sensitivity customers, nonprice incentives such as engineering assistance were used to pick up additional volume. In six months, the company achieved a 4 percentage point share gain overall while letting competitors lead a general 3 per cent price increase.

Timing pricing changes

The timing can be nearly as important as the changes themselves. For example, a simple tactic of lagging competitors in announcing price increases can produce the perception among customers that you are the most customer-responsive supplier. The extent of the lag can also be important.

In one company, an independent survey of customers showed that the perception of being the most customer-responsive supplier was generated just as effectively by a six-week lag in following a competitor's price increase as by a six-month lag. A considerable amount of money would have been left on the table during the unnecessary four-and-one-half-month delay in announcing a price increase.

Communicating pricing changes

This also has tactical ramifications. Even though deliberate advance communication to competitors concerning pricing changes is forbidden by law, competitors will closely monitor your price announcements. Publicizing a price increase is, therefore, generally desirable, provided care is taken to properly inform salespeople and customers in advance. It will position you in the eyes of competitors as the price leader.

The exception to the rule of publicizing price increases is the occasional customer. Routinely announcing price increases to infrequent customers will only tend to erode goodwill.

In contrast, price reductions that are widely announced can produce competitive retaliation and a downward price spiral. It is generally best to effect price cuts indirectly and to communicate cuts only through direct contact with customers by such methods as changes in terms of sale, reduced service charges, or revised discount schedules.

UNSEEN COMPETITIVE EDGE

At its best, tactical pricing is invisible to competitors. While a company's overall strategy (to be positioned as the highest-value supplier in the market, for example) may be obvious to all competitors, tactical thrusts (for example, low-visibility price cutting, off-list discounting, and so on), if effectively executed, should pass undetected.

With this in mind, companies that embrace tactical pricing sometimes completely do away with printed price lists and simply quote price directly on a case-by-case basis. While it may not be appropriate in all situations, the tactic never fails to create a good deal of uncertainty in the market, as competitors have much less to 'shoot at' in gauging where to set prices.

For example, an electrical components supplier, the share leader in its market, strictly adhered to a printed price list for its original equipment manufacturer (OEM) customers, along with a predictable discount structure for large accounts. As a result, the number two competitor knew what prices to beat with key customers.

In a year-long targeted sales offensive, the number two company cut prices and gained five share points in direct takeaways because the leader was afraid to match the new, lower prices for fear of losing margins and because of the misguided fear of legal problems with differential pricing.

Finally, fed up with the share loss and the overall price decline and assured that differential pricing was not an issue, given its customer base, the leader launched a three-part program. First, to protect existing OEM accounts, the leader linked its computers with customers' material-requirements planning and order-cycle systems; this provided a valuable service while effectively 'building a wall' around these accounts by increasing switching costs.

Second, the leader attacked number two's largest account with sharp discounts, sending a strong message to it about the consequences of a price war. While not winning over the customer, the leader's 'shot across the bow' was clearly understood.

Third, to disguise its pricing and create confusion among all competitors, the leader took its price list off the market and began pricing each customer on its own merits.

The end result: the leader stopped the share erosion among its existing accounts and switched some of its competitors' customers for a regain of six share points.

The basic principles of tactical pricing are not strikingly new. However, until the advent of widespread computerization, controlling and tracking the myriad factors involved in every transaction was nearly impossible for a company of any significant size.

But computers can now provide the speed and detail-handling capability needed to allow product- and transaction-specific pricing decisions. Systems can be as simple as a single personal computer or as sophisticated as a massive international management information system. Whatever its form, the objective of such a system is to help a company forecast competitive pricing and set its own price according to price/profitability tradeoffs. (Figure 17.2 depicts the data elements required for such a system.)

PRICING PITFALLS

Tactical pricing does entail risks. Chief among these is the danger of proceeding without accurate, detailed information on true cost and profitability.

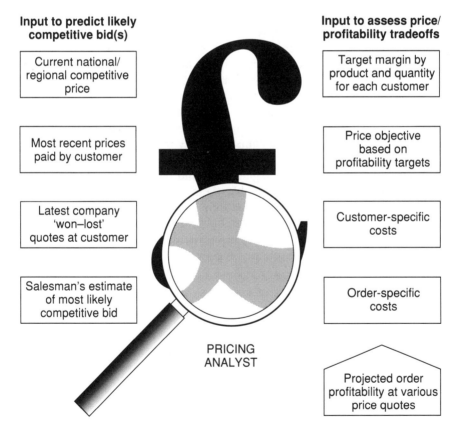

Figure 17.2 Information needed for price decisions

For example, an automotive components manufacturer based its pricing on the belief that small parts produced higher gross profit margins because of a greater price-to-materials markup (5:1 as compared with 3:1 for large parts). However, the manufacturing people complained that gross profit was not an accurate measure of product profitability because large parts absorbed more than their share of overhead. They reasoned that an extruding machine generated more pounds of product per hour of capacity for large parts than it did for small parts; therefore, the large parts required less labor and overhead per pound.

Dissatisfied with overall profit performance, management agreed to re-examine its traditional gross margin costing philosophy. It discovered that taking into account the relatively greater machine time required for smaller, more complex parts produced a radically different cost profile. Variable contribution margin per machine hour became the new costing basis.

Comparison of the old and new costing systems for recent orders produced some shocking results. With the new costing method, management discovered that several orders that had been rejected due to below-target gross profit would have generated excellent returns under the variable-contribution-per-machine-hour system. With the new costing structure in place, profitability, now much more clearly understood on a product-by-product basis, increased dramatically.

A second significant risk of tactical pricing is adopting the approach without first reorienting and, if necessary, retraining salespeople. Traditional salesmanship stresses making the sale above nearly all else, with the result that significant sums of money may be left on the table in the bidding process.

Salespeople must have clear guidelines and decision rules to follow, as well as information that will enable them to set price to optimize the selling opportunity by taking into account profitability and volume objectives, order-specific costs., price visibility and sensitivity, and competitive positioning. In some cases, the sales incentive plan may need to be changed to reflect profit as well as volume objectives.

Better information

The importance of accurate cost information and appropriate decision rules is illustrated in the example of a component supplier that attempted to control the pricing process through clear distinctions in pricing authority but little else. Under the assumption that discounts are inversely related to gross profit levels, product managers were allowed to authorize prices up to 35 per cent off list; marketing managers, 45 per cent off list: and the general manager, 60 per cent off list.

Sales were healthy, yet profitability was disappointing. Even though most individual orders met their profit targets, the overall gross profit objective of 40 per cent was not being met. Examining costs in more detail, management discovered that the gross profit measure did not depict the true profitability of its products; variable contribution margin was a better barometer. With hindsight, it was clear that well-intentioned decision rules had been subverted by inaccurate cost information. For example, variable contribution margin costing revealed that, for some products, a 35 per cent discount yielded only a 10 per cent contribution margin; for others, a 60 per cent discount yielded a 50 per cent margin.

In effect, the combination of misleading cost information and discounting rules allowed the product manager to unknowingly authorize prices below the corporate profitability objective. On the other end of the spectrum, this obliged the general manager to get involved in relatively unimportant pricing decisions.

Given the new information, the decision rules were changed to a 'cost up' profit orientation instead of a 'price down' discount approach (i.e. pricing decisions were kicked upstairs for reasons of lower profits, not solely because of higher discounts).

CONCLUSION

Pricing remains a 'black box' to many companies; misunderstood, under-managed, and virtually ignored. As a result, many companies continue to leave large sums of money on the table with their winning bids, miss opportunities to secure profitable volume orders, inaccurately assess true profitability, and unknowingly telegraph cost structure and pricing tactics to competitors.

Astute tactical pricing offers a major, untapped opportunity for dramatic and sustainable profit improvement for both industrial product manufacturers and for consumer goods companies. Those companies that successfully embrace tactical pricing will be among the winners of the 1990s.

NOTE

1 For a related discussion of transaction-based pricing and the pocket price waterfall, see Michael V. Marn and Philip J. Hawk, 'Memo to a CEO: managing transaction pricing', *McKinsey Quarterly*, no. 1 (1991), 90–105.

18 Pricing for a single market

Ralf Leszinski

As Europe moves toward a single market, lack of attention to pricing is a serious problem. The stakes are unusually high. Pricing, especially in a fluid environment, is the single most effective lever for changing corporate profitability. Done well, it can produce wondrous results. Done poorly, it can undermine years of hard work on fashioning strategy or pruning costs.

On average, a 1 per cent price increase results in a 12 per cent improvement in a company's operating margin. This is four times as powerful as a 1 per cent increase in its volume. But the sword cuts both ways. A price decrease of 5–10 per cent will eliminate most companies' profits. As the single market develops, decreases of this magnitude can easily happen: the existing price differentials across Europe for some products are in the range of 20–40 per cent.

THE MAGNITUDE OF CHANGE

The inevitable spread of price harmonization across Europe will hurt the market share and profitability of the unprepared and will benefit those that prepare for it. Take the example of a leading consumer goods manufacturer with a strong market presence in most major European markets. The company had several international brands, but the prices it charged its local distributors, after discounts and rebates, differed by up to 40 per cent between the lowest- and the highest-price country. It was common for a single customer with Europe-wide presence to pay prices that differed by up to 15 per cent between countries.

Only after the formation of an international buying group, consisting of at least one major customer in each important market, did distributors realize these price differences. The buying group put pressure on the company to level out its byzantine pricing system and charge the same amount for the same product in each market. If it went along with the pressure, however, the company risked losing as much as SFr100 million in revenues and between SFr10 and SFr20 million in overall contribution margin. Moving to national discount structures, systematically reducing the spreads between countries, and partially trimming some accounts helped minimize the damage.

Many companies in the European consumer goods industry already face – or will soon face – a similar crisis. At least 15 international buying groups have spring up, through acquisitions or alliances, just in the packaged goods sector. Nor is the consumer goods industry alone. For pharmaceutical companies, the potential threat is even bigger.

Price differences up to a factor of 10 can often be found for the same pharma product in different member nations of the EU. A basket of 100 leading drugs can easily show a price difference of more than 70 per cent between the lowest-price market, Spain, and the highest, Germany. If, as we believe, a substantial realignment of prices is going to occur, the financial impact will be a contribution loss of up to Ecu15 million for every Ecu100 million of revenues for some pharma companies.

The forces at work, however, will not all push in the same direction. They will have large, but quite distinct, effects on prices. Since, for example, the public procurement policies of individual EU countries will no longer favor local or national suppliers, stronger competition will in some cases lower prices. But in others, the elimination of cross-subsidies from previously protected markets will actually raise prices. The companies able to bid in newly opened markets will benefit; those that stand to lose from the elimination of captive markets will be hurt. The opening up of the US phone services market provides a useful precedent: price reductions of 38 per cent on long-distance calls, but increases of 43 per cent on local calls because of the elimination of cross-subsidies.

THE LEVELS OF PRICING

The effects of the single-market-driven changes will play out on one or more of the three distinct but interrelated levels of the 'pricing hierarchy'.

Supply and demand

The key challenge for managers is to understand how changes in supply (new plants and competitors), demand (demographics, consumer tastes, and substitute products), and costs will affect average industry price levels. The reduced costs of transport, for example, may allow large international players to better exploit scale economies in R&D and production. At the same time, the removal of past regulatory barriers may shift the demand curve. In the US airline industry, the ten years following deregulation saw an average drop in prices of 25 per cent.

Product market strategy

Within an industry, the challenge for managers is to choose a list price for a product that provides a tangible price/benefit advantage versus the competition. The greater the benefit, as perceived by the customer, that a product provides, the higher the price that can be charged. Therefore, understanding customer perceptions of relative benefits will be critical – an especially difficult task in what used to be protected niche markets.

Transaction

The critical issue is determining the exact price to charge each customer for each transaction – that is, which discounts, allowances, payment terms, rebates, incentives, and bonuses to offer. Calculated improperly, these adjustments can decrease revenues from a given transaction by more than 30 per cent.

In a truly single market, however, international customers will demand the equalization of price and discount levels at the lowest common denominator. If producers do not comply with such demands, arbitrage will force compliance. In consumer goods businesses, a price differential of between 3 and 8 per cent will attract such arbitrage; in pharmaceuticals, about 12 per cent.

PATTERNS OF REACTION

How managers respond to these changes will differ among and within industries. At whatever level of the pricing hierarchy the pressure for change first appears, it will trigger reactions on one of the other two levels. There are several possible scenarios.

Shifts in transaction prices leading to a realignment of overall product market strategy

In consumer packaged goods industries, as noted above, differences in transaction prices will be reduced by buying groups or arbitrageurs. This will destroy both the price positioning of certain brands and the profitability of certain markets. As a result, some players may exit from low-price markets or try to reposition their brands in line with the new price structure imposed on them. Others will more to harmonize their prices and discount structures across Europe within a range that makes unwanted third-party arbitrage unattractive.

Still others will try to prevent the customer from buying transhipped products by differentiating products with non-transferable service/product packages, for example, or local spare parts services – so as to make transnational arbitrage unattractive. By offering differently shaped bottles in various countries, a well-known beer producer ensures that the required recyclability of the products is guaranteed only in the intended country of sale.

Yet another alternative is to use different brand names and/or packaging in different countries. Today, of the top 300 consumer products sold in Europe, only 2 per cent are perfectly identical in terms of content, packaging, and weight across most EU countries. This approach would, of course, have little appeal to those companies trying to build or sustain global brands.

Shifts in industry cost curves leading to adjustments in product market strategy

As large players take advantage of previously unavailable economies of scale to apply price pressure on purely national players, the latter will be forced either to retreat into smaller market niches or to form international alliances to create their own scale economies. The French Roquefort cheese industry, for example, formed a cross-selling alliance with the Spanish cheese industry to improve its cost position against international consumer-goods companies. Similarly, regional distributors in several different countries undertook the joint development and production of brand-level yoghurts to better exploit economies of scale on an inter-national level.

Shifts in product market strategy leading to changes in an industry's supply and demand curve

Some customer segments that were previously too small to be served on a national level can now be served cross-border in a cost-effective manner – if segmentation is based not on geography but on lifestyle or buying behavior. Many English-language television channels have subcritical market potential in individual countries, but now have a viable business proposition by using international linkages to serve groups of national microsegments. In much the same way, insurance companies selling specialized products for dentists, say, or antique car collectors can now target these limited segments wherever they appear.

TURNING THREATS INTO OPPORTUNITIES

How quickly these patterns of reaction play out will, of course, vary from industry to industry. Such differences in speed depend on the nature of decisions taken in Brussels, the likelihood that cross-national buying groups or arbitrageurs will appear, the growing price sophistication of customers, the development by customers of sophisticated Europe-wide purchasing functions, and much else besides. Whatever their source, however, the question they pose for managers is how best to turn the inevitable ratcheting up of pressure on pricing into an opportunity to build or strengthen competitive position. To date, the lessons of experience suggest the value of the following approaches.

Being proactive

Because there is a true attacker's advantage in being the first to understand and exploit these changes, the most successful companies often
develop pricing strategies before their competitors do, identify their own
and their competitors' vulnerabilities, and act on them. When companies
wait for their competitors to make the first move and then try to catch
up, the most common result is the loss of market share and profitability.
During the deregulation and restructuring of the US airline industry, for
example, American Airlines was the first to offer an attractive frequent-
flyer program. This so enhanced brand loyalty that, even today, the introduction of similar programs by competitors has not been able to erode
American's advantage.

Understanding competitors

A corollary of being proactive is being aware of present competitors'
strategic degrees of freedom and, equally important, of those of companies that may use changes in prices to enter from a different industry.
Such caution is especially required of companies in restructuring and/or
newly-emerging industries. Remember, it was not the traditional automotive electronics suppliers or original equipment manufacturers (OEMs)
that took the lead in developing and marketing new car navigation
systems, but rather consumer electronics companies such as Sony and
Pioneer.

Improving skills

There is a clear, demonstrable need to develop new pricing skills at all
organizational levels along with the support systems for monitoring, inter-
preting, and managing prices across Europe. When deregulation hit the
US airline industry, American Airlines created a 100-person unit to
manage prices across the various regional markets. The company's verdict:
'We have been able to sustain a revenue premium higher than the rest of
the industry, most of which simply doesn't have the capacity to manage
seats as well as we do.' Similarly, when the US telephone services market
deregulated, MCI built its competitive advantage on differentiated pricing
among various customer groups – an approach based on specific point-
to-point economics, rather than on average systemwide costs.

Changing organizational structure

A commitment to effectively – and aggressively – managing prices across
the range of EU markets usually means that produce managers take on
greater responsibilities and power at the expense of local salespeople. To

facilitate and formalize such a power shift, a European supplier to the electronics industry changed from a functional to a business-unit orientation at headquarters and to a business-unit structure in the field. This improved pricing policies. Old internal transfer pricing rules had led the company, unsuccessfully, to try to sell a product at 20–30 per cent above market prices, even though its true costs were not significantly worse than those of its competitors. The lowering of prices made possible by the new organization structure stimulated sales enough to compensate for the reduced margins.

Understanding the risks

It is easy to underestimate the effort and time required to think through and execute such adjustments in pricing. Changing a price tag is not difficult, but assessing its impact on customers, competitors, and on financial results is. Senior-level time and involvement are essential. But these, in turn, may lead to quiet (or not so quiet) forms of rebellion among managers who are closer to the customers and who instinctively resist increased control by a centrally based business-unit or product manager. Getting the balance right takes a careful organizational hand.

There is also a danger in being too proactive. Altering price structures before ascertaining whether customers will be able to adapt and competitors unable to copy is a bad but common error. Monitoring readiness should be a continuous, not a one-time, effort. It can also help managers avoid the trap of restructuring their prices from a central headquarters perspective.

GETTING ABOARD

A systematic process of monitoring and adjusting prices is difficult to institutionalize. Few companies have the internal organizational structure and systems to do both in a variety of national markets. And even if they do, the organizational barriers set up by independent country managers often thwart attempts to strengthen Europe-wide co-ordination.

Doing nothing, however, is the worst of all alternatives. Deep changes in European pricing have already begun and will not be stopped by the inaction of even a major player. This train has left the station. The single market is coming. One day, not far off, when that company is suddenly confronted with the *fait accompli* of, say, a 5 per cent price drop in a national market, it will be too late to do anything but see most or all of that product's profit contribution wiped out.

Here, by way of summary, are three sets of questions that such companies should be asking themselves now.

Assessing industry changes

- At what level of the pricing hierarchy are industry changes most likely to occur? What will drive them? What will the effects on the other levels be? Because the driving forces in each industry will be subtly different, attributing price drops to new competitors instead of arbitrageurs can lead to false pricing conclusions with dramatic profit consequences.
- Where and how will competitors react? Which competitors are able or willing to lead the way?
- What is the right time to take action? There are costs to being too early as well as too late. Premature price adjustments, long before competitors have considered them, can lead to reduced profits if there is no disproportionate volume gain; excessively slow reactions can lead to a permanently defensive position.

Determining threats and opportunities

- In which market and by which products will current positions be threatened? Because the value of a company is largely determined by its cash flow, which in turn is heavily influenced by its operating margin, a pricing collapse can reduce the value of a company by up to 50 per cent within one to two years.
- Where are the pricing-related opportunities to expand into new markets? As new niches and markets are created, most will offer attractive returns only to the first entrant and average return to the followers.

Formulating a pricing strategy

- Is there in place a pricing strategy to translate all these threats and opportunities into concrete action plans? Is there a chance to be the first player to exploit the opportunities, and are there contingency plans ready for those markets where the company stands to lose?

19 Developing a global pricing strategy

Clive Sims, Adam Phillips and Trevor Richards

BACKGROUND TO A PARTICULAR PROBLEM

The formation and development of United Distillers presented problems and opportunities in many areas. Many of these stemmed from a fundamental change in operational philosophy.

Prior to the formation of United Distillers operations, from production to marketing and sales, were organised on brand lines. In one market place, therefore, there were many salesforces each concerned with one brand from the holding company's portfolio. All commercial energy was put behind the performance of a brand which differed depending on the brand company. The formation of United Distillers changed this orientations from a brand focus to a geographic or market place focus. In marketing terms this changed an important basic task from 'How to optimise the performance of a brand?' to 'How to optimise the performance of a portfolio?'

This change of task also led to a much greater focus on the total market. Brand orientation tends to lead to the assumption that the market will move independently of your brand activity. In other words, brand share is the key criterion. Portfolio orientation, especially when that portfolio represents more than 40 per cent of the market, leads to a realisation that your marketing activity, especially price, will affect the dynamics of the market, thus your actions effect both elements of the share quotient.

United Distillers therefore set out to understand the role of price in two major areas: (a) price and market size; and (b) price and brand share.

ESTABLISHMENT OF PRICE EFFECT

Price and market size

Before embarking on an analysis of this kind it is essential to have clear objectives, particularly with respect to what constitutes the relevant market, what time frame is appropriate and what the function of any resultant model will be. United Distillers objectives were as follows:

- to quantify the effect of price change on market and sector size;
- to establish medium- to long-term price effects;
- to restrict the analysis to the alcoholic beverages market and major sectors within it.

The impact of these assumptions is felt on the data used, in this case annual data generally from government and official sources, and in the model formulation. If the objective had been to build a predictive model for market size then the model formulation, the data requirements, and the tests of model adequacy could have been different.

Over the space of one year models were successfully built for eight major markets, the scope of the investigation being halted by available data rather than anything else.

The most important finding was confirmation that market size is significantly effected by the ability of the consumer to afford the goods. This ability depends on how much money they have and how much they are asked to pay.

In every sector of every market examined it was found that total market volume was significantly affected by changes in total national wealth relative to price inflation (usually Gross Domestic Product or total disposable income at constant annual prices) and changes in retail price relative to average price inflation.

These two factors, sometimes with the price of other competing sectors and dummy variables to allow for significant market events, produced robust and statistically reliable models.

A summary of results for one market sector across countries is given in Table 19.1. The results are expressed as long-run elasticities of real-price and real income.

In general the size of these elasticities is in line with what economists might expect for any market. In the case of Scotch whisky, the effect of changes in real price is relatively small; real income is a more important feature. The results also suggest a pattern where small price elasticity is

Table 19.1 Price and income elasticities – Scotch whisky

Market	Price elasticity	Income elasticity	R^2	D-W
A	−0.6	+1.0	0.97	1.96
B	−0.5	+0.7	0.99	1.90
C	−0.6	+0.3	0.97	1.70
D	−0.2	+1.4	0.99	2.14
E	−0.2	+1.3	0.89	1.42
F	−0.6	−0.9[a]	0.95	2.58
G	−0.4	+0.9	0.90	1.81
H	−0.5	+1.8	0.93	1.72

Note: Income elasticity indistinguishable from time trend

accompanied by high income elasticity. This seems to reflect the status of the market. Mature markets have a higher dependency on price than average. In countries where Scotch is still developing then income is comparatively more important.

Price and market share

As with the study of the effect of price on market size, the objectives must be clear. United distillers' overall objective was to quantify the short- to medium-term effect of a change in a brand's price relative to its competitors on that brand's market share. This problem was approached in two ways: (a) the statistical analysis of market data – mainly retail audit information; and (b) brand/price trade-off.

The statistical analysis of retail audit data

Retail audit information currently provides one of the best continuous sources of data on this industry, providing estimates of brand volume and price within specific market sectors in many countries. Over the years a number of time-series and cross-sectional approaches have been applied to retail audit data but people have tended to concentrate on modelling the price effect for one brand or the interaction between two brands. For reasons described in the introduction, United Distillers required a much broader model that allowed not only the estimation of a brand's 'own price' elasticity, i.e. the effect of a price change assuming all other brands in the market remained the same, but also the ability to simulate the effect of different pricing scenarios across a range of brands, taking into account their varying degrees of interaction.

After the discussion with personnel from the Henley Centre for Forecasting in London, who carried out the subsequent statistical analysis, United Distillers decided to opt for an approach borrowed from econometric theory known as the Almost Ideal Demand System which will be referred to in the rest of this paper by the unfortunate acronym AIDS (see Blundell *et al.* 1990; Deaton and Muellbauer 1980a, 1980b). In brief the AIDS approach sets out to estimate the matrix of parameters of Table 19.2.

Each of the brand equations is estimated separately using Ordinary Least Squares. The economic theory underlying the AIDS approach is then brought to bear. In general this leads to two key constraints:

1 the sum of a row $A_{i1} \ldots A_{in}$ must equal zero and the sum of any column $A_{1i} \ldots A_{ni}$ must also equal zero. In other words the losses of one or more brands must be gained by the other brands;

2 $A_{ij} = A_{ji}$. A change in the relative price of brands i and j must have the same effect whether caused by a movement in price of Brand i or Brand j.

Table 19.2 Brand price coefficients

Value market share	1	2	—	N	Trend	Market size
Brand 1	A_{11}	A_{12}	—	A_{1n}	T_1	Mt
Brand 2	A_{21}	A_{22}	—	A_{2n}	T_2	Mt
•	•	•	•	•	•	•
•	•	•	•	•	•	•
•	•	•	•	•	•	•
Brand n	A_{n1}	A_{n2}	—	A_{nn}	T_n	Mt

Note: Where A_{ii} represents the effect of a change in the price of Brand i on its own value share, A_{ij} represents the effect of a change in the price of Brand j on the value share of Brand i. T_i is a trend dummy to allow for any longer term growth or decline in the share of Brand i, Mt represents the coefficient applied to the total market size to allow for the fact that the share of some brands change with peaks and troughs of seasonal demand.

By a process of imposing linear restrictions on the coeffients of the individual equations and examining the validity of the assumption of interaction between brands, a final set of equations of the form described in Table 19.2 can be estimated. This process is repeated until a set of equations is produced that is statistically reliable and accords with economic theory and commercial common sense.

A more detailed explanation of the estimation process, the rules and tests governing the imposition of linear restrictions may be derived from the references below or from the Henley Centre for Forecasting, London.

To date this method of analysis has been successfully applied in six markets. Besides the complex statistical testing procedures, the estimated equations have demonstrated their effectiveness in terms of both tracking historic data and predictive ability. An example is shown in Figure 19.1.

The figure demonstrates a typical AIDS model fitted to actual market data. The last two points show the same model being used as a predictive tool to forecast future brand share and the comparison of the forecast share with the actual share achieved.

Trade-off

There are a number of problems with retail audit data from the point of view of building an AIDS model:

1 insufficient data for the major brands in the market;
2 incomplete coverage of major trade sectors;
3 imperfect competition in outlets due to non-random patterns of distribution;
4 the limited range of scenarios covered in real markets;
5 the inability to take 'snapshots' of the interactions in markets where large changes have occurred.

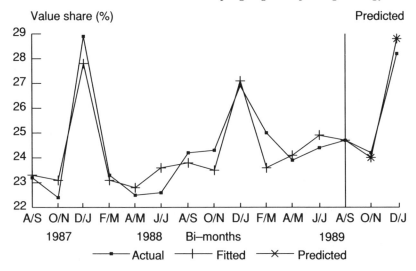

Figure 19.1 Brand 'A' tracking ability of the AIDS model

For these reasons an *ad hoc* technique was required which could stand alone and provide data where retail audits could not. The trade-off (conjoint measurement) approach was proposed for this task.

The brand/price trade-off technique is a powerful means of identifying, at the individual level, the trade-off between brand equity and price (see Morgan 1987). This enables a model to be build which can predict the effect of price on demand (number choosing) for each brand. By taking account of differential weight of usage by different respondents it is possible to build into the model a volume elasticity. As will be demonstrated, it also offers a means of identifying and quantifying market segments, in terms of brand utility or loyalty. This provides an understanding of the dynamics of price and what needs to be achieved in terms of building brand equity, to maintain a price premium or maximise a price advantage.

The main drawback of the brand price trade-off technique is its sensitivity to design, notably the design of the data collection task. This relates not only to the purchase occasion (for example every day vs. special occasion) but also to the brands which are included. For example, do cheap whisky brands compete with medium-prices brands and do these, in turn, compete with deluxe brands and/or malts? Is a cheap malt whisky more likely to compete with a medium-prices brand than other, more expensive malt brands? Other considerations, such as the effect of imperfect distribution and varying distribution patterns and the variation of price across different outlets, serve to add to the complexity of designing the project.

It is almost certainly these problems of presenting the respondent with a suitable task which have led some market researchers to be unhappy about the accuracy and reliability of this method of collecting price response data.

Because of this sensitivity to the design of the respondent's task, very careful piloting needed to be carried out in each market, prior to carrying out main fieldwork. This, coupled with analysis of data-concerned with distribution and price by outlet type was used to refine the technique and ensure that the brands and the purchasing context being presented to respondents were the most appropriate for the market sector being investigated.

For example, in the first market to which this approach was applied, piloting demonstrated very clearly the extent to which different sectors within the whisky market overlapped.

It became clear that consumers were using different brands for different purposes – medium-priced brands were bought in repertoire with more expensive, deluxe brands and drunk on different occasions. The medium-priced brands were more likely to be mixed (e.g. with soda) and, as such, this sector was more sensitive to price.

A further area of exploration in this first market researched was whether respondents should be presented with a fixed list of brands in the trade-off display or whether the display should be restricted to the 'salient set' for each respondent: that is the relevant set of brands in each respondent's repertoire.

Showing the same, fixed set of brands for each respondent would have the advantage of simplicity (a consideration when contemplating fieldwork in more far-flung markets). It would also provide the opportunity to simulate whether brands could be drawn into consumers' repertoires if their prices were reduced sufficiently.

The main advantage of the salient set approach was that it was likely to be more representative of each respondent's current choice process and would also, to some extent, reflect the relative awareness and distribution of different brands. The salient set approach also has the obvious potential benefit that markets with a large number of brands can be dealt with by respondents only seeing the seven or eight brands most relevant to them.

In order to provide a definitive assessment of the effect of these two approaches, a split-panel approach was adopted, with one panel of respondents being exposed to a fixed list of brands (in this case eight brands accounted for the bulk of the volume in the market). In the other panel, respondents were only shown brands in their 'salient set' (on average four brands).

The results were analysed using the ranks analysis method to model the likely demand for each brand. This procedure is well documented (Blamires 1987). The main reason for using this approach rather than the utilities approach was that price variation across brands meant that different price points had to be applied for different brands. Where this is the case, modelling from utilities is unreliable and not always possible. However, for brands which are similarly priced it is still possible to produce relative brand utilities which provide a direct measure of the strength of the brand equity.

In comparing the results from 'fixed list' vs. 'salient set' a pattern emerged which was common to all key brands (see Figure 19.2).

The salient set approach produced the stereotypical 's'-shaped curve which one expects to see in an established market (Frearson and Richards 1990). Moreover, the projected share at current prices was internally consistent with claimed last brand bought:

	Trade-off (%)	*Last bought (%)*
Brand A	18	16
Brand B	31	33
Brand C	30	30

The 'fixed list' approach projected a similar level of demand at current prices and above. However, the curve was closer to being linear and projected relatively heavy demand at prices below the current norm. In other words, forcing attention on a brand outside respondents' salient set inflated the expected demand. At the low end of the price scale the salient set approach generated elasticities which were much closer to those found in econometric analysis. It also showed more sensitivity when projecting likely behaviour at prices *above* the current norm.

It is possible to impose on the data, at the analysis stage, a 'pseudo salient set' – whereby choices of brands from the fixed list test which are not in a respondent's salient set are deleted from the data set. As can

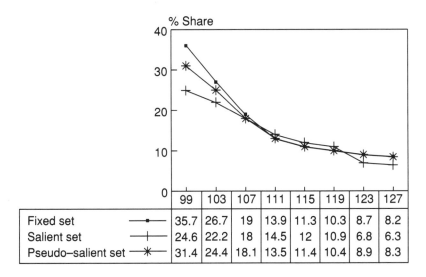

		99	103	107	111	115	119	123	127
Fixed set	■	35.7	26.7	19	13.9	11.3	10.3	8.7	8.2
Salient set	+	24.6	22.2	18	14.5	12	10.9	6.8	6.3
Pseudo–salient set	✳	31.4	24.4	18.1	13.5	11.4	10.4	8.9	8.3

Figure 19.2 Elasticity of brand 'A'

be seen from the figure applying this procedure did produce a curve which was closer to that derived from the salient set approach. However, the elasticity observed is still higher than that from the 'true' salient set.

The salient set approach was adopted for all markets subsequently explored.

A further element of exploratory work, carried out in several markets, is worth describing here. It had been noted that, for some markets, the brand price trade off approach would be inappropriate. This was the case for those markets where only a very small number of brands (two or three) were really relevant or where the competitive set was not readily definable. (The trade-off approach also involves a certain level of complexity which may be difficult to administer in less-advanced markets).

For this reason, it was decided to administer a Gabor–Granger exercise in parallel with the trade-off, for a single key brand in each market. This technique broadly involves establishing purchase intention for a brand at a number of different price level (Gabor and Granger 1965). An important refinement to the technique, applied here, was to provide respondents with a competitive context, with the prices of main competitive brands being shown, to ensure that relative price differentials were constant and explicit.

The simplicity of the approach lends itself to addressing the above problems. The disadvantage is that the interbrand elasticities are not distinguishable, but it affords an opportunity to extend beyond the price range covered by the brand price trade-off, as shown in Figure 19.3.

As can be seen in the figure and as was generally the case in the different markets covered, the Gabor–Granger approach gave absolute levels of demand which were substantially different (higher) than those projected by the trade-off. However, the *elasticities* which reflect the shape of the curve at a given price were very similar (see Table 19.3).

From this it was concluded that the Gabor–Granger approach gives a similar projection of brand elasticity to those from brand/price trade-off (although it should be borne in mind that the exercise was carried out among the same sample of respondents). However, absolute levels of demand cannot be projected accurately. The sensitivity to price context

Table 19.3 Brand elasticities around current price

	Market A		Market B	
	Trade-off	Gabor–Granger	Trade-off	Gabor–Granger
Brand A				
Number choosing				
at current price	21%	30%	25%	34%
Elasticity	3.6	3.8	4.2	4.3

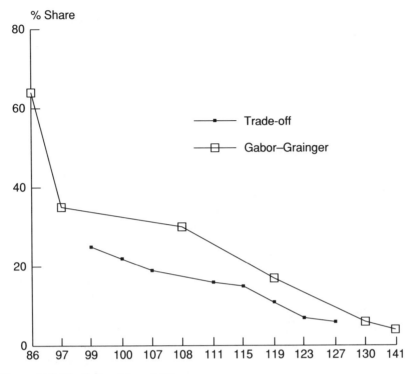

Figure 19.3 Elasticity of brand 'A'

of absolute demand projected from the Gabor–Granger approach has been demonstrated in other research (Frearson and Richards 1990).

Of course the brand price trade-off approach offers a much more powerful means of exploring 'what if' scenarios, with the facility to change the price of more than one brand when attempting to simulate demand.

The output from the brand price trade-off research fell into three main areas:

1 brand elasticity (demand curves);
2 gain/loss analysis;
3 market segmentation and consumer classification.

The last of these is dealt with on p. 287.

The price elasticity data or demand curves were produced for key brands within each market both for total sample (representing whole market) and with user groups (to examine elasticity among current franchise).

In each case, the elasticities for different brands were calculated around current average price ± 5 per cent and for current average price + 10 per cent. These elasticities were subsequently compared with elasticities derived from the AIDS analysis and this is described in the next section.

A further diagnostic 'spin-off' from the trade-off analysis is the facility to identify which brands are likely to gain or lose as a result of changing the relative price of a single brand in the market (see Figure 19.4).

This provides estimates for the interbrand elasticities needed in the AIDS analysis, as well as helpful simple data for local management on the impact of different pricing scenarios.

Comparison of techniques

The previous two sections have described totally different approaches to the problem of estimating the effect of price on market share. The conclusion United Distillers has reached is that both are valid and both offer complementary, different and valuable insights into the effects of price and market dynamics.

The key areas of difference are:

1 *Time* The statistical approach of AIDS estimates the average effect of price over the period of analysis. Trade-off estimates the effect of a price change subject to conditions prevailing at one point in time.
2 *Simulation range* Simulation of the effects of price variation outside the variation seen historically based on AIDS analysis can be dangerous because the elasticity is a single number and therefore produces estimates along a straight line. Trade-off can provide information outside the range of historic variation: for example, to evaluate the effect of repositioning a brand in terms of price. This is because the technique can produce a demand curve.

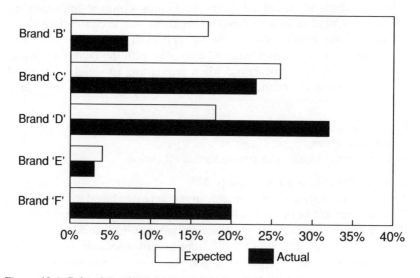

Figure 19.4 Gains from brand 'A'

3 *Use and cost* Statistical analysis of continuous data is less expensive and can be used as a monitoring device (e.g. to detect changes in underlying trend). Trade-off is an *ad hoc* consumer research technique but can be enhanced by the collection of usage and attitude information which helps to answer the 'What?' *and* 'Why?'. Also it can be used to provide comparable results in markets of the world where there is no retail audit data or similar continuous measurement.

Where both techniques have been employed estimates of the same parameter (i.e. own price elasticity) have been obtained. A comparison of results is shown in Table 19.4.

Table 19.4 Estimates of volume price elasticity – a comparison of results

	Market A		Market B		Market C	
	AIDS	Trade-off	AIDS	Trade-off	AIDS	Trade-off
Brand A	–3.8	–3.7	–4.1	–3.4	–2.5	–4.2
Brand B	–3.6	–3.7	–3.2	–3.2	–2.3	–3.7

The first and most important point to note is how much higher the estimates of brand price elasticity are than those for the total market. From all the work carried out the average 'own price' elasticity of a brand (i.e. the effect on volume of a price rise if all other brands remain at the same price), is about –4. Depending on market and competitive circumstances elasticities of –5 and –6 or even higher have been found.

The importance of this is that the evaluation of a price rise is critically dependent on the actions of competitive brands. If all brands move up in price by the same proportion the market elasticity can be used to estimate volume change.

In these circumstances the decline in volume will be more than compensated for by increased margin and therefore total profit will increase. However, if the competitive brands do not follow a price rise the volume loss can be so severe that total profit also falls.

The estimates produced for both brands by both techniques in markets A and B are very similar, both of these markets were stable over time and therefore the estimates produced from an analysis over time compared with a point in time are similar. The difference in results for market C might be explained by the fact that the market was relatively price stable for 75 per cent of the statistical analysis period and then, for various reasons, entered a period of price instability. The trade-off off fieldwork was conducted during this period of instability. The elasticity to be used for the evaluation of future plans is partially a judgement call depending on how long the period of price instability might be thought to continue.

SO WHAT?

'Price modelling'

The effect of price is significant and can be measured – but so what? Knowledge of this effect can be used in two important areas: (a) evaluation of future scenarios: forecasting, planning, 'What if?' questions; and (b) a better understanding of the past.

The first application is important and the most obvious. The second is often overlooked but equally important: what would have happened had price not changed.

Price simulation

Individual models have been incorporated into spreadsheets to enable the evaluation of different brand, or market pricing scenarios, tax changes, etc. One of the most useful however, has been to combine market and brand models.

The starting point for this combination is a brand-pricing scenario over time. The assumptions are an array of brand prices (see Table 19.5) where P_{ij} is the price of the ith brand in the jth time period. From the brand share models this array can be used to predict value shares directly. From these shares a change in average market price can be estimated and therefore, incorporating the market models, a change in market volume. It is then simple arithmetic to derive market value, then brand value, using the predicted value shares, and then brand volume, using the price scenario. Once the models have produced an estimate of brand volume it is again straightforward to estimate the effects of the pricing scenario on total profit thus providing optimisation criteria for pricing decisions.

Back-tracking

There is a tendency to view history in a univariate fashion, i.e. the market is growing or declining or a brand share is rising or falling, and to incorporate this 'fact' into future projections. Very occasionally people look at

Table 19.5 Prices by time period

	Period 1	Period 2	Period t
Brand 1	P_{11}	P_{12}	P_{1t}
Brand 2	P_{21}	P_{22}	P_{2t}
•	•	•	•
•	•	•	•
•	•	•	•
Brand n	P_{n1}	P_{n2}	P_{nt}

a market in terms of a total model which seeks to evaluate all factors, advertising, price, distribution as well as socio-political influences. There is great value in adopting a middle course that might be described as a residual approach; basically take out the effect of the factors that can be measured and look at what is left. Commercial reality dictates that decisions on marketing activities have to be taken whether or not historic effectiveness can be formally measured. It is often the case that insufficient data exists for all variables to be taken into account formally even if all relevant variables can be identified. Taking price into account, i.e. describing what would have happened if price had not varied, can make things much clearer.

Two examples are given below of how the conclusions drawn from history might, at least, be modified by considering that historic pattern without the effects of price.

The first example shows the annual volume for imported whisky in a market, the fitted values from the econometric model and an estimate, based on the model, of what the market would have been if real price had not varied and if real price and real income had not varied. This is an example of where the 'univariate' approach concluded that 'the market is growing strongly'.

The more realistic conclusion is that while market volume has undeniably grown the primary cause of the growth is economic rather than a general change in consumer tastes. Therefore, future market development

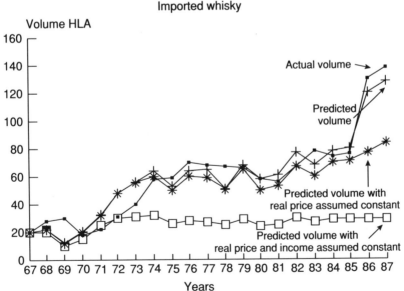

Figure 19.5 Whisky imports for market 'X'

is primarily dependent on the country's economic performance (see Figure 19.5).

Market dynamics

The application of these techniques has provided significant insights into market structure above and beyond the estimation of price effect. Some of the main conclusions are given below.

The second example is at brand level. Figure 19.6 shows the actual market share and an estimate of what the share would have been if the relative price of the brand had not changed. The implication of the model is that the brand increased and then fell for reasons other than price in 1987 and 1988. The current decline however, is due to its price becoming relatively more expensive. The underlying trend of the brand is stable.

These two examples show how a better understanding of the past can be achieved once the price dynamic is understood.

The process also represents a valuable monitoring device. If marketing activity changes in terms of either spend or content, then share movement that cannot be explained by a price change should be seen. A model established before the change should prove inadequate in predicting the positive share change if the change in marketing activity proves successful.

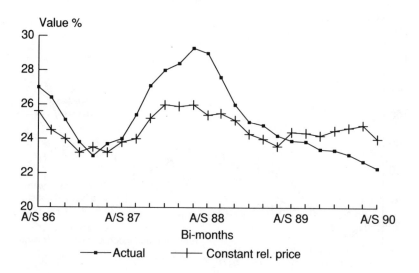

Figure 19.6 Brand 'X' value share: actual, and at constant relative price (moving annual averages)

Market segmentation

Both econometric modelling and trade-off provide useful information on market segments. From the trade-off data a gains/loss analysis can be done. Inter-brand utility can also be calculated and represented in the form shown in Figure 19.7. Each dot represents a consumer in the survey and the position shows the relative utility each consumer has for each of the three brands. Thus those in the middle of the triangle place more or less equal value on each brand, those at the apex would only choose that brand out of the three being analysed. Those along an axis would choose between two brands.

The array of coefficients from an AIDS analysis can be examined to give a measure of brand interaction with respect to price.

In the example in Table 19.6 it is clear that brand B interacts with brand A and little else. Brand A is effected by B, C and D and there is strong interaction between C and D.

Table 19.6 AIDS equation coefficients

Brand	Price A	Price B	Price C	Price D
A	−1.1	0.4	0.3	0.4
B	0.4	−0.5	0	0.1
C	0.3	0	−1.5	1.2
D	0.4	0.1	1.2	−1.5

Consumer classification

Another useful way of considering the market structure comes from trade-off data and involves classifying the respondents within broad brands of price utility.

This analysis approach has suggested the hypothesis that the price elasticity of a brand will differ depending on whether the brand share is growing or declining. As a brand declines a greater proportion of its franchise will be amongst the more brand loyal who, by this definition, have a low price utility.

It might be, therefore, that the price responsiveness of a declining brand will reduce over time.

As yet we do not have sufficient data to investigate this hypothesis formally. However, some circumstantial evidence to date suggests validity. Table 19.7 gives data for two brands in a market together with the estimated elasticity for each. As can be seen, Brand A is growing strongly in share and at a price premium to Brand B yet it is currently more sensitive to price.

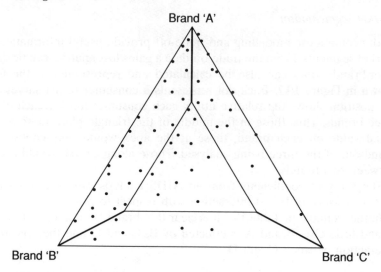

Figure 19.7 Brand comparisons and relative positioning

Table 19.7 Frame 14

	Market share year 1	year 2	Price year 1	year 2	Price elasticity year 2
Brand A	24.0	26.1	270	287	−2.8
Brand B	7.5	7.1	254	265	−1.7

If this hypothesis proves to be correct it is clear that the price elasticity of a brand is an aggregate measure of many brand features that could well change over time. The elasticity could be affected by:

- brand image and values;
- degree of competition;
- brand size;
- brand trend.

Clearly an area for more work.

A brand building hypothesis

The hypothesis of price elasticity being an aggregate measure of a number of factors that could change over time leads to some interesting hypotheses on how its measurement might help in the process of monitoring brand building or indeed tracking brand decline.

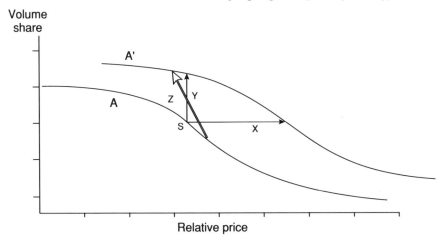

Figure 19.8 Routes between demand curves: a way to track brand development?

Figure 19.8 shows two price demand curves, A and A'. Curve A represents the brand share in a settled state. When price is the only variable (i.e. with no change in brand values) we would expect share to be described by curve A. If some action were successfully implemented to improve the status of the brand then the new curve A' would describe the share/price relationship. It is the route between A and A' that is of interest. Two simple routes are X and Y where Y describes an increase in brand share whilst maintaining price position and X describes an increase in price whilst maintaining share.

The results of both directions could lead to an increase or decrease of price elasticity depending on the starting position on S.

For the purposes of monitoring the progress of changing brand values the establishment of the starting position is vital. The 'expected' change in price effect could then be estimated.

Within the markets studied thus far United Distillers has identified a brand that moved along direction Z. A successful downward price repositioning led to a decrease in price elasticity (from –7 to –2) and an increase in share well above that predicted by curve A even at the historically high elasticity, in other words an implied increase in relative brand values.

As yet we have insufficient data to explore this hypothesis further. However, work will continue in this area because it provides a means of evaluating future plans and monitoring progress. Clearly progress along X or Y or any other vector can be monitored.

AN EXAMPLE

The recognition of the importance of price and the use of estimates of price effect now forms an important part of the planning process at United

Distillers, both in terms of the evaluation of future plans and the monitoring of events. Set out below is a brief example of how this process has been used.

The Scotch whisky market in country Y had four distinct price sectors. Figure 19.9 shows the structure of the market in 1988 together with the share the United Distillers' portfolio had of each price segment. It also shows the position in 1990 and the target position for 1992. It should be noticed from the price indices that the price of Scotch has been moving up steadily, particularly in the lower price sectors.

Given the position in 1988, it was clear that United Distillers was not competing in some important price sectors of the market. The decision was taken to develop our market share in two phases. The first phase in 1989 was to reposition two brands to compete in the lower price sectors. This had been successfully implemented by 1990. The total increase in United Distillers' volume share of this market between 1988 and 1990 as a result of this action was 10 per cent. The total increase in value share was 7 per cent.

The second phase is to create a new sector by taking a brand from the top sector to create a new price category and further develop the brands in other sectors. This second phase is being implemented during 1991.

A detailed knowledge of market dynamics, brand segmentation and price interaction has enabled United Distillers to accurately position brands in terms of price *vis-à-vis* intended competitors and to evaluate different future scenarios. Also, importantly, it has enabled the estimation

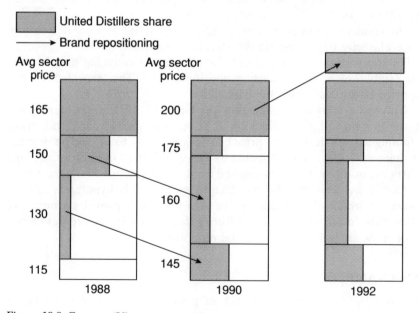

Figure 19.9 Country 'Y': category and share development

of the improvement in brand values necessary to accompany upward positioning. This has allowed the establishment of performance criteria for the marketing programme.

CONCLUSIONS

Price is a very important part of the marketing mix. Our work on portfolio optimisation has led us to a number of general conclusions:

1 *Ad hoc* techniques can provide essential information which cannot usually be obtained from retail audit or consumer panel data;
2 the role of price modelling in understanding the effects of historic marketing activity is at least as important as its role in forecasting the future and is vital when valuing the true impact of marketing activity;
3 brand elasticities can be much higher than market elasticities – we have observed elasticies of –7 or more;
4 there seem to be islands of stability defined by price sector within the spirits market. Brands can have different price elasticities within these islands from those which they have as they move between islands.

Over the next few years United Distillers intends to continue to increase its competiveness in the market place by making full use of the techniques described in this paper.

REFERENCES

Blamires, C. (1987) '"Trade-off" pricing research', *Journal of the Market Research Society*, 29: 133–52.
Blundell, R., Pashardes, P. and Weber, G. (1990) 'What do we learn about consumer demand patterns from micro data?', London: Institute for Fiscal Studies.
Deaton, A. and Muellbauer, J. (1980a) 'An almost ideal demand system', *American Economic Review*, 70: 312–26.
Deaton, A. and Muellbauer, J. (1980b) *Economics and Consumer Behaviour*, Cambridge: Cambridge University Press.
Frearson, W. and Richards, T. (1990) 'Margin optimisation throughout the brand life-cycle', paper presented to the ESOMAR Symposium on New Product Development.
Gabor, A. and Granger, C. (1965) 'The pricing of new products', *Scientific Business*, August, 141–50.
Morgan, R.P. (1987) 'Brand/price trade-off: where we stand now', paper presented to the ESOMAR Symposium on Micro and Macro Modelling.

Part VII
Regional markets

Those who see the world as but one market are indeed in need of glasses. The fear has been echoed many times, and one commentator in fact wisecracked that his greatest fear was that one day all the great shopping malls of the world would simply be joined up! A world without individuality is difficult to imagine. To those who believe there is a threat, it is not a real one. Given a world where everyone had the ability to buy, there is then the important question of choice. Certain products and services are indeed available worldwide but they are not mandatory. Companies such as McDonald's are global companies because they are successful in transferring their core strengths across nations.

In the first contribution in this Part, Jim Sherlock looks at the Single European Market which is presently twelve nation states, but under constant pressure to admit more, including in the not-too-distant future four from Eastern Europe: Poland, Hungary, Czech Republic and Slovakia. Sherlock reviews the origins of the Community and looks to the present day and beyond with further future expansion. He examines the harmonization process that has been underway throughout the European Union and looks at factors which he terms 'controllables' and 'uncontrollables' and offers alternative future scenarios.

Eastern Europe is now no longer, either as a political or as a geographical entity. The GDR (German Democratic Republic) has merged into a reunified Germany and there has been a tremendous lurch westwards by four nations in particular: Poland, Hungary, Czech Republic and Slovakia. What Stanley J. Paliwoda attempts to do here is to outline the substantial changes that have taken place and outline the very real differences to the marketing environment now existing in this region of the world. Product availability is everywhere and shoppers are surprisingly well-informed and sophisticated despite the rudimentary channels of distribution that have been hastily created to meet consumer demands.

The last contribution in this book is on the North American Free Trade Agreement (NAFTA) from a quite different perspective than usual. As the EU continues to enlarge, those outside start to look around for trading opportunities. Within North America, there are three separate countries: USA, Canada and Mexico, and a plan to harmonize in favour of free trade amongst them. What constitutes major differences relative to the EU is that NAFTA is US-driven and Canada and Mexico are being driven by their major trading partner, yet within Canada itself there is no real free trade across provinces. David Elton and Todd Hirsch offer a very timely assessment of the rationale for realignment within North America and assess its *raison d'être* from the viewpoint of the USA's closest ally, Canada.

20 A Single European Market?

Jim Sherlock

After 1992, Europe will turn in on itself and become a sprawling, sluggish entity about as relevant to the outside world as the Austro-Hungarian Empire – a decadent pleasure resort.

Anon.

As a British academic I should first of all say that I have no personal objection, in principle, to residing and working in 'a decadent pleasure resort'; in fact, it seems to be a pretty good idea. Unfortunately, it is unlikely that such a prophecy will actually come to fruition, at least not in my lifetime, but what is interesting about this rather extreme expression of opinion is that, whilst it defies accreditation to an individual, there is no doubt that its source was an economist, and not just any economist, but an AMERICAN economist. A case, perhaps, of getting your retaliation in first.

Right or wrong as an interpretation of the fate of 'Europe', it does presuppose that a 'Europe' will actually exist as a single entity and this does display a more confident perception of the future, from an American economist, than one would find from many of a similar bent actually operating in Europe. To put it another way, whatever form a future Europe takes, and whatever that will mean in terms of economic growth or decline, the question as to whether a single Europe can actually exist at all is one which has not necessarily been answered in the affirmative.

To be somewhat more pragmatic, there is no doubt that the, so-called, Single European Market does exist. The very words are enshrined in the legislation of the Single European Act and so we must assume that it does exist. The question is, of course, 'What form does this single market take?' That is, 'what exactly do we mean by *single*?'

A distinction between what is the same across the current 12 member states of the European Union, and what is, and may remain, different is clearly essential to any pan-European marketing strategies. It may even preclude any pan-European approaches completely and enforce the need for clear and complex segmentation criteria across the whole of Europe.

Whilst this may pre-empt any conclusions we may reach by dint of logical argument, a point worth making now is that those British companies who decided that the whole of Western Europe suddenly became part of their home market as Big Ben tolled in the new year of 1993, have found that perhaps they had been a little hasty, not to say precipitous. If the United Kingdom, being, reputedly, a European country, has clear problems in treating its European partners as an homogeneous extension of its domestic market, then it seem pretty obvious that non-European countries would find it even more difficult.

More of this later; but first it would be sensible, as all good management consultants would say, to examine just where we are now, and how we got here. A potted history of the European Union might seem to be of little constructive use to today's marketing executives, but it is hoped that you will come to see that wherever we are now, in terms of a single Europe, we are still carrying a lot of baggage from the journey, and it's what is in the bags that contributes to a real perception of Europe as she is now.

THE ORIGINS OF THE COMMUNITY

Two men in particular can be held to blame for the European Union, both of them French. Robert Schuman, who was the French Foreign Secretary at the end of the Second World War, and Jean Monnet, a fascinating character who was also a prime mover in the formation of the League of Nations and a high ranking civil servant when he wasn't producing cognac. Whilst it is difficult to understand now, they were committed to the avoidance of a Third World War. There had, after all, been two already this century, both of which they had lived through, and they were adamant that structures needed to be put in place to avoid further conflict in Europe.

Of the many ideas they put forward, only one actually got off the ground: the European Coal and Steel Community (ECSC) which was formed by the Treaty of Paris 1952. Other initiatives, such as a European Political Community, were considered too advanced (clearly not so in the 1990s) and the proposed European Defence Community was seen as pointless without the participation of the USA and led to the North Atlantic Treaty Organisation (NATO).

The logic of a Coal and Steel Community avoiding a Third World War may not be obvious, but there can be no doubt that it worked. It worked so well, in fact, that the ideas thought too advanced in 1952 were accepted by 1957. The logic of the ECSC was that international co-operation in the handling of the major source of energy – coal – and the major source of military power – steel – meant that one country could not unilaterally divert such resources into a war effort. Also, one of the major geographical sources of these resources was the Ruhr on the French–German border, and this Alsatian area of Europe had been a thorn in the side of

France and Germany for centuries. Strasbourg is at its centre, and is French now and will stay so. An illustration of how important the French consider Strasbourg, as the heart of the Community, is the fact that they have recently insisted that the European Parliament continues its plenary sessions there, despite the clear preference of the members of the Parliament for Brussels.

This first Community was composed of France (who started it), Germany and Italy (who lost the war and had no choice) and the Benelux countries (Belgium, Netherlands and Luxemburg, who are well known for joining almost anything). Likewise Britain, well known for joining nothing unless it is British, declined membership and decided to keep its coal and steel to itself.

The original six members in fact found the structure so successful that within five years the Treaties of Rome 1957 set up two more communities: the European Atomic Energy Community (EURATOM) which was an update of Coal and Steel (energy and armaments) and, perhaps most importantly of all, the European Economic Community. Originally operating through separate secretariats, the Communities soon developed into a single European Union, originally predominantly an economic one, but now with a much wider remit including monetary, political and social influences.

Eventually other countries saw the advantages and, in 1972, the United Kingdom, the Irish Republic and Denmark became members. Indicative of the role of the UK in Community activities is the fact that, whilst the Treaties were signed in 1972, the UK referendum regarding membership actually took place in 1975. Right from the beginning the UK has tended to plough its own furrow.

The Union became 10 in 1981 with Greece, and 12 in 1986 with Spain and Portugal, the only criteria for membership basically being the existence of a democratic government and, naturally, being part of Europe. In this context Turkey has been accepted as an associate member, being European, but Morocco was rejected as being African.

TWELVE PLUS?

The situation now is that an expansion of the Union is inevitable, and one of the fascinating areas of conjecture is: just how big can it get? Already the 12-member Union is the biggest single consumer market in the world with a population of approximately 345 million (including East Germany) and representing over 20 per cent of total world trade. It has free trade with the countries of the defunct European Free Trade Area (Austria, Sweden, Switzerland, Finland, Norway and Iceland) in the guise of the European Economic Area (EEA), which is almost a waiting room for full membership. Already Austria and Sweden have signed the treaty of accession and other ex-EFTA countries will follow early in the next century (which is not as far off as it sounds). Some have bigger problems than others; Switzerland, for example, will have to rewrite its constitution, which at the moment forbids it joining anything, and their rejection of full membership of the EEA in 1994 also slows things down a little.

It is not out of the question that other countries will become members before some EEA nations. Malta is no problem, but Cyprus will have to wait until Greece and Turkey have come to some understanding regarding its occupation. Most interesting of all is the commitment to 1 March 2002 as the date for Hungary, Poland and the Czechs and Slovaks to become members; and how about Romania, Bulgaria, Latvia, Estonia and Lithuania? Even Russia, Albania and whatever becomes of Yugoslavia are potential members.

We do have to accept that, following a number of occasions over the last 30 years when the Union was on the brink of collapse, it is now here to stay and will get bigger. The only contentious issues centre around the form of the developing Union and – back to our first question – just how far can we go in establishing a genuine single market.

LEGISLATION

The legislative backbone of the European Union is made up of the Treaty of Paris and the two Treaties of Rome, the main thrust of which has to be seen as purely economic, with an emphasis on free trade, even though the main Treaty of Rome contains many high-flown statements about co-operation and social cohesion. The real expansion of the Union out of its purely economic business orientated, role into a genuine frontierless common market, should it actually happen, will derive from the Single European Act 1987, designed to create 'an area without internal frontiers in which the free movement of goods, person, services and capital is ensured'. Clearly, a more ambitious aim than that of a free trading bloc with some economic co-operation.

Finally, the most recent piece of legislation, the Maastricht Act, is very much on the back burner (on a very low heat) even when it has been rat-ified by all member states. The UK has ratified part of it at the expense of a Prime Minister's reputation (or what was left of it), the Danes will only ratify a revised version, and many other countries are proceeding in the face of widespread disquiet. Even a totally ratified Maastricht is some-thing of a nonstarter, the only one of its elements actually to have had any effect being the increase in the power of the European Parliament. This addresses the so-called 'democratic deficit', which describes the fact that the only elected European institution, the Parliament, is clearly the weak-est in the face of the nonelected Council, Commission and Court of Justice. Of the other two elements of Maastricht, the Social Chapter proceeds, albeit slowly and without the UK, and the European Monetary System's target of a single currency by 1996, via the Exchange Rate Mechanism and economic convergence, has been blown apart by the power of the free market. It could be seen as quite ironic that the European Commission's much-vaunted freedom of the market should be the instrument for the destruction of the dream of a single European currency.

Whilst Maastricht might be said to be 'belly up', the single market, which officially came into existence on 1 January 1993, is a reality and the vast majority of the almost 300 proposals specified in the Paolo Ceccini Report 1985 have become legislation. The report, sponsored by Lord Cockcroft who, for his pains, was subsequently removed as a UK Commissioner, suggested that the direct costs of frontier delays between member states and of differing technical regulations added some 3.8 per cent to consumer prices throughout the Union and cost, in total, at least Ecu 200 billion per annum.

CUSTOMS UNION OR FREE TRADE AREA?

Before we attempt to identify what exactly is common throughout a single market we should first of all make a clear distinction between the European Union as a free trade area (which is where it started and where some members, such as the UK, might wish it had remained) and as a Customs Union, which is actually what it is.

Perhaps the best way to illustrate the difference is to compare the European Union with a pure free trade area such as the North American Free Trade Agreement (NAFTA) . The NAFTA has agreed general duty-free trade between its members, but how each member treats imports from non-members is still an independent national decision. Thus UK goods sold into Canada will attract different controls than if they enter the USA. The European Union has gone much further in, first of all, establishing a Customs Union with free trade between it members and, most importantly, a Common Customs Tariff against third countries i.e. non-members. Figure 20.1 illustrates the structure diagramatically.

Thus imports from outside the Union attract the same range of controls and duties in each member state. However, this has not yet gone as far as a harmonisation of national indirect taxes, such as value added (turnover) tax or excise. These differences are vital to an understanding of the future development of the single market. It has been asserted, by this writer among many others, that the only reason for internal frontiers to exist is fiscal differences between member states. The argument has now moved from 'the differences are so great as to make it impossible to remove internal frontiers' to 'a removal of internal frontiers will enforce a harmonisation of fiscal regimes'. In other words, if a country chooses to charge high indirect taxes on consumer purchases then they will lose revenues to cross-border shopping caused by purchases in low tax-charging countries. The American example suggests that differences of more than

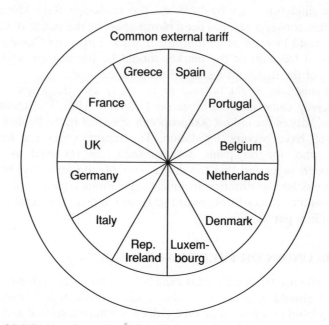

Figure 20.1 Penetrating a European Union protected by a common customs tariff

5 per cent in purchase/turnover tax from one state to another do distort revenues. The UK with just about the highest excise rates in the Union, particularly on alcohol, tobacco and hydrocarbon fuels, has great reservations about the liberalisation of consumer buying, but has lost the argument.

Therefore, the picture of the Union in Figure 20.1 illustrates the difference between internal frontiers between member states and a single, common, external frontier. What the Single European Act has done is simply to remove the internal frontiers, as shown in Figure 20.2. Raise the wall around the Union and you have the 'Fortress Europe' which still seems so attractive to some European politicians and civil servants, but more of that later.

SINGLE MARKET FACTS

So what can we identify as being realities in a single market? The Ceccini Report proposals targeted three main areas susceptible to standardisation, or at least harmonisation, and which were seen as barriers to the movement of goods, people, services and capital:

- physical:
  customs

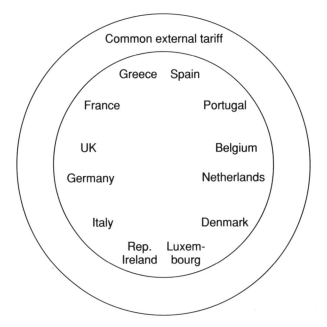

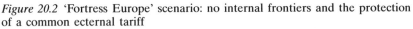

Figure 20.2 'Fortress Europe' scenario: no internal frontiers and the protection of a common ecternal tariff

    transport
 • technical:
    standards
    certification
 • fiscal:
    VAT
    excise

Many of the 270-plus ratified proposals have gone a long way towards the removal of most, but not all, of these barriers. What we can say is that, since 1 January 1993, a number of barriers to the physical movement of goods and people have disappeared.

The restrictions on road hauliers, the most common means of surface freight in Europe, have been reduced to such an extent that there has been created almost a free market for road freight throughout the Union. The restriction on 'cabotage' operations (foreign hauliers conducting domestic carriage) have been almost completely removed, allowing any EU-registered haulier to pick up and drop anywhere in the Union. The fact that, prior to this, something like one-third of heavy goods vehicles in Europe were travelling empty means a far more economic use of capacity, and a greater choice for the shipper. Further liberalisation of sea, air and rail traffic is high on the Commission's agenda.

Most influential in the long term must be the removal of mandatory customs controls at transit frontiers. Union goods and people are no longer required to undergo mandatory documentary checks at frontiers. The passport is no longer essential for travel by a Union resident in Europe, although the need to produce identification has not yet disappeared. This actually represents an unprecedented change in the attitude of European customs authorities. From the origins of Customs & Excise in Elizabethan Britain in the 1600s there has always been an assumption of guilt until innocence is proved. The production of a passport by every traveller provides proof that that traveller is actually free to enter a particular country. The deep philosophical change in customs controls from 1 January 1993 is that people and goods are considered to be innocent (noncontrolled) 'in the absence of anything to the contrary'.

This means that people and goods can be stopped and checked but that the vast majority will move through customs posts with no interference whatsoever. In fact, many customs posts have been permanently closed recently. Indicative of this is the 'Mattias Project' (named after St Matthew, the patron saint of 'revenue collectors'), which is concerned with the important job of retraining redundant customs officers. Another reality is the establishment of minimum Union technical standards in a very wide range of areas, entitled 'A New Approach to Technical Harmonisation', against which national standards can be approved. Any standard which is Union approved cannot be barred from entry into any member state. Couple this with a mutual recognition of testing bodies and certification authorities, and the situation which, for example, forced Amstrad to produce 11 differently modified PCs for the Union market becomes a thing of the past.

The third area of fiscal harmonisation is more problematic. Value added tax rates vary from 15 to 38 per cent within the Union, and the excise on a 75 cl bottle of spirits can range from £6.93 to £0.15. Such differences mean that it is not possible simply to agree a standard rate throughout the Union. The ways in which Union governments choose to raise revenue and the balance between direct and indirect taxes are not things that can be changed overnight. However, remove internal frontiers and allow unlimited cross-border shopping (as long as it is for personal consumption only) and the argument is that a levelling out of tax rates is inevitable. The droves of cross-Channel shopping trips out of south-eastern UK ports since January 1993 are proof of this.

It can be seen that the most obvious realities of the single market are to do with the physical distribution of goods. The situation now is that goods which originate within the Union, or which are imported customs-cleared and duty-paid, will move across the Union with no interference whatsoever, genuinely ignoring national frontiers, Those frontiers still exist as politically defined national boundaries, but as far as goods and people are concerned they are no barrier at all.

An interesting example of this freedom of movement in practice is provided by the author's driving trip to Sardinia in 1992. During the whole journey, which crossed Belgium, Luxembourg, France, Germany, Switzerland and Italy, passports were required only twice: once on leaving Hull, England, and once entering Hull on the return. The UK has attempted to hold on to passport controls longer than any other member state, but it is probable that such a journey now would be subject to no customs controls at all.

All these developments constitute important considerations for a company involved in planning marketing strategies for the Union, but we do have to accept that the elements of the plan most obviously affected are those of physical distribution and, to a lesser extent, product development.

CONTROLLABLES AND UNCONTROLLABLES

We could legitimately assume that a range of elements controllable by legislation have been rationalised to the benefit of most traders. The removal of expensive and unnecessary controls and restrictions does make Union markets more accessible. What has been removed are the bureaucratic and artificial barriers to trade which have distorted European markets for many years, and this should mean that those suppliers who meet market requirements better than others will be more successful.

However, what about the uncontrollables, those elements which will persist in resisting harmonisation and remain immune from any pan-European standardisation? Even a brief investigation soon leads to the inevitable conclusion that the single market may have gone a long way towards the removal of artificial barriers but the real barriers to marketing products and services are all still there. We still must accept that every member state, and the segments within each state, exhibits such a range of diverse characteristics that there are very few occasions where a pure undifferentiated marketing strategy could operate across the whole of the Union. So what differences might research reveal?

Language

The UK and the USA may well be 'two countries separated by a common language' but the nine distinct languages of the Union (English, French, German, Greek, Italian, Portuguese, Spanish, Dutch and Danish) clearly pose more of a communications problem. Add to them distinct regional, and often unique, languages such as Walloon, Flemish, Breton, Alsatian, Basque, Catalan, Welsh and Gaelic, and marketing communications demand differentiation.

The leakproof pen which 'prevented embarrassment' found an entirely new market when 'embarrassment' was translated into Spanish as '*emberazer*', which actually means 'getting pregnant'. Recently the launch of

Clive Sinclair's new innovation, the electric bicycle, was based on what was considered a single European name, the 'Zike'. Unfortunately, this turns out be be an (unprintable) crude word in Flemish. The list is endless: care must be taken.

Economy

Whilst all member states operate basically mixed economies, there are clear differences in the level of economic development. North–South divide in terms of economic development is a problem being addressed by the Commission in terms of targeted regional aid. Territories such as Portugal, Greece, Ireland and southern Italy have a long way to go before they can match the industrialised infrastructure of the more advanced members. It is important to note that France, Germany, Italy, Spain and the UK combined account for 87 per cent of the GDP of the Union.

The distinctions between large and small, rich and poor, have been a concern of the Union since its inception. Even the complex system of majority voting in the Council of Ministers is designed to avoid the smaller nations being swamped by the larger ones. The Danish rejection of Maastricht is a perfect example of the concern of smaller nations that they will lose their national identities, As a Danish student recently said to the writer: 'Don't forget, we are Vikings!'

A final point regarding economic considerations is that 1992 appeared to mark the beginning of a global recession from which the Union is not immune. The UK seems to have started the recession before most members and may come out of it first, but there is little doubt that the Union will have to accept very low (even zero) growth rates for the next year or two. This is aggravated by the problems being experienced by the strongest economy within Europe, that of Germany, linked to the cost of unification and the huge burdens placed on West German resources. A falling birth rate, ageing population and rising unemployment could also make speedy recovery somewhat more difficult.

None of this should deter us from the fact that the Union is a huge and developed market, and will continue to be so, but it could be that over the next ten years we shall see faster growth in the USA and, particularly, the Pacific Rim countries.

Culture

It is always difficult to define quite what is meant by 'culture', in fact it is probably a word best avoided by anybody involved in marketing; but it is useful here as an umbrella term which, it has to be admitted, covers a multitude of sins. There is no doubt that the centuries of disparate, and often conflicting, national developments throughout Europe have led to quite distinct and diverse tribes, all proudly displaying unique traits.

The complex historic developments which have created the modern Europe can be traced for over 2,000 years, from the Mongol hordes to the armies of Gengis Khan, to the Byzantine, Greek and Roman empires, through to the great European armies fighting territorial and religious battles. It all makes the current national structures seem a little boring in contrast. But the nationalism of member states should not be under-estimated, and most nations jealously protect their distinct inheritance.

A wide range of factors lead to a great diversity of national character-istics throughout the Union, linked to religion. climate, constitution, geography, natural resources and the ubiquitous matter of 'taste'. The European Commission gave up some time ago the idea that standard-isation of products and services was possible across the Union. In fact, there is now a far more sensible attitude which actually accepts '*Vive la différence!*'.

The examples of distinct national preferences are myriad and, once again, lead to the clear need for individual market considerations for most products and services. Even those products which appear to be generic and may be sold without modification are not necessarily so. Basic phar-maceuticals, such as aspirin, codeine, penicillin, and so on are used in distinct ways: most medicines in the UK are taken orally, in Italy by injec-tion, and in other countries by suppository. Brands of Scotch whisky are sold without modification all over the world, but the biggest seller in the UK, Bells, is hardly seen in Italy, where J&B is the most popular. What the British call 'chocolate' is quite different from the German version, and a china dinner service which lacked a pickle bowl would be pretty useless in Italy. There are many, many more examples of national differ-ences which, whether we list them under the umbrella of culture or of taste, cannot be ignored. True, there are products and services which can be sold in undifferentiated form throughout Europe and the world, often in technological and industrial sectors, but it has to be said that an assump-tion that differentiation is needed is a much safer starting point.

As a final point under the broad area of 'culture' we should note what appears to be growing nationalism throughout Europe. The increasing influence of nationalistic movements, particularly in Germany, France and Italy, the specific problems of the absorption of East Germany, and the growing resistance to immigration, are typical of countries suffering from recession and growing unemployment. This is leading to an insularity which is capable not only of enhancing an introverted nationalism, but also of promoting protectionist policies in terms of world trade. Whilst, on the face of it, the Union proceeds with a liberal policy of global free trade and the hard-core problems of the GATT appear solved, it takes only minor political changes, and perhaps a more protectionist attitude from the USA and Japan, who have similar problems, to turn the Union in on itself, and the 'sluggish entity' mentioned at the beginning is not impossible.

Even an optimistic view, which we have every right to adopt, cannot ignore the existence of xenophobia between one member state and another, let alone among members and non-members, which will always serve to hold back a total openness, even if only on a trading level. The British possess more than their fair share of this, and the much-quoted headline in a Victorian newspaper, 'Fog in Channel, Continent cut off', is still not an anachronistic joke.

SINGLE MARKET OR NOT?

We should not end on a pessimistic note. The European Union is now a permanent entity and is guaranteed to expand over the next 20 years into the largest free-trading consumer market the modern world has ever seen. It is certain to grow in size, although it is argued that each new, less-developed member will serve to slow down economic progress. It is certain to continue the removal of barriers between its members and to increase its influence in political and social matters. It is certain to negotiate, on a global basis, as a single trading unit.

What is not at all certain is how far this will go in terms of creating an homogeneous market which just happens to be made up of 12 (or 14 or more) political entities. The pragmatic view must be that 'the Germans will be Germans and the French will be French' and that, whilst there is a clear increase in the accessibility of markets as far as regulatory controls are concerned, there is absolutely no reduction in the need to differentiate between diverse, and sometimes contradictory, segmentary requirements.

Evidence that 1 January 1993 has not transformed the Union into a genuine 'common market' is already available from those UK companies who simply decided that the Union, overnight, became part of the responsibility of their home sales departments. The chaos that resulted, in the vast majority of cases, quickly dissuaded them from such a simplistic approach.

So where do we go from here? Like many questions of marketing strategies there is, of course, no single answer. If the question is: Can we treat the European Union as a true single market? the answer is:

'well, it depends, but probably not'.

Just what it 'depends on' could be as simple as what you are selling where; but then, all strategies depend on this. It is clear that certain products or services could legitimately span a pan-European market, without modification, and therefore greatly benefit from the removal of artificial barriers to trade. Evidence suggests that there is more likelihood of this in the industrial consumable and durable markets, particularly for those companies with large market shares. Consumer markets do not preclude this, but do make a non-differentiated strategy far less likely to succeed, and the sensible company will not take shortcuts in its market research on the assumption that a single plan will suffice.

THE FUTURE

The best scenario? An expanding European Union participates in the global development of free trade, following complete agreement on the GATT, benefiting from increased growth and employment, and plays its part, along with all developed countries, in the controlled industrialisation of Eastern Europe and the economic development of the Third World.

The worst scenario? A European Union, still riven by nationalistic differences and burdened by the cost on new members, reacts (or pro-acts) to protectionist measures by North America and Japan by manipulating its common tariff against non-members, and turning in on itself.

Perhaps the American economist we started with was right!

21 A new marketing environment as Eastern Europe moves westwards

Stanley J. Paliwoda

THE REGION DEFINED

The geographical scope is that of Eastern Europe minus the German Democratic Republic which has now been fully absorbed into a unified Germany, the new independent republics of the former Soviet Union and former Yugoslavia. The rationale for this is that, in the first instance, Germany is itself spending heavily on the former East Germany, upgrading its industries and societal infrastructure. This has effectively crowded out Western competition. Secondly, market conditions between Eastern Europe and the Russian republics have always been different from relations between Eastern and Western Europe; besides which, Russians had been told for years that they were suffering hardships because of their brothers and sisters in Eastern Europe. To Russians, Eastern Europe was where their national wealth was being squandered and all they received in return was colonial ingratitude and unsaleable goods. As to the former Yugoslavia, only Slovenia would rank at the moment as a possible investment base, there being too much uncertainty elsewhere.

Another factor here is the traditional degree of centralisation or decentralisation under central planning, and the extent to which the market was at all free to any extent was some measure of the ability of that particular society to create and cultivate an entrepreneurial spirit. In some countries it was always there and never died. In others, the entrepreneur has long been equated with the criminal class. Let us begin, then, with a look at Russia.

THE RUSSIAN ENTREPRENEUR

The environment in which the entrepreneur has to work is challenging, which explains why the entrepreneur often has to act alone. It is responding to a personal vision against an environment that is hostile, and none more so than the Russian republics; this is why we isolate them here for especial attention.

It is ironic that in the new situation that exists there are many myths and much disinformation which ought to be dispelled. This is ironic, because it was the Soviet Union which previously mastered the art of disinformation. Not until the Soviet Empire finally collapsed upon itself and realistic market analysis became possible did it emerge that the GNP of the Soviet Union was based on an economy no larger than that of Spain. The title of a 'superpower' that generations had been brought up to fear was based on military might rather than dynamic economic importance or cultural belonging.

In this system that existed there was no place for an entrepreneur, other than in the black market which is endemic to centrally planned communist countries. This created, therefore, a common view of entrepreneurs as black marketeers who made money out of the sufferings of others. Gratitude and the feeling of national salvation through the creation of a new class of entrepreneurs is pure fiction. Entrepreneurs arose out of the market opportunities that presented themselves, like entrepreneurs anywhere else in the world. In the former Soviet Union, they were never part of the official system and were provided with poor information like everyone else, had no legal status, and were denied being part of a system which was based on production not on consumption, and which separated research from production, and foreign trade activities from production. Production was seen as a pure function and not one which was deserving of the best brainpower. The best people were recruited instead for the state military and defence establishments which had their own universities. Research and defence were focused not on commercial applications but on military weaponry.

Entrepreneurs were not well perceived: they were seen to be wealthy when others were poor and so were viewed almost as part of the criminal class. This is far removed from the belief commonly circulating in the West that entrepreneurs are the salvation of the economy; to the Eastern populace their existence is viewed from their experience as parasitic. This is almost a tragedy, given the fact that has been witnessed the world over, of the power of entrepreneurship to provide employment and to bring to market goods that are sought after, quickly, cheaply and in amazing volume. The part that was missing in entrepreneurship as practised in the Soviet Union, compared with that practised elsewhere, was that in the Soviet Union there was no opportunity for new venture creation. Culturally, they were impeded and legally they had no real standing; for as soon as an enterprise became larger than a family enterprise and started to employ outsiders, it was seen not as a sign of success but as exploitation. Employment of workers was a form of exploitation. Dogma argued that the only form of acceptable exploitation was state exploitation because only the state could employ more than two people. Russian beliefs continue in the minds of many political leaders of its former satellites, most of which have now democratically returned leftist governments comprising former communists.

POLITICAL AND ECONOMIC UPHEAVAL SINCE 1989

Eastern Europe changed significantly and permanently after 1989. First, democratisation processes started to take effect, spreading from Poland. Next, as other countries started to demand free elections, East Germany merged with its neighbour to constitute a new unified Germany for the first time since the Second World War. Political processes have since continued to make any subsequent reversal of democratic gains highly improbable.

The economic face of Europe changed immeasurably with the EFTA countries signing a treaty with the EU to form a new European Economic Area, larger in size than North America and committed to the concept of free trade. Next, the issue of the security of national borders prompted Poland, Hungary, the Czech Republic and Slovakia to seek membership of the European Union and NATO. As regards NATO membership, Russia has objected to its neighbours and former allies being granted membership and so has wielded a political veto over such moves, in so far as it is able to do so.

As regards the EU, these four countries were granted associate membership, which is the level of membership presently enjoyed by Turkey. Poland and Hungary have since gone forward to apply for full membership of the EU. As a first step, Poland, Hungary, the Czech Republic and Hungary have formed CEFTA, the Central European Free Trade Area, to harmonise their trade structures, dismantle barriers to trade between themselves and help to bring themselves in line with EU practice. An EU plus Poland, Hungary, the Czech Republic and Slovakia is a formidable prospect not just for peace but for trade potential. Tremendous, irreversible change is taking place and gathering momentum. The impediments that previously existed to East–West trade no longer exist. The removal of strategic export embargoes by CoCom (the Consultative Committee for Multilateral Strategic Export Control), an offshoot of NATO, was deemed necessary to curb growth in high-technology areas of trade, such as in computers and telecommunications, in which all East European countries have for long been seriously deficient. In areas such as telecommunications and computerisation, the embargo was efficient but in other areas what was interpreted as being strategic was dependent upon the political mood swing of the day amongst Western leaders, and whatever the policy, soft or hard, this was rigidly enforced by civil servants.

Democratisation took place against a very painful transition from a command economy, with eternal subsidies and central planning; to a free market with weak distribution systems, which has thrown into jeopardy the future of entire national industries, such as armaments, which are also major national employers. It is indeed an irony that those goods which are most sought after have had difficulty reaching the market, whilst those generally available are commonly ignored. The means of bringing goods to market was lacking as was basic market research to determine what goods people were looking for, at what price and in what quantity. The consequence of this was a serious rift between what was produced and what people wanted, which meant industry was seriously out of tune with its customers. Marketisation policies created no comfort zone for these enterprises. Suddenly, all power was thrust at the consumer who was now able to choose between domestic and foreign competition for all their purchases. Domestic producers lost out completely once supply was no longer a problem and product supplier comparisons could be easily made.

Unemployment, combined with high levels of inflation which have accompanied all attempts to institute currency convertibility, creates social unrest. The net effect has been the restoration to power of former communists in practically all cases, except in the Czech Republic, Bulgaria and Romania, which never shook off communism in free elections. While no politicians actually disagree with the direction of the changes that need to take place, political debate has focused instead on the speed with which they are being taken. Poland, Hungary and the Czech Republic have been at the forefront of reform, setting the pace for others with these changes.

ACQUISITION, PRIVATISATION AND JOINT VENTURES

Dividing lines between these modes of market entry are becoming blurred. Acquisitions are taking place often as a result of liquidation sales mounted under privatisation programmes. Acquisitions therefore lead to privatisation, and joint ventures can lead to eventual acquisition.

A joint venture can help an incoming Western company to access the local market at less cost and more speed than would otherwise be the case, given the foreign nature of the culture and business environment. Wages are low but so is productivity. Acquisition may buy market share, but a greenfield site may well prove cheaper than investing in old and rundown plant that is cramped in terms of space and is unlikely to meet present-day regulations relating to hygiene and safety, or efficient utilisation of work space for employees or for production.

Using local management can help with the problems of local currency and of seeking to operate under local legislation plus the legislation specific to foreign-owned operations. In the past, these were distrusted because it was part of the culture to distrust all that came from the West. Now people are having to accept that for the last three generations they have been living a lie. Nowhere else and at no other time in the history of the world have people had to unlearn a culture that had for generations instilled values in them that were now seen to be totally false.

Joint ventures require care in selecting a partner, in negotiating with local management and with the state, and in common goal-setting. Language skills vary across Eastern Europe and, while management training is available, it is at an experimental stage only, introducing Western management concepts and practices into a hitherto alien culture with no real feel as to whether they will work better, or at all, compared with what went on before.

The downfall of communism and the introduction of legislation favourable to foreign investment has been necessary to fill a vacuum. The reintroduction of socialist regimes comprising former communists has done little to discourage levels of foreign investment in Poland, for example, which is being hailed by international observers as having staged a brave economic miracle. Yet the fact that the people think otherwise is evidenced in the presence of a former communist as Prime Minister of Poland. The case of Hungary is very similar. Trade and investment restrictions have fallen, but we are talking of relatively small amounts of foreign capital in total alongside that which has been drawn into China.

Joint ventures have changed over time and this is an important message to remember: from the 1970s, when we had a choice only of industrial co-operation, to today, where practically all the modes of foreign market entry available anywhere are available on East European soil. Over time and with the easing of restrictions, definitions have changed, and yet the term 'joint venture' continues to be used to describe the business relationship currently in vogue. Whereas in the 1970s joint ventures were understood to convey contractual joint ventures, in many of these economies today a joint venture may be seen as a form of creeping foreign direct incrementalism or back-door foreign direct investment (FDI).

Lawrence and Vlachoutsicos (1993) undertook a study of 33 joint ventures between Western and Russian enterprises and found that while many were very large corporations, size was not a success factor in itself. They found many talented local managers and a highly skilled and educated work-force who were capable of producing better things, and had the flexibility to solve problems. Encouraging Russian managers to use their own methods and only gradually and selectively introduce Western practices was a pattern found amongst the most successful of the joint ventures in operation. Empowerment has been an important part of their success. Curiously, although the law allows 100 per cent ownership, the best results are still being achieved there by joint ventures with less, where ownership encourages responsibility. It means also developing mutual trust across a cultural barrier which equates profit with surplus cash. Connections are important but have to be nurtured and used if they are to have any value. Identity is important and joint ventures should seek to maintain a good profile through citizenship within the community.

REASONS FOR INVESTING IN EASTERN EUROPE

These may be quickly summarised as a new set of emergent industrialising economies with latent potential that have only recently opened themselves up to the West after generations of trade embargoes and political and economic constraints to trade and investment. These markets are virgin territory for a vast number of possible goods and services. However, while the region as a while is still relatively untapped, the individual nation states vary in their ability to cope with payments that are now required in hard currency, a direct result of the free market economy changes. Prices are generally slightly lower than the European average whereas wages are significantly lower, perhaps around 10 per cent of neighbouring Western countries. At the same time, while literacy levels are high and there is a skilled work-force and professional elite, productivity is many times lower than the European average. Nevertheless, proximity to major Western markets such as Germany may now be sufficient to attract Western investment.

EAST EUROPEAN EXPECTATIONS

These vary between high expectations of economic salvation and low expectations, based on xenophobic mistrust of industrial and economic plunder by foreigners. In each case, the government is usually selling state enterprises through an agency but has to be sensitive to both sets of arguments. Access to new technology, skills, and on-the-job training are important. Early illusions have already been discarded as this process has now been ongoing for a few years.

There had been expectations of earning more and of fewer layoffs but this was an important part of the restructuring process to combat over-manning. In the short period that Western acquisitions have been present, there is evidence now to how that locals earn more when working for foreign companies.

FINANCIAL INSTITUTIONS AND THE DEBT CHAIN

Financial institutions in Eastern Europe are weak because the area as a whole traded only internally and in transferable roubles, which was not a currency but an accounting mechanism. Industries were controlled by state enterprise monopolies which were undercapitalised and, where successful, used as cash cows. The result has been the steady development of a debt chain led by these former monopolies now incapable of meeting their financial obligations without state help. Banks, too, are state institutions which are also undercapitalised and in the control of their major debtors, the state enterprises. The chain therefore had to be broken. An infrastructure had to be created which would facilitate domestic and international banking transfers and encourage the development of equity investment, and so Stock Exchanges were created first in Budapest, then Warsaw, then Prague. Presently, they handle only a very small amount of regulated business but their growth has been astonishing. The Warsaw

Stock Exchange set a world record for growth with its tenfold increase over the twelve months to the end of 1993.

The potential of these institutions is great, particularly to raise future finance internally through a flotation, but their impact in the immediate term is insignificant because so much money is now needed to upgrade inefficient industries that often resemble industrial museums more than productive enterprises of the twentieth century. This has been the legacy of communism: a system which drew so heavily on subsidies for existence that it finally collapsed like a tin can which has had the air drawn out of it. Multilateral payments have had to replace bilateral payments. Systemic change has accompanied structural change, so the transition in all cases has been very difficult. Psychologically, people still suffer from the communist past. Mind sets and attitudes do not change quite as quickly as politics or politicians. The civil servants in place are still the same as those who served previous communist masters, with some few exceptions. Mass privatisation plans are under development in all these countries, or else exist and await implementation. To take the example of Poland, this will see the creation of some 15–17 new national investment funds, created especially to administer the remaining state enterprises. The share certificates will be tradable and this will give a significant boost to the Warsaw Stock Exchange, likewise with the other East European countries as each approaches privatisation.

BUSINESS OUTLOOK

As regards doing business, the potential is for the long term. Political risk has greatly diminished and all forms of commercial undertaking are possible and generally actively encouraged. However, the demise of the central planning system, with the FTO (Foreign Trade Office) monopoly of foreign trade by industrial sector, means now that buyers are many and unknown. Previously, it took a long time to win business but, once achieved, there was open access to the entire industrial sector of the country. Now there are many buyers and most of them are new and untried without a known credit rating. Ironically, their own commercial future may be dependent on being paid by bankrupt state enterprises. The debt chain has now become a major threat to the newly established private sector. Commercial risk has therefore replaced political risk as the major concern for exporters.

There are democratic trappings everywhere but organisational structures are still built around communist models with all the excessive bureaucracy which that entails. Bureaucracy in some countries is still a nightmare despite a pretence to the contrary. Meanwhile the recession continues and people start to manifest thwarted ambitions which have given rise to the recently elected leftist governments. All goods are now available, at a price, where before there was scarcity. Generally, prices are just slightly under Western market price levels. However, East Europeans are paid Eastern wages and so the disparity between Eastern wages and Western prices is a very real one and gives rise for concern about continued social cohesion.

CONDUCTING BUSINESS

Conducting business in Eastern Europe brings special problems:

- People are generally very pleasant and courteous, so it may be difficult to understand the nature of the obstacle you have run into. It may be due to the lack of seniority of the people you are dealing with. It helps to clarify exactly where you stand if you believe you have an agreement, in which case this should be clearly delineated as to where the respective responsibilities of each partner lies. Otherwise, time passes and nothing happens. Understanding the nature of the impediments, you can help to force the pace of change and keep a relationship on track. Procrastination is endemic.
- Hierarchy and rank is a throwback to communism but is recognised as important. Society still recognises and has a special place for age, rank and protocol. In a negative sense, this can mean delays due to what appears to be officialdom.
- Mail is unreliable and people generally are not in the habit of sending letters to the degree encountered in business in other Western countries. Instead, much more business is transacted over the telephone and no record is, of course, kept of any understanding reached. The advent of the fax machine may change this.
- Distribution channels did not exist previously. A command economy with built-in shortages is not conducive to the creation or existence of many varied forms of distribution channel being targeted at the same customer. Customer orientation and central planning are mutually exclusive. Distribution systems have first had to be learned and then almost immediately implemented.
- Telecommunications are improving enormously with the total relaxation of CoCom controls and demise of CoCom itself. However, while Warsaw has cellular telephones, fax and satellite telephones, this is not equally true of Romania or Bulgaria, or of Albania which is perhaps the poorest country in Europe. It is not possible, therefore, to rely on there being such equipment available, as the number of telephones per 100 inhabitants is significantly lower than in neighbouring Western European countries.
- Transportation is generally difficult, rail travel is improving slowly, but an enormous infrastructural investment is required. Air travel by national airline is invariably not recommended by locals. Major highways are required, and the necessary investment in highways for Poland alone over the next few years is estimated at $3 billion.

- Shortage of telephone lines and of telephone sockets in which to insert fax machines, plus the general shortage of reasonably priced office accommodation with supporting infrastructure, makes hotel rooms appear agreeable as business offices.
- The business day starts early and finishes early, from any time after 6 a.m. till sometime after 2 p.m. This means that Western expectations of business visits in the afternoon are just not realistic. Expectations have to be shaped with regard to market realities and accepted practice.
- Convertibility has created pressures on many of these new democracies which have suffered successive devaluations and high inflation rates, resulting from perceived instability. The IMF, World Bank and banks generally are against countertrade, which they view as being an extension of bilateralism, and favour instead free, open markets. Nevertheless, the lure of countertrade is strong, particularly amongst the weakest economies, and so it will continue, but to a lesser degree that was known before. Other major changes include allowing the repatriation of earnings even where selling only on the domestic market. Unlike previous times under communism, no distinction is now made between domestic and export sales; all profits may now be repatriated.
- Industrial sectors under strain from successive years of underfunding and overmanning are in many cases still waiting to be brought into the nineteenth century before anyone can bring them into the twentieth. A deadly conspiracy of bureaucracy resulting from an inertia inspired by fear of widespread unemployment and officially condoned overmanning has prevented this happening. This necessary quantum leap is obvious in telecommunications and in some cases is working to their advantage as they absorb proven technology without having had to bear any of the development costs themselves. Modern-day Warsaw sees many pedestrians and motorists with cellular telephones.
- Marketisation does not mean that these people are unskilled negotiators. Quite the contrary. Negotiations are a forte of the East Europeans who employ silence and waiting very skilfully, but there are no state monopolies now and the increase in buyers plus the increase in market competition has influenced this situation for the better.
- Personal contacts are highly important and can same enormous amounts of time, but wining and dining is an important part of business life in this region of the world.

Generally, it is easier to find information on East European markets than ever before as all of the major market research agencies now have one or more offices in Eastern Europe and many market reports are now available on this region of the world. Consulates have never been very good sources of information because career diplomats are seldom conversant with technical requirements, being untrained in research methods, and consulates are usually understaffed. The net effect is the production of very general, usually dated, and rather useless, information. Actual site visits are important and it is vital to get out, talk to people and listen to what they say. In days gone by, the national trade show was all important, but these were only once a year, and the communists stage-managed the entire show. All important contracts would be delayed for signing at this annual event, so as to inflate the economic importance of the event. This is no longer the case; besides, with the removal of the need for visas, it is easy to make site visits. General market information may be obtained from consulates or libraries but the detailed specifics of a request or proposal can only be obtained from a site visit.

BUSINESS OPPORTUNITIES

There are a great number of business opportunities available in Eastern Europe. In production, these include packaging, food processing, computers, telecommunications, instrumentation, control systems and machine tools; and in services: finance and banking, accountancy (as they have traditionally used different accounting principles), law, advertising, and transportation and distribution. Retailing is currently undergoing a revolution as entrepreneurs enter the sector and add to the total number of outlets, while, at the same time, the outlets themselves expand in size and transform themselves in terms of their merchandising styles. Shopfitting units, designed especially to present merchandise in the best possible way to encourage sales, have suddenly become conspicuous every-where.

Shopping practices remain unchanged. People buy in small quantities daily, even for groceries, and they pay cash. Car ownership is lower than in the West and parking problems are often severe, ruling out shopping with the car which with its convenience has dominated North American shopping habits for generations. East European societies are still cash-dominated as the banking network is poor and the plastic-card revolution is still a couple of generations away. Plastic cards are being used and are accepted in most places but these are owned by foreigners. While East European banks now have the ability to issue these cards, they are charging so much and local people are so fearful of inflation that they are continuing to spend cash when they can.

Tourism is one of the most neglected of sectors, and yet an Eastern Europe in which one is free to travel has much to offer. Prague is popu-larly known as the Paris of the East and has a great deal of tourist poten-tial, as has Budapest, which comprises two cities built on opposite banks of the Danube. While Bulgaria has seaside resorts and ski resorts, what is missing is the infrastructural development without which Western tourists, with their different expectation levels, would be disappointed and would not return. General management training is needed everywhere, specifically in services marketing, production and quality control systems.

These needs are being met to some degree by a number of national and international initiatives which are sending management consultants and trainers into Eastern Europe to train the trainers, and in some cases to mount MBA programs.

Of all the areas of opportunity perhaps the most significant is environmental control and clean-up systems, as this is an area to which international funding has been targeted. Pollution is now an international problem and debt forgiveness programs in return for environmental clean-up programs are becoming more common, as nations try to deal with pollution both internationally and at source. Unchecked, it poses health risks and threatens agriculture, as is the case presently in the Czech Republic and Slovakia where overuse of chemical fertilisers has affected arable land, tainted crops and is affecting drinking water systems. The inability to deal with pollution will impede the development of tourism, one of the fastest-growing industries of the decade, and the one industry in which East Europeans could easily make the most significant gains in both the short and the long term.

THE FUTURE

Integration of Eastern and Western Europe means that we do not require and cannot expect a General Motors or General Electric plant in each nation state. Instead, nations are competing with each other to offer the best investment conditions. As one nation starts to offer something different, others follow, and so the investment climate improves. This has happened already in matters such as taxation treatment and avoidance of double taxation through international tax treaties. Planned harmonisation with EU practices will help companies large and small to foresee legislative and fiscal changes to integrate their European operations and to plan ahead an investment and payback strategy.

As regards economic projections, the economic growth rate projections for Poland are particularly impressive in that the OECD now forecasts that Poland, alone in Europe, will experience growth in this current recession. Coupled with the tenfold rise in its Stock Exchange over 1993 this augurs well for both the immediate and the longer-term future as it will entice new and non-traditional foreign investment into the country. The more dynamic nations are now forgeing a new region of economic growth in Central Europe and dismantling trade barriers among themselves. At the same time, the means of entering these markets has also changed. Instead of licensing, foreign direct investment is now welcomed, and by state enterprises which, although often for the wrong reasons, believe that this may bring salvation from their ultimate and very certain total demise. Joint ventures and privatisations now create new opportunities, making the trading atmosphere of the region more dynamic than it has been for years.

Issues such as applications to join NATO can only serve to enhance further the levels of foreign direct investment. Each nation state has gone forth into marketisation from a different base and, today, each has evolved a different set of conditions and regulations. Acquisitions, joint ventures and privatisations are the areas to watch as state assets become available cheaply on a once-only sale basis. Investment will continue for the next four to five years at least as the process of systemic and structural reform continues, albeit under formerly communist leaders.

REFERENCE

Lawrence, P. and Vlachoutsicos, Charalambos (1993) 'Joint ventures in Russia: put the local in charge', *Harvard Business Review*, 71(1): 44–51.
Paliwoda, Stanley J. (1995) *Investing in Eastern Europe*, London: Addison-Wesley/EIU Books.

22 NAFTA
Is it in Canada's best interest?

David Elton and Todd Hirsch

INTRODUCTION

Throughout the 1980s and early 1990s, the global economy has witnesses a transformation of international trading patterns, characterized by increasingly liberalized trade and the development of large trading blocks. While the degrees of liberalization have been beneficial to many trading nations, it has also become more important for those countries with smaller domestic economies to be aligned with one of the large trading blocks. The most significant trading areas are the European Union, the emerging trading area of southern Asia (ASEAN), and the recently implemented NAFTA – the North American Free Trade Agreement – which liberalizes trade between Canada, the United States, and Mexico.

This essay has three objectives: first, to outline briefly the historical development of the NAFTA; second, to provide an overview of the content of the agreement; and third, to assess the key arguments for and against NAFTA, thus providing the reader with the opportunity to assess whether NAFTA is in Canada's best interest.

HISTORICAL OVERVIEW

The Canadian government's decision to enter into a free trade agreement with the US was one of the most significant public policy issues of the 1980s. Free trade dominated the public policy agenda for most of the decade, and was the central issue in the 1988 election campaign. With the victory of the pro-free trade Progressive Conservatives in that year, the Canada–US FTA was implemented on 1 January 1989. It created a free trade area of some 300 million people and a GDP of nearly $US6 trillion.

During the same period that Canadians were debating the merits of free trade with the United States (1985–9), Mexico was undertaking substantive economic reforms such as joining the GATT (General Agreement on Tariffs and Trade), privatizing many of its previously centrally controlled sectors, and other measures to open its economy and attract foreign investment. This constituted a dramatic change in the

Mexican economy. For decades the Mexican economy was based upon a high degree of government-owned corporations, government owned farm land, and protectionist and interventionist policies regarding international trade.

Over the decade of the 1970s, largely as a result of high oil prices, Mexico experienced rapid economic growth accompanied by galloping inflation. In 1982, world recession hit Mexico extremely hard, marked by falling commodity prices, rapidly growing foreign debt, economic stagnation, and price instability. By the mid-1980s, it became clear that the existing economic policies of the government of the day were not working – protectionist policies, industrialization strategy through limiting imports, and massive state intervention had obviously been the wrong medicine for Mexico during the 1980s.

Although trade had began to open up in the early 1980s, and Mexico joined GATT in 1986, the effects were limited. In 1988, the new administration under President Carlos Salinas de Gortari instituted a new era of privatization, less government involvement, and the liberation of trade policies that built on reforms which had begun in the mid-1980s. An important spoke in this plan of trade expansion was to secure a free trade agreement (FTA) with its neighbors, particularly the United States.

Even though a plurality of Canadians remained opposed to the FTA following its implementation in 1989, and the two opposition parties in Parliament remained strongly opposed, when the Canadian government learned of the Mexican desire to enter into a free trade agreement with the US, the Canadian government began to promote the idea of a North American Free Trade Agreement. The primary argument for undertaking this initiation was that Canada wanted to make sure the US–Mexico agreement would not jeopardize the trade agreement Canada had made with the US.

Formal talks between Mexico, Canada and the US began in 1990. In June 1991 in Toronto, the leaders of the three countries met to negotiate a North American Free Trade deal, and by August 1992 they had agreed to a draft text for the agreement (Govt of Canada 1992: 1).

By 1993 Canada was entering its third year of recession, and was experiencing high unemployment (10–12 per cent). The FTA of 1989 was the obvious and easy target for the economic downturn, and many Canadians – both those for and those against the FTA – argued that the deal should not be extended to include Mexico. Canadian public opinion data throughout the negotiation period indicated that a plurality of Canadians opposed NAFTA. Opposition to the agreement was particularly strong during the 1992–3 period, as evidenced by the data in Figure 22.1, which shows Canadians opposing NAFTA by a 2 to 1 margin.

The fact that public opposition to NAFTA decreased dramatically in the four-month period between August 1993 and December 1993 (even though opponents of NAFTA sought to make it an election issue in

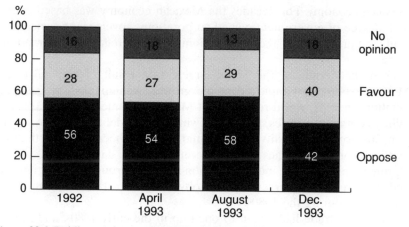

Figure 22.1 Public opinion on NAFTA, 1992 and 1993

Source: Gallup Poll, 1 January 1994

October) is evidence of how quickly public opinion can change on an issue when the opinions of a significant segment of the population are based upon weak impressions rather than deep-seated convictions.

In Washington, ratification of NAFTA faced a much steeper uphill battle. President Bill Clinton, whose campaign platform on NAFTA was obscure, embraced the deal as good for the United States even though it was initiated by his predecessor George Bush. His challenge was to counter the anti-trade sentiment felt by many Americans and fanned by populist 1992 Presidential candidate Ross Perot, prominent labour leaders, and many members of his own party. But in November 1993, faced with a time limit imposed by US fast-track legislation pertaining to NAFTA, the House of Representatives passed NAFTA by a vote of 234 to 200, clearing the way for the tri-lateral agreement to be put into place on 1 January 1994.

The agreement is noteworthy for a few reasons. First, it is a precedent-setting example of a developing nation (Mexico) being allowed free market access with two of the most industrialized and wealthiest nations in the world. Second, it creates the world's largest free trade area as measured by market size and economic output. Third, it came just prior to a turning point in world trade relations: the Seattle Summit of November 1993 that sought to expand trade liberalization throughout the Pacific Rim, and the continuation of intense GATT negotiations in December 1993. The ratification of the NAFTA provided examples of both successful negotiations and international co-operation for the Seattle Summit and the GATT talks.

As illustrated in Figure 22.2, the NAFTA encompasses a market of over 360 million consumers, and a combined GDP of over $US6 billion (Govt

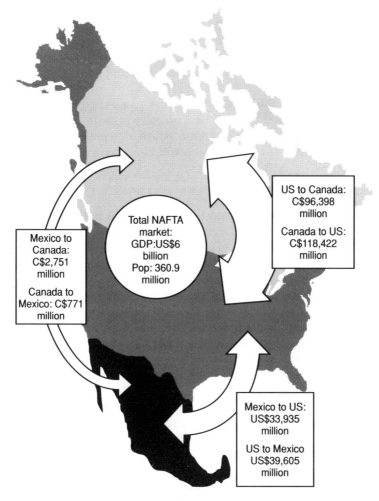

Figure 22.2 NAFTA market: Canada, US and Mexico, 1992

of Canada 1993: 3). Trade flows between the United States and its neighbors are sizable, with over $C96 billion of exports to Canada (first largest trading partner) and $US39 billion of exports to Mexico (third largest trading partner). Canadian exports to the US are also very large, but trade between Canada and Mexico is very limited. Canada has a merchandise trade surplus with both the US and Mexico.

CONTENT OF THE NAFTA

Basically, the NAFTA is an agreement-made-law by the three countries to liberalize trade within North America. This will be done primarily by eliminating trade barriers, particularly tariffs and quota limits on imports. As well, investment is covered by the deal so as to give fair treatment to foreign investors from one of the NAFTA countries investing in another NAFTA country. Also, the agreement has a built-in dispute-settlement mechanism, loosely based on the dispute-settlement panels established by the FTA.

It is not possible in this paper to list every sector affected by the agreement and the implications of the deal in every area, but below are a few of the more prominent issues or sectors which are contained in the agreement and the affects that these issues will likely have in Canada.

Agriculture

This sector is different than most because, prior to the NAFTA, agricultural goods entering Mexico faced trade barriers of quotas and licensing regulations (i.e. licenses to import), rather than tariffs. Under the NAFTA, Mexico will have to initially reduce, and subsequently eliminate, quotas on most agricultural imports from Canada and the United States. This elimination process will take place over a period of 5 to 15 years, depending on the particular item. Produce items exported from Mexico into Canada and the United States will also face reduced barriers, although almost all goods being imported into Canada were already traded freely. American citrus fruit growers, sugar farmers, and other warmer climate fruit and vegetable growers are likely to face the largest adjustment with the Mexican competition.

Grain and livestock farmers in Canada should experience modest gains from freer trade with Mexico. Wheat and barley exports in particular are expected to rise as the quotas are eliminated, and it is anticipated that pork and beef will do well as Mexican incomes rise. Dairy, chicken and poultry farmers were unaffected by NAFTA as these supply-management items were excluded from the agreement (as was the case under the FTA). However, under the December 1993 GATT agreement, these sectors are facing the loss of import protection; it is unlikely, though, that the increased competition from imports will come from Mexico.

Energy

Both Canada and Mexico export significant quantities of energy products to the United States. But the NAFTA is not truly a tri-lateral deal in this area; that is, rules governing trade between Canada and the US are not the same as those governing trade between Mexico and the US. NAFTA preserves and even strengthens the rules of the FTA by guaranteeing Canadian energy exporters access to the large American markets, and preserving the requirement that Canada can curtail its exports for reasons of conservation, national security, and so on, *only in direct proportion to its domestic consumption.* With Mexico, the agreement is a bit different. Because of Mexico's entirely state operated energy sector (under the oil company PEMEX), and because of the constitutional and historical importance of energy resources, Mexico is required to accept the NAFTA pricing provisions, but (unlike Canada) can restrict exports at will. This asymmetry is viewed by some Canadians as a flaw in the agreement, and an unfair victory for Mexico's state-operated monopoly.

The Liberal Party led by Jean Chrétien took a strong stand against the energy provisions of NAFTA during the fall 1993 election campaign, which was consistent with their strong opposition to the energy-sharing provisions of the FTA in 1988. In November 1993, after winning the election, and following the critical vote in the US Congress, the Liberal government requested that the energy provisions of NAFTA be revised by withdrawing the section which requires Canada to continue supplying the US market in the event of energy shortages in Canada. The US rejected this request which forced Canada's Prime Minister to save face by declaring an unenforceable, unilateral declaration to placate the opponents of NAFTA in Canada (*Alberta Report* 1993: 9).

Canada's energy sector will likely be unaffected by the NAFTA because it basically follows what has been established under the FTA. Also, Canadian exports of natural gas to the US are growing, not shrinking. Increased natural gas exports to the US are expected to become the backbone of Canada's energy export industry for the remainder of the 1990s.

Investment

The FTA contained four basic investment elements: national treatment; reservation of certain sectors (culture in Canada, transportation in the US); the retention of a review mechanism (the US Exon–Florio measure and Investment Canada); and the prohibition of 'performance requirements' such as export requirements. The NAFTA expands upon this framework established under the FTA in investment (see Rugman and Gestrin 1993: 1–2), and improves the agreement in five general areas:

1 the definition of investment (which under the FTA included only foreign direct investment) under NAFTA includes virtually all forms of investment such as equity and debt investment, real estate, or any interest entitling the owner to a share of the income/profit;
2 NAFTA increases the security of investments in North America by providing for binding, enforceable international arbitration for dispute settlement involving investments by member countries. This is particularly important for Canadian and American investors in Mexico with its unpredictable court system;
3 signatories to the NAFTA are granted most-favoured-nation status for investments in the other two NAFTA nations, which means that these

investors are to be treated by the host nation *no less favourably* than investors from any other nation;

4 Canadian provinces and US and Mexican states are given two years (from 1 January 1994) to create a list of measures under their own jurisdictions to be exempted from various NAFTA provisions for investment;

5 NAFTA will impose no performance requirements of foreign investments, such as export requirements, minimum domestic content, technology transfer requirements, and exclusive suppliers. The last two of these were not prohibited under the FTA.

In general, these provisions of the NAFTA are seen as improvements over the FTA's rules governing investments. The regulations are clearer, expanded, and more transparent to discrimination.

Financial services

Chapter 14 of the NAFTA deals with trade in financial services. This area of trade was difficult to negotiate both because of the widely different types of financial regimes existing in the three countries, and because there is generally more regulation in this sector than in other traded-goods sectors. Basically, NAFTA seeks to liberalize trade in financial services among the three members. Liberalizing financial services does not only apply to the rights and allowances of banks and financial institutions doing business in the other two countries, but also of the right of *establishment* in other countries. NAFTA includes provisions for equality of treatment of these services which establish in member countries, which was typically an accepted practice but is now enforceable under the agreement. Also, the agreement allows for the maintenance of each country's own system of financial regulations, which is significant considering the three systems and their varying stages of development. One significant improvement for Canada is the extension of the NAFTA dispute settlement mechanism to cover some financial service disputes which were not covered under the FTA. Also, the NAFTA ensures that national sovereignty in regards to monetary policy and exchange rate control are upheld, and are unaffected by anything in the agreement (see Chant 1993: 1–2).

Dispute settlement

Chapters 18 and 19 of the FTA set up a dispute-settlement mechanism which has been generally successful in its operation. Under these chapters, if a complaint is filed by either the US or Canada regarding general violations of the FTA, dumping or countervail, a temporary panel of five arbiters is established, with no less than two arbiters from either country. The panel passes judgment on the complaint, and develops a subsidies code which both countries are obligated to accept. The panels have been successful in that both countries have generally respected their judgments, and very rarely has the panel split along nationalist lines. Under the FTA, if there is evidence of misconduct by one of the panelists, an Extraordinary Challenge Committee (ECC) is to be established by three judges or former judges, to review the complaint and the panel, and to make a final judgment.

Some changes to the dispute mechanism will be made by the NAFTA. The NAFTA will liberalize the access by which complaints can be brought to the level of an ECC. While this will increase the validity and quality of the dispute mechanism, it will also increase the number of complaints brought before an ECC, and thus increase the time and process involved in settling disputes. Also, whereas under FTA each country chooses its own panelists, under the NAFTA the panelists from country A will be selected by country B, and vice versa. This small change is likely to develop a more consensual approach to resolving disputes. Other changes include the replacement of the Canada–US Trade Commission with the Free Trade Commission, a standing body which will be responsible for the oversight of the entire NAFTA. By and large, the changes to the FTA dispute mechanism under the NAFTA are seen as improvements, with the possible exception of the increased time and paperwork element from the broadened access to the ECCs, and that NAFTA still does not deal with clear rules regarding what constitutes a subsidy (see Cadsby and Woodside 1993).

Labour and environment side agreements

Some fears and concerns surrounding NAFTA's effects on labour and the environment were addressed in two side agreements. These were negotiated late in the process and were seen largely as symbolic gestures enabling President Clinton to support NAFTA and obtain passage through Congress. Both these side agreements call for the establishment of governing Councils – one for labour disputes and one for environmental issues – which will meet at least yearly. The Councils will have a presence in each area through established Secretariats, and will be responsible for responding to complaints of unsafe or unfair labour policies or environmental distress caused by an offending business. Panels will judge complaints, and if the offending business does not comply, the Councils have the authority to impose monetary penalties or allow trade sanctions.

There are some differences between the agreements on the environment and labour. The environment agreement, in addition to the establishment of a Council, will establish the Joint Public Advisory Committee to accept and review complaints from any party, including individuals, on violating environmental practices. On the other hand, there is no equivalent to this committee in the labour agreement, and complaints of unfair labour practices may be filed only by a government.

The most contentious issues in establishing these side agreements hinged on dispute settlement and enforcement. On the one hand, the US Congress insisted on policies which would not give Canadian or Mexican firms an advantage by noncompliance with the arbitrating panel's decision. On the other hand, Canada and Mexico wanted assurance that their larger trading partner would not be constantly harassing their firms and penalizing them with dumping or countervailing actions. For the bill to pass, these side agreements needed to be a 'watchdog with teeth, but on a short leash'. In the end, the agreements were negotiated so as to minimize the possible number of instances in which these measures could be imposed. If no agreement can be reached by the two disputing parties, a panel will judge the complaint, and decide what action should be taken. If an offending firm refuses to comply with this agreement, a monetary fine is levied. If the firm does not pay the fine, then trade sanctions by the complaining country will be allowed (but even then, tariff barriers must be kept to the most-favoured-nation level).

Significantly, Canada was exempt from this latter aspect of the agreements in two areas. First of all, even if a fine is not paid, no trade sanctions will be allowed whatsoever against Canada. Second, any fines imposed against Canada because of an offending firm will always be charged to a government, not a firm. These same concessions do not apply to offenses by Mexico or the United States (Cadby and Woodside 1993).

CANADIAN ARGUMENTS FOR AND AGAINST NAFTA

Arguments in favour of NAFTA

Canadians supporting NAFTA utilized six main arguments:

1 hub and spoke argument;
2 theory of competitive advantage;
3 humanitarian considerations;
4 huge potential market;
5 global competition;
6 minimal cost.

The hub and spoke argument

This is perhaps the strongest and most often recited argument in favour of Canada joining NAFTA. Regardless of Canada's participation, Mexico will be seeking a trade agreement with the US. If Canada opts out of NAFTA, the US will become the 'hub' of North American trade, and Canada, Mexico, and likely other South American countries will become the 'spokes'. Under such an arrangement, the US will be the optimal location to do business because of the wider free market access available to it. If Canada does participate in NAFTA, it will not be yielding this advantage to the US. Also, it is essential that Canadian representatives be at the negotiating table of North American trade. This would not happen if NAFTA was rejected by Canada.

The theory of comparative advantage

This argument is one that only economists are likely to make, but supports the idea of freer trade among nations. Its basic principle is that resources are used most efficiently if nations export those goods which it has a comparative advantage in producing, and import those for which it is less advantaged. Mexico, with its large labour force, is likely to have a comparative advantage in producing labour-intensive goods such as textiles, machine parts, etc. Canada, on the other hand, has a smaller but much more educated and productive workforce; its comparative advantage lies in high-tech goods, engineering, environmental management, and other services. The argument is that free trade will benefit all countries involved by allowing each to produce what it is best at producing, and import those goods which are inexpensively produced elsewhere.

Humanitarian considerations

The best way to raise Mexico's standard of living is through trade. This argument is based on the fact that, as Mexico's markets are opened to the US and Canada, their exports will rise and the price of imported goods will fall. This will act as a double-edged sword in raising the income and standard of living of the Mexican people. Money and aid to the developing nations has helped, but has not been able to provide sustained growth in incomes. Opening up markets to these countries and allowing them to compete will provide sustained income growth.

Huge potential market

Over the next decade the Mexican economy is expected to grow dramatically. This means increased demand in Mexico for water-treatment plants, pollution control services, communication facilities, and so on: all products and services that Canadian firms are able and willing to export. It is argued that turning down preferential treatment in this market would be near-sighted in the extreme.

Global competition

Canada will face increased competition from Mexico with or without NAFTA. As mentioned above in the 'hub and spoke' argument, Mexico will attempt to secure access to the US with or without Canada's participation. It is therefore useless to try and protect Canada's markets for exports in the US by rejecting NAFTA. Mexico is displaying the same global competitiveness that has raised the economic fortunes of many small Asian countries such as Taiwan, Thailand and Korea. Canada will not change this by rejecting the agreement, and is best to position itself strategically *with* the new trading order, not *against* it.

Minimal cost

Canada's trade barriers against Mexican imports are already very small, so in this respect the costs of opening trade with Mexico are minimal. Fears of Canadian factories closing down on the day of NAFTA's implementation or a flood of jobs lost to Mexico because of the deal are not based in fact. Canada already has very low tariffs against Mexican imports, and if this flood of jobs and investment were going to happen, it would have happened already. To some degree, it *has* happened, but it has been part of the longer and broader process of industrial restructuring which both Canada and the US (as well as Japan and Europe) are currently undergoing. NAFTA will not cause some floodgate to be opened, but will, rather, secure the flow of trade to which all three countries have been adjusting.

Arguments against NAFTA

Opponents of NAFTA utilize four key arguments:

1 low Mexican wages;
2 human rights violations;
3 environmental degradation/cost advantages;
4 erosion of Canadian sovereignty.

Low Mexican wages

This argument claims that Canada won't be able to compete with low Mexican wages, based primarily on the observation that Canadian wage rates are approximately 7.5 times higher than wage rates in Mexico. However, proponents of NAFTA counter this argument by pointing out that, as well as wages, Canadian productivity is far greater, with a ratio of about 6.5 to 1 (Department of Finance estimates; see also Watson 1993: 5; Figure 22.3). It was also noted that labour wages alone are not the sole basis for location decisions. Depending on the type of plant, all sorts of factors will be under consideration such as distance from markets, transportation facilities, political and economic stability, the prevailing legal system, availability of communication and electrical facilities, etc.

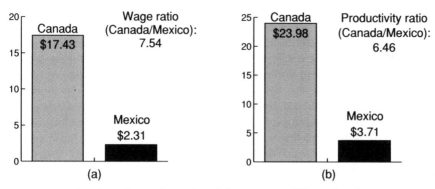

Figure 22.3 (a) Canadian and Mexican labour wages (C$ per hour)
(b) Canadian and Mexican productivity (GDP in C$ per hour worked

Source: Canadian Department of Finance

Human rights violations

Opponents of NAFTA point out the appalling state of human rights in Mexico. The exploitation of labour, lack of adequate living conditions, and limited personal freedom of expression is arguably more than a consequence of poverty, but rather the result of an oppressive and, at times, corrupt Mexican government and legal system. In Canada and the US, personal freedoms and rights of expression are highly valued. Is it appropriate for Canada to engage in a free trade agreement with a country whose citizens are treated with a level of human respect intolerable by our own standards? Some opponents of the deal insist that Canada wait until the Mexican government improves its record of human rights violations and labour exploitation before engaging in free trade.

Environmental degradation/cost advantages

The assertion is made that NAFTA will result in environmental disaster, and that Canadian firms won't be able to compete with Mexico's slack environmental laws. Flagrant examples of environmental degradation can be found in Mexico, particularly along the Mexican–US border. Opponents of NAFTA point to this environmental crisis and argue that with free trade, pollution and ecological damage will only worsen. Also, the lower standards for pollution control in Mexico may give industries in Canada, with its more stringent regulations, an unfair cost disadvantage, and as a result industry may shift to Mexico. These fears of environmental damage and an unlevel economic playing field were partly addressed by the side agreement on the environment, which seeks to prevent any of the three countries from gaining an advantage through slack pollution regulations. Whether it actually accomplishes this objective remains to be seen.

Erosion of Canadian sovereignty

NAFTA opponents argue that participation in the agreement will speed up the erosion of Canada's sovereignty started by the FTA. This argument is based on the premise that NAFTA reduces the Canadian government's ability to set its own national goals and objectives. Given that, any sort of international agreement necessitates some weakening of sovereignty (otherwise it would not be an agreement that needed to be negotiated). This objection is a valid one. Whether this is a valid basis for the rejection of NAFTA, though, is a matter of opinion. Take for example the following observation:

> The NAFTA may recognize that national sovereignty is shrinking, but it is not the cause of it. And it's not just in Canada, but everywhere, that national sovereignty is shrinking . . .
>
> National independence is shrinking because global interdependence is growing. And if the nations and peoples of the world are increasingly interdependent, they must of necessity be increasingly less independent. The only independent person in this world is the hermit in a cave, and his is the independence of hunger, hardship, and ignorance.
>
> (Gray 1993: 74)

CONCLUSIONS

Canada is much more trade-dependent than its largest trading partners, the US and Japan. While merchandise exports constitute only 7 per cent and 9 per cent, respectively, of these economies Canada exports almost one-quarter of all it produces (Statistics Canada; *Canadian Global Almanack* 1993). Also, Canada is a world leader in seeking reductions in trade barriers, and NAFTA is consistent with the example Canada sets. NAFTA will hasten Canadian firms to increase their competitiveness, a necessity for Canada to remain competitive on a global basis. The acceptance of NAFTA will provide a pattern for the international community and for the GATT of successful international trade agreements. NAFTA will also help to stem protectionist sentiment in the US which threatens Canada's access to large markets. As well, the emergence of Mexico as a potential market will provide Canadian businesses with expanded opportunities to export professional services, information and communication services, high-tech products, and so on.

This essay has explored the historical development of the NAFTA, examined briefly the content and intention of the agreement, and presented arguments both for and against liberalizing trade. Whether the NAFTA is in the best interests of Canada depends upon how much weight is placed on increased trade opportunities (and a probable increase in economic activity in the three countries), as compared to environmental, national sovereignty, and human rights considerations.

If you believe that increased trade results in an increase in standards of living, and that increases in living standards result in improved human rights and environmental standards, then NAFTA is in the best interest of all three countries. If, on the other hand, you are convinced that Canada's sovereignty is irreversibly damaged, that its standard of living will drop due to an exodus of manufacturing to Mexico, and that Mexico will become a haven for polluting companies, then NAFTA is clearly a colossal error.

We are convinced that the NAFTA will benefit Canada. But, as with most benefits, there will be some painful adjustments in certain sectors which compete directly with US or Mexican production. Canadian industries facing decline should not be callously ignored but, on the other hand, the benefits to the country as a whole from NAFTA should also not be denied because of a few sectors of the economy which will face adjustments, decline or disappearance. The important point is that these (sometimes painful) changes are part of a wider process of global industrial restructuring which will continue to evolve, regardless of Canada's participation in NAFTA. The liberalization of trade within North America will improve Canada's ability to adapt to a rapidly changing global economy.

REFERENCES

Alberta Report (1993) 20 December.

Cadsby, C.G. and Woodside, K. (1993) 'The effects of the North American Free Trade Agreement on the Canada–United States relationship', *Canadian Public Policy*, 19(4): 450–62.

Canadian Global Almanac 1993, ed. John Robert Colombo, Toronto: Macmillan Canada.

Chant, J. (1993) 'The financial sector in NAFTA: two plus one equals restructuring', in *Assessing NAFTA*, Vancouver: Fraser Institute.

Government of Canada (1992) *North American Free Trade Agreement: An Overview and Description*, Ottawa: Government of Canada.

Government of Canada (1993) *The North American Trade Agreement at a Glance*, cat. no. E74–56/1–1993E, Ottawa: Government of Canada.

Gray, E.W. (1993) 'NAFTA will ratify our shrinking sovereignty. Thank God!', *Canadian Speeches: Issues of the Day*, 6(10): 74.

Rugman, A.M. and Gestrin, M. (1993) 'The investment provisions of NAFTA: the NAFTA network', in *Assessing NAFTA, Vancouver: Fraser Institute.*

Statistics Canada (1993) *Exports by Country, January to December 1992*, cat. 63–003, 50(4), Ottawa.

Watson, W. (1993) 'The economic impact of the NAFTA', *C.D. Howe Institute Commentary*, no. 50 (June).

Index